Shadow of My Father

John A. Gotti

In the writing of this book, some names have been altered to protect the identity of certain individuals. In some cases, information in this book has been provided from third-party sources.

Cover painting by Michael Bell.
www.MBELLART.com

Design and formatting:
www.12on14.com

ISBN 978-0-692-39588-2

Dedicated to the grandchildren of my parents

FOREWORD

Throughout half of the 1980's and into the early 90's the principal target of the FBI's New York Office was John J. Gotti, the notorious Boss of Bosses who ran the city's most powerful crime family. Recently, after spending a decade in the research and writing of four investigative books for HarperCollins on the counterterrorism and organized crime failures of The Bureau* I came to realize that I had something in common with his son: John Angelo Gotti. Over the years both of us had become experts on the misconduct of various special agents and prosecutors working for the U.S. Department of Justice.

There's no doubt that *Shadow of My Father* will upend many of the public's assumptions about that mysterious secret society of criminals J. Edgar Hoover mistakenly dubbed La Cosa Nostra. Written in John Junior's own hand, it offers a rare inside look into "the underground kingdom" that was the Gambino family.

---

* *1000 Years For Revenge: International Terrorism and The FBI The Untold Story* (2003); *Cover Up: What the Government Is Still Hiding About the War on Terror* (2004); *Triple Cross: How bin Laden's Master Spy Penetrated The FBI, The CIA and The Green Berets* (2006-2009); and *Deal With The Devil: The FBI's Secret Thirty-Year Relationship With A Mafia Killer* (2013).

This isn't some ghost-written apologia told by an ex-wise-guy who cut a deal with the Feds and now lives under the protection of U.S. Marshals in the WITSEC program. It's the unvarnished personal story of "The King of The Volcano's" first born son.

The Boss of Bosses

In preparation for this Foreword I spent weeks interviewing John Jr. whom his family calls "Johnny Boy." I thought I knew his father's story, but the more he opened up, the more I realized how incomplete the historical record has been.

"When people think of my father," says John Jr., "they remember this bigger-than-life godfather in the Brioni suits and the razor cut hair; the boss who carried himself like a movie star; who went from being a knuckle gangbanger in the Fulton-Rockaway Boys to the cover of *Time Magazine*.

"They remember how it took four prosecutions to finally bring him down, and even then, the Feds had to rig the game by denying him access to Bruce Cutler, Gerry Shargel, Jimmy LaRossa and every top New York criminal lawyer.

"My father committed many sins," he told me. "But in the end, he was unapologetic; defiant to his last breath. He went out handcuffed to a bed, waving away the priest and choking on his own vomit and blood. That's what his death certificate says, 'choked to death; asphyxiated.' His bones were rotted around his neck from cancer and the decade he spent in 'the hole.'

"Many of our leaders start wars all over the world. They commit random acts of wholesale slaughter and they never pay for their sins. In the end, my father paid for his. He paid the highest price. And he didn't apologize. He went out like a man. That's why I felt it was important for me to tell at least that part of the story."

But this book is so much more. In fact, as colorful and tragic as Gotti senior's life was, the self-told chronicle of his son's odyssey reads like an epic worthy of Victor Hugo. What's little known outside the world of the New York tabloids is how, after cutting a deal with Junior in which he effectively pledged to withdraw from the Life and after he served nearly six and a half years, paying millions in fines, the Justice Department came after him again with four trials and a separate tax prosecution—five, not four—attempts to send him away for life.

In fact, one indictment included a death penalty eligible crime.

In the end, Gotti Junior proved to be "The Teflon Son." He got through all of that with his father's iron-willed tenacity. But if you met him today as he approaches his fifty-first birthday you'd find a man with none of the brass or unrepentant contempt his father had for law enforcement.

The son, whose DNA draws on the Neapolitan blood of his father and his mother's Italian-Russian ancestry, is downright self-effacing and reflective. He's witty and quick, with the same capacity for strategic thinking that propelled his old man from a driver for Gambino capo Carmine Fatico at 17 to head of the nation's most powerful crime family.

Continental and Cristal

The Bureau of Prisons reportedly tested his father's intelligence and learned that he had a genius level 140 I.Q. and in this case the apple didn't fall far. There was a time in the late 1980's after his lightning-strike coup d'etat over Gambino boss Paul Castellano when John Sr. reportedly grossed millions of dollars a year.

He'd leave his humble Howard Beach home in the morning with a fat stack of $10,000 to blow playing Continental at his beloved Bergin Hunt and Fish Club and end his nights in the wee hours at Regine's downing bottles of Cristal; all the while thumbing his nose at the Feds and managing a criminal enterprise with more than 200 "made" members and thousands of associates.

But Junior, the heir-apparent who was in line to succeed his father as boss, had a change of heart. "I was a full-fledged believer in the Life," he told me. "I idolized my father, I loved my uncles and I was going to follow them until the day I died. I used to tell everybody, 'It's an honor to go to jail for John Gotti.'

"But once I got married in 1990 and had my first child, my perspective slowly started to change. And why? Because my whole life, my father was in and out of prison, and I saw the effects it had on all of us kids and my mother. At the time my father died, my mother had spent twenty-three years in an empty bed by herself.

"I write in the book how one time at a wedding it struck me how sad this whole picture was. My uncle Gene's daughter had just gotten married and the women out-numbered the men two to one, because the men were all dead or in jail."

So in 1998, for the sake of his wife and his children, Junior made the decision to withdraw, renouncing his title as his father's successor.

New Cause for Headlines

For my most recent book, *Deal With The Devil*, I spent more than six years documenting the FBI's thirty-year relationship with Gregory Scarpa Sr., a murderous, Machiavellian Top Echelon informant who, by his own account, "stopped counting" after 50 homicides while operating at the "boss level" of the Colombo crime family.

Over the years, in the course of my research I've digested more than 50,000 pages of FBI memos and trial transcripts. I've conducted dozens of interviews with active or imprisoned "made" guys, not to mention FBI agents still on the job and retired. With those unique insights into the conduct of the Bureau's elite organized crime squads in The New York Office,

I can say with certainty that John Junior's memoir will make headlines on multiple fronts:

First for what he reveals about the way his father conducted business as an old-school, hard-core gangster. He relates one never-before-told story about a remarkable plot in which Gotti Sr., then serving time in state prison, ducked out of lockup and in a manner of hours, tracked down the remaining witness to one of his most notorious rub outs and "put two in his hat." He even found time to get back to Howard Beach for a home-cooked meal and make love to his wife before slipping back into prison.

Another cause for news coverage will be the untold details in this book of how Junior turned his back on the Life after he'd risen to Gambino heir-apparent following Senior's conviction in 1992. While his father was locked up in Marion federal prison, dying from cancer, John Jr. got his reluctant permission to withdraw; to go "on the shelf for life," as he put it; to step down from "the panel," that ruled the Borgata. He even got the blessing of the other New York families that if he never again "flew the Gambino flag" and left the enterprise forever, he could retire.

But the U.S. Department of Justice simply refused to let him go. Even after he made a plea agreement to minor racketeering and tax charges, paid millions in fines and agreed to serve 77 months in prison, they put him through five more prosecutions, keeping him locked up or confined in total for *nine years of his life.*

During those long prison terms he spent almost a third of his time in solitary confinement and twice he was subjected to what inmates call "Diesel Therapy," repeatedly transferred from lockup to lockup in the Bureau of Prison's system, effectively hidden from his family and his lawyers.

Team Fed just wouldn't give up unless he agreed to capitulate on their terms. If he did, they promised to pay back the millions in fines he'd paid and clean his record.

"But I stood strong and incurred their wrath," he told me. "They came with five cases against me in four years. See, the government didn't want other guys in the Life to know we could walk away on our own terms. They had to write the script—control the play. But with me it was different and I paid the price."

An Astonishing Account of Government Misconduct

The last chapters of the book reveal the desperate lengths that senior FBI agents and federal prosecutors went to in order to keep Gotti Jr. behind bars for life—embellishing and mischaracterizing evidence, suborning untenable testimony from murderers, intimidating witnesses, and going so far as to paint a target on Junior's back—falsely suggesting to wiseguys on the street that he'd agreed to "cooperate." In effect, after failing to silence him legally in court, the government was sentencing him to death.

As you will read, in July of 2004, just weeks before he'd completed his 77 month term with nearly a year in solitary, the Feds came up with a new racketeering and murder conspiracy indictment that they would pursue over three more trials. Each trial ended with a deadlocked jury and finally Justice announced it would stop prosecuting him.

But then, in the early morning hours of August 5, 2008 John Jr. heard the rotor of a helicopter over his Long Island home and within minutes a dozen agents in full combat load-out, came over the fence to arrest him in front of his wife and children.

"It was like a scene from a bad B-movie," he told me. "Even when they came up with this new indictment on fabricated charges, they could have called my lawyer Charlie Carnesi and I would have willingly surrendered. The Gottis always showed up in court.

"By then, I'd been out of the Life for over nine years. But

they had to make this theatrical show of force to suggest to the media that I was somehow dangerous. And that wasn't the worst of it. Because after they'd failed the first three times, in order to make these new charges stick, they stooped as low as any federal prosecutors have ever gone."

Locking him up on murder conspiracy, racketeering and drug dealing charges out of Tampa, Florida, a part of the country where Junior had never done business, Team Fed produced as their "key witness," one John Alite, a self-confessed murderer, home invader and torturer who was so low on the Mafia food chain that he had to leave the room when any significant criminal business was discussed. But throughout the upcoming trial when it came to the crimes in the indictment, his mantra would be, "John ordered me to do it."

A federal judge concluded that this was little more than "forum shopping," a bold-faced attempt to get the Gotti scion in front of a Deep South jury. So he quickly sent the case up to The Southern District of New York where the first three had been tried.

And once again, though no Gotti, father or son, had ever been a flight risk, they refused to grant him bail. Even worse, they moved him in rapid succession from federal jail in Brooklyn to lockups in Kansas, Texas, Oklahoma, Georgia, back to Oklahoma, then Georgia again—even New Hampshire—before he finally got back to New York.

During those weeks of "Diesel therapy," his family had no idea where he was and he couldn't meet with his lawyers to prepare for his own defense.

A year later Trial Four began with Mafia-beat reporters like George Anastasia in Philadelphia and Jerry Capeci in New York predicting that Alite might well be the Feds' magic bullet and this time Junior could go down.

Earlier Alite had pled guilty to his involvement in two murders, four murder conspiracies, at least eight shootings and two attempted shootings, not to mention a series of armed home invasions in New York, New Jersey, Pennsylvania and Florida.

Those crimes, one which was death eligible, should have earned him a life sentence, but as payback for testifying against Junior, he drew a wrist-slap, 10-year sentence, most of which he'd already served and the Feds knocked that down by 20 months, ultimately releasing him in January, 2012.

But not before defense lawyer Charles Carnesi subjected Alite to days of blistering cross examination in Trial Four, exposing lie after lie in the government's case.

"Alite was the government's own house of cards," says John Jr. "He actually testified that he was my unmade underboss; my 'Sammy The Bull.' But, in truth, he was a low-level gutter rat. Consider the logic: The Gambino Family had a strict rank and file structure. At the very bottom were associates. Italian associates, on their father's side ranked higher than people like Alite who was Albanian. He could never be a made member. He even used the name Johnny Aletto to try and pass himself off as a *paisan*, but he was never, ever, any more than a dog who chased the scraps.

"The pecking order was non-Italian associate talks to Italian-associate who talks to a soldier who talks to a capo and then it goes to the management. I was on that level at the time and he's saying that I'm ordering him to do crimes like murder. It defies belief."

Sure enough, after eleven days of deliberations in Trial Four, the jury deadlocked again and set John free. "Enough is enough," said one juror later. "If they try him again it'll be an abuse of prosecution." Perhaps most significant, all twelve jurors were unanimous that the least credible witness for the Feds was John Alite.

A Different Kind of Racketeering Enterprise

After publishing those four investigative books for Harper-

Collins that served to document the multiple counter-terrorism and organized crime missteps of the FBI—fully annotated works encompassing 925,000 words over 2,200 pages—I thought I'd seen everything when it came to Justice Department misconduct.

But reading through Junior's epic story, I was repeatedly shocked at just how far special agents and assistant U.S. attorneys were willing to go to take his scalp. As such, this book should serve as a cautionary tale to any American who believes that the criminal justice system can be easily manipulated by the wealthy and the powerful or that when it comes to trying Mafia figures, the only standards for federal prosecutors and FBI agents are the rules of evidence and fair play.

By the time you get to the end of *Shadow of My Father* with jaw-dropping revelation after jaw-dropping revelation you'll wonder whether a case couldn't have been made by Gotti Jr.'s lawyers for charging *the Feds* under RICO: The Racketeer Influenced and Corrupt Organizations Act. That's the notorious 1970 end-run around the U.S. Constitution in which federal prosecutors began getting indictments, not for individual *crimes,* but for *a pattern of behavior*; i.e. acts performed as part of "an ongoing criminal organization."

To convict under RICO the Feds merely have to prove the violation of at least two "predicate crimes" within a 10 year period. They include state offenses like extortion and bribery and various violations of Title 18 of the Federal Criminal Code, including fraud and obstruction of justice.

Now as you read this book, consider the lengths Justice went to in order to "get" Gotti Junior. They handed down a series of indictments and conducted trials spanning nine years in an organized enterprise that included obstruction, fraud, witness tampering, the mischaracterization of evidence and the effective "bribery" of cooperating witnesses: i.e. mob killers like Alite, facing life in prison who were treated to a quid pro quo.

If they testified against Junior they'd be set free or have their sentences drastically reduced. You'll come to see that Team Fed conducted their business with the same bare-knuckled duplicity as the most brutal Mafia boss, only they did it in league with The FBI whose official seal contains the words: Fidelity, Bravery & Integrity.

The Bar Fight that Changed His Life

Meanwhile, this book is full of untold revelations in Junior's personal story. "This Life was not the path I had originally chosen," he told me. "I graduated from New York Military Academy on June 5th, 1982. I was looking to go into a ROTC compatible college. I needed two more years of ROTC and that would qualify me as a Second Lieutenant in the Army. That was where I wanted to go. That was the career choice I had made.

"But fate had a different life in store for me. A couple of weeks into my 19th year I was involved in a bar fight. There were some kids there from Ozone Park, high on Angel Dust. We were from Howard Beach. One of my friends dated a girl who hung out there. One thing led to another and this kid kept shoving into me. We got into a fight, and I hit him. Pretty soon it erupted into a free-for-all. I got stabbed. Several other guys got stabbed and one poor kid died from his wounds. That changed my life forever.

To keep an eye on him, John Jr. says his father "remanded me to house arrest" at the Bergin Club.

"'Sit right over here,' he said, 'so I can watch you and you ain't gettin' into trouble.' And pretty soon, hanging out there, I was sucked into that way of life. Once I was exposed to John and those people, it became intoxicating. The respect they were getting, the way they comported themselves, the laughs they had and the stories they told . . .

"So I went from trying to be a military officer to looking up to these guys. I would listen to them around the table as they were playing cards and breaking balls, and they all had jailhouse stories. Jail sounded so fun, it really did. Listening to these guys talk, 'Remember when we were in Lewisburg together that time?' I always said to myself, 'Someday I want to have my jailhouse stories. I want to have stories like these guys.'

"Years later when I'm locked down in some hole pissing blood from my kidneys I had a dream and I heard this voice say to me, 'Hey John…Are you havin' fun now?'"

The New Alcatraz

His father was convicted in 1992 and sent to the U.S. Prison in Marion. Illinois. It had opened in 1963 to replace the notorious "Rock"—the penitentiary on Alcatraz island—and it was built to house the most hardened inmates. The highest maximum security prison in the system for decades, Marion soon developed a reputation as the worst.

In 1983 after two guards were killed it went on "permanent lockdown" for 23 years with inmates held in their cells for twenty-two and a half hours a day. Amnesty International condemned the prison for "habitually" violating the United Nations' Standard Minimum Rules for prisoner treatment.

Worse, evidence developed that the 280,000 gallon-per-day water supply drawn from the nearby Crab Orchard Lake (an EPA Superfund site) was laced with cancer-causing PCB's (polychlorinated biphenyls).

"My father hadn't smoked cigarettes in 27 years," says Junior, "and after a few years in Marion they took his commissary privileges away and he was forced to drink the tap water. That's when he developed head, neck and throat cancer.

"Anyway, while I'm visiting my father in prison, I realize how alone he is. He's deprived of human contact; allowed to talk to us only by phone, through bulletproof glass. He's held only one of my six children—Frankie—and that was while he was still free.

"Seeing him at Marion got me thinking. If I ended up in federal lockup doing a life bid my own kids would be thousands of miles away. When they came to see me it would be under conditions like this. I had to decide between my blood family and the one I was sworn into. I began pulling back in '95, '96, '97, and then I was arrested in 1998."

The indictment charged Junior and 39 others with a series of crimes, including extortion and fraud, alleging that Gotti Jr. and his associates had virtually taken control of Scores, the Upper East Side topless nightclub. The case soon became a prototype for the kind of abusive and unethical conduct by the Feds Junior would experience over the next decade.

"One of the government's top cooperating witnesses," says, Junior was Michael Blutrich, a lawyer who'd been indicted in Florida for bilking hundreds of millions from senior citizens." Blutrich had also been outed as a pedophile in a *Penthouse Magazine* article by former NYPD detective John Connolly.

"So we subpoenaed all of the notes on Blutrich's interviews with the arresting FBI agent named Jack Karst," says Junior "and when he came to court he told the judge, 'I shredded them all by accident.'"

Karst was later demoted for destroying the documents. He had developed Blutrich as an informant after the alleged lawyer/pedophile bought Scores with money he and his partner Lyle Pfeffer stole from National Heritage Life Insurance Company of Orlando, Florida. On that same case, Vincent Heintz, an assistant U.S. attorney, was dismissed from the case for reportedly leaking information adverse to Gotti Jr.

In years to come, during the four federal trials the Feds mounted after this case, there would be a similar pattern of media leaks. More revealing was the evidence Gotti Jr.'s defense team uncovered suggesting that FBI agents had hidden or destroyed what, per Bureau protocol, should have been *dozens* of debriefing memos recounting Alite's meetings with special agents in the years before he became a formal cooperating witness.

Ultimately in that Orlando case, Blutrich and Pfeffer pled guilty to 22 racketeering, fraud and money laundering counts. Prosecutors admitted that they were responsible for $237 million in losses. Blutrich was sentenced to sixteen and a half years in prison, but in return for his agreement to testify against Gotti Jr. he was given a new identity and allowed to enter (WITSEC) the witness protection program.

That was in sharp contrast to the fate of Shalom Weiss, another participant in the Heritage looting scheme, believed to be the largest insurance failure in U.S. history at that time. Unable to trade with the Feds and deliver dirt on Gotti Jr., Weiss was sentenced to a staggering 845 years—the longest known sentence ever for a white collar criminal.

"To make my case," says Junior "the Feds not only got in bed with the likes of Blutrich, but the lead FBI agent had to destroy his notes, documenting their back-door dealings. Using Blutrich against me was the height of hypocrisy and my father begged me not to take a plea in the case. He felt with that level of misconduct we could win it."

The Fateful Encounter at Marion

"I had more faith in the Justice Department and their willingness to play fair, than he did. He understood their capacity for treachery. But I kept thinking of my kids and I wanted out. So I went to see him. It was February 5th, 1999. I'd just been released on bail for the Scores indictment and the Marshals took me to Marion on the order of a federal judge. It's on videotape. And what I'm looking to do is to take a plea and go to jail. At that point they were offering me seven and a half years. If I pled to minor charges, I could come home.

"I'm thinking, my kids will still be teenagers. I can save them. But John's a dyed-in-the-wool gangster. He's talking about the rules. 'When a man chooses a path in his life—even if he comes to the realization at some point in his life it's the wrong path—you stay on that path because that's what a man is, that's what it means to have this in his heart.'

"And in the end, as it happened, I was wrong and he was right. Because even though I took the plea and did my 77 months, the Feds never intended to let me go."

Presenting False Evidence

Just weeks before his release in September, 2004, the U.S. Attorney for the SDNY unsealed a new 11-count indictment charging Gotti Jr. with counts ranging from attempted murder to racketing and extortion.

The central focus of the case was an alleged plot in which the Feds insisted that Junior had conspired to kidnap Curtis Sliwa, the founder of The Guardian Angels, who, as a radio talk show host, had railed against Gotti Sr.

For Trial One federal prosecutors trotted out Joseph "Little Joey" D'Angelo, a Gambino soldier who had posed as a cab driver in the failed plot to kidnap Sliwa outside his apartment building. They also called "Fat Sal" Mangiavillano, a Gambino associate who testified that D'Angelo had grabbed Sliwa on orders from Gotti Jr.

"That's when we uncovered more misconduct by the Feds," says John Jr. "In Fat Sal's interview with FBI agent Ted Otto, the case agent, we learned from Otto's notes that Mangiavillano had said Sammy Gravano planned to reward D'Angelo for Sliwa by getting him straightened out. In other words, inducted into the Gambinos. That was the government's position.

"The problem was the Sliwa shooting was in June of 1992 and my father had been convicted on Sammy's testimony the previous April. Gravano had been working with the Feds since the previous year, so how is he supposed to be ordering Joey to get his button from witness protection? It was the first of many lies and the jury deadlocked."

"John was acquitted on some counts," says Charles Carnesi

who signed on to represent Gotti Jr. in Trial Two. "The jury had acquitted John on some charges including stock fraud, and hung eleven-to-one against John on the rest. The government was confident that they would prevail in a second prosecution. But we decided to put on a vigorous defense and this time, on virtually the same evidence from the Feds, the jury hung eight to four in favor of *acquittal.* Now they got worried."

New Press Leaks and Alleged Witness Tampering

"Between the second and third trial," says Carnesi, "things really start to change. That's when the FBI crosses the line. Some agent intimately involved in the case must have had a relationship with a *New York Post* reporter named Kati Cornell Smith and she starts writing a series of articles with revelations she alleges are coming from a law enforcement source."

In the first piece, headlined "Gotti Pal In A Bind-Perjury Rap Looms," Smith reported that Joseph Fusaro, "...who surprised the feds by testifying in support of John 'Junior' Gotti could soon face perjury charges as prosecutors gear up for the former mob big's third trial... If Fusaro takes the witness stand again, he'll be doing it with an indictment hanging over his head,' the source said... Testifying in Gotti's defense in Manhattan federal court, Fusaro said the feds hounded him about cooperating. 'Every agent... every lawyer that I ever spoke to, the first words out of their mouths were, "If you tell me about John... you can go home,"' he said."

"So this article is published," says Carnesi, "quoting a law enforcement source as saying that there's a grand jury going on investigating Fusaro for perjury in John's trial and that should he come to the third trial and testify, he will be coming with a perjury indictment. If the source is from the government, then by any definition that is *witness tampering* and *obstruction of justice.*"

The Death Threat

Carnesi says he soon got a call from Joon Kim, assistant U.S. Attorney on Trial Two who was gearing up for Trial Three. "He tells me that they have information that there may be a contract on John's life," says Carnesi. "And that the mob is very upset with us and the way that the case has been presented. I ask him where did it come from and what's it about and he says 'I can't tell you any more than that.'"

Three months later, Smith filed another story with the headline: "Junior Had A 'Singing' Tryout—Turned Canary In Futile Bid to Stay Out of Prosecutor's Cage."

"The younger Gotti," she wrote, "disregarded the Mafia oath of silence and ratted out members of the Gambino crime family during a day long proffer session with federal prosecutors in the spring of 2005, sources familiar with the meeting told *The Post*."

"That was a complete mischaracterization," says Junior. "I never agreed to cooperate. It was that very principal that I stood for in suffering through the time I had served. But the government was relentless in trying to turn me."

"Implicit in this," says Carnesi, "is that now we've now got problems from two directions: from the government which wants to put him away for life. And now, even if he wins, he'll lose because, in effect, he can't be safe on the street. That's the pressure."

Like a Scene from *The Godfather*

"Around this time," says Carnesi," Ted Otto does the unforgivable. He goes out and serves subpoenas on people in the mob who the government believes are the most likely to want to hurt John at this point. In the process of serving those subpoenas, these people are specifically told, 'This is from John. You can thank John and Charlie.'"

Like the earlier "singing" story, the subpoenas were soon followed by another Kati Cornell Smith piece in the *Post* quoting law enforcement, under the headline: "Blame It On Gotti Subpoenas." She reported, "Lawyers for John 'Junior' Gotti say the FBI is delivering an unusual verbal message along with its subpoenas for a sweeping grand-jury probe of the Gambinos."

"It was like that scene in *Godfather II*," says John, "where Frankie Five Angels Pentangeli is sitting in a bar and a guy walks up behind him and throws a garrote around his neck with the words, 'Michael Corleone says hello.' This is a federal agent using tactics you'd expect from the mob. An unbridled attempt to get me killed."

"So we go into court," says Carnesi "and we challenge Kati Cornell Smith to disclose the source of the leaks, believing that they came from Ted Otto. She invokes the New York Shield Law which protects reporters' sources. But when asked if she *does* have a 'law enforcement source,' she affirms under oath that her story is truthful in that regard.

"Once there's been an indictment returned there's no reason to call people to a grand jury. So we present the article and tell the judge (Shira Shindlein) what was said to those who got subpoenas. She's outraged. She calls it the equivalent of 'letting the dogs loose.' She questions the AUSA and he says, 'If there's a grand jury, I don't know about it.'"

The "Ted Otto Special" in Trial Three

"We got to the point," says Junior, "of calling these stunts by Otto, 'specials,' and one of his most outrageous came in the third trial when he testified to a snippet of audio from a recording my father made when he was dying at the prison hospital in Springfield, Missouri. It was March 31st, 2001 and he was talking to Joe Corozzo Jr., a lawyer."

Otto testified that the tape was evidence that Senior

was appointing his son to a panel of Gambino leaders who would succeed him, including his brother Peter Gotti, Jackie D'Amico and Nicholas Corozzo, the lawyer's father. In the Trial Q&A with Otto attempting to authenticate the tape, an Assistant U.S. Attorney is questioning him:

> AUSA: Okay. And you hear Mr. Gotti use the expression...
> "Shake it up. Shake it up the way you want."
> OTTO: With a gesture. He's shaking his hand with three fingers.
> AUSA: Right. Okay. And you're interpreting the gesture in a particular...way, right?
> OTTO: My interpretation is that he was giving Peter Gotti the latitude to name whomever he wanted, listing John, Jackie and Nicky.
> AUSA: That's your interpretation, right?
> OTTO: Yes.

But the audio cited by Otto was virtually unintelligible, so the Gotti Jr. defense team called in Thomas J. Owen, an audio specialist who was the Chairman Emeritus of the American Board of Recorded Evidence. When he enhanced the recording it became clear that in the same snippet of audio when Gotti Sr. and Corozzo were supposedly having the succession discussion, Senior mentioned "Jimmy Brown," Failla, a former Gambino capo who had been dead for years at the time. So the cross examination of Otto by Carnesi went like this:

> CARNESI: Now Jimmy Brown in 2001 is deceased, right?
> OTTO: I think he died a couple years before.
> CARNESI: Right
> OTTO: He was no longer with us in 2001.
> CARNESI: Right. So any discussion with Jimmy Brown in that conversation certainly didn't have anything to do with any changes in the hierarchy of the Gambino family, right?
> OTTO: Not in that portion of the conversation, no.

" I'm a former prosecutor," says Carnesi, "And with respect to Ted Otto's misrepresentation to the jury of what was on that tape I would say that it was inaccurate and intentionally misleading. You can't have a conversation of appointing people to new positions and naming a dead guy."

Another Deadlocked Jury

Finally, after six weeks of trial and days of deliberations, the jury in Trial Three hung once again. It was the third time in just over a year and John Jr. was finally set free.

Quoting a "federal official," *The New York Times* reported that "the prosecution was unlikely to retry Mr. Gotti unless new evidence turned up, a decision that would all but end an expensive and highly publicized organized crime prosecution in a startling defeat for the government."

Even Fed-friendly Kati Cornell Smith seemed resigned to the fact that Junior might finally escape his father's fate. "Prosecutors in the John 'Junior' Gotti case threw in the towel yesterday," she wrote, "announcing they won't seek a fourth racketeering trial for the mob scion. 'The government has concluded that a retrial of defendant John A. Gotti on the pending indictment is not in the interests of justice in light of the three prior hung juries,' U.S. Attorney Michael Garcia said yesterday."

"So it looked like I could finally breathe," says John Jr. "Go on to live my life as a civilian. And then, just twenty months later, early in the morning as I fed my infant son Joe, I heard that helicopter hovering overhead and I knew that they were coming for me again."

Showdown in the Southern District

The details of the government's failed attempt to convict John Gotti Jr. on tax charges and the riveting testimony in his fourth trial are so compelling that I don't want to rob the reader of what promises to be a page-turner worthy of John Grisham or Scott Turow.

In the tradition of an opening statement though, I'll say that in the last chapters of *Shadow of My Father* you'll read an account of Charles Carnesi's devastating cross examination that caught John Alite, the Fed's star witness, in multiple lies. Among them allegations that:

–Alite had acted as John Jr.'s "Sammy The Bull" vs. the low-level associate that he was;

–John Jr. had ordered *multiple murders* when, in fact, Alite was the principal;

–Alite had made up to $10 million selling drugs, when, in fact, he was virtually broke at the time;

–Alite had had an affair with Vicki Gotti when, in fact, she had previously passed a polygraph to prove him wrong;

–Alite had denied wrecking a gym he'd invested in, only later to admit his involvement;

–Alite implicated Gotti Jr. in the torture/shooting of a contractor he'd hired; an allegation that both the jury and the press found implausible.

That electrical contractor's only offense, was having sex with his girlfriend at Alite's house while Alite was away. But then, when he got back, Alite said under oath, that he lured the electrician back to his home with the promise of more cash.

Facing the jury and telling the story almost proudly, Alite testified that, "I stripped him down. I piped him. I broke his ribs, his jaw, I believe his arm, and I threw him in my lake. It was about 30 degrees. I said, 'You want to make an asshole out of me, I'm gonna make one of you.' I was shooting at him, and I told him to stay under water... Then I took him out of the lake, tied him up naked, put him in my garage, and I had all the security dogs (12-to-15 of them) so he couldn't leave the garage, and I went to dinner...."

Even Jerry Capeci who had excoriated the Gottis over the years in his *Gangland* column, seemed taken aback by the story. "A few days later, on cross examination," he wrote, "defense lawyer Charles Carnesi raised the incident in an effort to stress how wildly Alite 'reacted' on his own because he felt he had been made a fool of. That's when Alite suddenly recalled that before he 'hurt the guy' he drove to Queens and 'got permission' from 'John Gotti Junior.' The convenient interjection of Gotti's name in a story that had been told in excruciating detail the first time around must have served as a bright red warning flag to jurors about the government's top witness."

In fact, Alite performed so poorly that the Feds decided not to use him as their star witness in the upcoming trial of John Burke, a Queens gangster charged in the murder of two drug dealers. Burke was the last remaining defendant in the Alite-inspired Tampa case that had spawned Trial Four, but in a column headlined "Team USA Benches John Alite," Capeci wrote, "Brooklyn federal prosecutors have figured out how to keep the flawed mob turncoat John Alite off the stand."

The Devastating Testimony of Joe O'Kane

Perhaps the ultimate demonstration of government misconduct in the epic series of Gotti prosecutions came after Ted Otto visited former Gambino associate Joseph O'Kane in prison where he was serving 15 years to life on racketeering & murder charges. Testifying now in Trial Four, O'Kane told the jury what Otto had reportedly told him:

"I understand you're doing a life sentence and we want to give you a number, which means that... I would either get 5 years, 10 years, time-served...something like that..." O'Kane said, describing Otto's alleged offer.

When asked how he responded, O'Kane said, "I told him to go fuck himself...and I walked away. I didn't ask what the number was and he didn't state what the number would be."

Even Assistant U.S. Attorney Jay Trezevant who was the lead prosecutor in Trial Four underscored the significance of Otto's offer: "If you provide any information here in this courtroom against Mr. Gotti, there are consequences that can happen to you, correct?"

O'Kane answered him truthfully: "If I was going to provide information towards John Gotti, I would probably be home with my family and son right now."

But he refused to give false testimony. In fact, O'Kane, a longtime friend of John Alite, testified in detail how the Albanian associate had lived "on John Junior's reputation." He also recounted how Gotti Jr. had a falling out with Alite over drugs.

"Alite beeped me," said O'Kane, "I met him and he said that he had a serious argument with John...that John told him to stop selling drugs... 'I don't want you around me anymore. If you're going to do that (John told him)...' John despised people that took drugs or sold drugs...

"After (that) Junior chased Alite pretty much from New York," said O'Kane. "His finances dried up because he was no longer selling drugs. He was broke."

Joe O'Kane, who had every motive to lie against Junior—in return for the same kind of reduced sentence promised to Alite—stood firm and returned to prison. As you'll read in this book, the fate awaiting him when he got back behind bars was shocking.

Why Does It Matter?

Apart from the stunning examples of federal misconduct documented in this book, perhaps the most astonishing aspect of it all for me, was that it played out in New York City, home to the FBI's New York Office (NYO) the largest concentration of special agents outside D.C. and the office of the U.S. Attorney for the Southern District of New York (SDNY) the most vaunted federal prosecutor's office in America.

Among its alumni are a U.S. Attorney General, a Supreme Court Justice, two FBI directors (Louis Freeh and current Director James Comey) not to mention Rudolph Giuliani, the mob-busting former New York mayor and presidential contender.

The multiple prosecutions of John A. Gotti and his father took place not in some Mississippi backwater or an Eastern Bloc courtroom, but front and center on Foley Square in Manhattan; cases that were investigated and prosecuted by "the best of the best" in the U.S. Justice Department.

After John J. Gotti's acquittal in 1987, he became "the top investigative priority" of the FBI's NYO and he remained Target Number One for the next five years. Tens of millions of dollars were expended prosecuting the Gottis, father *and* son. And much of that happened while an al Qaeda cell, funded directly by Osama bin Laden, was metastasizing in New York and New Jersey.

Given the fact that the SDNY and NYO served as the two Bin Laden "offices of origin," charged with protecting the U.S. homeland from terrorism, the surplus of moneys and manpower expended to "get Gotti" demonstrates the price that America paid for the Feds' misplaced priorities.

As I documented in *"1000 Years For Revenge: International Terrorism And The FBI,"* my first book for HarperCollins, both assaults on The World Trade Center: the 1993 bombing and the "planes-as-missiles" attack of 9/11 were carried out by the same cell of al Qaeda terrorists who had set up shop in Brooklyn as far back as the summer of 1989.

In fact, as early as 1991 the FBI was onto a check-cashing store in Jersey City run by Egyptians called Sphinx Trading. Ten years later, two of the hijackers who flew AA Flight 77 into The Pentagon on 9/11 got their fake ID's at that *precise* location.

How difficult would it have been for the Bureau to devote *a fraction* of the resources they'd spent in their round-the-clock surveillance of John Gotti Sr. to watching that store on Kennedy Boulevard? If they had, with the combined "chatter" and intel picked up in the summer of 2001 it's fair to argue that the Twin Towers might still be standing.

So why is Junior's rewrite of history important? Because like the investigation of counter-terrorism it serves as a kind of minority report to the conventional narrative that the Justice Department has sold to the mainstream media for years.

With respect to 9/11, the goal of that narrative was protecting the reputations of the FBI special agents, supervisors and counter-terrorism officials who had been outgunned for years during al Qaeda's murderous juggernaut.

With respect to Gotti Jr. it was the Feds' steadfast refusal to admit that he'd actually done what he said he would in 1998 when he took the plea, withdrew from the mob and went to prison. The "King of The Volcano's" son *actually believed* that if he did his time and exited the Life, the government would reciprocate and honor their pledge.

Now, as you turn the pages of this book you'll understand the price he paid and why he's now determined to set the record straight. He owes it not just to his children and the memory of his father, but to history.

Peter Lance
www.peterlance.com
Santa Barbara, California
December 15, 2014

INTRODUCTION

Reflections in an October Sky

.

Through the hanging willow trees in my back yard, I could see the stars.

It was one of those nights in my favorite season of autumn, when we are offered crisp pure air, and cold clear black skies dotted with sparkling white dots that are in reality large boiling suns in some other solar system.

Not everything we perceive, not everything we are told or shown, conforms to the actual reality of the thing. This applies to individuals also. I hope to prove that in this book you are now reading.

If the above description might seem a tad philosophical and poetic for the someone that you might think I am (or was), perhaps you are right, but I will plead guilty with an explanation.

Often, the inspiration for poetry or philosophy comes from suffering.

I remember many years, that for me, there was no open night sky, no stars, no crisp pure air. The view from solitary confinement is somewhat more limited. I'm taking notes now on a cushioned chaise lounge by my pool. In jail the mattress is less comfortable; the nearest thing to a pool is the stainless steel toilet sink combination.

There were times I was confined in a maximum security terrorist wing, where five times a day I would hear the Muslim prisoners' *adhan*, the call to prayer. I was never accused of being a terrorist, although I'm sure, had they wanted to, the government could have produced a willing witness that I was.

There were times I writhed in pain curled up in fetal position on a cell mattress from untreated kidney stones. Medically neglected by the Bureau of Prisons. Blood in my urine, pain worse than being stabbed—and I have been stabbed more than once.

Now, as I write this, I am smoking an excellent Dominican cigar, with full access to competent medical care anytime I want it. Both mind and body are at peace, in a state of comfort. I no longer spend every waking hour wondering whether or if I will ever be free, ever see my children again outside of the confines of a prison visit.

The government in four trials and one violation of parole hearing tried to convict me. They couldn't. No matter how much legitimate or perjured testimony they paraded in front of a jury or judge.

Please don't imagine that I am gloating. I am not. I am immensely grateful to those jurors who fulfilled the duty of a juror to the utmost, despite great pressure to do otherwise.

Both in the case of my father's final trial, and in my fourth (and hopefully final) trial, the judges had a tendency to find reasons to remove defense favoring jurors. Yet those that remained still did their duty.

For three weeks in my last trial the jurors deliberated my guilt or innocence, and in the end, they couldn't—more were for acquittal than conviction however. The government was less than pleased, but in the press the public was of one voice—don't try John A. Gotti again.

Those who read this may make up their own mind about my guilt or innocence. Some will believe I have reformed, others will doubt it. I can not change minds that have pre-judged a question. I can offer evidence and explanation to those who are of an open mind, who have not yet decided, who require more facts prior to making a determination.

Ergo, this book. In a venue where I can speak freely, without any artificial rules of evidence to constrict communication, without any arbiter in a black robe to tell me what I can and cannot offer as proof.

My father and I have been lionized and demonized, depending on the viewpoint of the people passing judgment on us. Believe me, what you may have read in the papers, what you may have heard from law enforcement "authorities" is not one hundred percent accurate.

Thus, I must set the record straight and answer the question, "Who was John Joseph Gotti and who is John Angelo Gotti?"

SHADOW OF MY FATHER

CHAPTER ONE

John Joseph Gotti

On October 27, 1940, my father, John J. Gotti, was born. The next day Italy invaded Greece. The former event, while not related to the latter, was to be of longer lasting consequence. It has been just about seventy-four years since my father's birth, but I would daresay that more people today are familiar with his life and doings, than the fact that Greece was once invaded by Italy.

Of course, while what is in the popular knowledge, what is printed in various media, may on occasion be accurate, sometimes the tales told are not true. It is my hopes herein to set a true account of the life of a man who rose from a birth in poverty in the Bronx, to a time when he was the king of New York City.

San Giuseppe Vesuviano, in Naples, was the home of his ancestors. His father was a laborer, often unemployed, his mother, Philomena, was a housewife, and later a part time butcher.

Including my father, there had been eleven brothers and sisters that survived; two others had died at a very young age. They were dirt poor. My father attended PS 209 in Sheepshead Bay in Brooklyn. When he was twelve, the family moved to

East New York. At around thirteen, he was placed in a youth home.

Along with the poor on those streets, was a significant amount of people who lived a life of crime.

John Joseph Gotti went to Junior High School 178, with more impoverished youths. They shared a common fascination for the Mafia, the guys in The Life who managed to rise from poverty to power. To become men of respect; at least in the neighborhood.

Although my father has been recorded as having a 140 IQ, school was not where he wanted to learn. The streets were to be his school, and he soon joined a neighborhood gang, the Fulton Rockaway Boys. It was here that he became friends with Angelo Ruggiero.

The gang became a surrogate family for the members, a place where they were accepted, a place where they obtained a feeling of belonging.

It was also handy for planning crimes and cons. Neighborhood protection rackets, loan sharking, gambling—the requisite courses for graduation when one got a degree in tough and street smart. One also gained the respect of one's peers because the fifties were the prime days for the outlaw kid, the biker, the Wild One, the rebel.

The image was attractive to young females—one being my mother, Victoria. Many years later, during the trial of 2009, one of my attorneys asked her what the attraction to my father was. "I guess I always liked the bad boys," she said.

★

My father was ambitious. He moved up from the petty criminal activities of the gang to more significant criminal activity. His smarts and toughness did not go unnoticed in the neighborhood. Mob guys Carmine and Danny Fatico, members of what was later to be known as the Gambino family, took a shine to him. Took him under their black leather wings.

Later, Neil Dellacroce, a powerful figure in the family, would become a mentor and surrogate father to mine.

My father brought Angelo with him. It was to be a lifelong criminal association and the continuance of a deep friendship of the men, that ended with Angelo's death of cancer.

★

My father's first formal milestone in professional crime came in 1959 when he was arrested for unlawful assembly. He had been caught in a gambling raid. Soon a disorderly conduct charge was to follow. His first bid was in 1964, a short time after I was born. He did several months in Riverhead, at the Suffolk County jail, in New York.

But at times, he went straight. He worked as a coat presser in a Brooklyn coat factory. But crime always beckoned, and soon he was busted again for possession of a weapon (club) which got him twenty days in jail.

Upon release, legitimate employment seemed to elude him, and back to crime it was. Gambling. Truck hijacking. One incident landed him again in jail, this time for three and half years in Lewisburg. He arrived in 1969, and "graduated" in 1972, an older and wiser, up-and-coming gangster.

He assembled his crew. Loansharking, gambling, extortion, and more nefarious activities on occasion. The staples of crime. The proceeds from these activities enabled my father to move my mother and the (then) four kids to a better part of Brooklyn. Canarsie.

Later in this book, we will learn the truth of the McBratney killing that endeared my father to Carlo Gambino, head of the family, and that also landed him a four-year bid in jail. Upon his exit from "college" he became a made man, as the books had once again opened up. (More on that later.)

You will read about the steps of his meteoric rise to king of the streets in an upcoming chapter; and about his meteoric fall, and reaching the final destination to which we all eventually journey.

In one lifetime, a man went from dirt poor to the most powerful mobster in the most powerful crime family in the United States. John Joseph Gotti.

In about half a lifetime, I, his eldest son, turned the other way, leaving The Life at thirty-four, leaving millions of dollars of my street money behind for the remaining vultures to scavenge.

While my father was in jail, I was a capo. Then, in 1998, I realized the errors of my ways, that the myths of the mafia, the supposed brotherhood, the supposed loyalty unto death, were untrue—as rat after rat had testified against my father, and were then lined up to testify against me.

I met with my father one final time in Springfield, Missouri, while he was suffering from multiple cancers, and told him in a prison conference room I was from thereon in going to be just a citizen. A civilian, a man who will achieve honor and, hopefully, respect by *not* committing crimes.

You will hear those conversations in this book. You will feel the tension between generations, as a dyed-in-the-wool gangster—a man who walked in that life "all the way to the gate," to use his expression—heard from his first born son, that The Life was no longer for him. John Angelo Gotti.

CHAPTER TWO

Father and Son Reunion

The cancer was advancing, and the once dynamically handsome face bore evidence of the ravages of the disease, and of the surgeries that had been performed to remove what parts of it that they could.

The heart and mind had remained hard, tough, and smart. Nothing could change that. He lay there on his prison hospital cot and remembered the days of the camaraderie of old and tested friends, the parade of willing women, and the oceans of *Cristal* that had served as a social lubricant. Great days.

Days when he was king of the streets.

"Hey John?"

He recognized the voice of the Hack, and opened his eyes.

"You've got a visitor. Cuff up."

★

Both my attorneys, the prosecutor, and myself were amazed when during my 1998 case, Judge Parker had agreed to allow me to visit my father in Springfield.

"Why shouldn't he be allowed to visit his father?" the judge had rhetorically asked.

Carol Sipperly, the prosecutor, protested the visit because she alleged that my father and I would be communicating in code.

The judge replied, "Nonsense."

★

I had heard from a fellow inmate about how my father had originally been brought to Springfield.

A black armored van—more government vehicles with smoked out windows.

Manacled.

My inmate friend told me how he watched in amazement at the show being put on. This was a prison transfer, but it looked more like the lead up to the invasion of Poland. Prison guards bearing automatic rifles dressed in full riot gear. Orders being shouted.

Deputy Marshals ran up to the black van, surrounding it with their weapons ready. The doors were yanked open, and a heavily chained man in an orange jumpsuit was led out, black boxed, wrist and ankle shackles.

Even though he had severe restriction of his movement, I was told that the swagger was still there. Only my father could still strut in chains. Even in a cage, a lion is still a lion.

Now I had been brought to Springfield to visit with my father. To see the lion.

I was excited about getting an up close and personal visit with him. Possibly the last one I would have. It had been two years since I had seen him, eight years since I had touched him. I went through the front door, showed my ID, my escort showed his, then we went through the metal detector, and were escorted to the conference room.

I took notice of the video and audio recording equipment. Then after about fifteen minutes, I heard a clanging of chains and the movement of men. It was my father shackled up and escorted by an entourage of guards.

When I had first arrived, two FBI agents approached me. One of them asked to be in on the visit with my father. After all, he reasoned, the visit is being taped anyway, so what was the harm.

I refused. I shook their hands and said no. That wasn't going to happen, and I reminded them that the judge's order didn't say anything about FBI being present on the visit. I informed them that my father would not set foot in the room with agents present and there would be no visit.

While I was refusing their demands, I heard the clanking of chains and manacles, and my father came to the door of the conference room, saw me in the presence of two agents, and immediately stopped. The agents went to shake his hand, and he refused. These were his enemies. My heart dropped. Here I was on a visit, and the first moment my father sees me, I'm in the presence of two FBI agents. What must he have thought? His son on a visit, court sanctioned, in the presence of two agents. Did his son turn?

"What can I do for you?" my father asked in a tone that clearly meant, "What the hell are you doing here?"

The agents said they were going to sit in on the visit. My father said no they were not. There would be no visit if they were to be present. He turned to me and said, "I love to see you and I love you pal, but I won't sit in any room with these individuals."

My father was taken back out by the guards.

The Lieutenant present at the time, had phone calls made and people contacted to see what to do about this impasse. One of the marshals had the judge's order, and informed the agents again, that nowhere did it say anything about agents attending our visit.

Finally prison officials convinced the FBI to make themselves scarce.

He had been again escorted to the conference room where we would meet. Eight guards deposited him at the table.

Now that the FBI was gone, we could converse.

I did rather well in hiding my shock at seeing what years of medical neglect had done to him. I knew that what started out as a set of bad dental implants, through numerous neglected infections, had eventually turned into mouth and throat cancer. I knew there were signs in Marion, where he had been housed, that warned people who weren't prisoners not to drink the water. It was carcinogenic.

The poisonous waters of Marion Prison had been long known to the government and non-governmental organizations. The water for the prison was drawn from Crab Orchard Lake, which is located in a toxic waste dump. The water contains huge quantities of PCBs and lead.

The city of Marion had stopped using Crab Orchard Lake water for drinking in 1982.

But the water and the Bureau of Prisons could not easily or quickly kill my father, and there he was right in front of me, a shadow of his former self—physically.

This was a man who had endured years of solitary confinement, and yet prior to the cancer, had looked bull-strong, and physically about twenty years younger. He had been sent as his final prison destination to the maximum security facility directly after sentencing. He had spent more time there—without being considered for a reduction of the stringency of his confinement security conditions—than any other inmate who had never committed any infraction of prison rules.

As always, whether it was DOJ or BOP, my father was a special case (as I would be). Not in the good sense of the word either. But even though emaciated, even though suffering from advanced stages of cancer, here he was and here I was.

We embraced across the table. They had allowed us that much, briefly. The guard had the decency to deflect the angle of the video camera during our embrace. I had come bearing a message in response to which I knew my father would have a strong negative reaction. Of course we were being videotaped, but at that moment, there was no one in that conference room except my father and myself.

"Look at me," joked my father. "Like I was Hannibal Lecter or something," referring to the excess of guards and restraints. The voice was raspy from the disease and the treatments.

I tried not to stare.

"The fucking trifecta," he continued. "Jaw, throat, and neck cancer. But despite the cut and paste job they've done on my face, I'm still me. Still standing. Still motherfuckering them every turn."

I smiled. Until he showed me the huge scar on his chest where flesh had been removed to graft on to his face.

"I got my tit on my face now," said my father. "Have to do one armed pushups now, 'cause they took the whole muscle."

It was getting tougher to keep smiling.

"Fucking government butchers." I couldn't help from saying.

"Bullshit," he said. "Cancer has maybe made my body betray me, but not my mind." He pounded his chest like a gorilla. "Not my heart either. Never happen."

He had stared directly into the prison video camera when he said that last part. He turned back to me. "What's up?"

I looked at the camera, then looked down at the conference table. Couldn't find any additional courage in these places. So I returned my gaze to my father's eyes. Eyes that knew me as only a father and a boss in The Life could know me. I was expecting the lion to roar—when I said what I had to say.

★

I was about seven at the time I visited my father in Lewisburg Penitentiary. He was there on a hijacking bid; and my mother, my brother Frank, and my two sisters were there to see him. I didn't understand the concept of jail, so seven-year-old me believed my father when he told me that the place was a barracks and he and his friends there with him were constructing it. He would be home when the construction was finished.

With him in jail were his lifelong friend Angelo Ruggiero, as well as Frank DeCicco, Mickey Boy Paradiso, and George Remini. When I went there to visit, it was like a family reunion. As kids, we were allowed to visit from table to table in the visiting area, which you can picture as being similar to a school lunchroom type setup.

It was around Halloween and my father asked me during the visit, what I was going to be—for Halloween.

"Officer Mike, down the block is going to let me use his nightstick and policeman's hat. I'm going as a cop, dad."

I saw his entire expression change—wide eyed, he bit his fist, which I came to learn was a gesture indicating, shall we say, extreme displeasure. He looked at my mother, who already knew what the gesture meant.

"What the Hell is the matter with you?" he asked my mother. "What have you done to my kid? He wants to become a cop?"

"Johnny," my mother said, "he's just a kid."

"If I ever hear you let my son or any of my kids, or you for that matter, talk to that cop, or any other cop, I'll kill you."

My mother tried to placate him. "Relax, he's just being nice to your son."

"Butch," he said looking at my mother, "don't make me repeat myself, I have my standards, and that's that." ("Butch" was the nickname my father had given my mother after they saw the movie, *Butch Cassidy and the Sundance Kid*.)

Then it was my turn. He gave me the cold angry stare. "You don't dress like a cop, you don't act like a cop, you don't talk like a cop—understand?" He gripped my forearm tightly, and I was so scared I wet my pants.

He realized he had come on too strong with me, and pinched my cheek to ease the tension. In lighter terms, he explained again that I was not to be a cop on Halloween.

Needless to say, I didn't dress up as a cop.

★

This time around, I wasn't dressing up as a cop. I had something to say far more likely to have him bite his fist, on this, our potentially last visit together. In response to, "What's up?" I told him.

"They allowed me a visit. I thought at best I'd get a phone call, but Judge Parker ordered that I get the visit."

"And they didn't just do it out of the kindness of their hearts," said my father. "So, I'll ask you again. What's up?"

I hesitated for a second. "I'm thinking of taking a plea, making a deal."

Some silences can be deafening.

★

It is strange the memories that come to you in times of significant stress. Me at seven, telling my father I wanted to play dress up cop, me at eight, seeing my father back in the neighborhood.

One of the things my father used to do when I was a little kid, (although I didn't know it at the time) was to hijack trucks from local airports.

He didn't always get away with it, and as I already mentioned, in 1968, when I was around four years old, he pleaded guilty to hijacking, and did a three and one-half year stretch at Lewisburg, which was the prison I visited when I wanted to dress up as a cop. (I was to later go there myself for a short time while en route to other places.)

While he was away, and back then I didn't even know what *that* really meant, I was sometimes taunted by other kids about having an absent father. I would always say he was coming home soon.

So you can imagine my thrill, in March 1972, after having my father away for so long, when I saw what to my eyes was a block-long, brown, brand new Lincoln Mark IV drive up in the snow on our block, while I was playing outside with the other kids. I had told my friends, "My father is coming home today." But they doubted me.

Well, here was the Lincoln, here was today, and here was my father.

He spotted me, stopped, rolled the window down, and said to me, "Hey Dad, where's the house?" (My father used to call me "Dad.")

To the other kids, I shouted, "There's my father," pointing proudly at the Lincoln.

The other kids' parents came outside to watch; some of them doubted that my mother had ever had a husband. I pointed to the house, and he said to me, "Okay, I'll see you down there."

I walked quickly towards the house, excited that my father had come home, as he drove the Lincoln to the house, parked it, and got out—resplendent.

He was dressed in a chocolate brown overcoat, which matched the color of the Lincoln, and underneath the coat he had a brown suit on covering a cream-colored mock turtleneck sweater. Perfectly coiffed hair.

To my future eyes, he was Tony Curtis with muscles, but back then, even though I couldn't put a name on it, I knew my dad was star quality. When this man was the head of the mob and out on the streets, no matter how many paparazzi, journalists, or Federal Agents took his picture, he always appeared immaculate. A King of the streets.

I felt his hand grab me by the back of the neck, and together—father and son—we walked into the house. As I write this, I am reminded of that 1961 song by Shep and the Limelites, *Daddy's Home*. (But unlike the song, my father wouldn't be home to stay.)

The whole family came out to greet him. He spent a few minutes talking with each of us individually. He asked us how we felt about him being home, and whether or not we minded if he lived in our house. (At the time, I was the happiest kid on the block—if not the world—that Daddy was home and living in our house.)

He went to my room, and saw the posters of the Mets. "You like the Mets?"

"Yes, Dad," I said. "What team do you like?"

"The Yankees."

Soon after that conversation, I tore down the Mets posters, and put up a Yankees poster.

But daddy wasn't to be home for long. Sometimes a door opens and closes on a new beginning for a man. Sometimes a door opens and closes on the last day of a man's existence, either literally, or figuratively.

★

"First of all John, what are their expectations of you in this plea?"

"Five and a half to seven years," I said.

My father looked at me sideways. "Five and a half? Seven? Which the fuck is it?"

I shrugged.

"I go buy a house. I ask the guy selling how much. Does he tell me somewhere between five hundred and fifty, and seven hundred thousand?" My father shook his head. "What number you think he's going to want?"

"They want their pound of flesh, that's all they want," I said, then realized that this expression had a literal meaning in this conference room for my father.

My father contained himself, but I could see the anger inside of him.

"I don't want you should do one motherfucking day in jail. I'd rather have this cancer than you have a cold."

I began to reply, but he cut me off with a wave of his hand.

"I'm gonna tell you something. If I robbed a church and the steeple was sticking out of my ass, I would deny it."

"I know."

"I'm telling you as a father, not as a boss, but as a father, you say you're innocent, I believe you. So why stand up in front of all those motherfuckers and say you're guilty?"

"I take the plea, and it's over. I get closure."

"Closure? What kind of mealy mouth word is that? You think they'll say 'thanks' and then give you a pass for the rest of your life? They'll be back on your ass again, and again, and forever."

"I've got to do this."

"John," he said to me, "when they had taken me from Marion do you know what the only thing was that I brought with me?"

"No."

"Your indictment. That's it. I brought it because I could give a fuck about this cancer, or what they are going to do to me. What's going to be will be. I'm only concerned for you."

"I know," I said, controlling my emotions.

"I must have read it fifty times and I don't see it."

"I know dad, but I'm thinking of my family."

"And what about your four hundred brothers and cousins, what about thinking of your whole family?"

Yes the whole family.

★

When my father was out of jail from Lewisburg, prior to going back to prison for reasons I will detail shortly, he practically lived at his club. The Family's club.

The Bergin Hunt and Fish Club, in Ozone Park. A place for friends to hang out.

Angelo Ruggiero, my father's closest friend, my uncles Gene and Peter, Carmine Fatico, Danny Fatico, Willie Boy

Johnson, Willy Chisel Chin, Skinny Louie, Tony Roach Rampino, Patty the Bookmaker, Jimmy Butch, and others were to be found in attendance at the Bergin with my father.

Oh yeah, back at this time, there was another nefarious character seen hanging around the club. Me.

Now, you may think that a little kid in a mob social club might be a little ill at ease, but not me. I thought the environment was totally normal. I mean, what did I have to compare it to? Hell, I thought it was amazing.

I would be all dressed up, brought into the club, and I became the junior center of attraction. Guys would come up to me and ask, "How you doin' pal?" They'd slip me a dollar, sometimes a five dollar bill. Obviously, little me, liked going to the club. A lot.

Maybe once or twice a month, when I was really young, on Saturdays, I'd be brought into the club. As I got older, I went more often. Usually, I was the only kid there, but sometimes my father's friend, Angelo Ruggiero, would bring his son, my late close friend, "Johnny Boy."

At club events, for holidays, barbecues, everybody brought their sons. Twice every summer, they would have old men vs. young men softball games. We'd also go on at least one fishing trip a year each summer, to Captree, on a boat, the Blue Albatross.

Most of all, the Bergin was a social center for the guys. They'd play cards, cook pasta, barbecue outside on decent weather days. Break balls, have a drink. Play stickball outside, that kind of thing.

I remember asking my father one time in the car on the way back home, "How come these guys are always giving me money, Daddy?"

He gave me one of his million dollar smiles and said, "'Cause you're a great kid and they like you."

★

It wasn't candy time, as I looked back at my father's eyes. What was there? Anger? Disappointment? One of each? I wasn't sure.

"A fucking plea?"

"My sons are kids. I do this deal, I am back with them when they're teenagers. I lose at trial, I'm doing twenty years. Like they never had a father. Remember Neil's kid Buddy? How he got fucked up? I can still be there for my kids."

"Sometimes you got to do things that fucking hurt." He had raised his voice when he said that. He pointed his finger at his chest. "Part of living like a man, not some guy who is looking for closure."

He leaned forward. "My freedom and my life take a back seat to my duty and manhood. These are *my* standards, John."

He leaned towards me, paused, and pointed a finger at me. "You remember when you told me that you'd follow me off a cliff?"

"Sure dad," I said, as I looked into his eyes.

He leaned back in the chair saying nothing, but his eyes saying everything.

★

Near the Bergin was an abandoned piece of train track. A biker group had taken up residency there, and they weren't part of the chamber of commerce. One time, an elderly woman caught the ear of Carmine Fatico and my father, and complained of how the gang members had continually made lewd comments to her daughter.

Skinny Louie was sent over to instruct the bikers in matters of local etiquette. Fifteen or so of them indicated that they required no such instruction. My father sent me and my friend, Angelo's son, Johnny Boy Ruggiero, home—angrily telling Jimmy Butch to drive us. Then he had the Bergin boys take care of business with baseball bats.

I had heard about that day later on. The men of the Bergin, like soldiers marching off to battle. Hoisting their baseball bats like rifles. Coming back victorious while a variety of ambulances and EMTs attended to the now wounded, but wiser, bikers.

They had learned, and had moved on. They were replaced with another group of bikers, who were already wise in the ways of the neighborhood, and these guys became friendly with the Bergin fellows, helping out, and occasionally being given some constructive activities to engage in when the situation required it.

★

He looked straight into me and gave me some good advice.

"Listen to me," he said, "I chose my side over forty years ago, when I was sixteen and a half years old."

"The hardest thing in the world for me," I said, "would be to have to say goodbye to my kids, but sometimes, Dad, you have to give a pound of flesh."

He understood. "I don't blame you," he said, "I hate them John. [The government.] This is it, I'm gonna go out of this world with a smile on my face, John. Because I believe what I believe."

I thought about it later. My father remained ever steadfast due to his belief in The Life, fueled by his hatred for the government. I was wavering due to my love for my family.

★

There was many a time to remember when there were no guards, no orange jumpsuits, no restraints. A time when the lion roamed freely in his jungle. A time for example, when a certain Irish gentleman, was about to get bit—for the last time.

Of course, I didn't know it at the time, but my father was heavily involved with the Gambino Crime Family. That family, along with other mob families, had recently been subject to the kidnapping of its members, and the relatives of its members, to be held for ransom.

One time, Carlo Gambino's nephew was kidnapped and held for ransom. I had heard the details later on.

My father had been sent for by Neil Dellacroce, who brought him to Carlo Gambino's home in Massapequa, Long Island. He had met Carlo two times before with Neil in Manhattan. On the way over, my father was filled in on the details of what Carlo wanted.

The five Families had search and destroy teams out looking for the guys who had been kidnapping members of their Family. Neil had chosen my father to lead the Gambino team.

"You're head of the team," he said. "Understand?"

"Understand," my father said.

"You're not only doing this for Carlo, but for all of the families."

At the house, Neil had once again instructed my father on what was to be done, while Carlo quietly sat by. Then Carlo spoke, softly as usual.

"I want you to take care of this thing for me," Carlo said.

"It will be my honor. Done," my father said.

Emanuel "Manny" Gambino was kidnapped by Irish and Latino gangsters working together. This time however, after a ransom was paid for his release, it turned out that Manny had been killed. Heavily involved with the kidnap and murder was a James McBratney, a muscle bound Irish thug who had done time for armed robbery, and had the moral fiber of a cobra. Several of the kidnappers had been already dealt with by members of the Families, and McBratney, who was sort of a leader of these miscreants, would be the last to go.

My father, his lifelong friend Angelo Ruggiero, and Ralph "Wigs" Galione were sent to take care of McBratney. On May 22, 1973, they found him in Snoopy's Bar and Grill, and McBratney, after a struggle, was "brought to justice."

Leaving his machine gun in his car, McBratney had gone

to the bar for a drink. My father, Angelo Ruggiero, and Ralph Galione came in. They approached McBratney. Angelo on the left, Galione on the right. He had the gun. Angelo had the handcuffs.

The men came in designed to be taken for plain clothes policemen. My father came in, sat down, and watched the crowd as the two other men identified themselves as police officers and attempted to take McBratney out of the bar and into a waiting car.

"You're under arrest," Galione told McBratney. "Don't give us any trouble."

No such luck. McBratney, a brute and a brawler put up a tremendous struggle, and the patrons of the bar were starting to get involved. The plan of capture and removal was not working. McBratney was dragging the "cops" all over the bar in his struggle. My father rose from his position to assist. Before it was over someone had pumped three slugs into McBratney.

This was not the kind of justice that had been ordered. McBratney was to die a slow and painful death, brought to a warehouse to be tortured and to be interrogated as to any insiders who might have been involved.

On the way out of Snoopy's Bar and Grill, the site of the killing, my father noticed the barmaid calling 911. He signaled her to put down the phone and remain silent. She did that night, but in July, identified Ruggiero and Galione from a photo array. My father was not identified. He went on the lam.

Wilfred "Willie Boy" Johnson (whose father was nicknamed "Injun Joe"), an associate of the Gambino family (half Italian, half Native American), had contacted my father while he was hiding out and said he had a problem. Johnson had assaulted a made member of the Genovese family, which was punishable by death.

Willie Boy Johnson asked my father to intercede at a sitdown and help to (hopefully) save Johnson's life. My father, being my father, came to Johnson's assistance, and had a sitdown in Maspeth, Queens.

Willie Boy got his life saved that day. But someone had tipped off the FBI to my father's whereabouts, that he was in town at that moment, and my father, shortly after leaving the sitdown, was picked up and arrested on June 3, 1974.

Galione, himself, did not live much past the McBratney killing. He was murdered, December ,'73, in Brooklyn. Some say he had become a liability to the family and had to go.

My father made bail of $150,000. Angelo Ruggiero, at his first trial, had a variety of alibi witnesses, and the trial wound up with a hung jury. Next time around, my father and Angelo were tried together; and Carlo Gambino and Neil Dellacroce hired lawyer, and well known New York City power broker, Roy Cohn.

Cohn was the epitome of a power broker in New York at the time. A homosexual who stayed in the closet, Cohn was privy to all of the secrets of what has been called the "Velvet Mafia," the secretly gay people holding important positions at the time.

He had become famous from his association with Joseph McCarthy, and the prosecution of the Rosenbergs. His non-Mafia clients encompassed such diverse entities as the Roman Catholic Archdiocese of New York and Donald Trump.

He was disbarred in 1986, for unethical and unprofessional conduct, and died a month later from AIDS. But in the Seventies, Cohn was very much alive as a name to conjure with in New York City.

Cohn made a deal for a plea to attempted manslaughter, and on August 8, 1975, my father was sentenced to four years. First to Clinton, the highest level security prison at that time in New York, then to a lesser security level facility at Green Haven Correctional Facility. Eventually, Johnson was also sent there on an armed robbery conviction in an unrelated matter.

★

While at Green Haven, my father was to meet some interesting fellows—Arnold Squitieri, Irish gangster James O'Keefe, and others. He also (my father that is) became "friendly" with some of those in the prison who were in charge of granting prisoner furloughs. He was able to set up "dentist" appointments outside of the jail.

He would be escorted by marshals from the prison to the building in New York City where his dentist was located. Someone would be waiting for his arrival, and then give my father several hundred dollars to give to the guards, while my father enjoyed his furlough. My father would go up to the dentist's office, open his mouth, and then go out the back of the building, where one of the fellows would drive him away.

When it was time to return to the prison, my father's man would drive him back to the dentist's building, and he would emerge from the front entrance back into the custody of the marshals.

I remember once my mother had put out a big spread of food for my father, who was coming home. At the time, I misunderstood, and thought he had been released from prison, but I didn't know he was only free for a day.

So in comes my father. He spent some quality time with my mother, spent some time with us kids in the back yard. He came in with a green jump suit on from prison, and changed his clothes.

At the conclusion of the family visit, he took a shower, put his prison clothes in a bag, and, prior to returning to Green Haven, managed to kill an individual who was a last piece of business left over from the McBratney piece of work.

It was believed that this particular individual, a McBratney crew member, had given information regarding the McBratney killings to those in law enforcement, and was also responsible for tipping off the authorities to my father's whereabouts when he was on the lam from the McBratney incident.

So, a visit and a meal with the family, a killing, a change of clothes, and back to the marshals waiting to take him back to Green Haven. All in a day's furlough.

My father was released on July 28, 1977, and his crew bought him another new Lincoln Mark IV (white) to celebrate his release. Within days of his return, my father was taken in a car, by Neil Dellacroce, to be straightened out, or in other words, to become a made man.

★

My father getting made at this time was a significant event, not only for him, but in mob history. The "books" had been closed since 1957, which means for the twenty years prior to my father getting his "button" nobody was getting made.

There were several reasons for this. Carlo Gambino and the other leaders of the Five Families had closed the books:

One, made men were sponsoring their people for their own benefit, and not for that of the families. They brought in a guy as a favor, or as an outright deal made for money. That is not the key to engendering loyalty to the organization.

Two, the killing of Anastasia in the barber shop put the kibosh on inducting new members.

Three, the fiasco of the Apalachin meeting was another reason. The aftermath of that meeting brought much unwanted attention to organized crime, and much unwanted surveillance on those in power.

I am going to go into some detail on these, but first, let me dispel a common myth about getting "made."

No. You do not have to kill somebody. You do not have to "make your bones." You do have to have a history of loyalty, of doing whatever it takes for the family. But killing someone as the price of admission—no.

Anastasia? One of the reasons he was killed (other than

the ambitions of Carlo Gambino) was that he had supposedly charged fifty thousand dollars to get a man made. A man who buys his way in, can be bought by others who have interests contrary to the Family. Think about it. You pay fifty grand to get in. What if the Feds pay you double to get out? Loyalty is not purchased: it is at best only temporarily rented.

And the November, 1957, Apalachin meeting?

Even back in the fifties, mobsters were not unaware of the possibility of being overheard by those who were not in sympathy with their doings. Further, there were some two dozen families across the country, and it was necessary that they follow the rules. To insure that everything was being done according to "Hoyle," the meeting in 1957 was called.

Up close and personal.

Apalachin, New York, home of Joseph "Joe" Barbara, mobster. About a hundred American, Canadian, and Italian mobsters in attendance. Discussions about dividing the action of loansharking, narcotics, and gambling. The operation of the Families in accordance with the rules.

Now most of you reading this, probably never heard of the town of Apalachin. One reason is it is small. So when law enforcement types started seeing a bunch of high-end fancy cars coming into town with license plates from all over the place, they became suspicious.

Who were the strangers? Road blocks were set up, and the meeting was raided. Mobsters in silk socks were running through the woods to escape. Not everybody did, because around sixty mob bosses were indicted following the Apalachin meeting.

One of the most devastating effects of this fiasco was a confirmation of the existence of a body of organized criminals, a mob, a Mafia. Contrary to the lies that J. Edgar had been telling (for his own career benefit) that there was no mob, the Apalachin incident served as proof that there definitely *was* a mob.

Thus after something like that, after such a breach of security, it was understandable why the family leaders would want to "close the books" for a significant amount of time.

★

Now obviously, thirteen-year-old me at the time did not know any of this. I didn't know what my father did for a living, except what he told me, which was basically, "I do construction, and I gamble a lot."

I had my toys, the family ate, quite frankly, I didn't think or care much about what my daddy did to support his family. Little did I realize then the profound effect on my life that was to occur by reason of his *real* occupation.

I did realize then, however, that my father had special feelings for me. After all, while I wasn't his first born, I was his first *son*. He always told my mother, "All I want is a son, one son, and I'll be happy."

So on Valentine's Day 1964, I pop out into his world, and he goes out and gets drunk to celebrate. John Angelo Gotti is born.

One thing I did know about my father's "work schedule" was that it used to cause a lot of friction between my father and mother. They fought a lot. He would come home at four in the morning, and sometimes not until the next day. Clubbing, gambling, doing what men in his position do.

But in the end my mother accepted it. Didn't like it, but accepted it. He supported the family, always leaving her money for the household expenses. And there were certain family rituals. Every Friday we would have Chinese food in the house, and every Sunday the family dined together.

My father and I didn't have all of that usual "throw the ball around" time. Quite frankly, he preferred street life to home life. But we did spend some time together. Even when I was really young.

He would take me to a candy store, to the racetrack, to one of the social clubs.

★

Besides going to the club, when I was about thirteen, I participated in what was referred to as the Pop Warner football league. Kind of like the PAL. However, one of the good things about Pop Warner, is having age and weight classifications that reduce the chance of injuries to the kids playing.

Besides football, I fought a lot in school, which did not reduce the chance of injuries to the kids participating. I was a hot-headed kid, quick to use my fists. I remember one time, I gave a kid a black eye in school, and they called my mother in. She yelled at me, and eventually told my father.

By this time he was calling me "Johnny Boy." So, after my mother tells him about giving this kid a black eye, he said to me, "Johnny Boy, come in here. What happened?"

I told him that the kid who got the eye said something about my mother. I told him that I grabbed the kid by his hair and punched him in the face.

"Good," he told me. "Good. Anybody bad mouths your family, or picks his hands up to you, you leave him there. If they're too big for you, pick up a bat or a stick, and hit them in the head with it." (Words to live by, I thought at the time.)

My mother was somewhat less than pleased. "You're encouraging him, you're teaching him all wrong," she told my father.

He explained, "Keep quiet." *She* was now in trouble, and I was off the hook. Go figure.

I was attending Beach Channel High School at the time. Maybe the word "attending" implies more than the reality, because I was frequently not in attendance; instead playing pinball at a local hamburger joint and game room, the Bow Wow or hanging out in an underground "fort" we kids had made in the weeds by Jamaica Bay—sort of a kid's social club.

We financed our Christmas activities conducted at the fort by "borrowing" Christmas cards from mailboxes, and spending the proceeds on us. (I always liked Christmas for a variety of reasons. Nowadays, my reasons are all honest ones.)

When you were truant, you used to get "cut cards" sent home. I was paying the mailman two dollars a card for him to reroute the cards to me. It worked for a time, but one got through, and then my mother, shall we say, expressed her disapprobation in something more than a whisper. The school had also called her directly and informed her I was frequently among the missing (for months).

She grabbed me and took me to the school while I was all denials. We went to the principal's office and he called in the teachers. The first one he called was one who had promised he'd pass me if I *didn't* go to class. (He didn't like me.)

He said I did show up to class, because he sure as hell wasn't going to admit that he told me *not* to, in exchange for giving me 70s on my tests and assignments. I thought I was home free.

Nope. The next five teachers the principal called in didn't know who I was. Suddenly my denials lost credibility. Both teacher number one, and myself were kicked out of school.

CHAPTER THREE

NYMA Loyal Steadfast True

Since I was now persona non grata at Beach Channel High School, and I had to get my diploma somewhere, that somewhere became the New York Military Academy. My mother was eager that I get out of the neighborhood, far from "undesirables." My father approved also. He didn't want his son to be a gangster, but something with bragging rights. Lawyer, doctor, some kind of respectable profession.

I was eager to go. Military things always had, and still do have, a fascination for me. I now believe that had I never been in The Life, I would have made a military career for myself. The challenge, the discipline, the hierarchical structure appealed to me—almost as much as the need for strategy, tactics, brains, and courage. In some ways it was like being a member of the mob—except in the military, honor is paid more than just lip service.

★

New York Military Academy, located at Cornwall on Hudson, New York, was founded in 1889 by Charles Jefferson Wright, a Civil War veteran and former school teacher from

New Hampshire. He believed that military discipline was the key to academic achievement. Well, Donald Trump was a graduate, and he did alright.

I was found there when I was fourteen years old. I had chosen the place. I had also asked myself on my first day at NYMA, a deep personal question.

"What the fuck am I doing here?"

There I was, in a tan suit, freezing cold (I had arrived for the winter session), with two rolls of quarters my father had given me, in case I had to call home. I was assigned a room, complete with roommate, Joe Gross, and settled in.

My first night there, at a meeting of the new kids at the school, they explained the rules and regulations of NYMA. There were a lot of them. After that orientation, I hit the sack for my first night away from home.

My sweet dreams were suddenly interrupted at 5:30 AM by a thunderous blast of a recorded horn playing *reveille*. For those of you who have been in the military, or in military school, you most likely won't ever forget the first time your sleep, your ears, and your brains were assaulted by this wakeup call—better said—wake up *scream*.

It is designed for several purposes, this reveille. First and foremost, it exists to get you up quickly. Second, its purpose is to make sure you start your day feeling miserable at having to get up at such an ungodly early hour like 5:30 AM. (Heck, my father used to go to sleep at that time.)

So they sound the horn, and we are all up. Everybody is running around, hitting the latrine, getting ready for the day's rules and regulations to come. What the heck did I know? I get dressed, brush my teeth, comb my hair, and go outside with the rest of the boys.

Lined up and freezing, I was wondering once again, "What the fuck am I doing here?" (All of a sudden I was getting a warm feeling for Beach Channel High School.)

I then kind of got used to the idea of military school. It was like my version of prison. I, at that young age, had respect for people like my father, who had been in prison—I loved hearing the stories about it, so I was gonna do my time in NYMA and make the best of it.

I wasn't the only mobster's kid who attended NYMA. Many of those kids quit.

On the other hand, Raymond Patriarca's grandson was also there—who did quite well and graduated a Captain with honors.

I remember the day I met him.

One morning I was in the NYMA gym, when I was interrupted in my workout by my bunkmate who ran up to me to inform me that "two mob looking guys" were standing by our room, waiting for me. The kid, Chris Rebecki, was scared. I calmed him down, told him not to worry, that they were probably just friends of my father.

I put on my hooded sweatshirt, packed up my gym gear, and went to meet my visitors. Truth to tell, I was a little nervous myself. What were these guys doing here? What had I done?

One guy was in is forties and had lips like a fish. The other guy was in his sixties, slicked back silver hair, and had the blackest eyes I had ever seen. Next to him was a kid about ten years old, who looked like a younger version of the guy in his forties.

I approached, and the older man reached out his hand. "You must be John's son."

I said I was.

"You look just like him," he said. "Let me introduce myself. I am a dear friend of your father's. My name is Raymond Patriarca, and this is my son, Raymond Jr. [pointing to the other man] and his son, my grandson."

I said hello.

"He's just starting here at the school and we were hoping you could spend some time with him and show him around."

"My pleasure," I said. He turned out to be a happy-go-lucky kid, I enjoyed his company.

About once a month, my father would drive up to see me, and the Patriarcas would come up to see their kid. It always ended up with me following my father around campus as he and the older man, Raymond Sr., would walk arm and arm up the hills of the campus and across the colonnade discussing what must have been Family business.

Neil Dellacroce would be present at many of these meetings.

The Patriarca family was the ruling mob family of Rhode Island, and parts elsewhere. Raymond Sr. was nicknamed "Il Patrone," and the family was sometimes referred to as the "office." He had been implicated in an unsuccessful plot to kill Fidel Castro. He died of a heart attack in 1984.

Raymond Jr. was to take over and wound up participating in a mob war. One memorable thing about that Family, is it gave the government their first live recording of an induction ceremony in 1989, picked up on Federal bugs.

Raymond Jr. eventually got out from his position to become a real estate salesperson in Lincoln, Rhode Island. The Patriarca Family had close ties with our Family.

★

Even though I did not know at the time that *I* was a wiseguy's son, I noticed that when my father came to see me at the school many of the guys—who also wore overcoats and who also looked like they were in The Life, who were there to visit their sons or grandsons—would congregate around my father, and they'd go off on a walk talk somewhere. A black Lincoln slowly followed behind, trailing the men.

The other students were star struck when these men came up to the school. I would lag behind like a puppy, out of earshot, following. It wasn't only the students. Some of the faculty, including my football and boxing coach, Joe Sacco, would wait outside of their respective buildings to come over and say hello to the strolling men—mob legends. Patriarca, Dellacroce, and my father (who would soon rise to the top).

I would go home maybe two weekends a month. My father would visit me about two times a month, sometimes with Neil Dellacroce. He liked coming there. He liked meeting his friends who came up to visit their kids, and he liked the military atmosphere. And I could tell, he was quite proud to have his son in military school. I was proud that he was proud.

I joined the school boxing team, eventually making captain. As a matter of fact, I helped form the team. We competed with other schools, until some kid got busted up a little too badly in one of the high schools, and then we competed amongst ourselves. It was a good outlet, a legitimate outlet for my violent tendencies, and I honed my skills with my fists.

I even won some trophies for competing. Sometimes I honed my skills outside of the presence of a referee, and was disciplined at school for several fighting incidents. I also got jammed up for truancy—again.

★

I learned many things in my time at NYMA. One of the most important and profoundly effecting things I learned in my life was who my father was.

It was 1979. I was sitting in the dayroom of the academy, watching a football game with the guys. When that was over, there was an investigative news show that aired, which dealt with the Mafia and their infiltration of New York's garment center.

Various persons appeared as players in this infiltration, when, all of a sudden surveillance photos were shown of my father. He was wearing a gray sport jacket, bandage on his hand, standing outside a social club talking with Neil Dellacroce.

The reporter referred to my father, "John Gotti," as a rising star in the Gambino Crime Family, and made mention of his being partially in control of garment center operations.

Heads turned in the dayroom. Some said, "Hey, we seen that guy here."

They had seen him with me. My father was John Gotti, up and coming mob star. So now they knew who I was, who he was—and I knew who he was. Some of my friends were in shock, a lot of them thought it was cool.

For some inexplicable reason, after this revelation, the staff at NYMA treated me rather better. They would see my father pull up in his chauffeur driven black Lincoln, which followed us as we walked around campus, and they got the message.

Then, in March of 1980, I got a message that I never wanted to hear.

★

I was in the gym, boxing, sparring in the ring, when the officer of the day came and found me and said, "Gotti, you got somebody here to see you."

I took off my gear, climbed out of the ring, and saw two men whom I recognized from my father's club. I kissed them hello, and asked, "Is everything alright?"

"You gotta come with us," one of them, Charles "Charlie Deac" Dicanio said. He had done around seventeen years in jail for armed robberies, one of those jails being Lewisburg, where he met my father for the first time.

"Why do I have to come with you?" I asked.

"Your father will explain when you get home."

Well, at least I knew my father was okay. I went to my room, took a shower, got into my uniform, and signed out of the campus. I entered into the back seat of the car that was waiting for me, and the two guys took me back home.

When the car pulled up in front of my father's house in Howard Beach, I was instructed to wait by the car. I saw a lot of people in front of the house, and I sure wondered what was up. I had a feeling it wasn't good.

Finally, my father came out of the house, and walked over to me, with his brother Gene, and his friend Angelo behind him. We kissed each other in greeting, then my father said, "C'mon, you gotta walk with me."

We walked. My father, Gene and Angelo right behind. My father looked into my eyes, and said, "I gotta tell you some bad news."

I waited.

"Your brother is dead."

I collapsed. I was in shock, I couldn't believe it. Not twelve year old Frankie.

My father helped me up, grabbing me by my elbow. "You gotta be strong for your mother, it's done. Your brother is gone."

About six hours before my hearing this, my brother, Frankie was alive and well. A happy kid. Now he was dead. Just like that. An accident, they told me: struck by a neighbor, John Favara.

I walked into the house in shock. My mother was basically a basket case. Her beloved Frankie was gone forever. She broke a mirror in her rage and she had to be tranquilized. The whole family was crying hysterically. There were maybe twenty five people in the house at the time. Not a dry eye.

I never got any sleep that night. I was in a state of shock. I remember lying in bed, then getting up around three or four in the morning, and saying to myself, "Nah, it can't be." I went up to Frankie's room to check. Would he be there? Was this all a bad dream?

In reality, it was no dream. My brother was dead. I walked into his room, and sat on his empty bed. A bed that I knew, but couldn't believe at the time, would always be empty. I went back downstairs to my room. My door opened up, and there was my little brother, Peter.

When Peter had a nightmare, he would go to my mother's room and sleep there. Well, my mother was understandably in a state of shock, so Peter had come to my room to stay with me. To protect him from the nightmare that none of us would awaken from. He was five at the time.

The wake for my brother Frankie was held for three nights at Stephens Funeral Home. Those in attendance were like a Mafia Who's Who. Of course many of those who visited were not involved in The Life. But the point is, all kinds of people came from all over to pay their respects to my family, and bid their final farewell to my brother, Frankie.

I was numb. It was my first time (certainly not my last) seeing a dead body. My brother was that body. The happy, joking, ball-breaking kid-brother of mine, whose smile was like the sun, now motionless forever. Never to laugh, never to smile again. When the lid closed for the last time, never to be seen again.

Throughout the wake, my father was standing soldier straight, stoic. He would make sure that Frankie's hair was done right in the coffin, and loudly express his anger when it wasn't.

I remember him jumping down Angelo Ruggiero's throat, when Angelo said to him, "Who knows why God does these things?"

"Don't you ever say that again, there ain't no God, my son doesn't even have hair on his prick yet, and he's lying dead here."

So the three days of the wake, he arrived hours early, then made sure we all got there on time in the limo. Standing up straight and tall. In charge, like a General.

But later on, in the small hours of the morning, from the vent that was in my room, I heard him crying alone in his den. He would be alone, make himself a stiff drink, sit down, and cry. I heard that, and I was in shock all over again.

Of course, I never told him that I heard him crying.

Several months after my brother's death, Favara was reported missing.

Over the years there have been questions, accusations, and assumptions about what happened to Favara. Was he a victim of my father's vengeance? What I don't know for sure, is if my father was involved. After all I was only sixteen at the time of my brother's death. What I do know for sure, is it was something my father *could* have done—you hurt one of his, he's going to hurt you.

★

I was back in military school, but the important part of me, wasn't. I had lost all interest in my studies, my boxing. I started ditching classes. For the most part, I was getting a pass from the instructors. They understood what I had just experienced.

There had been a kid in the room next to mine. His mother and two brothers were killed in a car accident. His father came to get him, and the kid was walked out of the school crying hysterically. He came from a military background. A proper kid. Wanted to be a career type. A lifer.

I saw that, and said to myself, wow that's tough. I didn't know that next up at bat was me. I remember him coming into my room, and even though he was only a sixteen year old kid, comporting himself like a man. Brooks was his last name.

"You can't keep this bottled up," he told me. "I know it's tough. But, you gotta deal with this and let it all out. Get everybody away from you and have a good cry."

Despite his efforts at consoling me, I continued to screw up. My focus, my drive, was gone, just as much as my brother Frankie was gone. A part of me had died with him. Not the violent part however.

The townies didn't like the boys from NYMA. It was almost a sure thing that when we went into town in uniform, we'd be going to get involved in some sort of unarmed combat with the locals. A couple of our boys had gone into town one time on a beer run, and had been jumped by seven or eight of the locals.

Our troops didn't win that engagement.

Some of us from the Academy went into town via the river, known as The Ramble, and explained in physical terms to the guilty parties why we weren't going to tolerate that sort of thing. You see we didn't talk, we used hand signals. We weren't in uniform, but those townies knew where we came from.

This time, our troops won the engagement.

The cops came to our school, held a lineup, but couldn't pin it on anybody. Except for me, who had his fists all banged up. They wanted my assistance in learning the names of the other parties participating. I wasn't going to help them.

Well that incident was the icing on the cake. I was out of NYMA, but with a chance to come back.

I was accepted back for my senior year, but on probation. Some of my fellow students, who because they didn't have a gap in school were now outranking me as officers, were rather reluctant to give me orders according to school protocol.

One, a lot of them liked me; and two, a lot of them didn't want to try and boss around a hot head who had been captain of the boxing team. They had known me not only to be a good ring boxer, but from some of our more violent forays into the town, they knew I was street tough and tested also.

It was the second coming of me. I buckled down, studied, started participating in sports again, and straightened myself out. I graduated with what was called "Staff Rank." I couldn't be officer's rank because of my hiatus, but I was made staff sergeant in charge of all intramural sports. That was good.

While staff sergeant, I had my own room, my own refrigerator, life was good. My father couldn't have been prouder of his son than on that day I graduated, decked out in dress blue uniform, marching in line to receive my diploma.

So I finished NYMA with honor, and it was time to go home, and figure out what the Hell was I going to do with my life.

CHAPTER FOUR

The Road Not Taken

I was contemplating going to college, taking the rest of my ROTC requirements, and entering into a military career. But I started hanging around my father's club, the Bergin on 101st Avenue, in Ozone Park, and told him I wanted to take a year off, and think about what I was going to do with me.

It was a mistake. I got into my share of trouble. Bar fights. I was carrying a lot of anger because of the death of my brother, and military school and boxing teams are not known to make one reserved and reflective.

Well the year came to pass, but college didn't. I hung out more and more by the club. The camaraderie, the activity, all were very attractive. Maybe some sixty guys hanging out, cooking, drinking, playing cards, watching sports on television, breaking balls. It gave one a real sense of belonging.

I started to get involved with football tickets, and vending machines that *could* be used for illicit gambling. I used to deliver machines at $250 a week, and I used to collect the proceeds from the machines. Machines like Slots and Joker Poker.

I saw the handwriting on the wall, and invested in a few machines of my own. I found good locations for them, and bought more machines. They provided a good living. Had about a dozen of them, and was making a couple of grand a week—in the early '80s.

So there I was, football tickets, piece of a candy store, machines, and I kept my job as vending machine delivery boy for $250 a week to justify the fact that I had money, without explaining to my father about any machines.

But I wanted more.

Around 1984, I started Samson Trucking, delivering materials, mainly asphalt, to construction sites. At first, people from Local 282 of the Teamster's union were not pleased to see a non-union driver delivering materials. However, I talked to some people, who talked to some people, and the problem was solved.

My father had given me some money for my first truck, and some accounts from contacts he had in the construction industry. I then took ten grand of my own money and bought a second truck.

I had Samson Trucking until about1998; although I had changed the name to JAG Equipment Brokerage. The "Trucking" was getting too much attention—read that as harassment—from law enforcement types.

Now, at the time, it would have been a bad thing if my father knew about the machines, the tickets, and a small book-making operation I was running. So I gave those interests over to somebody else, who every week would give me a portion of the earnings. But it gave me plausible deniability, just in case.

But despite the machines, the trucking, whatever, what I really wanted to be, was just like my father.

March 11, 1983. A night that would change my life.

It was a Friday, and Friday nights I would normally go out and have drinks with my friends. Possibly meet a girl. So on this night, me, Johnny Ruggiero, and Anthony Amoroso (another friend of mine) wind up in a local Howard Beach watering hole, the Shellbank. It was a clam bar restaurant on the canal leading to Jamaica Bay.

After a few hours of drinking, Amoroso suggested we go to an Ozone Park bar, The Silver Fox. It was Ladies' Night there, and a girl he was dating would be there with some of her friends.

I reminded Anthony that most of the guys at that location were dust heads. Maybe we should take a pass on that place. So we made the decision to just pass by there, pick up the girls, and go to a place on Queens Boulevard.

Before we left, Ruggiero's girlfriend, Julianne, came by the Shellbank and insisted that Johnny Boy take her out. As they argued, I told him to go with his girlfriend, and we would catch up with him later on.

Amoroso and I left, and stopped off at the Our Friends, a social club in Ozone Park, to have a drink before going to the Silver Fox. It was about six or seven blocks from the social club. At the club, we met Mark Caputo and invited him to come along with us to the Silver Fox.

He was hesitant, as he lived close to the bar and it was filled with "dusties," people using Angel Dust. "Why would you want to go there?" he asked us.

"Ladies' night," I said. "Anthony's girl friend is there with her girl friends."

"Let's go," Caputo said, and he sprang off of his seat.

★

The place was unbelievably crowded. Dark and packed. So we made our way to the back of the bar and a space was cleared, where we could sit and drink. Several neighborhoods were represented in the place. Because of the crowd, we didn't notice the Massa brothers from Lindenwood along with several of their friends.

They made their way down the bar to shake hands with us. We all shook hands and began drinking together. So several of the girls, about six or seven of us altogether, spent about an hour drinking.

Then, a guy whom I recognized as "Elfie," came over and offered to buy me a drink. I refused, but he continued to insist. I felt that he was definitely high. I continued to refuse. Finally I grabbed him by the arm (I was a punk and had a chip on my shoulder), spun him around, and pushed him away.

Now Elfie was a tough kid who had survived many battles, and had been stabbed—multiple times in actuality—and he was still around. I think that was in 1980, by a guy named Peter Zuccaro, who was later to become a government cooperator.

So Elfie comes back at me, aggressively to my perception, and I hit him in the head with a beer mug that one of the girls had been drinking from. He didn't blink an eye, which confirmed my suspicions about his mental state. He jumped back at me and we started to fight.

Unfortunately this set off the whole crowd. At least fifteen or twenty people brawling in the dark crowded bar. Tables thrown, bottles broken, total chaos. People were getting hurt and the girls and most of the patrons were making for the door. That brought some of the fighting out to the front. Some of it remained in the back. Guys were fighting on our side that I didn't even know—confusion and pandemonium reigned supreme.

Something sliced through my jacket, by my left elbow, then another slice on the palm of my right hand. Elfie was down, from my fist or someone else's chair or something: then I notice the blood dripping from my right hand.

A friend of Elfie, a guy I believe nicknamed "Swifty," came to his aid. I believe he had stabbed me with a broken bottle. Next to me, under a table, was Anthony Amoroso, bleeding from a cut from behind his right ear. I reached into his pocket and pulled out his razor, swinging it in Swifty's direction, to keep him and anyone else away from me and Amoroso. I think I caught him with it at least once. He, along with everyone else, started running to the front door. I pulled Amoroso out from under the table.

On our way out, I had seen at least two other guys down. One was leaning against the bar, and another over a chair. Amoroso, Mark Caputo, and myself were now outside, and made it to my car. I don't know where the other people went. I was one of the last ones out of the bar.

Turns out, a man died in that fight. Daniel Silva. I did not know him, and I have no idea who killed him. Certainly nobody was bragging about it, or taking credit for it. Out of fear—not for law enforcement—fear of my father.

I will explain. Within hours of the brawl my father gets a call. It was about six in the morning, and I am in my downstairs room, full of the night's alcohol, and more recently Tylenol. Both my hand and elbow were wrapped with gauze. I was lying in bed filled with both physical and mental pain.

I heard my father's footsteps racing down the stairs after the call. I thought it was about the fight, and now I was in trouble. He pushed open my door. Unusual, because he usually respected my privacy, and would knock or call out my name. Then, of course, I would get up and respond.

"You!" he said. "Get up!"

I stood up. He noticed the blood soaked gauze.

"You had a fight tonight."

"Yes."

"Do you know that somebody died?"

"No."

He grabbed me by the back of the shirt. "Get the fuck out of my house!"

As he was dragging me to the door, my mother intervened, crying at seeing the blood, and said, "Johnny, at least let me clean him up."

He turned to her. "Go upstairs before I hurt him right in front of you."

"I'm alright, Ma," I told her, and walked out. I got in my car and drove to Angelo Ruggiero's house in Cedarhurst,

Long Island. By the time I got there he was already up. He opened the door as if he had been expecting me.

"What happened?"

I told him. Seeing my hand and elbow, he told me to get in the car. He woke his son Johnny Boy up and asked for his driver's license. I was driven to the hospital as Johnny Boy. So, I, now Johnny Boy Ruggiero, receive medical treatment for having fallen through a glass table. Ten stitches to my right hand, over twenty inside and out to my left elbow. Still have the scars today.

★

Three days later, I'm at Uncle Angelo's house and I receive a visit from my father.

"How are you feeling?" he asked.

"Good."

But not for very long, because he began to crack me all across the room. Angelo tried to step in, but my father tossed him aside. He grabbed me by the shirt, and tossed me on the couch. He supported himself by one hand on the armrest, and the other gesturing in my face.

"Do you cocksuckers know what you did?"

I didn't answer.

"Not only did a fellow die as a result of this, but you all just ruined your lives. This will follow you the rest of your life."

He got up, signaled Angelo to follow him out of the room, as I just sat there.

My father left the house without saying another word. Angelo returned and informed me, "Your father is crushed."

"I know," I said.

"No! You don't know. The sharks are circling. Cops are going to shake your father down. He will pay to protect you."

"I didn't kill the kid. Tell him not to give them shit. Whatever it is, I will answer for it."

He looked at me and just shook his head. "You stupid motherfucker, you have no idea what youse did."

A short time later, I temporarily relocated to Florida. My father wanted me away from all of this and the stigma of what had taken place. When I returned, I learned my father was right. My life indeed would be different. Any thoughts I had of attending a college ROTC program weren't going to happen. I was to go to work every day, and sit by the Bergin at night.

I had to account for my whereabouts 24/7. My life had indeed changed.

★

After the police investigation into the incident, the lead detective on the case, James McKinley, told the press, "It was a simple bar fight. You know how kids are. One says, 'You're standing to close to me. You're looking at me the wrong way.'"

Uncle Angelo was right, the bar incident, as well as the suicide of a supposed witness to the incident, John Cennamo, who was found hanging in 1984, outside of a laundromat—would follow and haunt me the rest of my life.

★

In late spring, 1984, I had just returned from a trip to Florida with Anthony Amoroso and a kid named Jerry. One of the neighborhood kids had told me that John Cennamo had hanged himself. I knew both John and his older brother, Vincent, although I knew Vincent better. I had played football with John on at least two occasions. Now learning of John's death made me concerned. Was the suicide somehow connected with the bar fight a year before?

Rumors began to circulate that it was connected. Later in the book it will be revealed how this rumor was manipulated to exact revenge against a suspected informer, and that the suicide was indeed what it appeared to be to the investigative team at the crime scene.

CHAPTER FIVE

Community Clean Up

You may have heard that the crime rate is low in mob neighborhoods. We want our wives and children to be safe, and we learned long ago that you can't always count on the efforts of NYPD to keep things neat and clean.

So we took things into our own hands at times. Sometimes we took other things into our hands—to make sure that neighborhood miscreants get the message that crime doesn't pay in a neighborhood where organized crime lives.

It also aligns the neighborhood residents with us, as we did what the police can't, or aren't willing, to do to keep them safe. With local loyalty, we were tipped off to the presence of agents in the neighborhood.

Take drug dealers. We didn't like drug dealers in our neighborhoods.

Take one Capo in another family, Joe, who was a close confidant of my father. He was on the way up while his daughter was on the way down with a drug problem.

She would score in Forest Park, where besides a variety of cultural performances going on, many drug transactions would take place. The sort of a place where you could get both Hamlet and Heroin.

This place was a veritable flea market for drugs. Joe was furious about the situation, sickened by what had happened to his daughter. She was being taken advantage of by street dealing scum. Susceptible to cheap drugs and cheap feels from the degenerates who preyed upon her.

He went to Angelo Ruggiero, because my father was in jail at the time. Angelo sent for one John C to organize efforts to rid the neighborhood of these drug pushing scum. Angelo gave the green light from the Bergin.

In the course of our getting the low down on these low lives, I was sent for to see if anyone I knew knew who the dealers were. I contacted some people, who were themselves involved in the drug trade, who on occasion hung out with some of us on a purely social basis—a distant social basis.

One guy was John Gebert, whose uncle was Joe "Mad Dog" Sullivan, a notorious killer who had done work for the notorious Irish gang, the Westies, and our family. Sullivan had brought Gebert to the Bergin social club at one time, which is where I met him for the first time. He brought the actor Jon Voight to the club with him, to meet my father. Voight was there because he was researching a role for the movie *Runaway Train*, in which a character modeled after Sullivan escaped from an Alaskan penitentiary.

In reality, Sullivan was the only man to have escaped from Attica, a penitentiary in upstate New York.

His nephew was crazy, out of control, although sometimes I viewed him as a kid who was sort of a lost soul, needing direction. Didn't really matter, because to us Howard Beach guys, these guys weren't equals, they weren't friends.

Our uncles and fathers were Mafia. In our minds we were future Mafia.

From time to time I would run into Gebert. It turned out he hung with someone named John Alite. I had met Alite when my brother-in-law, Carmine Agnello, was trying to sell a Lincoln of mine that was a lemon. Alite had come to

Carmine's junk yard to buy the car, and that is when and where I met him—around the summer of 1984.

Alite said he was a friend of Gebert. Gebert sold marijuana and, even though we on occasion socialized with him, we mainly shook him down. Alite sold cocaine. We shook him down also. (Years before Alite was permitted to come to the Our Friends social club.) Gebert, although not as smart as Alite, controlled him through fear. What Gebert told him to do, Alite would do.

Alite and Gebert knew who was who in the world of dope dealers at Forest Park, and provided information to us. They offered to set them up. They wanted to ingratiate themselves to our people. Alite showed us where to go when we hit Forest Park. I was in a van with John C and some other guys. Alite was at the bottom of the hill in the park. His offer to accompany us was declined.

Some twenty of us, Howard Beach and Ozone Park boys, participated in this neighborhood cleanup operation. We planned it like a military operation, we even communicated with walkie talkies (this was the eighties).

We got into vans. John C and I briefed the troops. Entrances and exits to the park would be blocked off, so the dealers could not retreat, and so they would suffer the most damage. Axe handles and Willie McCovey bats would be used.

We dropped our guys off at several entrance and exit points that led up to the top of the park, called "The Dome." This was an outside amphitheater where, back in the day, concerts and shows were held. It was also the main location for the drug dealers.

We had blocked off the exits. Everyone was to get a beating. We weren't there to *scare* them.

A full scale battle took place, us vs. the drug dealers. They came in second. Within five minutes it was over. Several of them wound up in hospital beds. Our casualties were light. One guy had a chipped tooth, another, a broken hand.

We returned in triumph to the Bergin Hunt and Fish Club. John C and I informed Angelo Ruggiero of what had taken place. He was furious that I had gone with the rest of the guys. "Your father will slaughter me, if he finds out," he told me repeatedly.

However, he was pleased with what had occurred. Nobody seriously hurt amongst us, nobody arrested. But Angelo made a point to instruct me never to trust Gebert or Alite. They weren't our people, they weren't Italian. Gebert was Irish, Alite, Albanian.

"They set up their own," he warned. "They are outsiders. What would they do to you?"

I never dreamed at that time, the treachery, the lies of which Alite would be capable. I was to find out in 2008 *what he would do to me*, which we will discuss in detail in a later chapter.

CHAPTER SIX

Changing of the Guards

It's strange how one event, distant in time, can be the originating cause, or at least a contributory factor, to another event, which might take place well into the future.

In 1957, mobster and labor racketeer, Albert Anastasia is killed in a barber chair. In 1985, Paul Castellano, then head of the Gambino crime family, is killed in front of a popular steakhouse. Twenty eight years difference, but events bound together by a way of life, the Mafia, and the life of an individual.

Neil Dellacroce.

Neil Dellacroce was a capo under Anastasia at the time of the barbershop killing. Afterwards, he was to lend his considerable credibility and the manpower under his control to Carlo Gambino, who became the head of what was afterwards referred to as the Gambino crime family.

Without Neil's support, it is highly unlikely that it would have been the *Gambino* crime family. (The forerunner to our Family was referred to as the Mangano family, as Vincent Mangano had been the boss since the '30s, until his untimely death in '51.)

For his support of Carlo, Neil was a target of an assassination attempt, but escaped from the assassin's bullets in time. While at the Ravenite, two killers walked in firing their guns. Neil and two associates, Frankie Barranca and Mike Catalano, turned a table over for a shield and returned fire. Neil was able to get out through the back door of the club.

Neil was to serve as underboss to Gambino, but in 1976, on his deathbed, Gambino selected as successor boss to the family, Paul Castellano, his cousin and brother-in-law. Neil was an old time gangster, well respected and well feared. He had grown up from the streets, a stone cold killer.

Castellano was more of a business guy, a capo unable to relate to the street guys, the rank and file. He had only done a few months in jail, and was virtually untested. Many of the fellows were sure that Neil would succeed Carlo Gambino, and many of them were infuriated at the deathbed selection of Castellano instead.

My father was one of these men.

Two factions were now present in the family. Those loyal to Neil (who had been given control of lucrative New York City rackets to keep the peace), and those loyal to Castellano. The street guys favored Neil, because he had been one of them, was old school, and a stickler for the rules of the family.

Neil was to be heard on tape, many times, telling others, "The Boss is the Boss." Whatever animosity Neil might have had towards Castellano, Castellano was the boss, and Neil was a loyal underboss—as Castellano had let him remain in that position after Carlo's death.

In reality, given the respect that Neil had amongst the family members, given his ruthlessness, he could have wrested control from Castellano any time he chose to. But that wasn't Neil's way. He was an old time gangster, and a firm believer in the rules.

You could say that Neil, who was a mentor to my father, was the buffer between my father and Castellano. Neil kept both factions in harmony. The head of the family was aware of Gotti's animosity, but dealt with it. He had even used my father on several pieces of work.

One time, Paul's daughter had some problems with her boyfriend. My father was sent for, to rectify that situation.

★

One of the rules of the family, since Carlo's time, was no trafficking in drugs. In theory, anyway. Castellano was the recipient of significant moneys that originated from drug operations, but turned a blind eye. Officially, however, drug dealing was a death offense.

Angelo Ruggiero, my father's lifelong friend, had a non-made brother named Sal. He was an extremely bright man who could have been successful in any legitimate endeavor he chose. But he, too, was drawn to the streets. He was smart with numbers, and knew that the returns from financing individuals who were in the drug trade would bring great returns.

But it also brought great risks. He had been indicted in 1974, and fled the jurisdiction, thus becoming a fugitive. While on the lam, Sal and his beautiful wife, Stephanie, were killed in a plane crash, on a private Lear jet.

Some say the plane was blown up over Georgia. Miraculously, or by design, their two small children were not traveling with them. "Sally" had left millions of dollars on the streets, and his older brother, Angelo, wanted to collect it.

Angelo got permission (in the presence of my father) from Neil, to collect the moneys. He wanted to take care of his late brother's children, and he was also to manifest some selfish interest in drug money. My Uncle Gene got dragged into this.

Angelo may have gone over the line, and may have gotten too comfortable with a drug dealer. This resulted in a massive indictment for narcotics trafficking, which included Angelo, and others. (Angelo was not aware that his house phones had been bugged, and would talk freely about family matters while at home.)

This indictment served to justify Paul's long term desire to break up the Bergin crew, either by dispersing the members, or via a more permanent solution. Paul wanted Angelo dead, and I believe he wanted my father that way, as well.

Dellacroce was dying of cancer at the time, and both Paul and my father knew that when he died, when that buffer was eliminated, they would have to deal directly with each other, and in all likelihood those dealings would be deadly for at least some of the parties involved.

It was expected by the members of the Dellacroce faction (which was probably half of the family) that after Neil's death, my father would become the underboss. That of course would be contrary to the interests of Castellano.

Neil died on December 2, 1985. Castellano did not attend the funeral, and contrary to popular and media opinions, this did not cause any fury in the family. It was expected that Paul would not show. Paul had been facing several Federal indictments, one regarding his having a seat on the Commission, (the governing body of American organized crime), another dealing with a car theft ring. It would not be in his interest to show up at the funeral. Surveillance video of his attendance would have been used against him at trial.

He certainly didn't want the underboss—that would have to be acting in his place while he was imprisoned—to be my father.

So he chose Thomas Bilotti, his capo and driver, as the new underboss. It was a short reign for both Castellano and Bilotti after that.

With Neil gone, with Castellano wanting at least the organizational (and more likely physical) destruction of my father's crew, my father realized he only had one move to make. A move he could never have made while Neil was alive, because as Neil said, "The Boss is the Boss."

My father would become involved with the elimination of Castellano. Among other things, Castellano had continually lobbied my father and Neil to kill Angelo. No way was my father going to be a part of any harm coming to one of his closest friends.

Angelo was facing trial on the drug charges and RICO. My father had said to Paul, let him have his day in court, and if convicted, put him on the shelf—don't kill him.

Paul wasn't buying it.

Angelo had been taped saying very insulting things about Paul. Insults that could be very dangerous. "Paul's a bitch... he shouldn't be the boss...Johnny should have killed him..." things like that. The people that Angelo spoke to might have also agreed with Angelo. Again, very dangerous.

Paul was aware of the tapes, and he was demanding them. My father and Neil advised Angelo to turn over the tapes. Angelo was refusing.

Angelo, who was probably the most loyal guy to my father, and a man that I had loved, had an amazing ability to get into trouble. The following is an excerpt from a tape recording of a 6/9/85 conversation between my father, Angelo Ruggiero, and Neil Dellacroce:

AR: I'm gonna tell you something. If you two never bother with me again, again in the rest of my life, I ain't givin' them tapes up. If you never bother with me, again, the rest of my life. I can't. I can't. There's good friends of mine on them fuckin' tapes. If it was some, some fuckin' asshole like Buddy, or somebody like that, I'd give it to them in three seconds flat. There's good guys on them fuckin' tapes.

ND: They're good guys? Don't call 'em if you need 'em.

AR: That's how I am. I don't say I'm gonna call them, John.

JG: Don't call them.

AR: I'm just telling you. I'm just telling you.

JG: Don't call them good guys, whatever you do, don't look for them when you are in trouble, the good guys.

ND: That's right.

AR: I'm gonna meet this guy. [Paul Castellano] I'm gonna meet him and his lawyer, and I want them to tell me how these tapes can help him.

JG: And let him tell you, maybe he can show you how. If he shows you how, he's the boss, while he's the boss, you have to do what he tells you. [Yelling at Angelo]

ND: That's what I'm telling you. That's what we want to hear. You see, that's why I says to you before, you, you, don't understand Cosa Nostra.

JG: Angelo, what does Cosa Nostra mean?

ND: Cosa Nostra means that the boss is your boss, you understand? Forget about all this nonsense.

AR: La Cosa Nostra, I'll tell my boss or tell me to turn against you, I won't do that.

ND: Forget about it.

AR: I won't do that.

ND: Forget about it.

AR: I won't do that.

ND: Forget about it.

AR: That's not Cosa Nostra, Neil.

ND: Forget it, forget about it.

AR: That's La Cosa Nostra, Neil?

ND: La Cosa Nostra. Boss is the boss is the boss.

AR: Tell me to set one of my best friends up. I won't do that.

ND: Ah, you want to make up stories.

AR: I don't want to make up stories.

ND: Sure you do.

AR: I want to say the truth, Neil.

ND: You wanna say nothin'. So of course you don't want to do it. You ain't gonna set up no friends.

AR: I ain't gonna do it.

ND: You ain't gonna set no friends of ours up.

AR: You bet your life I'm not gonna do that. I would never do that.

JG: Why don't you keep quiet, you ain't talkin' Cosa Nostra
now.

AR: We know I'm not.

ND: We don't need you to tell us that for Christ's sake.

AR: Neil, I don't understand you. I don't know I'll tell you
the truth, you're talking to me different right now.

JG: You don't know what the fuck you're talking about. So
keep quiet and shut the fuck up.

Angelo was a good stand up guy who wouldn't budge on
this issue.

So from the above, the only way that my father, his crew,
and Angelo could survive, would be to insure that Paul didn't.

★

My father had survived the Castellano affair—and now I
was staring across a conference room table at him in February
1999, in Springfield prison, trying to make him understand
that I, too, was fighting for my survival and the survival of my
family.

"I always want the best for you and your family, you understand me?" he told me.

"Yes, Dad," I said.

"The thought of you doing one day in prison makes me
sick," my father said, "But I don't know what makes me sicker,
you in prison, or you bowing to those pieces of shit."

I was hurt by that word. "What bowing? There's no bowing. It's a compromise. They get their pound of flesh for my
peace of mind."

He continued to look at me, but said nothing.

I continued.

"The peace of mind that I will be there for my family when
I am needed—that's what this is, not bowing."

He continued listening, his eyes fixed on mine.

"I've always felt in my heart that the day would come that

my family and I would be separated by prison. I'm only thankful it isn't for life. The plea would insure that."

He leaned over, putting his face closer to mine.

"Bullshit! How naive could you be? Once they get you in, you will never be free again. This time you can win, the next time, they will make sure you can't."

"There won't be a next time," I said.

"That's what you think. John, my heart's broken for you, but I will tell you this. Me? I raise the black flag—do you know what that means?"

"Yes, Dad. No quarter."

He leaned back in his chair. "That's right, the government, or the streets for that matter. When you go to war with me, I give no quarter, and I ask for no quarter."

I looked back at him, remembering how true he had been to that code.

★

A meeting had been called by Castellano to be held at Sparks Steakhouse in Manhattan. Midtown was resplendent with Christmas lights, bustling shoppers, and crawling city traffic. Frank "Frankie" DeCicco leaned on the bar at Sparks, looking out at the street, and listening to the Christmas piano music. *Silver Bells* was playing. It really was "Christmas time in the city."

Standing in front of Frank, with their backs to the window, were Jimmy Brown Failla, Danny Marino, and Tommy Gambino—all loyal to Paul's faction of the family. Tommy, in fact, was the son of Carlo Gambino and Paul's cousin.

But DeCicco wasn't just watching the shoppers in the street. He had his eyes fixed on the parking spot that Paul and Tommy Bilotti would be pulling into. Sure enough, at around five o'clock, Paul's car pulled into the spot.

But there were also others waiting for Paul's arrival. A team of loyalists to my father, all wearing white trench coats and black Russian *ushanka* hats, waited near the restaurant entrance. They were so dressed, so as to make witness identification much more difficult.

As the doors of the car opened, the identically dressed men moved towards Paul and Tommy Bilotti, his right hand man and chosen successor for Neil Dellacroce's position as underboss. The men commenced shooting at them numerous times. A crash car blocked traffic as the shooters moved off in different directions, their work for the evening having been accomplished.

Inside Sparks, Jimmy Brown Failla checked his watch, "Looks like Paul's running late."

Frankie had seen what happened, as the flashes from the gunfire illuminated the window of the restaurant. The others had their backs turned to the window. The men didn't *hear* the shots because of the music. Frankie, in response to Jimmy's comment, said, "Paul's here but he won't be making dinner."

He looked them in the eyes to make sure they got the message. "Everything is going to be alright. Follow me out," said Frankie.

The others were a bit confused, but followed Frankie out into the street. Lying in it were Paul and Tommy, dead from numerous gunshot wounds. Jimmy Brown said, "That could've been me. I was supposed to ride with Paul." Failla was in a state of shock.

"You would have been fine," Frankie told him.

So Castellano was dead in the street. The police would later cover the body with a sheet at the crime scene. The Archdiocese of New York refused to give Castellano a Catholic funeral.

My father, who was sometimes known to slightly embellish a story in his latter years, would always stand by his statement regarding Castellano's death.

"I don't know who hurt Paul nor do I care. He probably had it coming to him. But I can tell you this on my son Frankie's grave—If Gravano was within ten miles of Paul getting hurt, my son should rot in Hell."

I was in the Brooklyn office of my company, Samson Trucking, listening, as I always did, to WINS radio. Suddenly a bulletin came on, announcing the killing of Paul Castellano. I rushed from the office, and in record time, made it to the Bergin club in Ozone Park.

I was concerned about what might have happened to my father. Was this the start of a war between the Families? I was twenty-one at the time, and while I had a general idea about the goings on around me, I wasn't party to all the details. Many thoughts ran through my head as my car sped towards the Bergin.

I entered and didn't see my father. I became more concerned. I asked about my father, and my Uncle Pete told me he was okay. I was assured he was fine, everything was fine. The men all seemed relaxed.

I began to understand the situation.

About an hour later, Angelo Ruggiero came into the club, and also told me everything was fine. Knowing that, I didn't pursue it. The Bergin started to fill up with men. It became crowded.

Then my father walked in, with a serious expression on his face. Truth to tell, he swaggered in. A conquering hero. He was also relaxed. He left the club early that night.

The next day I met my father over at the Bergin, business as usual. But not for long. People started arriving that didn't usually come. My father assured all of the fellows that there would be a full investigation of the Castellano hit, and that they would get to the bottom of it all.

With Castellano and Bilotti dead, there was no boss or underboss. By protocol the consigliere was to be put in charge temporarily. Joe Gallo.* Temporarily.

---

* Joseph "Joe" Gallo, not to be confused with Joe Gallo of the Colombo Family.

For those who might not be familiar with the term of consigliere, this is the individual who advises the family and the boss on matters. He is also cast sometimes in the role of diplomat in dealing with the other Families.

If you saw the movie *The Godfather* (and who hasn't?), Tom Hagen was the consigliere to the Corleone family. Although in reality, this would never be a position held by a non-Italian.

★

It was obvious who the successor would be. My father, a very well respected capo, had long been the voice of Neil Dellacroce. Dellacroce was suffering from cancer, my father constantly visited him. What Neil wanted, was relayed to the men by my father.

Dellacroce was gone, Castellano and Bilotti were gone—my father was standing tall, ready, willing and able to take charge of the administration. To be the boss.

According to Sammy Gravano, as far as he may be trusted, my father was voted in by all of the capos at a meeting at Ceasars, a restaurant in Manhattan. Of course, the restaurant was closed at the time, and all of the people there were people in The Life.

The capos went in a few at a time. It was assumed there would be government surveillance. Although, as it was Christmas, it was less suspicious to have all of these men coming to a restaurant.

John Gotti won a unanimous election to boss. Were some of the men in their hearts opposed to his taking over? Certainly. There were loyalists to Paul. But for some reason, one that probably had much to do with good sense and the survival instinct, my father was universally chosen by the men. Also, my father was respected by the men, a gangster's gangster. Further, he had a reputation for being fair.

He then chose Frank DeCicco as underboss. It was DeCicco who "nominated" my father as boss. They had done time together as young up-and-comers in Lewisburg penitentiary, and had bonded closely. It was DeCicco who had introduced my father to Gravano. That was why he was accepted.

Joe Gallo was to stay on for a bit, as consigliere, but he had a case coming up, and he wanted to retire. My father wanted Dellacroce loyalist Joe "Piney" Armone as his successor. His crew was to be taken over by Armone's nephew, Jackie "the Actor" Giordano. Armone, who was from Manhattan, and who was respected by the men, was trusted. An old school gangster, Armone was to die in prison in 1992, always remaining loyal. My father needed a man like that.

Armone, at this time, could have renounced the Life, and gone back to his home and spent the Holidays with his family. But old soldier that he was, he chose to stay with the men.

Thus, at that restaurant meeting, the whole new administration was selected. Angelo Ruggiero became the new capo of the Bergin crew. Gravano took over DeCicco's crew.

My father, in the coming days, solidified his position—putting his loyalist men in place. He also had to get up to speed on family business. Old timers filled him in. All the while, my father was out on bail facing RICO charges and under surveillance. (These were days prior to the Bail Reform Act of '86. If it had been in effect, my father would not have been allowed to associate with known criminals, and when it did pass, he couldn't get bail.)

Quick story. While out on bail, my father, if he wished to leave the state, had to inform and get permission from the government. One time he had been granted leave to go to Florida, but the Feds didn't inform the courts.

My father was relaxing poolside at a Florida hotel, when he was surrounded by ten Federal agents and handcuffed for violating his bail conditions. His lawyer at the time, Bruce Cutler, straightened that out in a few hours, and my father was free again.

But this erroneous story about my father violating bail conditions had been all over the Florida news.

One of the Feds, in front of my father, had thanked the new manager of the Hilton hotel for his assistance. That was the last time my father stayed there. After that it was the Harbor Beach Marriott. The new manager, never got to be an old manager—he was fired for losing the considerable business that my father brought to the hotel.

Across from the Harbor Beach Marriott, was hotel and marina Pier 66. George Steinbrenner, owner of the Yankees baseball team, had his father's yacht moored by the hotel. Steinbrenner had learned that my father was staying across the street, and was anxious to meet him. He sent an assistant to camp out in the lobby of the Marriott, to see if he could catch someone in my father's party to arrange a lunch on the yacht between my father and Steinbrenner at my father's convenience.

One afternoon while we were returning from the hotel pool, my father and I and several associates, were approached by the assistant who walked over to Jackie D'Amico, and asked if he might have a word with him for a moment.

He identified who he was and who had sent him, and Jackie mentioned the invitation to lunch to my father, by whispering in his ear. My father responded to Jackie, "Set it up." (My father had always been a big Yankee's fan.)

The lunch was set up for the next afternoon.

We spent several hours evading surveillance that was continually upon us from the moment we arrived in Florida. We pulled into a garage in the Yankee Clipper Hotel, two blocks from the Marriott. There, an old Gambino soldier, Dave Iacovetti, who was running things down in Southern Florida for my father, and was not staying at the Marriott, had a rental car parked. From there he ferried my father to the yacht.

From what I understood from later conversations, George had rolled out the red carpet to my father and went out of his way to make him feel welcome. My father was super impressed with George Steinbrenner.

★

The meteoric rise of my father did not go unnoticed. Both by law enforcement, and by the men who saw my father in the process of righting what he believed to be the wrongs of the Castellano administration. Paul loved money, and was out for himself, not the men. My father had nothing but contempt for money, and was generous with the men.

He also became a frequent subject of press coverage. He didn't seek it—he didn't shun it. He was a twenty-four hour-a-day-gangster, and if the government was always taking his picture, why not the newsmen?

When my father became the boss, his Lincoln was retired and replaced with a Benz. That was about the only change in him. He was not embarrassed by who he was. He wasn't going to hide. He would say, "Rats, rapists, and child molesters—all the lowest form of life—should hide their faces."

Maybe he should have ducked a little, but his pride and ego wouldn't let that happen.

★

One of the trials that my father was facing in 1986, when he assumed the role of boss, was an assault charge against one Romual Piecyk. Piecyk, a burly bear of a man, accused my father of striking him in 1984, and accused my father and his friend, Frank Colletta, of taking more than three hundred dollars from him.

The beef started over a parking space by the Cozy Corners Bar in Maspeth, Queens. Frank Colletta, one of the fellows, and Piecyk got into a dispute. Frank was small and well into middle age. Piecyk was more than six feet tall and huge. He was verbally abusing Frank.

My father had been in the bar talking on the phone with his bookmaker. When he heard the commotion he came out of the bar, and, shall we say, schooled Mr. Piecyk in proper behavior. The punches and the kicks emphasizing the lesson.

My father then returned to the bar. (The bar was located in front of a social club on Grand Street, which had been a Gotti stronghold for many years.)

Shortly afterwards, Piecyk, in the company of some members of NYPD, enters the club, and accuses my father and Frank of assault and robbery. The cops, who knew who my father was, insisted that Piecyk "be sure" that it was my father who assaulted him, but at the time, Piecyk didn't get the message.

About a year later, with my father now recognized by one and all as the boss of the Gambino crime family, something happened to Piecyk's memory of the incident. Headlines at the time said that he "Forgotti."

Piecyk, incredible as it may seem, turned into a fan of my father, regularly writing him in prison, and even sending him a mass card several years later.

CHAPTER SEVEN

Challenges to the New Administration

April, 1986. The new administration is in operation, and it was my father's chief concern—running the Family. It was always number one to him. His own pending case, even his blood family, had taken a back seat to his duties as boss.

But other concerns would arise to deeply trouble him.

★

Frank DeCicco was the son of a Gambino crime family associate Joseph "Boozy" DeCicco. Frank was known among his criminal associates as "Franky D" or "Frankie Cheech." Like a lot of wiseguys, Frank grew up in the Life, seeing the guys hanging out on the street, playing cards in the social clubs, the whole scene.

He was lucky with women, *and* lucky at cards—being a successful gambler, and running gambling operations in Brooklyn and Manhattan. It was this environment in which he was to meet my father, and become his close friend. One thing about DeCicco, he protected his kids. He didn't want them involved in the Life.

But for Frank, it was a foregone conclusion. Frank did truck hijackings, jewelry ripoffs, strong arm stuff for shylocks and bookies. About six feet tall, muscular, he was one tough guy. He became a soldier in the Gambino family around the same time as my father.

He moved up, and got close to Paul Castellano, who took over as boss of the family after Carlo Gambino's fatal heart attack. DeCicco was involved also in construction rackets, heavily involved with the notorious Teamster's Local 282, the truckers who deliver the goods to construction projects—or don't, if payment isn't made to the right pockets.

DeCicco was the bagman for Castellano's construction racket efforts, often going to the "White House," which is what Castellano's home in Staten Island was called. He made good money, but unlike my father, he wasn't flashy. He drove a Buick Electra—and died in it, for his part in the plot to kill Castellano. It was DeCicco who set up the Sparks Steak House meeting in December, 1985, with Castellano. It takes more than one party to make a plot. In the world of politics, and in the world of crime, murder plots abound. Often, whether the plot is successful or unsuccessful, some of the plotters want to distance themselves from their actions, they want a fall guy.

Frank DeCicco was killed in order for other mobsters with knowledge of the hit on Castellano to distance themselves from the acts they had known about.

It was believed that at least Anthony "Gaspipe" Casso of the Lucchese crime family was in the know about the conspiracy to kill Castellano. It was DeCicco who liaisoned with the Lucchese family with respect to Castellano's murder. (Casso's interpretation of the events in his cooperation deal and his book differed from this.) Vic Amuso and Casso were, in reality, running the Lucchese family, with Tony "Ducks" Corallo on trial, in what was called the Commission Case. (This is the 1980's case where the government "proved" there was a Mafia, an organized crime group. One of the prosecutors was Michael Chertoff, the individual who was instrumental in the botching of Homeland Security's efforts during the Katrina hurricane relief. The convictions in the Commission Case helped skyrocket Giuliani into the Mayor's office.)

Vincent "The Chin" Gigante was a friend and business partner of Castellano's, and not involved in his killing. Quite the opposite, he wanted a full blown investigation into the killing of the mob boss, which, of course, was a flagrant violation of Mafia rules. There had been no "official" sanction of the Castellano killing, which was required before a hit could be "legitimate." That's the theory, but, in reality, it is rarely followed.

According to Casso, Amuso and Casso sought Gigante's support in their bid to take over the Lucchese family. Had "Chin" known about the knowledge of the Castellano plot, the relationship between the two groups would have changed significantly and Casso's life could have been in jeopardy. Castellano—who had been reluctant to endorse Amuso and Gaspipe in an acting administrative capacity while the Commission trial was ongoing—was instead pushing for Buddy Luongo, who was killed in December of 1986, and Neil Migliore who experienced, but survived, an attempt on his life about the same time, surviving a shotgun blast.

DeCicco also endorsed the takeover of the Lucchese family, because of the support given to he and my father on the Castellano hit.

In any event, DeCicco had to go.

★

Before I get into the details of DeCicco's death, I want to make a point. It is the popular delusion that DeCicco's car was blown up, because the bombers thought my father was riding with him.

Not true. The man who accompanied DeCicco to the Buick Electra on that fatal day, was Frankie Bellino, a vice president in the cement and concrete worker's union. My father was shorter, wider, and had a different hair color than

Bellino (who survived the bombing, losing some toes). My father was also a much sharper dresser than Bellino.

★

April 13, 1986, was Frank DeCicco's last day on earth. His Buick Electra was parked across from the Veteran's and Friends Social Club on 86th Street in Brooklyn, which had been Castellano's club.

Nearby, was the headquarters for the Lucchese family, The 19th Hole on 86th Street.

Herbert Pate, who placed the bomb under DeCicco's car, was parked near the club. (Pate was unknown to Gambino family members, which is why he was used on this job.) He had loaded the Oldsmobile he drove with two bags of groceries. Walking past DeCicco's car, he "accidentally" dropped the bags by the car, spilling groceries all over the street. As he picked them up, he managed to stick a magnetized improvised explosive device under DeCicco's car.

He picked up the spilled groceries, and walked on.

DeCicco exited the club with Bellino, and crossing the street, he entered the Buick. DeCicco sat on the passenger side, looking for something in the glove compartment. Bellino stood close by.

Pate detonated the bomb, tearing DeCicco apart. He was blasted all over 86th Street.

What follows is testimony at one of the trials from Michael "Mikey Scars" DiLeonardo with respect to the killing of DeCicco. (Transcript of testimony 2/22/2006 Southern District of New York):

Q. And who did John Gotti, Sr., make his underboss immediately after killing Castellano's underboss, Tommy Bilotti?
A. Frank DeCicco.
Q. Let me show you on the screen government exhibit 17. Who is that?

A. Frankie DeCicco.

Q. What became of Paul Castellano's social club, the Veterans and Friends Club, that we saw in some of those earlier photos, after Gotti and DeCicco murdered Paul Castellano?

A. Frankie took it over.

Q. So the social club stayed in operation?

A. Oh, yeah.

Q. And did you continue to go to the Veterans and Friends, even though Castellano was now dead?

A. Sure, yeah, I was close with Frank.

Q. I want to direct your attention now to approximately four months after the Castellano murder, April 13 of 1986. Do you recall going to the Veterans and Friends that day?

A. Yes, I do.

Q. And do you recall what time of day you arrived?

A. I believe 12:00, around 12:00, 1:00.

Q. Do you recall seeing anything out of the ordinary as you entered the Veterans and Friends that day?

A. Yes. I drove a up Bay 7th Street, towards 86th Street. And when you get to that point, you can either make a left or right. And directly across the street is a catering hall with a driveway to go to the back. And I seen a fellow sitting in a car with a baseball cap, leaning down in the seat in the car, looking back on his rearview mirror towards the club. And I said—I felt that was odd.

Q. And when you went inside Veterans and Friends, who did you meet in there?

A. There was about 50 or 60 guys in there at the time.

Q. What guys?

A. Gambino family guys; associates, soldiers, captains, Frankie DeCicco.

[Sunday was a gathering day for the Brooklyn faction of the Gambino family that were always close to DeCicco.]

Q. Once you got inside, did you tell anyone about what you had seen outside, that thing that you said was, seemed odd to you?

A. Yes, I mentioned to Pauley Zac. [An old time Gambino soldier.]

Q. What did you say?

A. I told him what I seen. And he said, he wrote it off as law enforcement.

Q. Meaning what?

A. We thought—we had the FBI sitting outside, or Kenny McCabe, or somebody like that taking pictures, which they usually did on Sundays—almost everyday.

Q. Just to be clear, who is Kenny McCabe?

A. He was an investigator with the government, and he would be tenacious fellow. He was on that club every day it was open, from beginning to end.

Q. What happened shortly after you went inside the Veterans and Friends Club that day?

A. Frankie DeCicco walked out with another individual named Frankie Heart, who was a soldier in the Luchese family. And within a couple of minutes, there was a huge explosion, rocked the whole club. And there was a—Frankie's car had been blown up with Frankie sitting in it.

Q. Did you go outside?

A. Yeah, we all ran outside.

Q. And what did you find when you got to DeCicco's car?

A. Car was blown up and on fire.

Q. Where was Frankie DeCicco?

A. Frankie DeCicco was still in the car. Garafola, myself, Gravano, and another fellow named Joe DeCicco ran across the street to the car. And they were trying to pull Frankie out of the car, but he was just falling apart, they said. And the other fellow, Frankie Heart, was blown across the sidewalk on to a fence, and his foot was hanging off.

Q. Either of those two men alive at that point in time?

A. Frankie Heart lived, and DeCicco died.

Q. Did Gotti, Sr. appoint a new underboss after the murder of Frank DeCicco?

A. Yes.

Q. And just to be clear, DeCicco was Gotti's underboss at the time he was murdered?

A. That's correct.

Q. And who replaced him as underboss of the Gambino family?

A. Joe Armone.

Q. A-R-M-O-N-E?

A. That's correct.

★

The powerful explosion rocked the neighborhood, shattering windows for blocks around. It is a testament to the insanity of Gaspipe Casso who would put innocent people at risk without a care or thought.

Sammy Gravano in his book and in his testimony said:

Frankie Hearts [Bellino] goes flying backwards. The blast blew his shoes off. And his toes. I go flying across the street. And there's Frankie Hearts with the blood shooting out of his feet. I saw Frankie DeCicco laying on the ground beside the car. With the fire, it could blow up again. I tried to pull him away. I grabbed a leg, but he ain't coming with it. The leg is off. One of his arms is off. I got my hand under him and my hand went right through his body to his stomach. There's no ass. His ass, his balls, everything, is blown completely off. I was wearing a white shirt. I looked at my shirt, amazed. There wasn't a drop of blood on it. The force of the blast, the concussion, blew most of the fluids out of Frankie's body. He had no blood left in him, nothing, not an ounce."

Was this the start of a war? My father knew better, and, for a time after the bombing, would drive himself around to see those in the Life that he needed to see—sending the message to one and all that it was business as usual, no war. That John Gotti wasn't worried, and that they shouldn't be either.

It wasn't always good to be the king, but duty was duty. While my father loved DeCicco dearly, his death couldn't interfere with family business.

★

Who else was involved with the DeCicco bombing?

At first my father thought it was Sicilian loyalist to Paul who had been brought over from the Old Country to do the job. American mobsters are forbidden to use bombs. Joe Armone met with several loyalists to my father and an investigation was initiated. A representative was sent to Italy to investigate there.

The hit didn't come from overseas. Tommy Bilotti's brother, Joe, was sent for and interrogated. He was released. It would be years before the truth behind the bombing came out.

It had been rumored and reported that Jimmy Failla and Danny Marino were in the know. Both Castellano loyalists. They had been talking with Casso about a "restructuring" of the Gambino family.

Administration Aftermath

Castellano was dead, my father was boss, and new challenges arrived in the new year. But what had to be dealt with first was actually an old challenge, the Bergin Crew case from the previous year.

My father and six of his associates were indicted for murder in March, 1985. Those of McBratney, and a man named Pate, who had been killed for Neil Dellacroce, allegedly by my father. Further charges included racketeering and conspiracy with respect to truck hijacking, gambling, cigarette smuggling, and loan sharking.

These were charges that encompassed a period of eighteen years. The men were facing forty years in prison if convicted.

My father and his friends were playing cards at the Bergin into the early morning hours. When the bust came down, the streets had been blocked off by law enforcement. My father was there with Tony "Roach" Rampino and Willie Boy Johnson, my Uncle Gene wasn't there, but was arrested at home. As was John Carneglia. Nick Corozzo was arrested in Brooklyn. Charles Carneglia was a fugitive from justice, and another arrestee was Neil Dellacroce's son Buddy. Neil, himself, who was first named on the indictment, was arraigned at his home, in his bed, due to his illness.

Leonard DiMaria, who had also been indicted, was already serving a sentence in Federal Prison, and was produced for the arraignment on the new charges.

At the arraignment, all were granted bail, with the exception of two people. Leonard DiMaria, who was already serving a sentence, and Willie Boy Johnson.

The prosecutor, Diane Giacalone, when Willie Boy came up to be arraigned and heard on the matter of bail, revealed in open court that he had been a government cooperator, and would not be safe on the streets. My father was shocked to hear this. A long-term and trusted friend was, in fact, a long-term turncoat.

Bruce Mouw, who had headed the Gambino squad efforts against my father, had practically pleaded with Prosecutor Giacalone, not to burn Johnson, as he was a very useful Confidential Informant. But Giacalone burned him—in the hopes that he would flip and testify at the 1987 trial.

My father, who now knew about Johnson's informant status, said he forgave him. He even joked with him, and assured Johnson that no harm would come to him.

But in reality, upon learning of Willie Boy's status as a CI, my father felt sick to his stomach. He had also learned that Willie Boy was responsible for his arrest on the McBratney killing. (As you remember, my father had been summoned out of hiding to save Willie Boy Johnson's life.)

My father was always of the opinion that he had been arrested due to one of the McBratney crew, but had now learned the truth.

He was disappointed. He had turned to Willie and asked why? No answer was forthcoming. Then, Willie Boy asked him, "If I stand tall John, do I get a pass?"

"Yes, but you will be a ghost to me."

"Swear on Frankie boy," Johnson said, "You won't kill me."

My father said, "I swear."

★

With respect to my father, who was originally granted bail, recent events had plagued his bail status. My father had been successful in getting the Piecyk assault case dismissed and enemies of the family had been successful in killing Frankie DeCicco. My father was referred to as a danger to the community, and thus bail was revoked. He was remanded to the Metropolitan Correctional Center, in lower Manhattan, to await trial.

He now wound up at MCC, along with Willie Boy Johnson.

★

My father was placed in solitary confinement. Nine South in the MCC. On occasion, he did have an opportunity to have contact with Johnson.

The purpose of putting my father in solitary wasn't the safety of the public. It was to seriously impair his ability to prepare a defense. The visiting conditions and restrictions in solitary are much more severe than lower levels of prisoner confinement.

There are restrictions as to what paperwork can be brought to an inmate, what can be removed by an attorney, and restrictions on inmate access to tapes and videos, if any, and limited phone access.

We had to go to court to get him released from solitary. As will be shown later, pretrial detainees have greater rights than convicts.

While my father was in the hole, Jackie D'Amico, at times would sneak food in to him, in his sock. He'd hide a prosciutto and mozzarella sandwich, or the equivalent, all chopped up, in a potato chip bag. There was access to vending machines so what looked like potato chips in a bag, was a whole lot better.

My father would get angry at D'Amico, and tell him not to do this, but Jackie felt guilty that he was out "eating good," and my father wasn't. "Don't worry about me," my father told him, "This is my second home."

While my father was in, Joe Armone and a panel of fellows were the representatives of my father on the outside. They were running the Family—of course—in concert with my father's instructions from jail.

★

The trial, which opened at the end of September, 1986, took seven months to complete. The jury had to wade through seventeen thousand pages of trial testimony. To even pick a jury, the lawyers had to go through six hundred and forty people.

Eugene Nickerson was presiding judge. A North Shore Long Island WASP type, he was used to more gentlemanly sparring than took place in this trial. Both the prosecution and the defense lawyers screamed at each other during the trial, and this epic battle definitely had put a strain on Nickerson—in addition to the flack he received from Washington for being so "liberal" with the defense in the case.

Many judges felt he had aged from this trial, and some court officials blamed Cutler and the other defense attorneys. This was held against him, and would later hinder his defense work. On the other hand, some had praise for Bruce for the job he had done.

The government cooperating witnesses, all seeking to

reduce their own sentences, and/or reduce government forfeiture of properties, were not adverse to lying to advance their own positions.

One of those was James Cardinali. He had been introduced to my father in jail by a man named Arnold Squitieri, and when Cardinali got out of jail, some time after my father, he was helped by my father, who found him some work.

Cardinali would occasionally hang out at the Bergin. He would also occasionally rob drug dealers in New York and Florida. In Florida, he had killed several drug dealers, gutted them, and threw them in the ocean to lose the bodies. Cardinali was eventually arrested and was facing a death penalty. Instead, the government offered him a pass if he testified against the Bergin Crew.

Especially against John Gotti.

He did. Under cross-examination by Bruce, Cardinali swore under oath that, "John Gotti was the finest man he had ever met in his life." That wasn't a lie by Cardinali. He told the FBI that, during his meetings with them. It was in their notes.

Another government cooperator testified against my father. A bank robber from Ozone Park, Matthew Traynor. But midway through his testimony, he switched sides, and started to testify on behalf of my father. He was used as a defense witness only for a short time, as he came up with ridiculous and vulgar testimony about the female prosecutor that was not helping the defense case. Cutler cut his testimony short.

The government case had other problems.

Diane Giacalone had alienated the FBI by exposing Willie Boy Johnson as their confidential informant, and the FBI didn't exactly cooperate fully with Giacalone after that. Federal Organized Crime Strike Force and State Organized Crime Task Force had to carry the ball without FBI help.

They dropped the ball.

★

During deliberations, when the jury had asked for thirteen verdict sheets, my father's lawyer was puzzled by that. My father, ever confident, told him, "One for the verdict and twelve for souvenirs."

The verdict for all defendants was not guilty, after seven days of jury deliberations.

My father pointed to the prosecution table and said, "Shame on them! I'd like to see the verdict on them too." He praised the jury for their verdict, and thanked them for what they had done to the prosecution.

Regarding the jury, Cutler observed, "I think they're tired of paid government informants who lie."

"How did you beat it?" a reporter asked my father as he left the courthouse in triumph.

He gestured back in reference to the jury. "Don't talk to me, it was these people here."

The attorney for one of the defendants, Leonard DiMaria (who was imprisoned for a previous conviction), in reference to the jury, said, "The verdict shows that the jury was tired of the government's magic show, and as magic sometimes does, this case went up in smoke. It shows the jury was serious about the evidence, and that they ignored the media hype."

It was claimed that one of the jurors in that trial was bribed, one George Pape. The story goes Pape, was a friend of a Westies boss, Bosko Radonjich, and through him Gravano was contacted to pay a sixty thousand dollar bribe which insured at least a hung jury.

Pape was later convicted of obstruction of justice, but there were twelve jurors on that case, not one, and each and every one voted for an acquittal. Pape was convicted based upon Gravano's testimony of what took place.

★

My father and Willie Boy Johnson, were released. Johnson had been kept in the hole to try and force him to testify; kept there for twenty two months. Even though he had been a long term cooperator, he did not break, and did not testify at the trial.

Let's go further into the relationship between these two men—how it started, and how it ended.

Willie Boy Johnson

At the age of sixteen, my father knew what he wanted. What he wanted was a piece of the action from a crew of thieves, who were ripping off warehouses in East New York and Brownsville.

The crew was protected by Wilfred "Willie Boy" Johnson, on his father's side, American Indian, on his mother's side, Italian—all tough guy through and through. He was known in the neighborhood as someone you *never* wanted to fuck with.

To establish his territory, my father, along with lifelong friend, Angelo Ruggiero, met up with the crew and administered a beating to the leader. Angelo watched my father's back. The leader's crew wasn't watching anybody's back, they just watched as their boss took a beating from a sixteen-year-old street tough.

He and Angelo were told that when Willie Boy finds out, "You both are dead." My father's response was, "Fuck Willie Boy."

Willie Boy went hunting the neighborhood for my father. He wanted the guy who beat up the crew chief, and had said, "Fuck Willie Boy." He wanted him real bad.

So my father decided to help Willie Boy find him, by getting word around to Willie Boy that he would be at an old vacant lot off Fulton & Rockaway—waiting for Willie Boy. (Such balls moved Willie Boy, who then decided merely to put John Gotti in the hospital, and not kill him.)

Sure enough, Willie Boy arrived at the lot, and saw my father leaning against the fence like he didn't have a care in the world. Willie Boy greeted my father with, "Hey, Cocksucker, you get your ass over here."

My father smiled back, and asked, "Cocksucker?" Then he walked over to Willie Boy and pulled out a small, broken, low caliber hand gun, and asked, "How about I put two in your hat?—Cocksucker."

Willie Boy was even more impressed with the balls on this sixteen year old kid. Their differences were resolved, and Willie Boy told me (I had known him all my life and even called him Uncle Willie Boy, when I was a kid), "I believed in your father from that point on. I said, 'This kid's the real deal.'"

I remember that when I was a kid hanging around the Bergin Hunt and Fish Club, Willie Boy would slip me some money, buy me candy, be my pal. I looked up to him. Things changed after the Giacalone revelation at his arraignment.

Willie Boy Johnson had a long history of hanging with mob guys. If he would have been Italian on his father's side, he would have been made, but he never could because he was half Indian, and perhaps that was what spurred him on to be a long-time informant.

When it was first revealed that Johnson was a rat, my father disbelieved it, thinking it a tactical ploy by the Feds—divide and conquer. But after he thought long and hard about it, it was clear to my father that the timing of busts could not be ignored.

A gambling operation just opened—bang! Closed. Agents knew just where to place their bugs to hear the big guys. Unsolved crimes were suddenly solved. The sad fact of Johnson's betrayal could no longer be denied. My father had tried to give him the benefit of the doubt, but the reality was now indisputable.

Willie Boy Johnson lasted a long time as a government confidential informant. (1969–1985)

So who was this man who was at the same time loyal friend, and disloyal informant?

Born in 1935, he grew up as a street tough, had a talent for strong arm stuff, and, by 1949, was running a gambling operation. In 1966, Johnson was doing time on an armed robbery charge. It was reported that his superior Carmine Fatico, had promised to support Johnson's family. He was a made guy that controlled most of the neighborhood in East New York, and then the Bergin club. But Fatico didn't provide the promised support, and the family went on welfare.

The FBI, whatever else they may be, have a sixth sense when it comes to potential informants. Sometimes it is almost a form of radar. When Johnson got out of jail, he was approached to become an informant. He had, of course, mixed feelings. But then, he changed his mind.

He informed on Paul Vario's hijacking operation, which was made famous in the *Goodfellas* movie. He also revealed the location of hijacked goods, collecting insurance company rewards in the process, as well as informing on other crews throughout the city.

★

My father kept his promise he made to Willie Boy to the letter, but not the spirit. He did not kill him. He allowed others to do it.

One of the groups that Johnson had a relationship with, and also informed upon, were the Bonannos. On August 29, 1988, a hit team approached Johnson as he left his home to travel to a construction site. Three men firing nineteen rounds at Johnson. Some estimates have him being hit at least ten times.

Johnson died instantly. In front of his wife.

A cooperating witness later testified that the Bonanno Family was actively involved with the hit.

Willie Boy was aware of the nature of the beasts in the jungle where he lived. Why he stuck around so long after the revelation that he was a CI, I will never understand. In any event, I cared for him, and was sorry to see him die.

I was at my office in Samson Trucking, when I heard about Willie Boy Johnson's murder. News reporter John Miller gave my father the news, outside of the Bergin. My father's comment was, "Everybody dies." When I learned of this, obviously, I had no comment. I got into my car and went for a ride, to think.

I felt this didn't have to be done, whoever was responsible. Johnson could have been chased. But it was not my place to make such a decision, and I had to accept the reality of what had been done—regardless who might have been actually responsible.

★

In the mob, power and money control. Territories are up for grabs, industries are subject to incursions, or even invasions, and there is almost no such thing as a friend. There are however rivalries, enmities, factions, and secret wars.

After my father's acquittal in 1987, his power and influence grew. He looked and comported himself like he was invincible. Many of the street people felt this way about him as well. He was handsome, smart, and tough. He had earned the respect of the men in the street because he had *taken* his power; it had not been bestowed upon him. He, in essence, was a self-made mobster.

At the apex of his power, it was reported that he not only held his Family in an iron grip, but had considerable influence among the other Families as well.

My father's influence over the Bonannos dated back to 1979, when Carmine Galante threatened to take control over their Family. The boss, Phil Rastelli, was incarcerated and while he was away, Galante plotted a takeover. Although my father had an enormous amount of respect for Galante, as an old-school, tough-as-nails guy, and even though they had done time together in Lewisburg, my father and Neil Dellacroce were backing Rastelli and Joe Massino's bid to kill Galante—who was shot to death, 7/12/79.

Massino, was a well respected Bonanno captain, who was close to the Bergin crew. Then in 1981, again, a plot arose to take over the Bonanno Family. Their capos, Alphonse "Sonny Red" Indelicato, Phil "Lucky" Giaccone, and Dominic "Big Trin" Trinchera. They too were eliminated, with the support of the Neil Dellacroce faction.

My father also had tremendous influence with the Colombo Family. His firm support had helped install Vic Orena as acting boss, and Joey Scopo as acting underboss.

Scopo, at first, had been a member of the Bergin crew, and was extremely close to the Gottis. In fact, he was the best friend of my Uncle Gene. But he was moved over to the Colombo family, solely because of the request of his father, who was a made man in that Family. Orena was in awe of my father, and the times that I was in the presence of both of them, it was clearly visible.

The DeCavalcante Family in New Jersey was headed by John Riggi. Upon his incarceration, my father pushed hard to have John D'Amato installed as acting boss. This was accomplished.

According to Fred Martens, who was the head of the intelligence division of the Pennsylvania Crime Commission, back in 1987, my father's reach extended deep into the Philadelphia crime Family.

In fact, when the Philadelphia Family underboss Phil Leonetti became a cooperator against his uncle, Nicky Scarfo, who was the boss, the government was going to use him to testify against my father regarding the Castellano killing.

But the government used Gravano to testify against my father instead. Leonetti would have testified that the Castellano hit was sanctioned by the commission. Gravano was to testify that there was no sanction—that my father had acted on his own. The government liked the Gravano version better, and they needed him to be credible, as he was the major link in their case against my father.

The situation was the same with respect to the New England Crime Family.

In 1989, there was a war within the Patriarca Family of New England. This was put to rest, according to testimony given by Sammy Gravano, by my father. He had summoned Raymond Patriarca, Jr. into New York, and told in no uncertain terms, "Settle this."

For the period of time that my father was free, this matter had been settled, for the most part.

William "Big Billy" D'Elia—who became boss of the Bufalino Family, in northeastern Pennsylvania in '94, and has been a cooperating witness—testified that he would communicate through a captain in the Gambino family to my father's administration, which evidenced his dependence and approval seeking from my father.

★

The influence of my father over so many families, made some in the Life, uncomfortable.

Vincent "Chin" Gigante, was a man who was used to being in control. With a whispered voice, and a point to his chin to signal that orders came from him, Gigante ruled over the Genovese family. Members, when referring to him, would point to their chins, so that all would know who was the voice behind the orders being given.

Gigante's method of command contrasted from that of my father. My father was up front and out there with his people. He was accessible, out in the field every day, while Gigante, enshrouded in his bathrobe, played the part of the crazy man. Men in the Life could see and touch my father; he was a real leader, and not hiding behind any facade.

"I would rather be doing life," my father would say, "than be like him." (Referring to Gigante.)

In my father's presence, the men were enthralled. To use a mob metaphor about my father, men in the Life would say, "When he shot, he hit his target, not grazed their head." (This referred to Gigante's attempt on Frank Costello's life, when he grazed his head with a bullet.)

This charisma, this effective and popular personal form of leadership exercised by my father, would obviously be threatening to other leaders, who preferred issuing edicts from the shadows.

On the other hand, I believe an intelligent man like Gigante, who had a sense of strategy, was in some way grateful for a John Gotti, because the attention he attracted by his style of leadership, deflected scrutiny of Gigante's own operation. My father was number one on the radar of law enforcement, obscuring Gigante's doings.

Gigante's insanity act had sufficient verisimilitude behind it to fool even government psychiatric evaluators. A man who was "crazy" might likely make a move against my father, but in reality, Gigante was crazy like a fox.

There was a belief, in 1987, that a move by the Genovese Family was in the works to kill my father. Gigante's New Jersey faction, based in Newark, according to reports, was given the go ahead to eliminate my father and my Uncle Gene.

However this conspiracy was picked up by the FBI, who in the course of their official responsibilities warned my father of the planned hit. Bruce Mouw and company arrived at my father's residence in Howard Beach to inform him of what was being planned. He responded with a noncommittal shrug, wished the agents a nice day, and closed the door to them.

A sitdown was arranged between my father and Gigante, with security being arranged by my Uncle Gene for my father, and I was told that Gigante's security was arranged by Quiet Dom Cirillo. At the meeting, Gigante denied any knowledge of any plot against my father, and said, if it were true, he would kill Louis "Bobby" Manna, the head of his Jersey faction, for attempting such a plot.

Gigante explained that tape recordings regarding my father and my uncle being dead, did not refer to any hit attempt, but referenced the strong likelihood of their conviction at the trial they were facing in 1987. With Gigante's word, an agreement was made and all parties left satisfied.

My father, ever the wise strategic thinker, investigated the facts behind Gigante's explanation. He issued instructions to his Newark, New Jersey captain Bobby "Cabert" Bisaccia, to monitor the actions of Genovese's capo, Manna, and his crew.

The investigation was cut short by the arrest and conviction of Manna who received an eighty year sentence. (He's due out in 2056. He was born in 1929.)

The truth of Gigante's explanation is known only to him.

However, according to Gaspipe Casso, Gigante did at times lend support to the aims of Casso and Vic Amuso. Casso had made claims that he had a sort of fifth column within the Gambino Family in the personages of Jimmy Brown Failla and Danny Marino, as has been said before.

With DeCicco dead, and should my father get a life bid, and should there be a further elimination of loyalists, then it could be Failla and Marino who could control the Family, in alliance with Casso's people.

This Machiavellian maze of treachery was to continue in existence into the nineties as it will be later shown.

CHAPTER EIGHT

Rebirth on Mulberry Street

*S*pringfield, Missouri, February 5, 1999, transcription of conversation *between myself and my father:*

JJG: John, when a man chooses a path, whether the choice be right or wrong, a man has to be true to himself, stay on that path, no matter how difficult it may be.

JAG: Well, Dad, that depends.

JJG: Depends on what, John?

JAG: Depends on the circumstances.

JJG: What circumstances might you be referring to?

JAG: Dad, every man's perspective changes. You can't say, for example, that you acted and felt the same way before you had children, than after.

JJG: That's where you're wrong, John. Do I love differently, yes. But how I feel about the choice I made for my life is stronger now at its most difficult time, than ever. When something's good, John, you can't say, 'This is for me,' but when it gets difficult, 'It's not.' Some decisions you make are for life, and a man—to be a man—stands by those decisions.

★

Probably all those who have an interest in organized crime, both as amateur historians, or professionals involved in law enforcement are familiar with the term *made man*. A person who has been formally initiated into the Mafia, and who with that initiation has certain privileges, and certain obligations.

There are many rules that the made man must abide by. A breach of some of those rules are punishable by death.

Now, when I was twenty-three years old, and doing what I was doing, involved with small time criminal activity, I knew that such a thing as a made man existed. I knew, but only from newspaper reports and television, that there was some kind of ceremony involved in becoming "made," but other than what the public also knew, I didn't know the details of the procedure.

I did know, however, that I eventually would want it. I wanted to be what my father was, at least as much as I was able to be. I wanted to be a part of the "Life," that meant everything to him, as my father meant everything to me.

I was first approached by my Uncle Gene, and asked if I wanted to be a part of the Life. That was in 1987, when I was a twenty-three-year-old. To be honest, I was taken a little bit aback by the approach, for in my mind these people (my father and men like him) were giants.

I was intimidated in a sense. My response, which today seems incredible to me, was "I'll let you know." (The chutzpah of the young knows no bounds, apparently.) Obviously, after that response, my uncle looked at me incredulously.

I was later approached again, maybe a half a year later, by my Uncle Gene and my Uncle Pete, and I was told, "If this is what you want, now is the time."

One thing I want to make clear, during this time period when I was being considered to be "straightened out," to become a "made man," my father never mentioned this to me, he never spoke about it to me. It was my uncles, including Angelo Ruggiero.

Not that I think he had any reluctance for me to become initiated, but it wasn't like him to put any pressure on me for this important step into what was to be my future for ten years. Additionally, he wanted plausible deniability with respect to his shepherding my entry into the Life, as he had promised my mother that he would keep me out of it.

What I did know about my father, was his special appreciation for Christmas time, and how he would like to schedule momentous occasions involving the Life around the holidays. So I had an idea, that if I were to be initiated, it would most likely be Christmas time. It would be a special time.

Now, here it was Christmas Eve, 1988. Normally, we would spend part of the evening at the Ravenite Social Club in Manhattan, and I would be dressed up for the holidays. We would pay respect to Neil Dellacroce, say hello to the rest of the "fellas" and then make our way back to the Bergin Club in Ozone Park. The guys loved the holidays, over one hundred people at the Bergin, same with the Ravenite.

But for this particular Christmas Eve, when I was hanging out at the Bergin social club the night before, my Uncle Gene advised me to "Make sure tomorrow, you are wearing a red tie and pocket square for good luck." I knew then, that the next day, was the day of my initiation.

So, on Christmas Eve, I wore a good black suit, white shirt, and the red tie and pocket square.

I was picked up at the Bergin, on the morning of Christmas Eve, driven to Manhattan with my dear friend Bobby Boriello, and my Uncle Gene. We arrived on Mulberry Street in lower Manhattan, and we entered an apartment.

I had never been in the place before. It was a normal apartment, owned by Joe "Butch" Corrao. I was told to wait in one room, and in the living room, was where all of the "fellas" were. There were to be five of us initiated that night. One of them was Michael "Mikey Scars" DiLeonardo, who was to later testify for the government as to the ceremony.

Out of respect for my father, I was to be the first inducted. I was also the youngest, and the youngest at that time, who was made in the Family.

The room where the men were assembled was dimly lit. There were roughly a dozen men sitting around a table. There were open seats at the table for the new inductees. Around the table sat various capos in the Gambino family. My father was not there. There would be no show of nepotism here, and there could be deniability if needed later—my father was not to be the one who had straightened me out.

Sammy Gravano and Frankie LoCascio had chaired the ceremony.

I was brought up to the front of the room by the table where the administration sat, and was asked a series of questions.

"Look around the room," they told me, "Do you know everybody here?"

I said yes.

"How do you feel about these men?"

I replied I liked them.

"Do you know who we are?"

"I have an idea," I said.

They confirmed my idea.

"We are a society, and we live by *our* rules. We are a brotherhood. We honor and give loyalty to each other. We wonder if you want to be a part of us?"

I replied yes.

"You didn't choose us, we chose you," they told me. "We have watched you all these years, and we chose you. And that's why you're here today."

A pin pricked my "trigger" finger. A drop of my blood was put on a picture of a saint, which was then burned in my hand. I moved the flaming picture from hand to hand, until it was totally consumed by the fire.

Some words were said, indicating my pledge of loyalty to the Family. I went around the table, and kissed all of the assembled there. We all locked hands. It was referred to as "tying in."

The whole initiation ceremony for me, took maybe ten minutes. For the next ten years, those ten minutes affected my entire life—in *the* Life.

As I was the first inducted that night, I was present when the other guys got made.

There was a standard litany in this ceremony. Even if you knew what was going to happen to you...where you were going...when they told you, "Dress up"... you were supposed to say, "No," when they asked you in the induction room "Do you know why you are here?.."

Obviously, when asked about how the inductee felt about the people in the room of the ceremony, he wouldn't answer in any negative fashion. One amusing incident with an inductee, was when Craig DePalma got made, around 1992.

When they asked him if he knew why he was there, he honestly answered, "Yeah."

Eyes rolled. They asked, "Yeah, why are you here?"

"To get straightened out," he answered.

Eyes rolled again. This time, DePalma caught on and said, "Well, I'm not a hundred percent sure." (Bless his heart.)

★

Once everybody had been inducted that Christmas Eve night in 1988, the administration instructed the inductees on the rules governing made men. When I was in military school there were rules too, but if they were broken, they weren't punished by execution.

Some of the rules in the Life *were* punished in such a manner.

We were not allowed to deal in stolen stocks and bonds. (Too much government attention.)

We were not allowed to have any romantic relationships

with any wife, mother, or daughter, or other blood relations of a made man.

The use of car bombs was forbidden.

We were not allowed to raise our hands to a fellow made man. That was punishable by death. As was involvement with narcotics.

When sent for, a made man cannot come with a weapon.

The inductees all acknowledged the rules, and were told who our boss, the *representante*, was. John Gotti, my father.

The other capos were identified to us. We were told as well who the representatives were for the various families. A formal introduction had to be made. We were told the protocols of meeting a fellow member. You couldn't just walk up to him and say, "Hi, we're members of the same outfit." Somebody had to tell the person that the other person meeting them was a "friend of ours," which meant they were made. You had to be introduced first.

After being read the rules, we were asked to leave, and the persons who sponsored each of us left with us. My Uncle Gene had been my sponsor, although it was Frank LoCascio who had approached my father about my getting straightened out. Both men were present at my initiation.

Most of us ended up at the Ravenite, which was only blocks away from the apartment in which we had been inducted. Knowing we were likely to be under law enforcement surveillance, we did not all leave at once.

I was brought to "meet" my father at the Ravenite as a newly made member. I walked into the club and nodded a quick acknowledgment to the people in the front room who offered their congratulations.

I was led directly into the backroom by Gravano, the room where the boss was with the other "skippers." As a soldier, I was to be introduced to the *representante*, my father. I quickly walked to the back room, and embraced my father, and then the other skippers. My father hugged me, and whispered in my ear, "I'm proud of you."

Then to the front room to meet with the rest of the guys, now being introduced as an *"amico nostro"*—a friend of ours. In the front, it being Christmas Eve, the tables were filled with food, and bottles of booze abounded. The men whispered in my ear, "Congratulations." The FBI was busy snapping cameras outside of the club, and listening to whatever devices they had. None of them offered congratulations.

After several hours at the Ravenite, we repeated the process at the Bergin, in Queens. The Ravenite was the club of my father's mentor, Neil Dellacroce, and the Bergin was my father's "stronghold."

Every Christmas Eve, the tradition was to go from the Bergin to the Ravenite, then back to the Bergin. Then around eight or nine at night, we'd all go home to have dinner with our families.

But this day was special. Prior to going home that night, I had to stop by Angelo Ruggiero's house, who was out on bail on a pending case, and was confined to his home. He had not yet been put on the shelf, as my father sought to delay that as long as possible. I was "introduced" to him. He was my godfather. We spoke for about twenty minutes then I went home to have dinner with my father, mother, and the rest of the family.

With the exception of my father, nobody in my family knew what had occurred. It wasn't their business, and I certainly didn't want it to be any of their concern. My now wife, then girlfriend, Kim, was sitting next to me at the dinner table, when a neighborhood friend who had married my cousin, came up to me and whispered in my ear, "Congratulations."

Kim asked why I was being congratulated. I told her, the guy had a good Christmas. That sufficed at the time.

The food at the house was abundant and excellent, fish dishes, lasagna, turkey, ham, lamb. There was so much food, we had to do the meal in two seatings. There were about twenty-five people at the house that night, and nobody went away hungry.

Despite being made that night, I did what I usually did on Christmas Eve at home. I bartendered. My father entertained his guests in the living room with the fireplace going, and the Channel 11 *Yule Log* on the television.

Prior to being made, I had to report to my Uncle Peter with respect to my crew's problems or business. Once being made, I reported to my Uncle Gene, then my Uncle Pete, for a short while.

When I was made capo in 1990, I reported directly to my father—the administration. It would be about four years later, with my father in jail for the rest of his life, that as captain and heir apparent I would lend assistance to a panel of men in charge of the family.

CHAPTER NINE

Uncalm Seas

Anyone can hold the helm when the sea is calm—Publilius
Syrus

He was my father's best friend since their childhood, but problems seemed to gravitate around him. I am talking about the late Angelo Ruggiero.

He had a long standing feud with Lucchese capo Anthony "Gaspipe" Casso. When it came to light, around 1983, that Ruggiero had been caught on tape talking about mob business and mob personnel, and that these tapes were going to provide the government with some highly effective prosecutorial ammunition, Gaspipe had said that Angelo was "no better than a rat."

Calling someone in the Life a rat was perhaps the worst possible thing you could call a man, because the penalty for being an informant was death. It also was a severe attack on his manhood. So this, of course, did not sit very well with Ruggiero, who decided to take care of Casso.

Supposedly, between the efforts of Lucchese man Vic Amuso, and my father, the "hatchet had been buried" over this incident, but that was not the case. With my father now head of the family, and in jail, Angelo put out a hit on Casso.

He contacted via a middleman, a local psycho named Jimmy Hydell, who was known for walking attack dogs, and carrying two pistols in his belt at all times. This was done to give Ruggiero distance and deniability in case the hit went wrong.

One day in September 1986, Casso is in his car eating an ice cream cone when Hydell comes driving up alongside, repeatedly shooting at Casso. Casso, wounded, managed to exit the car, staggered into a restaurant, told the owner to call the cops, and then hid inside a meat locker.

Due to the crowds around the shooting site, Hydell didn't bother to finish Casso off, but sped away. It would prove to be a fatal mistake for Hydell.

Through connections with crooked cops, Casso had found out that Hydell was the shooter. Casso had heard of this kid, and knew he was tough and nuts. So he wanted the cops to stage a phony bust of Hydell, in order to take him alive so he could be interrogated as to why he tried to kill Casso, and who was behind it.

Hydell hung out, with his pistols and dogs, at a candy store he owned. The cops came there, told him to ditch the dogs, (Hydell hid the pistols), and they cuffed him up and took him away. Hydell recognized the cops as cops from the neighborhood, so he didn't immediately suspect that this was anything other than a legitimate arrest.

But when the car pulled into a parking lot, and Hydell was told to get out of the car, he no doubt realized he wasn't headed towards a precinct house, but instead he was headed into Hell. They tossed him into the trunk of the car, and pistol whipped him when he tried to resist.

I had heard about the incident from FBI 302's (the FBI form used to report or summarize interviews), that were obtained in discovery in my cases, from Casso, himself, Al

D'Arco, and, while I was incarcerated, from some inmates who knew of the story.

Hydell was brought to a house on East 73rd Street, in the Mill Basin section of Brooklyn. Casso tortured him to find out who was behind the hit. Tarps were already down on the floor, so that the blood wouldn't mess up the floor.

The cops involved were Louis Eppolito and Stephen Caracappa, perhaps the two most evil people ever to hide behind a badge.

Casso, while a cooperator, later admitted that he shot Hydell some fifteen times, but not to kill him. Hydell was tortured with cigarette burns, bullets, and other implements of pain, but held out for a long time before giving up the party responsible—Angelo Ruggiero.

Upon learning this, according to Casso, he immediately contacted Joe "Butch" Corrao and Jimmy Brown Failla, from our family, brought them to the still living Hydell, who repeated it—Angelo Ruggiero had been responsible for the attempted hit on Casso. I had learned about this from Jimmy Brown himself.

Hydell kept saying that he was Danny Marino's nephew. Casso had kept Hydell alive long enough for Jimmy Brown to send word to Danny to let him know what was going on. Danny, panicking, denied any knowledge of this, and had added that he had chased Hydell away a long time ago. He washed his hands of the kid, and didn't care what happened to him. It wouldn't have mattered anyway.

Then Casso shot Hydell in the head, and afterwards the place was cleaned up, and Hydell's body disappeared.

To do an unsanctioned hit on another made man from another family, was not only a serious breach of mob protocol, it could easily have sparked a war between the Luccheses and the Gambinos. A lot of fellows would have been killed.

Ruggiero, acting out of personal malice, could have been responsible for a great deal of carnage in the streets. By protocol, he should have been killed himself, but that was not going to happen.

An appointment was set up with Vic Amuso, Gaspipe, and my father, who by this time had been acquitted in the 1985 Federal case. They wanted Ruggiero turned over to them for execution. No way was that going to happen, my father informed them. Ruggiero, despite his dangerous mistakes and breaking of Family rules, was a lifelong friend of my father's, and he wasn't getting killed by anybody.

Fortunately, Amuso, who like my father, was a street tough guy, had a great deal of respect for my father, and agreed to my father's solution to the problem—Ruggiero would be placed on the shelf, out of the Life, with nobody to approach him again.

For a lifelong, dyed-in-the-wool gangster like Ruggiero, this punishment was worse than death for him. Amuso was satisfied with this. Casso was not, but had no other choice but to accept it. (At least that's what was expected.) My father, when Casso was out of hearing range, told Amuso, "This I appreciate." So my father, with a very heavy heart, had placed his loyal friend on the shelf.

Amuso had known that even had he kicked the matter upstairs to the commission, my father had sufficient support from some of the other Families to defeat Amuso's petition to have Ruggiero killed. My father had sufficient influence with the Bonannos and the Colombos to overturn the sympathetic votes that Amuso might get from Vinnie "the Chin" Gigante and the Westside, nickname for Genovese group.

(It is believed that the days of protocol, ruling panels, and commissions are now just history. What remains of the Life are mainly individuals who are old and tired, returning from prison, or newcomers, the majority of which are frightened at the prospect of long prison terms—we used to refer to them as short timers.)

Enraged that he could not get satisfaction, over time, Casso wound up covertly killing some people. This included a kid,

Patty Testa, who was a close friend of Amuso. Casso tried to make it look like the Gambinos did it. Out of animosity to Vic Amuso, Casso wanted to start a family war.

But it didn't happen, fortunately.

★

The order had come down from my father—stay away from Ruggiero. But I didn't. I was his sole support, bringing him money on a regular basis. He was my "uncle" Angelo, he was now suffering from cancer, and I loved him dearly. I wasn't going to abandon him.

Unfortunately, one time, somebody eyeballed me sneaking in to visit Angelo. It got reported back to my Uncle Gene who then told my father, and I was sent for.

There I was in the Bergin. About forty other fellows in the room. My father first, in a low tone, asked me if it were true, that I had been visiting Angelo in violation of his specific orders. I admitted that I had.

His lips were pursed, he paced up and down. I knew I was in for a full blast from him. I waited for it. I was not to wait for long.

"Let me get this straight," he said. "Your Uncle Angelo, I declared him persona non grata, I put him on the shelf. Me, I issued a rule. Nobody is allowed to see him. *Nobody! Nobody! Who the fuck are you to violate my fucking rule?*"

"Dad," I said, "the guy is almost like a second father to me. I love him."

"*I don't give a fuck!*" he said, biting his fist in emphasis. "*I told you fucking something, I told everybody something!* My rules are the gospel, that's the way it is, John. That rule was made with a heavy heart, but it had to be done. Who are you to violate that?"

"You're right, you're right dad."

"Don't ever let it happen again," he said. "Don't let me hear it happens again."

With that, he stormed out and walked into his office. I left the club. Later on, when we were alone, when I had come back to apologize for what I had done, he said, "John, I know you love him, I love him, but what I did, I had to do. If I let you violate my rules, the principles that we live by, it weakens me, and it weakens you, if some day you are in my position."

I understood why he had to make an example of me in front of the men. It was for future strength for the both of us, not to tear me down. I stood still.

"Something you want to say?" he asked me.

"Dad, how could you ask me to stay away? Since I was a kid I loved Uncle Angelo. How could you ask me to turn my back on him?"

He looked at me and said, "John, pray that I don't know about it. I love him too."

Until Angelo died, I sneaked visits to bring him money. I hired a driver to take him to and from the doctors, and to run errands. Nobody else did.

★

My first contact with Casso was in late 1989. I had just become involved in a construction dump in the Bronx, called Oak Point. I had had a dispute with a soldier in the Lucchese family, named Maselli, who was trying to gain an in with the dump.

He and I just couldn't see eye-to-eye. So I reported this to my captain, who at that time was my Uncle Pete. (Gene had just been incarcerated.) Maselli reported this to his captain, Al D'Arco.

A meeting was set on Mulberry Street, in Little Italy, New York. Pete had taken a passive approach. Then Al D'Arco and I began to disagree on the issues related to the Bronx dump.

With Pete unsure of himself, nothing at this level could

be resolved. It was then kicked upstairs. A meeting was set in Brooklyn. For the Lucchese family it was Maselli, his captain, Al D'Arco, and their underboss, Gaspipe Casso.

For the Gambinos, it was myself, my Uncle Peter, and Sammy Gravano, our underboss at that time. Maselli had made an accusation regarding a conversation that we had had, and I verbally jumped all over him. Under the table, Sammy kneed Pete who in return, kneed me. That was the signal for me to shut up. I did.

Gaspipe then spoke, "I would like to apologize on behalf of our *borgata* for any error made by our soldier."

Sammy then spoke. "We accept, and anything we can do to accommodate you and your Family at the dump, we will."

We all said our goodbyes and left. Later that night, I was summoned to the Ravenite. As I entered, I walked straight to the back to greet my father first. I didn't get the chance to greet anyone else. My father said, "Take a walk with me."

I did.

He walked me around the corner, away from all of the fellows, and proceeded to ream my ass out. It was for speaking up at the sitdown. He said, "Who are you to speak your mind when there were superiors at the table?"

"I thought that's why I was there," I said.

"No!" he shot back at me. "You were there to listen and learn! That sitdown was resolved two days ago, when I sent Sammy to sit with Gaspipe. It was won then."

"I didn't know," I said.

"You don't have to know, John," my father retorted. "Your skipper should have shown you when to talk and when not to talk. What you see in this Life isn't always what it seems. Do you understand?"

"I understand," I said.

"Also John," he explained, "how you feel about an individual in this Life is your business. You can think and feel it, but when you speak it, especially to people you can't trust, it is not only careless, but dangerous. You understand?"

"Yes," I said.

"Good, don't let me hear it happens again."

Lesson learned. Incidentally, looking back now, I see how right my father was. Of the six men at that meeting, at least three became cooperators: Casso, Gravano, and D'Arco. The dump and all its workings were memorialized in 302s from the various cooperators. Al D'Arco testified to this in several cases, and was scheduled to testify against me in the '98 case.

Assassination Attempt

The life of a street guy hangs by a thread. Factions on both sides of the law are gunning for him. Once, in the spring of 1987, a lone gunman, not connected to any Family, nor working for any Family, decided to try and take out my father.

The Our Friends social club, in Ozone Park, around the corner from the Bergin, was the locus of the action that day.

Now, in an urban environment one hears all sorts of sounds. There is much traffic, usually some kind of construction or repair going on—the usual sounds of a city. Sometimes we might hear a noise that sounds like something, but is something else. A car backfiring, someone lighting off a firecracker, and, sometimes, somebody shooting a gun.

On this particular day, I saw someone dressed as a construction worker standing around by a florist shop, appearing like he was picking up garbage. I looked towards the Bergin, saw the door open up, and my father step out.

As soon as he stepped out, I heard a loud *bang*! Was it a car backfiring, a firecracker, a crash of some kind? I wasn't sure when I heard the first one. On hearing the second *bang* closely following the first, I realized what it was.

A shooter. Shooting at the same time my father had left the club. I put two and two together and realized that my father was the target. I couldn't make out where the shooter was, but I heard cars screeching, and without further thought, I raced over to my father.

He was pushing away club members, who were trying to keep him in the club, because he wanted to go after whoever was shooting at him. Ten, twelve seconds later, I heard another shot.

My father was fine. He smiled as he dusted himself off, and said, "What's this guy got a pea shooter?"

So who was the shooter, the would be killer of my father? It turned out he was Jeffrey William Ciccone, a distant cousin of Sonny Ciccone, a close friend of my father. Sonny confirmed that his cousin was a complete bug.

To get more details of the aftermath of this attempt on my father's life, let's go to newspaper accounts and government documents.

Pursuant to an FBI investigation, and agent notes pertaining thereto, it appears that (according to interviewee Dominic Borghese, a cooperating witness), Ciccone was quickly apprehended by my father's people, and was being held for questioning. He had been brought to a social club in Staten Island, where he was tortured for hours.

Borghese went on to state that he and others were summoned to clean up the scene. There were men mopping up the floor of the kitchen—a floor covered in blood. It required a significant cleanup. Further, he testified that there were wires hanging from the ceiling from which, presumably, Ciccone had been hung.

Borghese said Ciccone was later brought to a sweet shop in Staten Island, where, after more torture, he was killed. The participants in the killing wanted to bury the body under the cement of the sweet shop basement, but lacked the necessary tools to do so.

Someone was sent to get the equipment needed. As luck would have it, while the people involved were absent, somebody broke into the sweet shop, saw the mangled body of Ciccone, and called the police.

When the fellows returned to the scene, they saw the cop cars, and took off. They saw that the police had kicked in the front door.

In the newspaper reports:

Organized-crime experts said that the apparent attempt to shoot Mr. Gotti appeared to be amateurish and bore no signs of a well-planned gangland slaying.... Detectives said Mr. Ciccone had been shot four or five times in the face after he had been placed in a body bag on the floor of the basement. A rubber-coated white clothesline was used to tie his hands behind his back and his feet and clothesline was also looped around his neck. Bruised and Lacerated. (Selwyn Raab, *NYT* 5/1/87 "Body is found after attempt on Gotti's life")

Eye on the Sparrow

Tommy "Sparrow" Spinelli was a soldier in Jimmy Brown Failla's crew, and his cousin. He was subpoenaed before the grand jury related to an investigation of mob activities. He was severely shaken up by having been called to testify. "I don't know what I'm going to do," he said.

Failla told him, "What are you going to do? Take the Fifth, and if you have to go to jail, you go."

"I don't want to go to jail," vowed Sparrow.

"Who does?" asked Jimmy.

That, of course, did not escape Failla's notice, and he brought the matter to my father's attention. My father told him to keep an eye on Sparrow.

Sparrow was a cousin to an acting captain in Jimmy's crew, Louie Astuto, who was also related to Failla. Word came down that Sparrow had had two meetings with law enforcement. Astuto said the FBI had probably come to visit Sparrow, just as a probe, which was not unusual for us. Agents would drop by and leave their cards, making sure that everyone knew they had an ear for anyone wishing to tell them something.

Failla was concerned. Two meetings with FBI, but Sparrow hadn't told anybody about it? Failla went to my father and Sammy Gravano, and informed them. He questioned why Sparrow had not revealed this FBI "harassment." He heard that the agent had spent five minutes with Sparrow.

"Five minutes? That's not harassment. That's a conversation," my father said. "It takes five seconds to tell someone to get the fuck lost."

He turned to Failla. "What do you think, Jimmy?"

Jimmy Failla said the obvious. "He's got to go."

Sparrow was summoned to meet Failla at a glass factory. Failla gave him one last chance. "Any word on the subpoena?" he asked him.

Sparrow sealed his doom by seeming unconcerned about it, in contrast to his first reaction. "When that comes, it comes. I'll deal with it."

Failla asked him, "So what's going on with you?"

"Nothing," said Sparrow, just before his brains were blown out.

Stutman Seeks Street Justice

Gus Farace was a marijuana and cocaine dealer who had done time, in 1979—for having killed a young homosexual who had propositioned him in Greenwich Village. It is reported that Farace killed the boy, and severely beat up his companion.

He was a big, muscle-bound, low-level thug in the Bonanno family. He met a man, Everett Hatcher, in February, 1989, during a drug transaction. But Hatcher wasn't a user, he was a DEA agent. He also was an African-American. Farace didn't like blacks, and he might have been suspicious of Hatcher, so he shot him in the head a few times.

Farace wound up on the FBI's ten most wanted list. Robert Stutman, who was DEA chief for the New York area, was putting pressure on NYPD and FBI to find the guy who killed Hatcher. They, in turn, started putting pressure on us, showing up at social clubs, bars, restaurants we controlled. They wanted Farace, and they wanted him very badly.

In the summer of 1989, answering a knock at my parents' door, I see Stutman standing there. I was visiting my parents' home, and now I am looking at a DEA chief agent. He identified himself and asked to speak to my father.

"I'll see if he's home," I said. Then I told my father who was at the door. Two minutes later, I went back to the door and told Stutman and the other agents who accompanied him that my father would be right down.

After a few minutes of mutual, silent, staring my father appeared downstairs, resplendent in black silk pajamas, and a black and red Sulka robe. Stutman asked my father if he had heard about Hatcher's murder. He had. He stared quizzically at Stutman.

"It would be appreciated if Farace wound up in the street where he belongs," Agent Stutman said to my father.

"Meaning?" my father inquired.

"Face down in the gutter."

"I'm sorry for the loss of one of your agents," my father said, "This *babania* pusher I don't know, and I don't want to know. As far as this garbage pail ending up face down in the gutter, you are going to have to do your own killing, so if you will excuse me..."

My father turned to me and said, "Let's go," pointing his thumb in the direction of the inside of the house.

On November 17, 1989, Farace was killed. A van had pulled up to him—shot him eleven times. He died in the ambulance to the hospital. Later, two Lucchese associates plead guilty to the murder.

O'Connor

The restaurant was under construction in the early months of 1986. It was called Bankers and Brokers, and it was located in Battery Park City. The place was under the wing of Philip Modica, a Gambino family member.

The workers weren't union carpenters, and that did not sit well with the carpenters' union, or John O'Connor, then business agent of Local 608. They protested this non-union work by sending a crew of thugs in to bust up the place. Around thirty thousand dollars in damage was done, and I respect-fully remind the reader that the damage figure was in 1986 dollars.

This, of course, did not sit well with Modica, who went to my father, seeking redress.

The government was to allege at a trial concerning these events that my father contacted members of the Westies to take care of O'Connor. What was supposed to be a beating turned into a shooting, and O'Connor was wounded in his posterior on May 7, 1986. The shooter was alleged to have been Westie Kevin Kelly.

O'Connor survived, and, in fact, was arraigned in Sep-tember, 1986, for coercion and criminal mischief with respect to the damage which was visited upon Bankers and Brokers.

It wasn't until January 24, 1989, that my father was arrest-ed for the O'Connor assault and attempted murder. He was walking along a Soho street when Joseph Coffey, an officer from the Organized Crime Task Force of New York, caught up with him, almost pushing him through a plate glass window before cuffing him.

That's what Coffey claimed. Never happened that way, and there were dozens of witnesses. Coffey was a great one for embellishment, especially of his own exploits.

Coffey had referred to my father as a moron. My father had a 140 IQ.

When my father was arrested, he told Coffey, "I'll lay you three to one I beat it."

Coffey claims he told my father in response, "Forget it, jerk off, get in the fucking car." These words were never spoken by either man. For the arrest over two dozen officers had closed off the street where my father was arrested. One was disguised as a hot dog vendor. The arresting officers were extremely polite. We had witnesses to the arrest, including my Uncle Pete.

So my father was arraigned along with Angelo Ruggiero and the late soldier Anthony Guerrieri. At the time of the arraignment, Angelo went to Beekman Hospital where he was getting chemo. He was to die before the trial began. After that, my father permitted everyone to go to the funeral, relaxing the rule that, while he was alive, nobody was to see him.

My father was a big hit with the other detainees in jail who applauded him when he entered the courtroom. The Prosecutor, Cherkasky, demanded that the judge hold my father without bail. He noted that my father was facing 25 to life if convicted, and had the financial wherewithal to leave.

Cutler replied that my father never ran away from a problem, and that the defense would win the case. My father was let out on $100,000 bond, leaving the courtroom—to fall into an ocean of reporters.

Jury selection took eleven days, and those selected were ordered sequestered by Judge Edward J. McLaughlin. Jury sessions were to be held six days a week.

With two informants and a pile of tape recordings, the prosecution felt confident. Vincent "Fish" Cafaro, former Genovese member, testified as to how the Five Families operated. Then tape recordings were put into evidence, including the tape where my father was alleged to have said with regards to O'Connor, "We're going to bust him up."

Of course, OCTF had some problem explaining why, if they had heard these tapes, they didn't warn O'Connor in advance of his assault. One of the agents explained that the tapes weren't clear enough to identify O'Connor as the target.

Very bad move. If it wasn't clear enough for law enforcement, with their expert listeners and tape enhancement facilities, then how on earth did they know the discussions referred to O'Connor?

Not good enough for OCTF, then obviously not good enough to convict my father, Shargel, his attorney, argued.

The next informant up for the prosecution was a former Westies member, James Patrick McElroy, who had been convicted in 1988 for, among other things, assaulting O'Connor. He was facing ten to sixty years in Federal prison. Obviously, he joined "Team America" to try to reduce that sentence.

McElroy testified that the order to get O'Connor came through Jimmy Coonan, of the Westies, who received it from my father. Under direct examination, McElroy testified to having murdered two men, shooting two others, and slitting a man's throat.

He gave details about how the assault on O'Connor took place.

During the shooting, he said that O'Connor was "spinning around in circles trying to get to the elevator."

Then it was cross-examination time. Attorneys Gerald Shargel and Bruce Cutler ripped into McElroy. So much so that Cutler had to be, on occasion, warned by the judge. (Shargel was a long time Gotti attorney, who was one of the top criminal lawyers in New York.)

Then the "bust him up" tape was played for the jury, to indicate that my father had ordered the attack on O'Connor. The defense claimed that the tapes were tampered with. The sound quality was terrible.

In a bold move, the defense called the supposed victim, John O'Connor. He admitted on the stand that he had many enemies; that he was never warned by law enforcement about a potential attack; and that he didn't have the slightest idea who did it. "I don't know Mr. Gotti, he's probably a fine gentleman. I never did anything wrong to him, and I don't think he ever did anything wrong to me," O'Connor testified.

Summations were contentious, with lawyers on both sides engaging in ad hominem attacks. Jury deliberations commenced, but not without strife. Judge McLaughlin was given a note that one of the jurors evidenced bias. The judge brought in the jury and addressed the issue. "You can't get twelve New Yorkers to agree on anything," he quipped.

★

During the trial, my father's attorney, Bruce Cutler, had often spoken with the court officer who would bring in the jury. He became friendly with him. Once, on the day before the verdict, Cutler asked how he was doing with respect to the jury deliberations. The officer said, "Eleven tuna fish sandwiches, one roast beef."

My father,upon hearing that from Cutler, took it as a bad sign. He now expected to go away on this case. Bruce became depressed. My father met with many of us at the Ravenite. He also held all night meetings above, in the Cirelli apartment. He began to give instructions of what he wanted to happen after he went to jail.

Frankie LoCascio had suggested that after my father goes in, I was to be made a captain. It was seconded by Gravano. However, it was not to be done until after my father was incarcerated. My father went outside and took me for a walk-talk. "It's eleven-one against me," he told me. He then explained what he needed me to do after he went to jail. It was an emotional walk for me.

However, he wasn't convicted. On Friday, February 9, 1990, my father was found not guilty on all counts. My father was amazed, and anyone watching the delivery of the verdict on TV could see the emotion in his eyes. That almost never happened with him, but he was sure he'd be found guilty—he was most happy to be found incorrect. To those who thought the jury tampered with, no. Just no. My father was sure he was going away until the verdict of not guilty was read.

Courtroom spectators applauded. The judge threatened them with contempt. It was over, and my father had emerged from the courtroom, not only free, triumphant.

On the way to the car, which waited to take him from the scene, he pumped his fist in the air to celebrate the victory. Later, on Mulberry Street, fireworks, barbecuing, and cheering people greeted him. The block was roped off, and the celebrations carried on throughout the night.

Several nights later, my father and my mother, my Uncle John and his wife, Mary Lou, myself and my future wife, Kim, went to a restaurant in New York, Maxims. The men in tuxes, the women in cocktail dresses. It was required on a Saturday night.

One of the owners of Maxims was Pierre Cardin. The place was open from 1985–1992, and was one of the hottest upscale places to go in Manhattan. It was housed in the Carlton House Hotel by Madison and 61st street.

We were celebrating the victory, and my upcoming twenty-sixth birthday. We then went to the legendary night club, Regines (owned by a woman named Regine, housed at 502 Park Avenue but now closed). When he entered, the DJ played the Gypsy Kings, his favorite group. My father suggested that I get up and dance with Kim. I politely declined. Then my father turned to Kim, and said, "Go ahead honey, why don't you get up and dance and have a good time?"

She looked at me, and I shot her a look that meant "no," and she said, "No, I'm okay." Later on when my father got up and went to the rest room, I followed him. He stopped short of going in, turned to me, and said "What was that all about?"

I said, "Dad, I don't feel comfortable here with my mother and my fiancée."

"Listen John," he said, "life is about making memories, you got to make as many as you can. Now, this is one of those evenings when you can create some good memories, for you and your future wife, because at the end of the day, John, that's all you're going to have, understand me?"

★

I took it as meaning when you are in prison or at the end of your days, memories are all you're going to have.

On July 5, 1990, O'Connor took a plea and received a prison sentence of one to three years, but not for his actions at Bankers and Brokers. Those charges were dropped as part of the deal.

It is ironic that the FBI wanted my father to win the state case involving O'Connor. They wanted my father's head all to themselves. Word came down from D.C. that there was an unlimited checkbook when it came to getting myfather.

After the O'Connor victory, my father realized that, with all the past trials, with all the surveillance, with all the manpower and government money dedicated to getting him behind bars, it was time to do some succession planning. He elevated certain chosen individuals to the rank of captain. He straightened out certain people.

Government surveillance cars would be parked along the streets where the Ravenite was located, to catch intel from walk-talks. Eavesdropping devices in the cars, were turned on as my father strolled past them. In fact, during one of the walk talks, Bobby Boriello noticed a van with a television set. My father is on the TV. Bobby stares at it, his face pressed against the van window. Looking right back at him from the other side of the glass is an agent.

Despite all the eyes and ears on him, my father continued to be right out there, an in-your-face type of gangster. Didn't hide in the suburbs, didn't turn down the dress up. He was who he was, and would continue to be so, regardless of government harassment.

★

The bugs in the club were easily defeated by loud televisions, white noise generators producing static, and other means. The FBI needed clearer tapes. They finally figured out that when my father's voice was no longer heard, and a door was heard slamming, he must have been going to another part of the building.

After continued visual surveillance of the club, the FBI noticed that at certain times, an elderly woman would be seen leaving the building—there were apartments above the club. And they found out that the woman was the widow of Mike Cirelli a Gambino family soldier.

Once they discovered it was the Cirelli apartment, and once their special collection team was able to break in and plant bugs (on a rare occasion when Ms. Cirelli was visiting friends), the tapes began to roll, and the sound was loud and clear.

DiBono

Louie DiBono was a soldier in the Gambino family, and involved in construction. He was a wheeler dealer. He had various partnership interests with Sammy Gravano in construction related industries.

Sammy hated him. There has been a question about who was responsible for DiBono's death. Some thought it was Sammy. Others thought it might have been my father.

In any event, there was a government recording, taken from the Cirelli apartment above the Ravenite, where my father was heard saying, "You know why he's gonna die? He didn't come in when I called him."

Here is the segment of the tape related to DiBono that was played for the jury:

GOTTI: He didn't rob nothing. You know why he's dying?

He's gonna die because he refused to come in when I called. He didn't do nothing else wrong."

LOCASCIO: "You have that meeting yet?"

GOTTI: "No. Gonna have it tomorrow."

LOCASCIO: "Because at the meeting, I predict that he's gonna bring you fifty."

GOTTI: But I wouldn't take nothing. The cocksucker! I wouldn't take nothing from him. He's gonna get killed because he, he disobeyed coming…

On October 4, 1990, as Louie DiBono pulled into the parking garage at the World Trade Center. A lone gunman with a silencer approached him after he parked his car, and fired multiple shots into his head and torso.

But two weeks after that recording, DiBono came to the Ravenite, and came again. My father was getting along fine with him, but for one reason or another, DiBono was killed. (Later on, I would be accused of involvement in the Dibono murder.)

CHAPTER TEN

Wedding Bells

Kim Albanese and I had been dating since we were teen-agers, and I guess I always knew—we'd be married one day. Through all the trials and tribulations, we still are, some twenty-four years, as I write this. Not a lot of couples who faced what we did can say that.

We had been engaged for about two or three years, and, in 1990, it was time to officially tie the knot. So I had a meeting with my father. We discussed it, and he was all for it.

Where we differed, was on the ceremony. I just wanted a simple, civil, City Hall wedding, and then dinner with the mutual families afterwards. Not my father. It wasn't going to be City Hall for his son. No way.

"Listen," he told me. "I am somebody, you are somebody, and now that you are going to marry her, she is somebody too. We have to do this the right way." So he took charge of the details.

Those details brought our reception to the Helmsley Palace. My father was friendly with Leona Helmsley—they had had a mutual attorney at one time. (More on that later.) But let me tell you about the proposal. This was an offer she *could* have refused, but didn't.

One night, on taking Kim out to dinner, me being me, I took out a ring, tossed it to her, and said, "See if this fits." I had purchased the engagement ring (and the wedding ring) from a friend of my best friend, Bobby Boriello. Bobby was also to serve as my best man at the wedding.

The church where the actual ceremony took place was located in Williamsburg Brooklyn, where the presiding priest, was a cousin of Angelo Ruggiero. He was called "Father Seppe."

We would be able to have more of a respite from the press and law enforcement surveillance there. I believe the official name of the church was St. Mary's. We would be able to get married behind closed doors, away from prying eyes that did not wish us well.

Father Seppe was a good, old-time, cigar smoking type of priest, and in his church, just the family members were there to witness our wedding. We gave him a box of his favorite cigars, and in fact, I remember that the day of the wedding he appeared in the church with an unlit cigar in his mouth.

He wasn't very formal for a priest. He did his best to put us all at ease with his lively sense of humor. A very down to earth guy—a rare quality in a priest, and a welcome one. He set his cigar down on a pew bench, told a few jokes, and then said, "Okay, let's get this done."

★

For days before the actual wedding, the press had camped out at my house, and at Kim's residence. How they knew about the wedding was anybody's guess. My guess? An informant. Also, it wasn't exactly a secret that we had booked the Helmsley Palace for a wedding reception on April 21, 1990. A place like that you don't book at the last minute.

Now the FBI, of course, was eager to penetrate this reception. They first approached Leona Helmsley and directly asked to have their men within the catering staff at the wedding. She said no. They then surreptitiously started to apply for jobs as catering help with the Helmsley for the reception. As far as I know, none of them got hired, because both the hotel people and our own people screened any new faces suddenly applying for work.

One thing you have to say about Leona Helmsley, she had guts. She was tough, and stuck by her guns. For my reception, she flew a twenty-foot square Italian flag from the Hotel, something normally done only for diplomats and other high level Italian VIP visitors to the hotel. She caught some flack for that.

She didn't care. She flew the flag, and she kept the cops out of the reception. The FBI threatened her repeatedly with a tax case, but she held her ground. They later brought the tax case. She got a sentence, at the age of 71, of four years imprisonment, repayment of some $8,000,000 and 750 hours of community service.

The government claimed she had defrauded the IRS with respect to a million dollar renovation to her house. She had paid millions in taxes, offered to pay the taxes on the renovation, but they still imprisoned her.

She served in a woman's Federal prison in Kentucky, the same location where Westie Jimmy Coonan's wife served time. Edna Coonan. My father had sent word to make sure that Edna took care of Leona. She did.

Of course, depending how you look at it, there *were* a lot of visiting VIPs at my reception. Representatives from all Five Families, capos. Also, well known lawyers—Gerald Shargel, Bruce Cutler, Richard Rehbock, Barry Slotnick. Every family had their own table. The lawyers had theirs too.

Now, we did have a photographer at this wedding, of course, but he was carefully instructed on where not to point his camera, given the attendees. It wasn't a problem, as we had hired a photographer recommended by Tommy Gambino. He knew where to focus his camera—and where not to.

The flowers were done by one of the biggest outfits in the five towns, Stefans. Any provider of services to our wedding got the gig because they were well known, well connected, and well trusted.

Everybody was screened, even members of the orchestra that backed up Jimmy Roselli. After all the son of John Gotti didn't get married every day. Jay Black and the Americans played. Comedian Lou Baccala. Italian singer Renato di Roma, and other Italian singers all performed.

The performers were all family friends. Roselli performed as a favor, refusing to take money. My father had done a solid favor for Roselli in the past—I will tell you the story.

★

Frank Sinatra's mother, Dolly, wanted Roselli to perform at a charity show, but she didn't ask him herself. Roselli had told the people asking him to have Dolly give him a call, because he was already booked up. Sinatra took offense at this, and via his connections, insured that Roselli's songs didn't get played or sung in this country, until my father brokered a truce.

But the Chairman of the Board sometimes needed to be reminded of things.

Back in the late 1980s my father, me, and some of my father's friends were at the *Savoy Grill* in Manhattan. I feel sure that Sinatra remembered that night for the rest of his life.

Sinatra was due to perform in New York that night, and had sent some complimentary tickets to the Ravenite, for my father and several guests to attend the performance at Carnegie Hall. Sinatra had met my father several times before, when my father ascended to the top position of the Gambino family.

At the last moment, Sinatra canceled the show, due to "illness," and my sisters and their husbands, along with other guests, were disappointed to say the least. These were personal invitees of Sinatra, who were to see him back stage and have dinner with him.

He didn't apologize, and it turned out he wasn't all that ill, because he popped into the Savoy Grill with his entourage, smiling and joking, and looking rather healthy.

This did not go unnoticed by my father. He sat at a table in an alcove with Jackie D'Amico, Jackie the Actor, Joe Watts, and some other fellows. He had full view of Sinatra's arrival with his best friend Jilly Rizzo and others. Rizzo was our liaison man with Sinatra. Messages to Frank went by way of Rizzo, usually.

My father was less than pleased that his friends and members of his family had waited in line to see Sinatra's concert, only to find out it had been canceled. To now see Sinatra come in to the Savoy, looking the picture of health, enraged my father.

My father sent Joe Watts to talk to Rizzo and Sinatra. He went over to their table, and "suggested" that Rizzo and Frank join him for a private conversation, away from the table. Watts proceeded to tear Sinatra a new asshole, and Rizzo too.

Sinatra had previously shown disrespect by failing to come see my father when he was requested to do so. He had dragged his feet in resolving the beef with Jimmy Roselli, getting him back into the clubs and casinos to perform. The show cancellation was the last straw.

"The next time John sends for you," Joe advised Frank, "and you make up an excuse, I will be the last face you will see on this earth."

A very nervous and frightened Sinatra turned to Rizzo, screaming at him, and blaming him for not getting these messages from my father. He then asked permission to go over to my father and personally apologize.

Nothing doing. When my father wanted to hear from Sinatra, he would send for him, Watts informed him. Watts then turned to Rizzo and told him that he could make sure that "by this time next week you're in a hole some place."

Watts told my father that the error might have been Rizzo's fault regarding Sinatra's previous no show for a meet with my father regarding Roselli. Sinatra and company quickly exited the restaurant. Now, for sure, the Roselli matter was settled.

So Roselli showed his gratitude, giving a free performance at my wedding, singing one of my favorite songs, "Little Pal." (This song is about a father going away to jail, telling his son to remember him. Obviously for those in the Life, it has a special meaning.)

Even though Roselli refused to charge for his singing, my father, being the gentleman that he was, bought Roselli a diamond and gold watch that had inscribed on the back, "Thank You, Your Pal, Johnny." Roselli would always wear that watch when he performed.

★

Wherever there are Italians, there is food. When there is an Italian wedding, there's a lot of it. At mine, there were tons of it. All kinds. Lobster, shrimp, Beef Wellington, caviar, of course. You name it, you could probably find plates of it at the reception.

We aren't talking lasagna and chicken francese here. This was a very elegant, $1,000 a plate affair. In 1990 money.

The reception took place on two floors in the Palace. The main ballroom was for immediate family and distinguished guests. The friends of the families were upstairs, guys from the neighborhood, and the lesser lights of the *business*.

We had three rooms at the Helmsley. The main ballroom held up to 300 people, and two smaller rooms on the floor above held a total of about two hundred. The smaller of the two, which held about 75, was for those less close to us.

The upstairs rooms had their own bands. We had reserved many hotel rooms for the guests. The suite where my father, mother, and brother Peter stayed had three floors. The first was a living room with a baby grand piano, fireplace, kitchen, dining room, and maid's quarters. The second floor had three master bedrooms, and the third floor contained a study with fireplace, and a terrace of 1,500 square feet that overlooked St. Patrick's and the New York City skyline. Just prior to my father's arrival at the suite, the room was swept for listening devices, supervised by Jackie D'Amico.

My suite was two bedrooms, located right beneath my parent's suite. A third consisted mainly of a sunken living room with player piano, it's floor to ceiling windows overlooking Manhattan.

That suite was to serve a special purpose.

James O'Keeffe, known as Jimmy Irish, trusted caretaker of the Bergin club, was entrusted to protect this suite for our use. While the rest of the suites were booked well in advance, this one was not. Leona Helmsley used it for her own meetings. The day before the wedding, we had it swept for bugs; then Jimmy slept there overnight until the wedding to make sure nobody came in and put new listening devices in the suite.

While bands played and most of the party goers were enjoying themselves, it was a workday for the Bergin crew. We had to ensure our guests were taken care of, that all went smoothly, and that the Chief, my father, looked good.

We stood around long enough to show respect to Jimmy Roselli and Jay Black, the performers, but after dinner, we began ferrying fellows through a back entrance leading to a private elevator, which led to the suite aforesaid.

Bobby Boriello had given Jimmy Irish notice to put on a suit and join the party, we needed to use the room for business. Boriello conducted our "special" guests, three at a time, into the suite. Members from the New York Families and guys from out of state too.

I was excused from the meeting, and my father held court: sort of a state of the union for the Mafia. Everyone's pulse was felt. Since they were all there for the wedding, it was an excellent opportunity for this get together in private. (Gravano 302 12/27/91)

★

There were over 500 people at this wedding. Outside of the Palace, every law enforcement agency that was an interested party, was taking pictures of the comings and goings. Inside, everybody was enjoying themselves, and they showed it with several hundred thousand in wedding gifts.

Two of the many revelers at the wedding joked and drank to each other's health. They danced with their wives together. Bobby Boriello, and Anthony "Gaspipe" Casso. Their merriment at this affair would later turn out to be both tragic and ironic. But at this moment they were the best of buddies, celebrating my wedding together. What happened later between these two will be detailed in later chapters.

All in all, it was a most beautiful affair, my wedding. It was great to see everyone have such a good time. All the fellows eating and drinking, resplendent in their tuxedos.

But now, looking back, it was probably the last moments at the pinnacle of *our* existence. Soon, life as we knew it would change—deceit and treachery would lead to arrests and murder of many in the Life.

On the morning after the reception, my father and I and the entire family went to brunch at a restaurant in which he had an interest, Da Noi. Da Noi was a restaurant frequented by actor Anthony Quinn, usually on a Tuesday or a Thursday night, when he was in town. He would often meet my father there for dinner. My father always enjoyed his company. In later years, in the HBO movie, *Gotti*, Quinn was to play my father's mentor, Neil Dellacroce.

We left the hotel on the way to the restaurant. The press and the FBI were still there, snapping away at us with their cameras. They had camped out overnight.

★

My wife and I received mountains of cash gifts. We didn't get to keep it, so it turned out.

In 1997, $350,000 of wedding gift money, along with items of personal jewelry, were found in the basement of a building, along with a list of the wedding gifts, too. At the time, renovations were being done on my home, and I wasn't going to have that kind of money lying around. I had given the wedding money to a friend of mine to hold.

He put the money and jewelry in a safe in his mother's house. However, the woman died, and his family got into a battle over ownership of the house. So the safe was moved to a building in Ozone Park, where I had a first floor office, and a very secure basement in which to place the safe.

The FBI raided the Ozone Park location, and found the safe. They sought to do what they always do—have the property forfeited. However, our lawyers challenged them, and when it was revealed that none of the currency had been printed later than 1990, the wedding money argument stuck. It was true, and sometimes the truth will win out, even with the FBI doing their best to stop it.

Of course, they gave back the jewelry, and kept the cash. It was part of my forfeiture agreement with the government, which will be detailed later on. Thus the FBI became the beneficiary of what were my wedding gifts.

★

We never had a honeymoon either.

I had not lived with Kim prior to our marriage, and after the wedding, we moved into my Massapequa home. Now if you think that married life made a big change in my lifestyle, no. I came and went as I pleased, just like when I was single. My wife at times challenged me, but not often. She knew it would not do any good in any event.

My days were occupied for the most part with my businesses,

and my long nights usually began in the Our Friends social club, and could end up in a variety of locations. However this changed, with the birth of my first child.

The pride and excitement of having a son, began the process of changing my perspective, and I started spending more time at home with my wife and child.

Chapter Eleven

Fourth of July
Dad and RICO

There were numerous Italian social clubs in Ozone Park, Queens. Of course there was the Gambino flagship in Queens, the Bergin Hunt and Fish Club, there was a Bonanno club on 96th Street, another Gambino club, the Friends Club on 99th Street. On 101st Avenue there was Joey Scopo's club, which was a Colombo family club. The Genovese family had a club between 102nd and 103rd, called Cafe 2000. And another Gambino club on 106th Street, which was called the Painter's Club.

In short, it was a Mafia neighborhood. But the club that controlled Ozone Park, and all of Queens was the Bergin. The Bergin was full of tough guys, and it housed the largest crew in Queens, if not the whole of New York City. It was the hub of activity.

★

Independence Day. I always looked forward to it as a kid, and even as an adult. It would be fireworks and barbecue at the Bergin. We would close off 101st Avenue from 98th to 99th

Street to party, to celebrate. The streets were blocked with Police horse barricades. It was a tradition since 1970.

Heck, even the city buses had to re-route. The fire company down the street stood at the ready in case something happened. Local cops would, at times, attend the festivities. At times, they even brought their families.

Free food abounded. There was truly an *abbondanza.* The aroma of grilling burgers, hot dogs, chicken, sausages made everyone hungry. Much of the food had been donated by Western Beef, which had been a Castellano family business. The fruits, salad, condiments, and bread were donated by the Sciandra family, who owned Top Tomato.

We rented Mister Softee ice cream trucks for around the clock ice cream, and had rides for the kids. T-shirts were given out. But the highlight of the day and evening was the 9:15 PM fireworks display. The news reported that some ten thousand people were in attendance.

Fun times in this working-class neighborhood. Was it legal—the block party was, we had obtained a permit. The fireworks? No. But uniformed services and politicians turned a blind eye. They joined in the fun. It was good press and good politics. Everybody enjoyed themselves, it was harmless fun.

But authorities have a way of screwing up the enjoyment of the people they are supposed to serve. It was 1990, and the Teflon Don designation, given to my father by the press, was in full force and effect. Hell, even the authorities let him close off streets and set off fireworks with impunity.

Since politics is all about public perception (as much as about to performance), it was time for those in power to reel things in. On Independence Day, 1990, there was a tremendous police presence in Ozone Park, and they weren't there to join in on the traditional fun. Officers on each corner of the streets, and mounted policeman also were found in an abandoned lot a block away from the celebration site.

The Captain of the 106th precinct appeared and demanded

to talk to who was in charge of the festivities. My Uncle Pete told him that he was.

"Set off one firecracker and that guy who did it is getting locked up," the Captain told him.

"You know, we have done this for years and never had a problem," Pete answered.

"Yeah, I know," said the Captain. "But the orders come from upstairs, and believe me, I am not happy about it."

"We've got thousands of people here expecting fireworks," said Pete. "How do you plan on handling that?"

"That's your problem."

"Right. No, it's your problem," Pete said and walked away from the cop.

My uncle went to my father and told him what had happened.

"Make sure all the lawyers are on call tonight, and have plenty of cash for bail," was my father's response. He went back to reading the newspaper.

Our tough guys were put in charge of the fireworks display, and when 9:15 PM came around, you could feel the tension in the summer night air. We had ten and twelve inch mortars ready to blast. One of the guys in charge of the works was a decorated Vietnam veteran, Trevor Dunwell. He knew about tension and explosives.

So there it was. The Gambino family, friends and neighbors, and loads of cops. Journalists too, of course, ready to get it all on video, whatever was going to happen in this standoff between neighborhood guys and cops.

It started. Locals started to shout, "Cops go home." The response came from the police captain's bullhorn, through which he shouted, "There will be no fireworks tonight." The ten thousand some people that were there for the fireworks display were not pleased. There was a growing potential for a riot.

Finally, my father left his office. The neighborhood crowd went wild. They shouted, "John Gotti! John Gotti!" The Captain walked over to my father.

"Listen John," said the Captain, "I don't care how angry this crowd gets, there isn't going to be any fireworks."

My father turned to my Uncle Pete, and indicated to start the works. Pete gave the thumbs up to the guys waiting for the signal, and the sky lit up with multi-colored lights and thunderous sounds. The stuff was launched from rooftops and train trestles. I coordinated the shoot-off via walkie-talkie.

The crowd went wild. "Now," said my father to the Captain, "how do you want to handle this?"

The Captain shook his head in resignation and partial disbelief. "Can you cut it down to an hour?"

My father gave him a big smile and said, "No problem." As the Captain left, he turned and said, "John, it wasn't me." My father nodded his head in understanding.

Not every tradition lasts. Years later, with my father locked up forever in isolation, the fireworks stopped. The times they were a-changin'.

★

A storm was now brewing. My father received information from one of his sources that arrests were to be made within a month. Sammy Gravano went on the lam, but my father refused to do so. When I had suggested this to my father, he bit my head off for proposing such a thing. My father would *never* run.

While the arrests were being considered, another problem arose for my father, which came in the person of Eddie Lino.

Lino was one of the Gotti loyalists, a feared man in Brooklyn, no stranger to killing for the mob.

Lino, in 1987, had been put on the carpet by my father for threatening to kill Sammy Gravano, who had been hounding Lino about a debt owed. Lino was a man who would have been an opposing force in the event of a coup against the Gotti regime. He was a co-defendant, with my Uncle Gene, in a 1989 case, and was acquitted.

On the evening of November 6, 1990, Lino was pulled over on the Belt Parkway by an unmarked police car. He stopped his car when he saw the flashing red light, and two cops, who were something more than cops—they were mob hirelings—got out of the vehicle.

Louis Eppolito and Stephen Caracappa . They showed Lino their badges, and as Lino reached into his glove box to pull out his license and registration, Caracappa shot Lino in the head several times. (Eventually the two cops were convicted of Lino's murder.)

My father was compelled to investigate the reality behind this hit, as he had done in the DeCicco bombing, but he was to run out of time.

The Bell Tolled

On December 11, 1990, my father was again arrested. I remember, it was a Tuesday night.

Over two dozen law enforcement officers charged into the Ravenite to make the arrest.

I had followed my father from the Bergin to the Ravenite, where we said hello to the fellows, had some drinks, and did what we usually do there. We were getting ready to leave, to go see Frank Sinatra perform at Carnegie Hall, as he had invited my father.

I was with Bobby Boriello, Michael DiLeonardo, and if memory serves me, another friend of mine, Frank Radici. We were to have our own table at Sinatra's performance. I was going as my father's representative, as he wasn't one to stay put at a concert for any length of time. My friends were going with me, and I was sure this time, Sinatra wouldn't be canceling.

En route to Carnegie Hall, we were listening to the radio, when the program was interrupted by a news flash that John Gotti had been arrested at the Ravenite. The story was being updated every two minutes.

We turned the car around at the first announcement, and headed back to the Ravenite. By the time we got back, he had already been taken away. We got the lowdown from the remaining people in the club, then drove back to the Bergin club to start strategizing as to what to do next.

My father had been arrested with Frankie LoCascio, and Tommy Gambino. Also, Sammy Gravano. We started meeting with attorneys the night of the bust. First I met with Bruce Cutler and Richard Rehbock. Bruce would handle the arraignment, and Rehbock would stay to advise me.

We also got Tommy Gambino's lawyer, Mike Rosen, on the phone. LoCascio was using Dave Greenfield, and Gravano had Nick Gravante, from Gerald Shargel's office.

I did not attend the arraignment, as my father had given instructions that I was not to be in court. He never wanted me there, if I had any choice in the matter. My uncle Peter and Jackie D'amico, and maybe one or two guys from the club, went in support of my father at the arraignment.

While he was arraigned the morning after the arrest, the bail hearing was put off until the following week. My father was being housed at the Metropolitan Correctional Center in lower Manhattan. In the hole. Locked up 23 hours a day.

I was able to visit him once a week on a one hour visit. Some of the guards, who liked us, let me stay longer. Eventually, LoCascio and a short time later, Gravano, who also were in the hole, were transferred to less stringent confinement conditions. Not my father, however.

In January, 1991, after a motion by his defense attorneys, Judge Glasser, the judge assigned to the case, decided that keeping my father in the hole was unconstitutional. He was moved. Glasser was no doubt aware, that had he ruled otherwise, we would have appealed to the Second Circuit, which would have delayed the trial.

The boys in D.C. wanted a conviction soonest. So, Glasser made the proper decision vis a vis my father's housing conditions. I fully believe, that Glasser, before deciding anything in this case, had to wait for instructions from Washington.

Now that my father was out of the hole, I was able to visit him twice a week. One of those times each week, I was accompanied by my mother and my siblings. On the other weekly visit, it was just me, my uncle Peter, and maybe one or two of the guys from the club.

The government's next move was to deprive my father and his co-defendants of the attorneys they had chosen. AUSA John Gleeson (now Federal Judge Gleeson) made a motion to have Shargel, Cutler, Pollock and others removed from the case. Other high profile defense attorneys were listed as potential witnesses, such as Jimmy LaRossa, which precluded them from serving as counsel for us.

Gleeson claimed there was conflict of interest that the attorneys were acting as "in house" counsel to the Gambino family, and were liable to be called as potential witnesses in the case. This was not an unexpected move by the government. They had tapes. My father was aware of the likelihood of something like this being done.

The government was not unaware of the close relationship between Cutler and my father, and the level of comfort between them. They had both a professional and social relationship. My father would meet Cutler for dinner at least once a week, whether or not there was some kind of case going on.

There was a sort of telepathy, a chemistry between them that had grown out of their relationship. They dressed alike, they moved alike, and Cutler looked up to my father as a surrogate older brother. Cutler was at his best when he was representing my father, he gained energy and enthusiasm from him, and the government wanted to remove Cutler from the picture, as they felt it would weaken my father's position.

And they did.

Judge Glasser granted the motion, and the defendants had to go shopping for new counsel. This further weakened Gravano, who lost the Shargel firm representing him. The government knew that would happen because of their cooperating witness, Pete Savino, who advised them.

Savino had been partners with Gravano when they were both associates in the Colombo family. They got out of that family, with its infighting, and moved to greener pastures. Gravano wound up as a Gambino member, and Savino ended up with the Genovese family. (My father used to refer to the Colombos as the "Cambodians," with all of their internal violence, of which you will hear more about later.)

Savino advised the Feds, which can be found in his statements, that there were two steps they had to take to get Gravano to turn. Take away Shargel, and move him away from Gotti in the MCC. Savino noted that Gravano couldn't do time, never did it. "Move him and he'll flip," advised Savino.

One of the major pieces of evidence that helped the government ditch the attorneys, and perhaps the final straw that got Gravano to flip, were the recordings they had obtained from the Ravenite and the apartment above the club. As we mentioned before, their black bag types had installed listening devices in the Cirelli apartment above the club, as they were aware that the more sensitive conversations took place there.

We believed it was a mob informant who was an additional source to the FBI regarding the use of the Cirelli apartment.

The bugs installed there by the government brought a treasure trove of recorded evidence for the trial. Some of that treasure included negative comments about Gravano. My father was heard speaking to Frankie LoCascio regarding complaints from the skippers, about Sammy. It appeared that Gravano was exploiting his relationship with my father to monopolize the various construction businesses that our family controlled.

The tapes had been unsealed, and, according to the "rule of entirety," they were fully played in the courtroom during pretrial hearings. The whole tapes, not just selected passages. Gravano, of course, heard my father's criticism of him.

Contrary to journalistic reports that this was one of the factors in Gravano flipping, it was not. Totally untrue. My father and Gravano lived in the same unit at MCC, these tapes were played at their co-defendant meetings and in court, and Gravano never said anything.

But hearing the tapes did help to make him turn towards the government side, because he was dead on these tapes—there was unequivocal evidence on the tapes of his discussing his criminal activity.

But the main reason he became a cooperator was he had never done time.

Joe Doherty (a member of the Irish Republican Army), who had been locked up with my father and Gravano, said to my father that "This guy can't do time, all he does is complain and whine."

My father had taken a strong liking to Doherty while they were in the MCC, and, in fact, had sent me to buy suits for Doherty, so he could appear well dressed in court. Thus, Doherty's approach to my father was not a breach of etiquette, but a communication between men who had become friends behind bars. Sure enough, shortly after, Gravano was moved, and then he became a cooperator.

Gravano had become friendly with my father through Frankie DeCicco, who was close to both men. It was to prove a mistake. When DeCicco became underboss, Gravano was part of his crew. Actually, there were two crews, and upon Frankie being elevated to underboss, Gravano headed up one, and George DeCicco, Frankie's Uncle, headed up the other one.

After DeCicco was killed in the car bombing, Gravano became underboss out of respect to DeCicco and his men, who were Gotti loyalists. Gravano was eyes and ears in Brooklyn,

Frank LoCascio was same for the Bronx, Neil Dellacroce's crew was same for Manhattan, and my father was same for Queens. As my father had control over Dellacroce's crew throughout the years, basically my father's voice *was* that of Dellacroce.

★

My father always preached a unity among co-defendants. A unified front, because, as a student of strategy and military history, he was very aware of the doctrine of divide and conquer. Once, when well known attorney Barry Slotnick was representing a co-defendant on trial, and a statement had been made by another defendant, Slotnick asked the witness, "You didn't hear *my* client say that did you?"

When Slotnick sat down, my father schooled him rather severely, instructing him that such kind of questioning was strictly verboten. You maintained a unified front. "We all walk together or we all fall together," was my father's motto. He also suggested to Slotnick, "Next time you do that go to the window and count the floors to the ground, 'cause you won't get the chance when I throw you out of it."

Gravano. He had never done jail time. My father had been advised, and believed, that you surround yourself with tested men—men who had successfully done time and withstood it. His mistake was bringing Gravano in the fold, and he paid dearly for it.

He had admitted this to me and my uncle when we came to visit. While they were in close proximity to each other, my father kept Gravano strong. Once the government moved him, my father predicted that Gravano would shortly flip.

★

After Cutler was bounced, he was still paid as an advisor. He helped select his successor. I knew we needed a tough RICO experienced attorney. F. Lee Bailey's name came up, but was rejected. I had met with him, and was concerned that his own legal problems, and close relationship with the bottle, would be serious distractions if he were to represent my father. We eventually found Joe Bonanno's attorney, Al Krieger, from Florida. Excellent attorney—in *Florida*.

New York isn't Florida however, and I wasn't sure if Krieger was fully armed for that particular war zone. I had advised my father that if possible, we needed a New York experienced RICO defense attorney. If we couldn't find a native guy, we should look to Chicago, Boston or Philadelphia.

The state of Florida was not mentioned. Krieger would not have been my choice, with all due respect to him. Krieger looked like Cutler's older brother. Bullet shaped shaved head, and a similar aggressive gait. But Krieger himself was surprised at the New York venue's act. We'd meet and strategize at Harry's Bar in the Helmsley Palace. "I've never seen anything like this in all my years of practicing," he'd tell me. "Motions I should win, I lose, my cross-examination interfered with by the judge. My witnesses bounced."

Frank LoCascio hired Tony Cardinale, an experienced Boston mob attorney. There was nothing but high priced talent. On Al Krieger alone, my father went for a million dollars. (Krieger would bill everything—his food, his toothpaste, anything he purchased while staying in New York on this case.)

My father also footed the bills for private detectives, transcripts, and experts. John McNally, was the head private investigator, accompanied by Stan Kochman, and Vick Juliano. For a tape expert, he hired Ernest Ashkenazy one of the best. My father easily spent over two million dollars in the defense of this case.

★

I had found out when Gravano flipped, on a visit to my father. I showed up for a regularly scheduled visit, and saw a look on my father's face. "What's up?" I asked.

He looked at me and said, "They took that punk out of here last night."

"Who?"

"Gravano."

The guards had walked Gravano out of his cell. Gravano, the witness for the prosecution.

One of the guards came to my father and told him, "Hey Chief, they just walked your friend out of here."

"Who?" my father asked.

"Gravano," the guard said.

"When?"

"Ten minutes ago—2:00 AM," the guard told him.

Sammy the Bull was becoming Sammy the Rat. They grabbed him, escorted him to a meeting area with the Feds, and then drove him to Quantico, Virginia, where he was housed. The location is also known for being FBI headquarters.

Neither my father nor myself were surprised. I never liked nor trusted Gravano. I had made reference to the fact many times with my Uncle Peter. I never understood how my father could be close to an untested guy like this, when it had been a maxim of my father's to surround himself with battle tested men.

My Uncle Peter told me, "Sammy's one of us, don't ever let anyone hear you fucking say that again."

★

During the jury selection for the trial, there were fliers being left on cars outside the courthouse, depicting Gravano as a liar and a rat. I was aware of this. It hadn't come from us, some kids from the Bronx were responsible. Frankie LoCascio was from the Bronx. He had loyal supporters there.

But that wasn't the only propaganda campaign being conducted for this case.

The media, which had lately depicted my father somewhat favorably as a fashionable Robin Hood character, were taken to task by the Feds, and basically told to change that tune or their sources in law enforcement were going to become very dry. No law enforcement sources, no articles. No headlines. Circulation goes down.

Suddenly the press attitude to my father changed. It turned negative.

In any event, a jury was selected, and AUSA Andrew J. Maloney gives his opening statement. He tells them that their star witness, Gravano, committed nineteen murders. I knew that wasn't the case.

There were two he had forgotten, as well as other crimes, as we learned from interviewing members of Gravano's crew. We could have used this information at trial, but my father said no. He felt like it would be a rat move, and wanted to protect Gravano's crew members.

Also during the trial, there were several bomb threats to the courthouse. I believe they might have been orchestrated by the government, just to poison the jurors' minds against us. The government would use any method available to demonize my father. They did not want to lose again. (On the other hand, so as not to appear to be a conspiracy theorist, it is possible that the bomb threats were called in by a lone nut case watching the daily press reports about the trial.)

Just maybe they handpicked the judge in this case to make sure.

Judge Leo Glasser was another prosecutor in a black robe on my father's case. He precluded five defense witnesses from testifying, he bounced jurors who might have been favorable to the defense, and he allowed AUSA Maloney to make an outrageous statement in his summation that any other jurist would have found to be more than adequate grounds for a mistrial.

Here was Maloney's statement:

...this is the leadership of the Gambino Crime Family. If you accept the proof of what you are dealing with here, the boss of a murderous and treacherous crime family and his underboss, you would be less than human if you didn't feel some personal concern.

Dirty pool. Greasy kid stuff from this drunken bum of an attorney. Of course the defense jumped up and wanted a mistrial declared. If my father's name would have been Gottlieb, or O'Grady, it would have been granted.

But, as I said, I believe from the bottom of my heart that Glasser was handpicked by the government as the trial judge to get my father, and he denied the mistrial motion. Incredible, but true. You people reading this, please believe me, I make no excuses for what my father was, for what I *once* was, but if you are laboring under the delusion that the government and its law enforcement agencies are composed of White Hats with high ethics and scruples and morals— forget it. Not so.

Without tainting the Bureau itself, some rogue federal agents have condoned murders. (More on that later.) Some New York City cops have performed murders. (More on that later.) It is a very dirty world when you lift up the slate and look at what's underneath the rock; and when you pick it up, sometimes some of the bugs slithering around in the dirt have badges, and are called "law enforcement."

When my father had defeated the government several times in court, what started as a law enforcement project, became, in Washington D.C., a public relations disaster, especially when *Time* magazine had my father on the cover.

When something like that happens, a win at all cost mentality takes hold of those in politics who then send pressure downwards to law enforcement on the local level to get a conviction at any cost—including the total violation of the constitutional rights of the targeted defendant.

With respect to this issue, it later turned out "like father like son," and we will visit that in a forthcoming chapter.

With all of the machinations behind the scenes by the government, it was no surprise that my father was found guilty on April 2, 1992.

★

June 23, 1992, my father was sentenced. I was not in the courtroom, pursuant to my father's mandate, but I was outside with the rally of "Free John Gotti" supporters.

When the life sentence was handed down, Gotti supporters outside went loud but not initially wild. They were egged on by others. Cars were overturned, and a few cops made it to the hospital. I was blamed for the near riot.

Not true. We had coordinated what was to be a peaceful rally with the attorneys. We informed law enforcement authorities that people would be there. It was to be a peaceful protest, with people wearing T-shirts, and carrying signs that said "Free John Gotti." Fellows were there with their wives and kids, showing support.

We had arranged buses, bagels, banners, coffee, and strict instructions to our supporters to keep the peace. But there were people out there at our protest that began physically assaulting the protesters.

Although we had some rowdies in our camp that I'm sure exacerbated the situation, there is a possibility that some of the hitters were plain clothes cops. We had our private detectives dig up all of the photographs taken at the protest of the attackers, and we demanded to know who these individuals were.

No. They wouldn't give us the time of day; which kind of worked in our favor because any of the protesters who were arrested that day were acquitted—at trial. I was not arrested, but my cousin Joseph and others were arrested, and they walked—because they should have walked.

At the time of the trial, and now, I believe that we spent top dollar on a sub-par defense.

With all due respect to Al Krieger, who is an excellent attorney, in New York on this case, he seemed out of his depth. In his defense, the way he was treated by the judge could not but interfere with his effectiveness.

Glasser treated the defense attorneys like second class citizens, often forcing them to shut up and sit down—or risk contempt. Bill Kunstler and Ron Kuby had come at the sentencing to put in their "friends of the court" statements, but Glasser tossed them out of the room.

Frank LoCascio, who was also found guilty along with my father, read a statement into the record, denying his guilt with respect to the charges against him. He did say, however,

> I am guilty though. I am guilty of being a good friend to John Gotti, and if there were more men like John Gotti on this earth, we would have a better country. And you, Your Honor, know that I am not guilty of these charges; in your heart you know I'm not guilty. There was no evidence to convict me of these charges.

The judge only tangentially replied to this, remarking that the sentence being handed down was not within his discretion.

★

Kuby visited my father in the bullpen, immediately after his removal from the courtroom. He was combing his hair with the aid of a plastic mirror.

"How are you feeling?" Kuby asked.

"I feel great," said my father. "Five life bids, no problem, but the fifty dollar fine, that judge really knows how to hurt a guy." He flashed his million dollar smile at Kuby and shook his hand heartily.

After receiving his life sentence, my father was brought

back to the hole at MCC. At two o'clock in the morning, in a convoy of armored vehicles, my father was brought to Teterboro Airport.

In the pitch black night, suddenly there was a flashing of headlights. A plane was coming in for a landing. A small Lear Jet. Six marshals come out with shotguns and flak jackets. My father was shackled and belly chained.

The plane landed in Williamson County Airport in Marion, Illinois. Four armored vehicles were waiting for my father. The costumed participants, on behalf of the government—flak jackets, camouflage. What nonsense, what theater.

This armored convoy drove eight miles to the prison, where they delivered my father to the warden.

★

At the time of my father's arrest and trial, his incarceration was not the only tragedy I faced. There was the matter of my best friend Bobby Boriello.

CHAPTER TWELVE

Farewell to a Friend

In some mob movies, in fact in many of them, there is a scene when somebody in the Life is killed. Often in these movies, that scene is filmed in slow motion, with "appropriate" background music, making the murder a dramatic, stylized event. Almost an artistic performance.

No. In reality, it is usually a matter of a few very ugly seconds when someone is brought over the bridge from life to death. There is no musical accompaniment, there is no slow motion. There is only murder and the death of a target.

And the agony and anguish of those left behind who might have loved the deceased. Wives, children, siblings, and friends.

★

I had become friendly with Bartholomew "Bobby" Boriello from our mutual attendance at the Bergin. I met him through my father and uncles. Bobby was an associate of the Gambino Family. He was originally a member of my Uncle Pete's crew, (after my Uncle Gene went away), and eventually, after I became made, Bobby became a member of my crew. More like an advisor and older brother.

He had previously been involved with the Gallo gang, as

a driver for Larry Gallo. After Joe Gallo was killed, Bobby left the inner turmoil of the Colombos and became involved with the Gambino family. He got made in the '80s.

My father first met Boriello when my father went away on the McBratney killing. They were both in the courtroom at the same time, my father for McBratney, and Boriello for something unrelated. Might have been an armed robbery case, I am not sure.

When Bobby saw my father walk in, dressed to the nines, in the company of then famous and powerful Roy Cohn, his attorney, (he told me later) he thought, "Here are the big guns." He also told me, "at that moment I just fell in love with your father."

Boriello walked over to my father, to introduce himself and shake his hand, and my father said to him, "What are you here for kid?"

Bobby told him he was taking a plea and headed for Attica. My father told him he had friends up there, and to make sure to mention his name. He did, and it helped his time there.

Bobby was a big, handsome guy. Six foot two. Imposing. Tough as nails, but with a jovial personality—always joking, always busting balls. Always first to pick up a dinner check. The more I saw him at the Bergin, the more I grew to like him, even though we were twenty years apart in age.

Boriello was my father's driver and more or less bodyguard, but when Bobby wasn't driving my father, he'd pop by the Bergin, and he'd often invite me out to dinner. So from our repeatedly hanging out together, we became very close. He was the gatekeeper at the apartment on the day I got made.

He became my closest friend, and was the best man at my wedding. Bobby and his wife Sue, had asked myself and my wife Kim, to baptize his newborn son, Bobby.

★

Bobby would go out of his way for a joke. When he was my father's driver, he would pick him up at the Bergin, after having the car cleaned and gassed up. My father went through his daily ritual of haircut, dress up, and wait for Bobby to pick him up.

But on one day, the usual Lincoln didn't show up.

"Where the fuck is Bobby?" my father asked.

We are all looking at each other, because we didn't know.

All of a sudden, Boriello comes pulling up on a motorcycle, wearing on his head, a helmet with a spike on it, and a roach clip in his ear.

"C'mon Chief, you ready?" asked Bobby.

My father gave him an incredulous look, and Bobby cracked up hysterically. My father might have had a few unkind words to say at that moment, but I doubt that he meant them. He was doing his level best not to crack up himself.

He had the guy who followed him in the Lincoln drive off with the motorcycle, and Bobby took my father to the city.

★

Boriello was very protective of my father. If my father was at a function, and went to go to the john, Bobby would follow him. He was a solid, loyal guy, right to the end. On the other hand, between his bad gambling habits, and his generosity, Bobby could cause himself money problems. Never complained though.

A real sport, a real street guy. But not everybody loved him. Some people killed him.

★

It was a Saturday afternoon, about a week shy of the first anniversary of my wedding. We were hanging out at the Bergin, eating. It was a tradition that, on Saturdays, we would have lunch at the Bergin. Maybe fifty guys would show up. My father was in jail by this time, and we wanted to hold on to our traditions. Out of respect for him, out of respect for what we were.

Some of the guys who visited my father in jail would speak of how strong he was, how immaculate he kept himself, even in prison. We would, at times, relay his thoughts and desires to the men, which would be the topic of some of our "walk talks." Even though he was away, the spirit of my father was still with all of us.

Many would just come around to the club to hear how the Chief was doing, if he needed anything. They also came to be seen, for they knew my father would inquire who was showing up, and in the event of him getting free again, they did not want to have been found wanting.

This time around it was lasagna and veal cutlets for our meal. For the sauce, Jackie Cavallo, a long time friend of the Gottis, was in the back of the club making his special sauce. Jackie was an excellent cook, and we all loved his sauce.

In fact, that day, Bobby Boriello asked Jackie for an extra jar of sauce to take home with him.

Bobby was hanging with me, cracking jokes as usual. As I said before, he was one of the funniest guys I ever met, and tough. We were trading zingers back and forth, discussing family business, eating and drinking, all of that male bonding stuff.

After eating and hanging out, at about a quarter to seven in the evening, Bobby said his goodbyes to us and headed home.

"If you need me I'll be home," he told me. "Sue's making me pasta tonight, I got Jackie's sauce, who's better than me?"

"I'll catch up with you tomorrow," I said.

"Yeah, tomorrow. I'll meet you here tomorrow afternoon, give you a ride to the cemetery to see your brother, and then we'll get something to eat."

Those were the last words I heard him say and it was the last time I was to see him alive. April 13, 1991. There wasn't going to be any tomorrow for Bobby.

After Bobby left the club, I went down the block on 101st Avenue, to J. V. Carter & Company, a local jewelry store, to get something for my wife for our first anniversary coming up in a week. I window shopped for about forty five minutes or so.

At the same time, the phone in my father's office rang, and one of the guys who answered it, came after me down the block.

"John," he said, "You have to come back to the club now. Sue [Bobby's wife] is on the phone, hysterical. Crying."

I raced back to the club. I picked up the phone, and heard to my horror, "They shot him, they shot him."

"Who? Who shot who, Sue?" I asked.

"Bobby. He's lying outside. They shot him. He's shot."

We raced in the car to Bobby's home in the Bath Beach section of Brooklyn. The block was roped off. Cops everywhere, EMS, and Bobby's bullet ridden body lying in a pool of blood in his driveway. I ran to speak to his wife, to calm her down if I could, and find out what the fuck had just happened.

They had shot Bobby in front of his two year old son's eyes. The kid heard his father's car pull up, and excited to see his father, he ran to the window, from which, at his age, he could barely see over the sill.

But he saw enough. Seven bullets pumped into his father by persons (at the time) unknown. His father slumped down on the driveway. Sue, his mother, had been in the kitchen when it happened. She didn't see it.

"I heard him yell at somebody," she told me. "'What the fuck are you doing here? Get the fuck—'"

Then she heard the shots. She ran to the door and saw cars speeding away from the scene, and her husband dead. She thought she saw two or three shooters.

Turns out, Bobby had time to throw the jar of Jackie's sauce at his attackers.

I spent hours that night with Susan, trying to calm her, and, if any way possible, comfort her. Michael DiLeonardo came by, as he lived close by. Jackie D'Amico was also there. We finally left her in the care of her father, and went to pick up Bobby's ten year old son, to tell him the news.

I remember when I got word that my brother was dead, when my father walked me down the street. I was sixteen. What the Hell was it going to be like to tell a ten year old kid that his father just died?

I took the kid for a walk. I told him something happened to his father, and he didn't make it. It took a while for it to sink in to the kid, and then the kid sunk. He cried. I cried. I took him home to his mother.

Of course, we didn't want to bring the kid home with his father still lying in the driveway, and when we approached the house, we saw that that was the case, so we drove around a bit, killing time, until the body had been removed.

I was with the family the next few days. I made the arrangements for the wake and burial along with DiLeonardo and D'Amico. I was with the body of my friend, in the back room of the funeral home, where they plugged the holes that had been shot into Bobby. I was there to make sure that he was buried with the right suit, the right tie, his watch and jewelry, that his hair was done right, all of that.

Racuglia's Funeral Home in Brooklyn. Lines were down the block. Except for those that were at the time incarcerated, almost all of the Gambino family members were in attendance. Limos in lines, huge flower arrangements. Bobby was acting captain in my crew, and they gave him a funeral worthy of a capo.

I will miss him as long as I live.

★

We knew what, we knew when, we knew where. Now it was time to find out why and who did it. Bobby had had a rival in his area of operation in Brooklyn. A competitor. They didn't exactly love each other. Preston Geritano, a Genovese associate, although at one time the two men were close.

Bobby had once told me that if he ever got whacked, it would be Geritano who did it. He was a hot head. So we investigated. Boriello had experienced problems with Geritano several months before Bobby was hit.

If it were Geritano who did it, there would be justice extracted. I set up a meeting with accused Genovese man Liborio "Barney" Bellomo. Through intermediaries, and to avoid possible government surveillance, we arranged to meet at Rockaway Beach, in Queens, at three o'clock in the morning. The Genovese, after their own investigation said that Geritano had nothing to do with it. Geritano got the word out that he had nothing to do with it. He fled.

As it turned out, he was telling the truth. Geritano would later meet his death at the hands of his brother-in-law, thirteen years after Bobby died.

So who was responsible and why?

Around 1992, a Lucchese family member rolls into MCC, and is smitten with my father. He gossiped. This was the beginning of our suspicion that Bobby's murder might have had Lucchese fingerprints on it. Just like the DeCicco and Eddie Lino hits.

So that was who. What was the why?

Couple of different possibilities.

Rumor had it they thought Boriello had participated in the Castellano hit. I never heard this to be true. The real and Machiavellian reason that the Lucchese clan had Bobby hit was because Bobby was close to my father and me. That was it. The press, at the time, was touting me as the next leader of the family, so it made sense to hit someone who was a close associate and friend of mine. It could weaken us, and possibly open the door to a Lucchese takeover.

But who was it in the Lucchese family that orchestrated these hits? After investigation, all signs seemed to point to Lucchese psychopath and serial killer, Anthony "Gaspipe" Casso. He had two crooked NYPD detectives in his pocket,

Louis Eppolito and Stephen Caracappa. They had helped to set up the Boriello hit. Eppolito had gone to his house, gun in hand, knocked on the door "in his official capacity," and confirmed that Bobby was indeed living there.

Here's a part of the indictment against these two detectives who were stone cold killers:

RACKETEERING ACT FOURTEEN

(Murder Conspiracy/Murder/Depraved Indifference Murder)

60. The defendants STEPHEN CARACAPPA and LOUIS EPPOLITO, together with others, committed the following acts, any one of which alone constitutes racketeering act fourteen:

A. Murder Conspiracy

61. On or about and between January 1, 1990 and May 1, 1991, both dates being approximate and inclusive, within the Eastern District of New York and elsewhere, the defendants STEPHEN CARACAPPA and LOUIS EPPOLITO, together with others, knowingly and intentionally conspired to cause the death of Bartolomeo "Bobby" Boriello, in violation of New York Penal Law Sections 125.25(1) and 105.15.

B. Murder

62. On or about and between January 1, 1990 and May 13, 1991, both dates being approximate and inclusive, within the Eastern District of New York and elsewhere, the defendants STEPHEN CARACAPPA and LOUIS EPPOLITO, together with others, with intent to cause the death of Bartolomeo "Bobby" Boriello, caused his death, in violation of New York Penal Law Sections 125.25(1) and 20.00.

C. Depraved Indifference Murder

63. On or about and between January I, 1990 and May

1, 1991, both dates being approximate and inclusive, within the Eastern District of New York and elsewhere, the defendants STEPHEN CARACAPPA and LOUIS EPPOLITO, together with others, under circumstances evincing a depraved indifference to human life, recklessly engaged in conduct which created a grave risk of death to Bartolomeo "Bobby" Boriello, and thereby caused his death, in violation of New York Penal Law Sections 125.25(2 and 20.00).

The hit had been well orchestrated. Cars had boxed in the ends of the block he lived on. A car of killers followed him up to his driveway. As big as Bobby was, the seven bullets that hit him brought him down forever. Forty-seven years old. In the prime of life, now in the unforgiving arms of death.

CHAPTER THIRTEEN

Foul Deeds Will Rise

Casso was to have one more piece of business he wished to take care of, and we'll talk about that later.

As an aside, the flipping of Gravano had significant negative financial consequences for the family. Fellows were afraid to collect moneys, "solicit" commissions on construction deals, everybody was afraid of exposure and arrest. This scenario made the maintaining of order within the family more challenging.

★

After my father's incarceration, it was an extremely trying time in the streets. Within several Families, the ambitions of certain members to rise to power, and internal disputes, gave rise to numerous murders of made men.

While my father was at liberty there was stability within the Families. Other than the cowardly murderous acts of Casso, the Families were pretty much at peace.

Once my father commenced his life sentence, the situation changed. The Colombo family had an internal war which claimed over a dozen lives. Casso purged the Lucchese family of those he thought would cause problems. As an example of the instability of this individual, Casso had a man killed that he had *dreamed* had been a rat.

Members of the DeCavalcante family killed their acting boss, John D'Amato; and in the Philadelphia family, a war between John Stanfa and an outfit of young Turks was ongoing. The internal strife in the New England family, which my father, while free, had settled, flared up again.

When my father was free he would make these issues his. He loved the Life, and would have used all his resources to quell these problems, for the preservation of the Life. On the other hand, Gigante, who was free, never lifted a finger to stop the internecine wars. With his power and influence, I believe he could have. Just like nobody at that time would want to defy John Gotti and the powerful Gambino family, so would it have been for Gigante.

At this point, several high ranking members of all Families had flipped, and I guess Chin was more concerned for himself, rather than the Life.

But John Gotti had made the Life first and foremost.

★

As I mentioned before, my father had installed an ad-ministration panel. The two constants on the panel, up until 1993–94, were Jimmy Brown Failla and Joe Arcuri. Several captains assisted them, and also engaged in watching them. Arcuri was a by-the-book guy, put there to counterbalance Jimmy Brown, in case Brown thought his current position was other than temporary, and joint.

But even so, Brown's position could not be solidified, unless certain people would be imprisoned or killed. My father had deeply entrenched loyalists in the family. If a move were made by Jimmy Brown to seize control, these individuals had been instructed to react accordingly.

However, it wouldn't stop some others from trying to make this a possibility.

★

But now, the fallout from Gravano flipping had to be dealt with.

As a result of Gravano's cooperation, my father had sent word out immediately that all the fellows should check the metal of any associate whom they felt was not built right. They should be chased. My father knew that Gravano turning would bring a firestorm.

The men stood by most of their subordinates, but not all.

★

Around this time, a soldier named Tony "Pep" Trentacosta brought in information that a police source of his had said that John Alite (a non-Italian who hung around the perimeter of our family) was a confidential informant.

Alite was an Albanian. He was a non-Italian associate, basically the bottom of the totem pole, and could never be made. Alite was not a denizen of the Bergin, but floated between the Our Friends Social Club in Ozone Park, and JoJo's City Line club (on the border of Queens and Brooklyn), as well as other crews and places in the area. So if Alite was truly a CI, this would be a local matter in the neighborhood, not a Family issue. After seeing all of the surveillance tapes taken of the Bergin, you would see Alite once or twice going around the corner to the club—and we're talking from '84–91.

So we asked "Pep" if he was sure about this information regarding Alite being a CI. He was sure. A few weeks after receiving this information, Alite was sent for. He was put on the carpet, he was fucking up all over the place, using drugs, dealing drugs while flying our flag, and robbing drug dealers. As an example of this, from a 302:

it was reported by government source 3507–98 Michael DiLeonardo says Gotti Jr. asked him to go see Gravano about a situation where a Danny Fama, a drug dealer was going to be robbed by Alite and a rival gang of drug dealers. Gravano told DiLeonardo not to say anything to Gotti Sr.

This would have to have been before November 8, 1991, the date Gravano became a cooperator. Obviously, had Alite been a member of the Bergin crew instead of a floater, this report would have made no sense. He was also involved in the killing of some guy he said tried to kill him, Bruce Gotterup.

Alite was verbally abused by me while my then brother-in-law Carmine Agnello, Johnny Boy Ruggiero, and a guy named Tommy "Sneakers" watched. Alite was chased from the neighborhood. People were instructed to give him the "shoulder," if he came around.

Now, I had said that Pep and his police source were wrong about Alite. He was being chased for the drug dealing and the other shit he was doing. If I had put my stamp on the CI story, Alite would have been killed. Chasing him was sufficient. He had a wife and two little kids, and at the time, that was something that I felt shouldn't happen. His wife was a friend of my wife.

I would later regret having protected him.

★

Being John Gotti's son, and possible heir apparent, made me a target for the Casso faction of the Lucchese family. Jimmy Brown Failla and Danny Marino saw me as a liability. They wouldn't be sorry to see me go.

I was being watched. According to Casso, he assigned a soldier in his crew to do the surveillance, and gather as much information about me as possible.

Casso wanted instability in the family. In an attempt to instigate a war, he had done a hit on a member of his own family who was close to his boss, Vic Amuso, and tried to make it look like the Gambinos were responsible. He also conspired to kill Vic's brother, Bobby. He wanted me out of the way to further destabilize the family. Casso's appointed spy was also friendly with Greg DePalma, an acting skipper in the Bronx, with Lou Bracciole Ricco, who ran gambling. Greg's son Craig was a good friend of mine, and was in my crew. Casso's man would regularly pick Greg's brains about me—did I have a girl, where I would frequent, where he meets me.

Greg took it like the man idolized me. He told me that this guy must have been infatuated with the Gottis. I was suspicious. Suspicion is a good thing to increase one's longevity, especially in the streets.

I later had all of my suspicions confirmed. While I was doing time in Ray Brook, a member of the Lucchese family close to Casso, was housed with me from 1999–2003. It was here I learned more of the relationship between Marino and Casso, and the conspiracy against me.

Another member of the Lucchese crime family confirmed the conspiracy while I was at Ray Brook. We had become very close in jail, as we were housed in the same cell block from June, 2002, to July, 2004. We ate together, played cards, worked out together.

Paranoia is another good quality to keep a street guy on the right side of the dirt. I never followed a routine, never drove home the same route. Sometimes I had a driver, sometimes I didn't. Different cars.

Wait.

There was one consistency in my routine. Three days a week I would go visit my father in the Metropolitan Correctional Center in Manhattan. I brought others with me, and I was under surveillance.

But that big target was still on my back.

In 1993, I caught a couple of breaks that helped keep me alive to tell you about it in this book. In the beginning of '93, Gaspipe Casso was arrested in Mount Olive, New Jersey. Found during the arrest were materials that showed Casso had an interest in me. It was later confirmed by Casso, that there was a conspiracy to kill me.

With Casso imprisoned, it was time for Jimmy Brown Failla and Danny Marino to play. They were joined by Joe Watts.

Watts was Italian only on his mother's side, so could not become a made man. He had survived several administrations through his ability as an earner, and (according to his best friend, turned cooperator, Dom Borghese) killer.

According to Borghese, Watts had killed more than ten individuals. Watts even bragged that my father took him on his first piece of work, when Watts was a young buck in the seventies. When Borghese had flipped (which we will cover in more detail later), Watts was devastated. As usual, however, he survived.

Now, it appeared he had aligned himself with Jimmy Brown and Danny Marino. It was reported that these men may have had Genovese and Lucchese support in principal, but not support as in fire support.

So on their own, Failla, Marino, and Watts plotted to kill me.

There was something "funny" about certain meetings they wanted with me. I later learned that I was to be killed after my father lost his appeal, which he did on October 8, 1993. This I learned when Fat Dom Borghese flipped. It was in his 302's.

Borghese was scheduled to testify against me and so I had access to his 302's.

What are 302's you ask? When FBI agents conduct interrogations, or want to memorialize any information, they take notes. The notes are used to produce a summary, known as a 302 form. These forms are used by agents when they testify, and are discoverable by the defense in a criminal case. The process is terribly flawed, as we will get into later.

But the three took a back step in their plans to kill me.

In 1993, Failla and friends were busted. Failla, who had been the head of the Association of Trade Waste Removers of

Greater New York, extorted players in the industry, dividing up routes, causing New York City to have the most expensive trash collection in the country.

He was charged with murder conspiracy of a grand jury witness testifying against the Gambino family, Tommy Sparrow. Danny Marino and Joe Watts, along with Fat Dom Borghese, Phil Mazzara, and Louis Astuto were likewise charged.

There were certain individuals who had strong concerns about the Gravano loyalists in the family, after Gravano had testified at trial, but had a deal not to testify against said loyalists. Jimmy Brown was always insistent that all good guys would go to jail, and Gravano's crew members who were free, would always have a soft spot for Gravano.

He felt threatened by the Gravano crew members, and believed they should be killed.

So now he put his focus on getting rid of Gravano followers. I wouldn't support it. My Uncle Pete and Jackie D'Amico stood on the sidelines on the issue. So who-was-supporting-who was brought to my attention by George DeCicco, the uncle of Frank DeCicco. He was also an uncle to Frankie Fappiano who was a soldier in Gravano's crew, and one of the guys who Jimmy Brown wanted hurt.

I told Jimmy Brown, unless the order came from my father, it wasn't happening. I met with several powerful captains and enlisted their support. I arranged a meeting with Failla and his followers in a warehouse in Queens.

I arranged transportation and security. Failla and company were picked up in front of Russo's On the Bay, and driven to the warehouse. They each had arrived in separate cars—obviously, they had their suspicions too.

I faced my opposition and asked them to answer one question for me. Depending how they answered, either I would stand down, or they would. (I had, prior to attending the meeting, stationed some of my crew outside the warehouse, armed. One of the crew who went with me in the warehouse was also armed. That was a major breach of our protocol, but I really didn't care about that at the time.

As Jimmy Brown and I stood face to face in the warehouse, I said to him, "I'm gonna ask you a question, and regarding the answer one of us is going to stand down. Did the chief order this?" (Did my father order it?)

"No," was the answer.

"Then I suggest you stand down my friend," I said.

"You're prepared to defend these guys?" Brown responded.

"No, I'm prepared to defend my father."

This created more bad blood.

★

I believe that one of the attempts to do away with me almost took place in a Chinese restaurant in Manhattan. Joe Watts wanted to meet with me and convey some information he had which dealt with the Genovese family. He also told me he had information that could help get my father a new appeal.

The meeting was set at Chin Chin, a restaurant on East 49th Street. The instructions were to come in the back door of the restaurant and go into the basement where the meeting would be held.

Johnny Boy Ruggiero drove me to the location, and I immediately noticed that the back of the restaurant was on a tree lined street, basically dark and deserted, as was the alley way leading to the basement door.

It would be a perfect place to dispose of me. The door had steps going down to the basement. Nobody would notice it if I was suddenly dispatched there.

I told Johnny Boy to keep going, and drop me off several blocks away. I instructed him that in the event of something unfortunate occurring, he was to let our people know where I was.

One of my security measures was to park a car several

blocks from any meeting I was to have, and then either walk to it, or get on the train and arrive that way, so as to minimize the chance of my being surveilled, or worse.

Contrary to my "instructions," I walked into the restaurant via the front door. A guy, who was Joe Watts' driver, did a double take when he saw me walk in. I gave him a look that wasn't very friendly.

I passed by a waiter and told him I was headed downstairs. He must have thought I was crazy, but I passed by him, and went into the basement. Watts was waiting. Danny Marino was also supposed to be there, but wasn't. I didn't like that. I told him to come upstairs and have some dinner. He didn't want to, and I didn't care.

We went upstairs. It was obvious that Watts was ruffled by the change in his expected scenario. It crossed my mind that the basement meeting could have been my last. Watts made conversation and questioned me about things that made no sense under the circumstances.

He asked me how I got to the restaurant. I told him someone drove me.

He asked who, and I said what does it matter?

He said invite the driver in, I said no.

He must have perceived that I felt something was going on. We spent about three quarters of an hour eating then I left.

I had tipped the waiter by the door fifty bucks, and told him to get me a cab. I had the cab take me a few blocks away from where Ruggiero was waiting in the car for me.

CHAPTER FOURTEEN

Don't Worry Dad

As part of my duties it was required that I, along with other captains, meet with the rank and file, to insure that we were all on the same page.

My father was now imprisoned for life, and I was busy coordinating efforts regarding his appeal. I met with top flight lawyers around the country, and with his New York attorney on a regular basis. I also visited my father in Marion every six weeks.

But I had other responsibilities as well. The primary threat was dealing with Gravano and planning how to neutralize his expected testimony.

When Gravano flipped, people began to panic.

The flow of money stopped. Several of us had numerous meetings with the rank and file to find out what Sammy knew. His former crew members were of tremendous help. They cooperated with our lawyers and investigators to help stem the tide of whatever ocean of destruction Gravano's testimony might cause.

Monies were collected to establish a war room and a huge data base to help combat Gravano's treachery. Jimmy Brown Failla, Joe Watts, and Danny Marino were already arrested, and were spearheading this effort.

"We ain't taking no pleas," they said. "We're going to trial."

In a room in the suite of attorney Jimmy LaRossa, shop was set up. Gravano crew members filed in one after the other to give information we needed, with my assurance that they would be protected. Information that Gravano was not going to testify to in court, to protect his own interests. Vallario, a close confidant of Sammy Gravano, participated too, realizing that it was his duty. "I feel like a rat," he said, "but I got to do this."

Vallario had been removed as head of Gravano's crew, but he was of tremendous help, leading his former crew members into the war room one at a time. At the end, after Gravano turned traitor, Vallario had no great deal of affection for him. Another Gravano crew member who hated Sammy was Eddie Garafola.

At this point, regarding the Sammy Gravano crew affair, as well as other issues, there was a tremendous amount of friction between me, Failla, and others. But what there wasn't was any intention of going to trial anymore, after a fantastic plea offer was made.

Six years imprisonment for *murder*. They grabbed this deal. But not Joe Watts. He said he will fight. At the time, I thought that at least all of the effort and expense of the war room was not wasted. It would serve Watts.

He, however, at the eleventh hour before the trial, took a six year plea for multiple murders. It was an amazing offer I didn't blame Watts for taking it. Perhaps it was too amazing.

Whether he did or not, it was believed that Watts had tried to broker a deal for himself, with my father and I as barter. Watts may have been partially responsible for keeping my father in twenty-four hour lockdown. (In a 1994 memo, reportedly originating from Watts, regarding a telephone call from my father to an attorney: Watts was in the room with the attorney, and communicated with my father, in violation of the prison rules.)

Later, an article appeared in the press that he was a CI who had had a falling out with the government. Watts, through my father, had placed his best friend, Fat Dom Borghese, in my crew, even though I didn't want the guy. He became a cooperator with the government, against me.

When it turned out that Watts, who denied being a co-operator, would not testify, the government, after his plea deal, began hitting him with racketeering charges that were not covered by his plea. He put up a good defense, and only received a few more years jail time.

When he was released, he was accepted back to the streets without any problems. Watts had a reputation for being a very capable guy, and as I had said before possessed an enormous amount of wealth. (In 2009, he was indicted for a 1989 murder; and after conviction, received a thirteen-year sentence.)

Looking back, is it possible that Watts was not a cooperator? Yes. I learned a hard lesson about this. He may have thought he was smarter than the government, and played a dangerous game. However, I had a hard time forgiving and forgetting, and when we speak of events in 2005, this will become clear.

★

I mentioned that my visitor meetings were monitored after 2003, and here I will provide some of the actual conversations which were recorded. JAG is myself, John A. Gotti, SK is a friend of mine, Steven Kaplan, and JR was (he is deceased) one of my closest friends, John Ruggiero.

When you see U/I, that means unintelligible, in other words the transcriber couldn't understand what was being said.

The conversations related to events in the nineties.

Regarding Joe Watts

JAG: And that's the way it's supposed to be. And that's the way it's supposed...you got a loyal friend, you got brothers, you got my brother, you got people that are loyal to you. (U/I) There's no loyalty here, John. It's all just a figment of your imagination. That's all dead. That camaraderie between Bobby Boriello and me, that was real. We loved each other. The love we had in our club was an exception.

We had the world here. Believe me, John, we genuinely grew up loving each other. Other than me being abusive and getting mad, but at the end of the day you got to hurt me twice before I hurt you. You understand me. You got to hurt me before . . . (U/I) That's the way it was with us. And you got to hurt Bobby before you hurt me. We had that camaraderie in our club. Nobody else has that.

This is all an angle. I've seen people (U/I) getting ready to go to war. I can't believe this. Brothers shooting brothers. We were so fortunate we didn't need this. This should have never happened. I wish when I was twenty three years old my Uncle Gene would have just left me alone. I really wish now, looking back, he just left me alone.

We had a good crew of guys around us, we minded our own business, didn't want nothing. (U/I) it's fake, there's nothing real about it anymore, any honor any dignity died with my father. My father, my father on the street, made you want to be a part of this because he was that kind of guy. You had to be a part of this. You wanted to feel as close as possible to him. The only way, was by being that. You, you wanted to be it. When he left, John, the picture changed.

I survived more conspiracies and more angles, I'm gonna show you 302 material, I'll mail it to your house. You're gonna read about shit and you're gonna say how'd this happen when did this happen—treachery.

SK: Why would Joe Watts want to (U/I).

JAG: He was making up a story cause he knew he couldn't get me. He knew I already had the push on him and (whispering) if you remember, when he came to me and said we asked around for money on his defense to attack Gravano and nobody's helping us. I says, Joe, you guys are millionaires. You want people who don't have, to help. I would appreciate some help, (Joe Watts). Me, Tommy Gambino, Big Lou, we all put up $8,000 a piece and gave it to him to put together, so did other skippers—a main base a war room, to attack Gravano. He took the money and did whatever he did with it.

There wasn't any war room. And he went around telling Dom Borghese that I'm shaking down the skippers. "John's got the capos afraid, he's shaking them down. Did he ask you about any business that I'm doing?" Borghese said, "No, he never asked me anything about your business, nor my business either for that matter. He doesn't ask, You're sure? Positive? Well, he's got some guys nervous here, you know, and ah, we're just waiting for our time and we are gonna take him out."

★

I had settled down into married life, and was living in Massapequa, on the south shore of Long Island, in Nassau County. By 1993, my wife and I had three children. Two boys and a girl. So along with my responsibilities to the Life, I had significant duties with respect to my own family; trying to be the best father I could be.

The FBI and Organized Crime Task Force obviously were concerned with where I came and went, because every day when I left the Massapequa house, there were two cars of agents following me.

I knew that I was a target for several investigations. Back in the late '80s my company, Samson Trucking, was investigated. For many years later I was regularly hit with subpoenas. In fact, between 1985–1998, I was an annual target for the grand jury.

In case anybody reading this is not familiar with the function of a grand jury, I will briefly explain. Sixteen to twenty three citizens are summoned to hear evidence presented by a prosecutor. It is for the purpose of seeing whether or not there is sufficient evidence to charge someone with a crime—not convict them. A defendant may testify (usually not wise), but his lawyer cannot actively participate in the proceedings, he can't object, he can't directly address the grand jurors, he can't cross-examine witnesses, like he would at a trial.

Think of it this way: the grand jury is the initial process in prosecution, not a final determination.

★

In Queens, their cops would pick me up. I'd leave from my mother's house in Howard Beach, I was followed. They followed me everywhere, and one reporter at the time, John Miller, who had conducted a surveillance on me for a long time, said in the press that I was trying to shake my tails.

Actually, the Miller incident that gave rise to that wrong conclusion was my driving around, trying to find a place for my first born son to go to the bathroom.

Miller was on my tail for a whole week. After the incident above, the following day, I was walking my son on his tricycle. This had a handle on it so I could keep him from straying, and I held this in my right hand. In my left hand was a Partagas 150, which I was enjoying smoking.

All of a sudden, speeding around the corner of the block, came a black Jeep Cherokee with smoked-out windows, and a black Ford LTD, also with smoked-out windows. As they raced towards me, my first thought was this was a hit.

Using all the strength in my right arm, I flung my son into the nearby bushes, with the tricycle, and walked towards the two vehicles so they wouldn't miss. Out jumped John Miller, and his news crew, with cameras rolling.

He asked me about my cigar, and I started to scream at him for scaring my son. "Are you out of your fucking mind?" I yelled at him.

"What did you think we were; assassins?"

I ignored his question, grabbed my son, walked towards my home, and handed my son off to my wife over the fence.

The next morning, John Miller came by the Bergin Hunt and Fish Club, and apologized.

"You scared my son," I said.

"He seemed more concerned about his bike," said Miller.

Like John Miller, law enforcement tails would be downright inconsiderate, rude, and threatening. In 1997, when I had my kids in the car, taking them to school, I got boxed in by the OCTF, who were there to serve me with a subpoena.

My kids were crying, terrified. "Who are they?" they asked. "Friends of Daddy," I said. I told my "friends" I would be right with them. Ignoring the commands of the OCTF, I brought my kids into school, and then came out, and quite frankly told them what I thought about their actions.

The language I used might have been a tad coarse.

★

In May of 1994, my wife had given birth to our fourth child, our son Peter. My joy at this event, as I left the hospital, was turned to surprise, as I was confronted by two detectives from the Brooklyn DA's office, who served me with documents evidencing a wiretap on my office phone, and clandestine transmitters in my office and other places. I was curious why Brooklyn was involved, when the base of my operations had always been Queens.

In 1995, along with this Brooklyn case, there were two federal investigations into my doings.

Bruce Mouw, the head of the C-16 squad of the FBI dedicated to taking down the Gambino family, stated that I had become a top priority target. Throughout the nineties, up until the time of my arrest in '98, surveillance on me was constant.

The surveillance and the subpoenas to certain business

customers of mine caused me to lose income from my legitimate endeavors. Nothing scares a customer away like a Federal Subpoena. This was one of the goals of the government—to bankrupt me.

I formally complained about this government harassment and the financial devastation it was causing me. Of course, that did nothing.

Between the Family business and trying to salvage my businesses, a toll was taken on me. I have a decent amount of strength and resilience, but I am only human, and I fully realized that fact.

★

I was at my Uncle Gene's daughter's wedding. Jeanine. Me and my Uncle Pete were walking around making sure everyone was having a good time. Gene was in jail doing a fifty year sentence. So I'm playing host, when it hits me, and I stop. There were twice as many women in the catering room than men.

Death and jail had consumed many fellows. We were really selfish. Wives with no husbands present, children with no fathers present. They were the innocent sufferers for our guilt. With the increased media attention to mobsters, the children of men in the Life would be teased, ostracized.

What the Hell were we doing? My aunt Rosalie, the mother to the bride was slow dancing with her second daughter, Dina. I saw Dee Scopo, widow of Colombo underboss Joey Scopo, seated alone. Looking alone. Her husband was killed in October 1993, the last casualty of the Colombo wars.

He had been machine gunned in front of his Ozone Park home, with his wife and son present in the house. After the hail of bullets, and the screeching of cars getting away, Scopo's teenage son and his wife ran out to the dying man.

He looked at his son and said, "Take my jewelry off my hands."

The son removed the ring and watch, which were the last mementos of his father's life he was to have.

Then there was my mother, who at this point had spent some sixteen years alone, being married to my father. Now her husband would likely die in jail. So I walked over and asked my mother to dance with me. It made her evening, and distracted me from these dark thoughts.

A short time after the wedding, a crisis arose. John "Jackie the Actor" Giordano, a capo in our family, and nephew to Joe Piney Armone, was on a regular visit to see Louie DiFazio up in Lenox Hill Hospital in Manhattan. DiFazio was an associate in Ralphie Bones' crew—a skipper from Astoria, Queens. Cancer was slowly killing DiFazio.

It was the regularity of the visits that helped gunmen cripple Giordano in April 1995, as he waited in his car—at his usual space, at his usual time. 7:19 PM. He was hit three times. Chest and spinal cord injuries put him in intensive care.

Was this the opening of another war? We grilled Giordano's crew, we made the rounds. All my father's men were told they could now carry firearms. But after an arrest was made in the shooting, it turned out not to be a war, but a personal beef from an associate who hired Latino gunmen to do the job.

Giordano was to remain a paraplegic until his death in 2009.

★

Joe Arcuri was starting to tire. He was being assisted by several other captains. I was engaged in helping my father with his new appeal and trying to keep my businesses afloat.

Arcuri was to stay on, and a fellow by the name of Stephen "Stevie" Grammauta, an old timer who was made capo in 1994, and took over Giordano's crew, and part of the ruling panel in 1995, was to join Arcuri on the panel. He had done time with Joe Piney, and had been a soldier in his crew for 25 years.

But he was somewhat of a mystery man, not too many

people knew all that much about him. He didn't even show up as a soldier on any of the charts of the government. At the time of joining the ruling panel he was nearing eighty. (He was born in 1916.) But still strong and sharp. He rarely went out, and was often home taking care of his sick wife.

Grammauta was believed to have been one of the shooters that killed Albert Anastasia in 1957. Rumor had it, (Grammauta never said it) that he had put two shots in Anastasia's head—in the same hole—and then took the subway home.

I felt a sense of freedom, I could breathe again. I remembered back in 1993, with my father the boss of the family, but caged up in a supermax prison, on his orders a poll was taken of the capos. Did they want him to remain boss?

A selfish part of me wanted a "no" answer. It would have taken much pressure off of me. But it was not to be, they still wanted him to rule. For life. A unanimous vote. He had hand-picked the men underneath him, and knowing the reality of jail for those in the Life, had determined who would replace who in that event.

The loyal men at one time, when my father was dying, had asked to change the name of the Gambino family to the Gotti family, but I felt that my father's grandchildren had suffered enough from the affiliation of that name with crime.

Now, I could catch my breath with Grammauta and other skippers assisting Joe Arcuri. I could now go full speed ahead on the appeal for my father. There were numerous issues existing that would have justified a new trial.

Gravano had denied drug dealing, yet through cooperators and stand up guys both, he was linked to one of the largest drug deals ever. The ship, *The Hunter*, was seized outside of Sheepshead Bay, loaded with heroin. He was also linked to two more murders other than the nineteen he had admitted to on the stand. One was a cop. He had also killed a sixteen year old kid, Alan Kaiser, with a shotgun, mistaking him for a member of a biker gang that had previously roughed up Gravano.

This alone would have merited a new trial. But no. We also provided all of our defense material to Vincent Gigante for his trial in 1997.

While Gigante beat most of the charges, he went away for twelve years on racketeering. In 2003, facing new charges, he took a plea and admitted his long time crazy act was an elaborate ruse to avoid prosecution. In 2005, Gigante died in prison.

I was feeling low at times, and I would visit my father, and that bucked me up. Cutler, my father's attorney, nicknamed my father "Grandpa," and he said when ever he was feeling down, he would visit my father and feel better. Get an energy boost. "I'm gonna see grandpa and get a shot of Poppa Schultz," he would say. Poppa Schultz was a nickname for my father that had been given him by Frankie LoCascio.

When I looked at him through the two inch thick prison glass in the visiting room, and spoke to him by the phone, he could see the fatigue on my face, my tired eyes.

"Relax," he said. "Go enjoy your family, and never mind the rest of this nonsense."

But I could see the concern in his eyes. He would get five day old newspapers, and he believed my arrest was imminent. The war drums were banging.

I told him a story about the time there was banging on my office door.

I was at my office in Sutphin Boulevard, in Jamaica, Queens, when there was a loud banging on the door. With me was my secretary, my partner in the phone card business, and a friend of mine, Steve Dobies, who was to later testify on my behalf several times at my trials.

My partner, Anthony Plomitallo, panicked. He saw that the building was surrounded by agents. They wanted in. The building, which was owned by my then brother-in-law, Carmine, had strong steel doors. The agents were threatening to break down the doors.

It didn't seem likely they were equipped to do so, however. I told Plomitallo, if they have a warrant or subpoena, let them in. They had. A dozen agents poured in to the office. I calmly sat at my desk and perused the warrant.

They were authorized to grab everything. Okay. So I got up, preparing to go out to lunch, instructing Plomitallo and Dobies to comply with the agents' demands; make sure they get what they need. I grabbed a cigar from my desktop humidor, and waved goodbye.

I grabbed my hysterical secretary, and told her, "Let's go grab some lunch." She had been intimidated several nights before, when agents went to her apartment and demanded she cooperate. They had rousted this single parent mom out of bed, but she held firm and wouldn't help them. Delmy, the secretary, was worried that she might have said something that brought the agents to my door. I assured her it was not.

I returned from lunch and looked at a bare office. Everything was taken. Wires were hanging from the walls where they had removed their bugs they had covertly installed. Computers were gone, files were gone, vending machines missing, hundreds of thousands of dollars worth of phone cards taken, but they did leave one phone.

But what ticked me off most? They had grabbed my humidor with the cigars. I had automatically made a grab for my humidor while seated at my now empty office, and my hand came up with air. I guess they didn't like my demeanor when they barged in.

So there I sat at the desk and chair they had left. Surveying the nothing that remained of my office, which had taken me a year to get to the comfort and efficiency level I had enjoyed prior to the invasion. They removed it all in a couple of hours.

While contemplating fate, I heard another loud banging at my door. Now what? Plomitallo goes to the door and asks "Who's there?" He hears FBI. He relays that back to me, but I don't believe it, I think it's my brother-in-law breaking my balls.

They have a warrant they say. I tell Plomitallo to relay this: "I'm not in the mood for him now, and tell him to find a Galliano bottle and shove it up his ass." Now my remaining office phone rang. I picked it up.

It really was an FBI agent. Bob Vendette. I knew him. "We are outside with a search warrant, and I don't want to take the door down. Further, I will not shove a Galliano bottle up my ass!"

I go to the door and let him and about eight other agents in. They come in and they see the place is bare-assed empty. They are amazed.

"What the fuck happened here?" Vendette asked.

"Don't break my balls, you know what happened," I said.

"I have no idea what you are talking about," he said. "I have a warrant. How did you know we were coming?"

"I didn't. Your friends from White Plains and New Rochelle FBI, along with the Secret Service, came and brought their friends from OCTF."

Wish I would have had a camera at the time to take a picture of the expression on his face. He made a confirming phone call. It was true. He left with the agents.

I bid him, "So long Bob, you be well and I'll see you tomorrow on the avenue."

He said goodbye, and from his body language, I could tell he was having a bad day.

★

In the next days that followed, they began to seize vehicles and take out the bugs that had been planted on them. My car had been bugged, so had Plomitallo's. One of the tapes they had made me seem like I was going to shoot someone, but no.

Here's what happened. I'm in my car with my driver. Government unmarked cars cut us off. Blacked out windows. You couldn't see who was driving. They box me in with two cars, to pull us over.

They were there to serve a subpoena. I thought it was an attempted hit, so I tell my driver, who was Plomitallo, "Keep your foot on the gas, if you don't see badges, blast them."

They get out, badges dangling around their necks. I tell Plomitallo to cool it. When I had said blast them, I meant ram them with the car. There was no gun in the car, none was found, and I didn't carry one.

★

It was clear, so by this time, I tell Richard Rehbock, my attorney, to start preparations for a trial.

I remember a visit with my father in Marion Prison in 1997, and the conversation we had.

"Well, what do you think," he said.

"I hope I at least make it to Christmas. I don't want to disappoint all of your grandkids."

"I'm sick for you right now."

"When they come, I'll be ready for them."

"You know John," he said to me, "I blame myself for this, for stealing your youth."

"You can't blame yourself. It's a choice that was made," I said. "They do what they want, it's a part of their agenda. I'm scripted in."

"As your father, I'm sick for you. I made you a grandfather and father and brother to too many people."

"Don't worry dad, everything will be alright."

CHAPTER FIFTEEN

Journey Through Valhalla

January 21, 1998, I was arrested with dozens of others.
Charges included loan sharking, extortion, mortgage fraud, and even a phone card scam.

After the fanfare of my arrest in 1998, after the various law enforcement agencies had their photo ops, I was taken to a nearby armory and printed and photographed again—for all of the law enforcement participants in my bust.

As I made the pic and print rounds, I was asked if I had any statements to make.

I declined.

At one point, I was in a room with my co-defendants, Greg DePalma, and his son Craig. We were waiting to be strip searched. Craig and I were bodybuilders, muscled up and ripped. Nothing to poke fun at. Craig's father, Greg, however, had survived several surgeries for hernia and cancer, and was in his late sixties. Needed a cane, a physical wreck.

"Too much pasta eh fella?" asked one of the agents, referring to Greg.

Now at this particular moment, I chose to make a statement.

"How would you like it if some snot nose asshole made that remark to your father?" I asked the agent. "You treat us all with respect and this can go smoothly, or you don't and we buck."

The agent's superior apologized, and things did go smoothly. After processing at the armory, after the media feeding frenzy as I exited, I was taken on a bus, along with my other co-defendants, and hauled to Valhalla, the county jail in Westchester.

Valhalla is a quaint hamlet in Westchester County, in the township of Mount Pleasant. The jail was neither quaint nor pleasant. Another thing that it is famous for is its Kensico Cemetery. Famous people buried there. Babe Ruth, Tommy Dorsey, Ayn Rand.

The prison had its share of bad publicity. About a year and a half before my arrival, a seventeen year old girl who couldn't make her $7,500 bail hanged herself in her cell with a bed sheet. In the nine months I spent there, several other inmates hanged themselves.

In a properly monitored, properly run, penal institution, that sort of thing shouldn't happen. Since it did, several times at least, that speaks volumes of the administration at Valhalla.

So, there I am, on the fourth floor processing center in Valhalla. Stripped, checked for lice, and given a tan jumpsuit to wear. I was sent to a single man cell, where I would await an opening in the long-stay prison wing. Federal inmates at Valhalla were usually housed on the third floor.

A place opened for me, and holding my bed roll and pillow, I go to the third floor. One man cell. Metal desk, metal bunk, thin mattress, stainless steel toilet and sink combo.

At least it was clean in Valhalla. It was also ice cold. Intentionally so, because when you have a bunch of frozen inmates, you have less trouble. Less violence. It's too damn cold. The blood flow slows, energy levels go down. Prisoners longed for an exercise period, not just for the open space, but for a chance to warm up.

Cell doors are electronically controlled. Unless otherwise directed, inmates can walk around the cell block, talk to other inmates, play cards. I played cards. Didn't talk all that much, because a prison can be infested with two legged rats—just waiting to sell what you might tell.

I also prepared for my upcoming case. Tough to do in Valhalla because, it being a county facility, it doesn't have Federal legal materials in its library. I ordered the materials I needed, and of course, I never received them.

Nevertheless, I spent hours each day in the law library. I had obtained a paralegal certificate, and knew my way around legal research. I also had the procedural assistance of an inmate who was a lawyer on the outside.

Of course, word soon got around that I was hanging out in the law library, and a parade of inmates would come by, telling me their problems, asking for help, or just wanting to meet me. I left the library and worked on the case from my cell.

I needed what privacy I could have to strategize and prepare for my defense. When I wasn't hitting the legal books or visiting with lawyers, I exercised. There was no weight pile at Valhalla so it was pushups and sit ups. Had to keep in shape.

I wrote to my family, as access to phones was difficult, due to the few number of them. There were no per se restrictions on phone use at Valhalla. The feds limit inmate phone time to 300 minutes per month; however, since Valhalla was a county jail, housing federal inmates pursuant to a contract with the government, I had more phone time than I would have had in the BOP prisons. I also received a visit from my Uncle Pete, and relayed to him to convey to the powers that be, that win, lose, or draw I was done with the Life.

★

I am denied bail at my first court appearance, and upon my return to the prison, I am sent to the hole. Six by nine cell, filthy, mice for company. A food tray slid through a slot to feed me. Locked up 24 hours a day.

I was sent there with no explanation as to why.

While there, guards and inmates tried to talk to me. I waved them off. I trusted no one, and that was a lesson I had learned at my father's knee. After several days in the hole, I was returned to my regular cell block.

About two weeks later, I had another court appearance. I walked past the first floor bullpens, and through the glass partition, both female and male prisoners recognized me. Some of the women flashed their breasts at me. Celebrity treatment, I guess.

My second shot at bail, I am in front of Judge Brieant. He seems disposed to granting bail, when, all of a sudden, AUSA Carol Sipperly drops the bail bomb. She informs the judge that I am conspiring to kill a co-defendant in my case, Michael Sergio.

Problem was, I didn't even know him, much less want to kill him. Where did they pull this particular rabbit from the hat? Turns out, an inmate next to me in the hole was looking to cut a deal with the Feds at my expense.

An in camera hearing was held. The judge doesn't believe the story. But me being me, a man in a position of power in the Gambino family, no bail for John. The prosecutor called me the acting boss of the family, a Super Capo.

Of course, several years before, the government said Nick Corozzo, a captain in the family, was the acting boss of the family. They had wiretapped conversations where he was referred to as the boss. But now, I was the boss, according to the government.

Tapes said it was Corozzo. But according to the government, Dominic Fat Dom Borghese, a soldier in the Gambino family, and Alphonse Little Al D'Arco, acting boss of the Lucchese family, said I was acting boss.

Were these guys reliable sources of information? Borghese, an obese, degenerate gambler, had a great sense of humor and I liked him. Like I said before, he was one of the attendees at my wedding, and a regular at the Ravenite.

Borghese got made in 1990, my father presiding at the

ceremony. But he became a cooperator, breaking his oath, as he had done since 1995. He also participated in two hits. According to Borghese, he didn't kill anybody, just helped dispose of the bodies. But, in 1995, he turned, when the Feds told him that someone close to him in the Life who was working with the Feds had implicated him in those homicides.

What about Al D'Arco? A convicted heroin dealer, admitted to killing ten people. He turned cooperator in 1991. He also admitted to participation in a plot (which never saw fruition) to wipe out the entire New Jersey faction of the Lucchese family. (They were planning a literal Last Supper for the fellows.)

He testified at numerous trials and didn't do time for all of his crimes.

I found out later on that both of these guys never actually pinned me as the acting boss of the family. During government debriefings, they referred to me as a capo, and said that the Family was ruled by a panel, which at times changed, not by any one individual.

★

So since bail wasn't happening any time soon, my attorneys answered "Ready for Trial." The judge said he didn't believe it. But we were. The government also answered ready (they weren't), and Judge Brieant set a trial date.

But two weeks later I am back in court, but where is Judge Brieant? Not there, but replaced by Judge Barrington Parker. He wants six co-defendants tried with me if we are to get our speedy trial. Judicial economy and all of that. (Actually, it was for the purpose of having me tainted by the brush of the other co-defendants, making a guilty verdict more likely—common prosecution strategy.)

I get five guys to come on board. I need one more, and I approach Jackie "The Nose" D'Amico. First he said yes, then he said no. Valhalla was his first time in prison. "What am I doing here, I don't belong here," was the noise being made by Jackie. "I don't belong on this indictment, I don't know these people."

"Neither do I pal," I told him. But he's only there three days, and he makes bail. Took a quick plea, and got eighteen months which he served at Fort Dix, New Jersey.

As I couldn't get my six, I didn't get my speedy trial. In the cell across from me, while I awaited trial, who do you think is assigned there? Michael Sergio. The man I was supposed to be looking to hit.

I tell him the government says I am out to get him. News to him also. He offered to write a letter on my behalf, but I respectfully declined the offer. I liked this guy.

But not everybody did. Sergio was in his sixties and cantankerous. Despite having cancer and needing a cane, he wasn't very polite. Made enemies of some of the Latin Kings; he talked to them with disrespect.

Come to think of it, the only guy he did treat with respect was me. The Latin Kings wanted to teach Sergio some manners. The sharks were circling around Sergio, ready to bite. I get word while I am in the shower, and quickly wrap a towel around me, and try to diffuse the situation. I stand between the Latin Kings and Sergio.

I take him back to my cell, after being able to get back there, and put some clothes on. I return to the Latin Kings and things got worked out. But Sergio continued to be cantankerous.

I had to physically break up a fight between him and Denny McClain, a pro baseball player that was doing time at Valhalla. I got them to shake hands and come out *not* fighting. McClain was best known as a ten season pitcher for the Detroit Tigers and one of only eleven men in the 20th century to win 30 or more games in a season.

Sergio was so grateful for my help that he turned government cooperator. The guy I took care of in jail, watched out for. I even made sure he got to watch his favorite show, *Jeopardy*, on the television.

★

Another individual involved in these charges was a popular nineties' DJ named "Goomba Johnny." Supposedly, he was involved with extortion with respect to Scores topless bar. He was also supposedly forced to give free ad time on the air to mobbed up topless bars. He was a friend of Greg DePalma. He was later indicted for tax fraud, and that was what he pled guilty to as part of a deal.

★

Jail food was, well, jail food. I did get used to the filet of fish and macaroni and cheese dinner. I also got regular care packages from the outside; we were allowed fifteen pounds a month from the outside. Italian cold cuts, cheeses, protein bars, supplements. Inmates pooled their packages and did some creative jailhouse cooking.

To get around the fifteen pound per month limit, I would have my office send my packages in the names of various inmates. However, a shipment of protein bars that was to go to a Muslim inmate bodybuilder was mixed up with prosciutto, which was to be shipped to an Italian inmate. The pork to the Muslim set off the alarms, and my packages were to receive extra scrutiny.

In any event, I ate well, I exercised, and adjusted well to prison routine.

★

Third time up at bat for a bail hearing. I am transported shackled, black boxed belly chained. In a van, guarded by marshals. I travel the forty or so minutes to the Federal Courthouse in White Plains.

Once at the courthouse, it's the old bend down, balls up, strip search routine. Put in the bullpen. Before Judge Parker, who looks like he is inclined to grant bail.

But wait. Now the government says it has come up with

other bad things I have done, and they need an adjournment to draft a superseding indictment. They get it, I go back to jail. I was accused of having robbed a drug dealer in 1996.

While in the Life, I wasn't short of money. The government had estimated my net worth at this time between seven and ten million dollars. I was living in an exclusive North Shore Gold Coast Long Island mansion, but I needed to rob a street drug dealer? They said I held a gun to this guy's head, took his money, his drugs, and only spared his life because I saw a picture of his children.

It seems that this particular drug dealer was facing twenty-five years in jail, and fourteen months after his arrest for narcotics trafficking, suddenly remembered I robbed him. Turns out he was selling drugs to a co-defendant on my case, Vincent Zollo. I found that one out later. Zollo stayed loyal by the way.

The dealer I supposedly robbed recognized me from the papers. The robbery took place in Ozone Park, an area of Queens where I am not exactly unknown. But he recognized me from the papers. He also agreed to testify against me so instead of twenty-five years, he cops to a misdemeanor plea from the Queens D.A.

He didn't get to testify, because I was never tried for this nonsense. Now Parker, in October, 1998, was disposed to grant me bail under certain conditions.

The price? Ten million dollars.

Chapter Sixteen

Government Bail Out

On September 15, 1998, Judge Parker approved of bail for me.

One of the reasons why the court had a change of mind was our use of the words of mob expert Joe Coffey.

Coffey was interviewed by Fox News reporter Penny Crone on March 12, 1997. She said of him as follows:

When it comes to organized crime, and the Gotti family, Joseph Coffey is the man who knows. If you're wondering if Junior is now acting boss of the Gambino Crime Family, Coffey says well you can forget about that...

Coffey offers his expertise with:

He's not even made. The kid is one quarter Jewish, you have to be 100% Italian to be made. He is not even considered to be a made solider in the Gambino family, much less the boss.

While his expert opinion was beneficial to me, it was wrong. I have no Jewish ancestry—Jewish friends, yes—but not blood, and yes, I was made.

On October 1, 1998, Federal Magistrate Mark D. Fox added some refinements to the bail conditions. I had just been let out from Valhalla on ten million dollars bail.

With additional conditions. I had to wear an electronic monitoring device on my ankle. It worked on radio waves and was tied in to a base unit connected to my phone. If I strayed more than fifteen feet from my property line, an alarm went off, and I would have violated the terms of my release and be sent back to prison. I was allowed off the property for doctor and lawyer visits, as long as they were was cleared by the government.

Every visitor to my property had to be screened and approved by the government. I was not allowed to have or use a fax machine or a cell phone.

I also had to pay for 24/7 guards to be with me. Once, while playing soccer with my daughter on the property, I strayed beyond the fifteen foot limit, and had to be accompanied to court with the guards to argue that I shouldn't be violated for this and incarcerated again. I wasn't. The guards cost me approximately $24,000 per month.

The government, however, had eviscerated most of my income at the time. Shortly after my arrest in January 1998, the government restrained my assets, my properties, my rental income, my bank accounts; were all off limits to me.

In addition, the government was billing me for the privilege of having government receivers manage my properties while forbidding me any payments from those properties. Several thousand dollars a month for their management. They were in charge of collecting rents, and they did what most government employees do. They performed very inefficiently, letting many thousands of dollars of rent arrears build up from the tenants.

Real property taxes went into arrears, and I would eventually be left to clean up the government issue mess.

In an attempt at economic survival, I moved to vacate the government restraining order. Originally, the government sought to restrain $20,000,000 in assets. Assets which I did not have; so they took what they could find. Fortunately, in March 1998, Judge Barrington Parker granted the *vacatur* of the restraint, but left the government time to appeal his decision. In other words he stayed the *vacatur*, which of course, allowed the restraint to continue.

Eventually, on June 5, 1998, Judge Parker signed a modified restraining order, keeping me away from $358,000 of wedding gifts, forbidding me from refinancing or selling my Mill Neck home, or my commercial property in Queens, or using the rents. I also couldn't touch my corporate bank accounts, or mortgage or sell my Pennsylvania property.

Besides the long range purpose of financially devastating me, the restraining order had the shorter range purpose of making sure I would fall in arrears on the payment of my guards. This, of course, could generate an order revoking my bail, for failure to meet its conditions.

It worked. On November 13, 1998, the government was notified by United Security the contract guards watching me, that they were going to terminate services because I owed them money. (Four weeks' worth of payments.) They also claimed that I had asked them not to report my arrears to the government.

The chances of me asking that are equal to the chances of them complying with my wishes. Zero. In fact, the guards that were monitoring me had told my attorneys that I never made such a request. But the situation read thus: Either I come up with an immediate payment of $10,000, or back to jail I go.

My former request to be subject to video monitoring, in lieu of in person guards fell on deaf ears. The electronic bracelet, 24/7 video monitoring, was not sufficient. Not enough for the government, even though there had never been an incident of a Gotti skipping out on bail. (With the exception of my father's youngest brother, Vincent, who had skipped bail on a case in the early eighties, and was eventually apprehended. Vincent at no time was a part of the Bergin crew, and in fact due to his actions and indiscretions was not permitted by my father, to associate with the crew.)

Carol Sipperly, one of the AUSA s working on my case, said in opposing papers:

> The Government is skeptical of the capacity of such a technique (video surveillance) to identify in a clear and timely manner all visitors to defendant Gotti's residence, and to monitor his contacts when not at the residence.

You might be thinking I was receiving special treatment. Maybe you are right. In my case, and in my father's case, I believe the Feds made it personal. It wasn't just a job, no, for them it was an avenue that could lead to significant career enhancement.

Prosecutor Gleeson, who helped put my father away on the 1992 trial, had become Federal Judge Gleeson. For life. The lesson did not go unheeded by others in law enforcement.

★

I did have a limited amount of money coming in from the rents on two properties. One of which I was only part owner. These generated significant rents, which partially paid for my guards' fees. Without the help of family and friends, I never could have survived economically while being allowed out on bail.

In March, 1999, I entered into a formal stipulation with the government that I would make timely payments for my guards. If not, back to prison.

Remember, this all took place *before* my being convicted of anything.

★

But I remained at home, planning my defense. It was definitely a better atmosphere than prison. Let me describe the property.

The house was a five thousand square foot white stone Colonial over two hundred years old. It sat on three and a quarter acres. There was a guest house, tennis court, reflecting pool, and 200 feet of dock on the water. It had once been owned by the family of Quincy Gilmore, a Civil War General.

When I bought it, the house was in a shambles. But with time, money, and the efforts of an excellent construction crew, the shambles became a showpiece.

There was also a cemetery adjoining the property. It hadn't been used in about forty years. It was in disrepair, grown wild with weeds, as forgotten as the dead who resided underneath the soil. Those who had been entrusted with its care had abandoned it.

Some of the graves dated form the 1700s. Being the history buff that I am, I took it upon myself to maintain the grounds. My landscaper friend, Angelo Noviello, assisted me. We put the graveyard back in proper order, provided a token of respect to the dead there, including the children that had been interred.

It was peaceful, that cemetery. I would sit and think there in between strategy sessions with the lawyers and investigators.

It was among the dead that I planned for what might happen the rest of my life.

★

Home.

I remember my first night home, out on bail. October 1, 1998. My wife had made a special meal, her signature dish of linguine and white clam sauce. My sister, Victoria, contributed her own renowned lasagna, my mother had supplied her famous shrimp balls, and my sister Angel provided her low carb crab cakes.

The whole family (with the obvious exception of my father),

was gathered at the table. But he even appeared telephonically, allowed to call from the prison. But he couldn't speak directly to me. He relayed his good wishes through my mother. He did speak with my wife and children. But I could hear his voice, and heard the joy in it that his son had been released on bail. It was as if *he* had been freed.

His phone time was limited. Two calls a month, nor any call more than fifteen minutes. Further, his throat cancer made speaking rather difficult for him. I will never forget that meal.

After dinner, I went upstairs for some alone time. Contemplation of my situation. But what continued to come to mind was my father's situation. In solitary, cancer slowly eating away at him.

I haven't often felt powerless in my life, but I did at that moment. I was out at least temporarily; he would never walk the streets again. I could eat fine meals, sleep in comfortable beds. Be with my family. He couldn't—ever again.

Those feelings strengthened my will to fight the government tooth and nail (at the time). I am a great believer in preparation and planning, and so I got ready to go to war.

In the house, a room had been set up as the "war room," where I would meet with attorneys, investigators, and, on occasion, co-defendants, and strategize. We would face the accusations, analyze the strengths and weakness of the case.

We would go to trial.

CHAPTER SEVENTEEN

Charged Up

My right hand was covered with chalk dust. I had been busy at the blackboard which was installed in my "war room" at the Mill Neck house. I was drawing lines between government allegations, co-defendant charges, and the accusations against me.

There were times that several co-defendants met with me and our lawyers at Gerald Shargel's office. In order to protect individual interests, these meetings were subject to written defense cooperation agreements wherein what was said in the office stayed there—unless otherwise agreed. It was required to protect attorney client privilege.

But most of the trial preparation would be done at my "war room" at my home, with the attorneys and the investigators. I would not invite men who were strangers into my home, being very protective of my family and their privacy. The vast majority of my co-defendants were strangers to me.

We were accused of the usual extortion, loan sharking, money laundering, obstruction of justice, illegal gambling, etc. The indictment alleged that these activities had earned the members of the Gambino crime family more than twenty million dollars over a period of some twenty years.

The main target of the indictments was me. I was prime target number one. Send me to jail for over twenty years, strip me of my income and property. This was the government's best case scenario.

You have already read about government tactics to have me denied bail while I was in Valhalla, but there was much more to come. I shelled out many thousands of dollars for lawyers, investigators, trial transcripts from other proceedings, tape experts, and more. If the government wanted to put me away, they were going to earn every second of time I was going to serve.

We had a heavy duty lineup of lawyers for this case.

Gerald Shargel, Jimmy LaRossa, Joseph Corozzo, Bob Layton, Sarita Kedia (who was with Shargel), Richard Rehbock. Shargel, Sarita, and Cutler were representing me. Soon they would be joined by noted Harvard Law Professor Charles Ogletree.

Rehbock represented Vincent Zollo, with Robert Layton as co-counsel, Joseph Corozzo represented Anthony Plomitallo. LaRossa had Greg DePalma, and his son Craig had John Mitchell. Jack D'Amico had Jimmy Kousouros and Salvatore LoCascio (son of Frank LoCascio) was represented by Jay Goldberg. Ron Kuby also represented one of the co-defendants.

The government had a bunch of cooperators lined up to testify against us, in order to escape or reduce their own jail sentences. There were thousands of hours of audio tape. (Very few of which had my voice recorded on them.)

If you think the government never plays games with its tapes, think again. The transcripts you are given leave out important statements, referring to them as "U/I" or unintelligible. The quality of tapes/CDs you get are like tenth generation copies.

So, if you want to fight fire with fire, you hire a tape expert. I hired Ernest Ashkenazy, an audio expert who had been involved with the Watergate affair. His analysis of the government tapes showed evidence of "start-stops" in other words, tampering.

Ashkenazy was surprised at the amateurish tapes the government made with so many obvious start stops. Conversations had sentences cut in half, either at the beginning or the end. My expert was looking forward to testifying at the electronic shenanigans of the government.

My brother-in-law, Carmine Agnello's auto parts businesses had been wiretapped; Craig DePalma and his friend Willie Marshall were bugged. There had also been a bug under the table at the Lindenwood Diner, a place I rarely went to. All of my businesses and vehicles were also bugged.

Prosecutorial Leaks to the Press

When it comes to my courtroom battles, the arena is not only the courtroom, but in the press. The prosecution, rightly or wrongly, will use their journalistic connections to influence a jury before they are ever picked, as a jury is composed of members of the public who are readers of the newspapers on a daily basis.

In my '98 case Special Assistant US Attorney Vincent Heintz was thrown off of the prosecution team by the US Attorney for the Southern District of New York, for leaking confidential information about my case to the papers, to potentially influence the outcome.

Heintz was one of the few prosecutors in Southern District of New York history dismissed from a case for unauthorized communication with the press. If it weren't for another journalist who had contacted both the US Attorney and my attorney, Gerald Shargel, about these leaks, we never would have known the source, and the government would have ignored the problem.

By informing both sides at the same time, this journalist served justice by precluding the prosecution from sweeping this under the rug. The individual who did the right thing, wound up being blacklisted for his efforts.

Cooperators Line Up

The lineup of cooperators included Michael Sergio, Willie Marshall, Michael Blutrich (an attorney con man and pedophile, whom I've had the pleasure of *never* meeting) were to link me to Scores topless bar. Joe Fusaro was to testify against gambling. Dom Borghese (a former soldier in my crew), Al D'Arco, Salvatore Gravano (of course), and Lucchese family member Frank Gioia were all batting for the Federal team.

We were scheduled for an April, 1999, trial, and here it was October, 1998. Not a whole lot of time to prepare. (The April 5th trial date was an adjourned date from an original January, 1999, scheduled trial.) We examined the charges, one by one. Have a look:

Scores

I was charged, but never convicted, of participating in extortion with respect to a "high end" topless bar, Scores. Never was there. This place came about around 1991 in an effort to create a classy place in New York City where women showed their tits to customers and danced on their laps for a price.

The owners figured, with a better class of clientele, there would be a better ring in the register. They were right. For example, Michael DiLeonardo, a former friend of mine who testified against me in several of my trials, was indicted in 2001 for extorting $100,000 from Scores in 1995. He was acquitted, however. A year later, he was busted again and looking to deal. (We'll have more on that later.)

So what gangster started Scores? None. It was an attorney, a Park Avenue pedophile, Michael Blutrich. He had been a law partner with former Mayor Cuomo's son, Andrew, in the eighties, who had no idea as to the character of this man at the time.

So Blutrich, with his political connections and a venture capital pal, started Scores, moving tits up on to the East Side. The $300,000 seed money that started Scores was earned "honestly" by Blutrich in his defrauding a Florida insurance company. He had become an owner of it Top officials in the company made him a personal loan of the funds.

There were other silent investors also. One of them was Shalom Weiss, and he bears some examination. He was a partner with Blutrich. Weiss had been a defendant in a criminal case where he was charged with defrauding an insurance company of $450,000,000. As the jury was deliberating his fate, he left the courthouse and the country.

He was eventually captured in Austria, and received a sentence of 845 years. His estimated date of release is 2754. This is neither a typo or the next Jewish New Year.

It is interesting that Blutrich started Scores. Dancers need music to wriggle to while chalking up huge credit card bills for ogling customers, and Blutrich had a musical background. He was a child actor and an understudy in the Broadway show *The Sound of Music*.

Blutrich was a basketball coach at the Brooklyn YMHA, where he was accused of molesting a seventeen-year-old boy in 1994. He wanted to trade the kid a bracelet in exchange for sex—at Scores no less.

He pled to disorderly conduct, and learned his lesson until he pled guilty in 1998 for downloading kiddie porn on his computer. Maybe this was the reason the government thought twice about using Blutrich as a witness against me.

John Jack Karst was both the special agent that arrested me on the '98 case, and the control agent for Blutrich. The character of Blutrich was such that this agent took it upon himself to shred notes of his conversations with Blutrich, which is completely in violation of both agent ethics and investigative protocol.

For this breach of duty, Karst was demoted from supervising agent to field agent.

We first found out about Karst and his actions, when pursuant to the discovery phase of trial preparation, we had demanded 302s and agent notes. None were produced, and when we kept pressing for them, the government said they didn't have any.

As this was both impossible and incredible, unless the agent in question had destroyed the notes and other documents, there was only one conclusion, reached by both our attorneys and the FBI, especially when Karst admitted to shredding notes.

This was not an isolated law enforcement incident when it came to prosecuting me, as we shall see later on.

If Blutrich had been used, he would testify to something like this: Michael Sergio contacted him during construction of Scores in 1991, and said that my father required payments from any club opening at the site. Not remotely true. Sergio had never met my father, and was a nobody in the Family. He was a personal friend of Frank LoCascio. Once LoCascio learned that his sons were cops, he disassociated himself from Sergio.

Perhaps Blutrich and his partner Pfeffer were gullible enough to believe Sergio, who was trying to establish himself under our flag, but their stupidity is not equivalent to truth.

But Sergio and Marshall were lined up to testify against me on the Scores matter, so the government wisely decided to pass on Blutrich.

Blutrich was later sentenced to twenty-five years in jail on the insurance fraud matter, but that turned into three year's probation and restitution of $82,000. (Do you see why being a government witness is so attractive to criminal defendants?)

It was claimed that the Gambino family was taking two hundred thousand a year out of Scores. Got it from the coat check room and the valet parking. Further, a supposed tribute of $1,000 per week had been demanded, as well as the right to pick the club bouncers.

I was, supposedly, one of the parties involved in extorting a million bucks from Scores over the years. Blutrich had his office and his phone bugged. Yet no tape ever had my voice on it. So what *was* going on at Scores?

Michael Sergio and his son, Sigmund "The Sea Monster" were taking from the coat room and supposedly from the dancers. Willie Marshall was also skimming money. He had been working as a bouncer. Marshall kicked some bucks back to Sergio and Greg DePalma.

I had no idea who some of the people named in the indictment were. On a tape recorded of my father speaking with my uncle Pete at Marion prison, the following is heard:

> JG: I can't even ID the people in the indictment. Sigmund the Sea Monster? Where do these creatures emerge from?
> PG: I don't know them.

★

I didn't know them either.

There was a manager of Scores, Craig Carlino, who had a dispute with Blutrich. Michael DiLeonardo came to me on behalf of Carlino and wanted me to adjudicate the dispute. I told him, in no uncertain terms, I was not interested.

DePalma was glad to hear that, and told Blutrich, for one hundred grand, the dispute would go away. DePalma got the money, kept $30,000 for himself and his son, and kicked up $70,000 to the Gambino family coffers.

From the $70,000, I divided this up with Michael DiLeonardo and several others. That was the only money the Family got from Scores, and I regret being dumb enough to take any part of it.

So there at Scores, you mix booze, broads, and testosterone

charged up men. As in any establishment, when these mix, violence occurs. That's why there were bouncers. Sometimes bouncers get out of control, situations get out of control, and people get hurt—or killed.

Some of the charges in the indictment against some of the defendants involved murder conspiracy. What had happened was the classy East Side Scores often attracted boys from the Bronx, who weren't all that classy. Albanian gangsters for example.

There are several versions of the story given, I provide both. I don't have any personal knowledge of what happened that night.

Willie Marshall got into a beef with some of the Albanians, possibly over some comment made to his girlfriend by one of the Albanians. Another of the Bronx types had lost an arm wrestling match and was being teased about it. He didn't like that. He got physical with the guy laughing. Marshall's girl-friend, Lori, screamed.

The Albanian suggested she be quiet, in rather adult lan-guage. Willie tells the bouncers to toss the Albanians. During the altercation, the bouncers are shot by the Albanians. Well, actually they shot and stabbed the bouncers.

Whatever happened, the Albanians were not impressed with Marshall. Marshall knew these two were hot heads and dangerous, knew that they often carried weapons. He could have diffused the situation, but didn't and, as a result, two bouncers lay dead on the floor.

The Dedaj brothers didn't exactly voluntarily surrender to the authorities. Finally, during a June, 1997, stakeout of a Bronxville apartment complex by FBI and Manhattan DA investigators, Simon Dedaj appears on the street. He was chased.

He took off, finally leaping into the Bronx River and swimming away. (From a *New York Times* Story p. 7 June 19, 1997.) He was finally captured on February 17, 1998, at a

New Jersey Motel, the Inn at Ramsey. The chase after him had lasted nineteen months.

His brother Victor had been captured in March of 1997 at a Valley Forge, Pennsylvania, motel, shortly before he was to escape to Paris.

The first trial ended in a hung jury. The second found Simon guilty of second degree murder, and his brother guilty of first degree manslaughter. Simon received a life bid, Victor received 25 years.

★

Greg DePalma pled guilty to (among other things) a conspiracy to commit extortion of the owners of Scores and a former manager. On the same day, his son Craig pled guilty, too. Marshal, in exchange for his government cooperation, received a pass from law enforcement.

Scores survived. Several lawsuits were initiated against it for overcharging customer credit cards. American Express sued them in 2005 for some $241,000 of unauthorized charges on a CEO's credit card. The exec in question admitted to $20,000 being authorized. Another suit looked for $28,000 and $129,000. In 2007, they were sued by one of their bartenders alleging that management was glomming the bartender tips. The same year, the SLA tried to close them down.

A computer check shows the club is alive and well, charging very high prices, but under new management since the Blutrich days.

I comport myself a certain way, whether as a former mobster, or a present day civilian. I didn't go to topless bars. I don't now, they personally disgust me. To me, there can be no high end topless establishment, just better looking whores, and drunks with larger expense accounts.

And remember, I was never convicted of any activities related to Scores.

Phone Card Scam

Another charge against me in the indictment, (dropped three weeks before the trial date), was that I was running a phone card scam. Prepaid phone cards were then popular. You'd buy a card with a certain amount of time on it. Up to 300 million of them had been issued by 1997.

Phone carriers had them, businesses used them to promote themselves, they became a sort of advertising specialty. Some buyers bought the cards wholesale to sell at retail. At the time in question, MCI was one of the major carriers that sold the phone cards to resellers. They were responsible for the telephone lines.

They sell large blocks of minutes to resellers, who breaks them up into smaller minute groups and resells them. It was claimed that I, as a reseller, was selling worthless phone cards. The cards didn't work because of the fault of the carrier, who was responsible for malfunctioning phone cards. Not the reseller.

If there was a victim of worthless phone cards, it was me. I had seen this as a legitimate profit potential activity, and my partner in the cards was a legitimate guy, a hard working, tax paying carpenter.

As a result of the indictment, his life was turned around, and not in a good way. So who was the racketeer? MCI was investigated in 1999 for running a $30 million dollar scam. Their financial manager was obtaining millions of dollars of bank loans based on phony documentation. Much of it went to the Caymans. He personally, allegedly, made $2 million.

MCI was also charging a full minute of phone time, even when a consumer might have used only five seconds. That meant if the customer got a busy signal or hung up, we, the resellers, were still being charged for a full minute of time by MCI. The resellers were losing substantial amounts of money, while MCI got the profits.

The fact that three weeks before the trial date the government dropped the charges against me, speaks volumes of their lack of bona fides in bringing the charge in the first place.

★

There were additional weaknesses in the government's case, and my father felt I should fight. I was torn between a trial and a possible plea. I remember speaking to my father about this at my 1999 Springfield visit.

JJG: John, there is no cancer in my brain and none in my heart.

JAG: [Shaking my head] You amaze me.

JJG: What I wouldn't give to walk in that courtroom just one more time [His eyes lit up] just one more time to show them what a man is, and break their holes. Show them what a man is, John, show them what it means to have this. [Pointing to his heart]

[At this point in the conversation, I nodded and stared at him, pausing. He broke the silence.]

JJG: We only have five more minutes John and I don't know when or if we will ever see each other again. I don't know if I got through to you or not, but you certainly have some thinking to do.

JAG: I know.

JJG: I miss seeing you.

JAG: You have no idea how much I miss seeing you.

JJG: Right now to me, this visit is worth 55 years hanging upside down in the corner of my cell because you know the way I feel, I love you and adore you.

JAG: I know dad.

[At this point, tears rolled down my face.]

JJG: So go do what you have to do and don't worry about me, because it doesn't make sense. What will be will be, so stay strong and keep your head up.

[I gave into my emotions and shed more tears.]

JJG: Don't give them the satisfaction—come on.

[He motioned to me to embrace him and say farewell.]

It was then that we embraced for what was to be the last time.

CHAPTER EIGHTEEN

On the Record

Gotti transcript of Ray Brook Conversations 10-5-03

JAG is myself, John A. Gotti; SK is a friend of mine, Steven Kaplan; and JR was (he is deceased) my closest friend, John Ruggiero. When you see U/I, that means unintelligible, in other words the transcriber couldn't understand what was being said.

JAG: John, if we are stupid enough to raise our children near this, then we deserve to die in jail. I'm sorry, but we do. My suggestion, John, to salvage our children, you gotta move away. You gotta move away, John. You gotta stay away from these people. You gotta stay away from these people.

JR. I don't see how to get out of here. How to get away.

JAG: John, you go to Canada, for every dollar, you get a dollar fifty. A million dollars is a million five.

JR: U/I

SK: It's tough.

JAG: I'm done.

JR: U/I out there.

JAG: I told my mother, I told my sister in law, I told everybody else too, I told 'em listen, if I'm fortunate enough to make it out of jail, I'm leaving. Youse can come with me or not. Your choice, I'm leaving, there's nothing here. Nothing in New York. 'Cause all that's gonna happen

In New York is one of two things: one, I'm gonna lose my cool and hurt somebody or two, they're gonna suck me right in again and make me the scapegoat, make me the scapegoat, and dump all the shit on me again, and I'm not having that again.

JR: You're smart.

JAG: I'm not gonna be... smart! Yeah, I'm real smart. I felt smart every day I gotta spread my ass in front of a cop's face I feel smart. Smart? Smart would have been running away a long time ago. Smart...

SK: It's gonna be hard.

JAG: I got trapped.

SK: I know.

JAG: All my father had in this world was me, and I was the only one who could go see him, and he had me for the lawyers, running around for the lawyers, and so on and so forth, I got trapped. I couldn't tell him, "Listen Dad, I don't want to live in New York, I want to leave. I want to move to Carolina."

SK: Did you ever have...

JAG: He would've looked at me like, "What do you mean?"

SK: Did you ever have those thoughts then? Back then?

JAG: Honestly, Steve, there was many times that I did. I didn't want to be there. I wanted to be someplace else.

SK: I remember.

JAG: I wanted to move to Florida at one point. How would I ever tell him that I wanted to pack up and leave? My father would've said, "Well, you enjoyed the beginning of the game, now in the middle you want to walk away."

JR: U/I

JAG: I got trapped, trapped, John.

JR: You wanna know something, John...

JAG: I couldn't disappoint the guy, I had to stay.

JR: Your father wouldn't have let you out. Your father would be more proud that his son, that his son went jail. And he knew, he knew, you know what my father said before he died my father said...

CHAPTER NINETEEN

Closure

After I left my father on the Springfield visit, I was once again eager to go to trial. But when I saw my children my emotions would swing. I was clearly a man torn between pleasing my father and doing what I felt was the right thing for my blood family. I felt that if I fought the remaining case and won—the racketeering case that my lawyers and I felt strongly that we would win—I would become the second coming of the Teflon Don.

There would be no release from the streets, because I would be perfectly filling my father's shoes. The government would view me as a much larger prize. The press would have shoved it in their faces as only they know how. (Like schoolyard instigators of a fight, they love to stir the pot.)

When would it end if I went to trial? How would it end? Life imprisonment? Maybe, as my father used to say, "If a guy don't abide by the code of this Life, he ends up with two in his hat and left in a dumpster."

Did I have the right to do to my wife and children what was done to my mother, my siblings, and me? I spent countless hours wrestling with these questions. Many sleepless nights. Then, on one fine Spring day, only days before Easter, I was sitting in my yard. (I was restricted in my movements by the electronic bracelet on my ankle and my bail conditions to ten feet from the property.)

My daughter came up to me, and, out of the blue, asked me, "How come Pop Pop never comes here?" That was the nickname for my father all of his grandchildren had given him. I told her he needed to stay where he was.

"Why?" My daughter Nicolette is rather persistent. Now I had to give my soon to be eight year old daughter an answer. The right one.

"Sometimes, Nic, when you don't always follow the rules that society (I had to explain that word to her), expects you to follow, or in other words you live by your own rules, they make you live in a certain place and you are not allowed to leave until they say you can."

"Could he ever come here or to my party this summer?" she asked. (Her birthday was in July.)

"Definitely not your party, but maybe someday here."

"If he doesn't come here daddy, I'm never going to know him?"

She ran off to play with her three brothers while I just stared off into space. She would never know him. It was at this point that I decided to consider a plea deal again. When I finally did make my decision, it was made with a very heavy heart. I felt that I disappointed my father.

It would be a long time before I came to terms with this.

If I could get a lesser chunk of time, in full satisfaction of everything, if I could put the Life behind me once and for all, and be free of government prosecution/persecution, then maybe, just maybe, I might take a deal.

I wanted my family to have a father that was present in the home. I felt, given the poor quality of the government witnesses, the lack of tape evidence against me, I had a decent chance of prevailing at trial. But there was always a risk.

If I could manage that risk with a plea bargain, I would consider it. If I got closure.

You will notice I am repeating myself. I want to make sure that the reader understands that my only reason for taking a plea was to have it be the plea that ended all future government attacks on me.

The government started to make reduced time offers, but not closure. I rejected those offers. Easter Sunday, before the trial was to start the following week, Sarita Kedia, from Shargel's office, had a phone conversation with AUSA Carol Sipperly. Negotiations were opened up again.

On Monday, Shargel and the government engaged in a marathon negotiation session. The point was repeatedly driven home that I would plead to less time if there was closure. They would get the unheard of gift of having me take a plea.

Drafts of the deal were exchanged back and forth, but the language wasn't sufficient to satisfy me. Finally, disgusted, I told Shargel, "Let's go to trial."

Shargel pleaded for more time, believing a deal could be made. Later, he came back with a smile on his face and a legal pad in his hand and informed me, "We got the deal John." Cutler agreed.

However, the deal was not written the way I would have it. The US Attorneys didn't want language too specific in order to avoid setting a precedent for future deals. But they agreed that the defense could make a statement about closure and coverage, and that being the basis for the deal.

So I pled guilty to bribery, extortion conspiracy related to the construction industry, mortgage fraud, supervising gambling operations, and to Eastern District charges of conspiracy to commit usury, and filing a false tax return.

Shargel, in his presentencing letter to Judge Barrington Parker dated July 6, 1999, put it succinctly:

By his plea of guilty Mr. Gotti has expressed his desire to end this battle the government has created because of his name. He wishes to lead an ordinary life, once he is released from prison, without constant interference and aggravation by the government and the media.

Shargel said at the sentencing:

One of the key purposes of this plea is Mr. Gotti's desire to have all this put behind him, so he can move on with his life, one of the essential reasons for this plea is finality and closure.

Shargel had been negotiating with an AUSA he knew, Mark Pomerantz, who was working under David Kelly, then head of rackets. Shargel had a good working relationship with Pomerantz. Kelly had OK'd the plea.

Then between 2004–2006, when Kelly had risen to the US Attorney for the Southern District, he had me tried for various RICO offenses.

★

You read about what I pled guilty to above, but that doesn't mean I was guilty of all of those things, it was just part of a deal. Plea bargains happen all the time where, for lesser time, or a lesser charge, a defendant "cops" to that lesser charge—even if he didn't do it.

Let's look at the mortgage fraud charge I plead guilty to. Before the bank meltdown, back in the late nineties and first six years or so of the 2000's, banks were lending money, mortgage money, to anything with a pulse.

There was no documentation, no asset check, no income check loans. As long as your credit was okay, and there was sufficient loan to value in the mortgage, no problem: you were approved. Mortgage brokers made up incomes to qualify for loans that would never be checked. It was standard industry practice.

One of my attorneys who handles real estate matters for me, told me how over ten years ago, he closed a deal one time that was not only "no money down" but the borrower got money back at the closing. There had been no income check or request for documentation.

So me? The indictment read:

> John A. Gotti filed a mortgage application in the amount of approximately $338,000.00 with Madison Home Equities in connection with his home at 33 Riviera Drive Massapequa, NY, in which he misrepresented the nature and amount of his income.

Obviously, given my job description at the time, I didn't want to declare the nature of my income. But I did truthfully declare my income for the mortgage to get a lower rate. (No-doc loans had a slightly higher interest rate.) I also fully intended to pay back the loan, and eventually did.

★

So I had pled guilty and received a sentence of 77 months, forfeiture of my wedding moneys, 89 acres of land I owned in Pennsylvania, property in Sullivan county, a RICO forfeiture judgment in the amount of 1.5 Million dollars, and restitution in the amount of $336,000.

While awaiting my date to appear at the Federal Correctional Institution at Ray Brook, near Lake Placid, I remained at home, supervising the sale of my residence at Mill Neck, and the construction on my new residence in Oyster Bay Cove. All in the company of security guards.

I was originally slated to go to the closer Otisville Prison, but it was somehow determined I had too many friends there, so my family and attorneys were now bound to make a twelve hour round trip to Ray Brook. Eighty miles from the Canadian border.

I had made a last minute request through my attorney, Gerald Shargel, to be sentenced to Marion or Springfield instead, so I could be with my dying father, but was refused. So on October 18, 1999, I kissed my family goodbye, shook hands with my attorneys, and headed North.

CHAPTER TWENTY

Ray Brook Days

Ray Brook houses over thirteen hundred inmates, though it was built to house only five hundred. In 1980, while it was under construction, it was used to house competitors at the Winter Olympics in Lake Placid. It's about eighty miles from the Canadian border, and, in the winter, to say it gets cold, would be a rather gross understatement. Cold as in fifty degrees below zero.

One of the cruelties of Ray Brook, whether or not intentional, is the inmates who are shut in, are occasionally afforded outside views of beautiful mountainous country. Civilians who are free get to ski in the mountains, swim in the lakes. Those of us inside get to view the sun through wires or a hole in the wall.

Ray Brook is a level four high security facility. There are six different levels of prison security. Only ADX Florence, in Colorado is a level six—the highest security. Before that, Marion was at that level. On level one you might have individual rooms or a room might be shared between two men. There might be four man cubicles. Not unlike old style military barracks.

In a level six scenario you are locked up 23 ½ hours, no contact visits with those who come to see you—you communicate by phones through thick Plexiglas. Phone privileges are limited to 300 minutes a month. My father had been in the first level six prison, Marion: that is it contained a level six lockdown facility within the prison. Marion was the flagship for level six prisons, and it survived investigations by Amnesty International and several court challenges.

However, at times there were some traces of justice being done. In May, 2006, a Ray Brook inmate, Keith Maydak, was paid $9,275 in damages for retaliatory abuse by guards against him for filing complaints.

He had been placed in a cell without food or water for five days, handcuffed and shackled for allegedly threatening the warden with a lawsuit. Well, the guards weren't all bad, they did feed him an apple and two pieces of bread in those five days.

In that five day period of his lockup, he was allowed to use the toilet once. Then they placed Maydak in a cell designed for two people. Problem was there were four other inmates there for a six week period. The floors were flooded with sewage, the food was spoiled, and as a result of water deprivation, the inmates were dehydrated.

Reality check: We are talking New York, part of the United States, not Guantanamo, or Abu Ghraib. Americans treating Americans in this manner. With full approval by the Bureau of Prisons.

So for a total of 47 days of being tortured, Maydak received the equivalent of $197 per day.

Maydak happened before I got to Ray Brook. While I was there, an inmate saved a guard's life. Gonzalo Mota-Rivera was awarded $100. Rivera was doing several years in for violating immigration laws. That's all.

★

So on October 18, 1999, at approximately two in the afternoon, in walks me, to commence serving his time in Ray Brook. I go through the doors to the Receiving and Delivery area. I was met by Lou Facciola (whom I had known as a kid from the old neighborhood), known there as "Captain Lou," for his fishing prowess, and several other friends and associates who were in the Life. They came bearing gifts. Sneakers, sweats, underwear, food. It was a customary act, a sort of Welcome Wagon for the newly arrived guys from the Life.

Lou Facciola had grown up in the East New York part of Brooklyn with my dad. He and his brother Bruno were friends with my dad as kids. As did most street kids from that neighborhood, they went the way of the Life.

Bruno was a soldier in the Lucchese family, and Lou was under him. Like others who served under the demented Gaspipe Casso, they would feel the Life's brutality.

In August 1990, Bruno, who was suffering from cancer, was summoned to a meeting in a Brooklyn garage by Casso. Upon his arrival, he was quick to realize that this was not a routine meeting but a hit. He was the target.

As he made a run for the door, he was tackled and dragged back in. He knew he was about to die and made a last request to his killers. He asked to make a last minute phone call to his daughter to tell her he loved her.

His request was denied, and he was strangled, then shot to death.

Once Bruno was killed, Casso began killing members of Bruno's crew. His brother-in-law, was next, then a close friend, and finally they were searching for his brother, Lou, who was in hiding at the time.

A month after my father was arrested, as I was standing outside of the Bergin, Bruno and Lou's sister, Carmela, approached me, crying, and asked me to please inform my father of what had been going on. "I beg him to help us," she told me.

I comforted her and promised I would pass the message along to my father. The next evening, I visited my father and relayed what had happened the previous day. He was upset about this situation, and instructed me as well as Nicky Corozzo to arrange a meeting with Al D'Arco, who at that time was the acting boss of the Lucchese family.

The meeting was set up at the La Bella Vita restaurant in Ozone Park. At the meeting, Nicky and I asked D'Arco to relay a message to Vic Amuso, who at this time was on the lam from an indictment that was handed down in previous months. The message was: John Gotti was asking the Lucchese family for a favor. Spare Lou, and release him to our group.

D'Arco promised to get back to me shortly. Three days later, I received a message that D'Arco wanted to meet. I had met him alone on Cross Bay Bridge in Howard Beach, at one in the morning. I was informed that his superiors agreed and Lou was to be spared and released.

He was then put with Nicky Corozzo, who also being from the old East New York neighborhood welcomed Lou to my father's group. Lou was the only Gambino associate at Ray Brook.

It was ironic, that an individual who had been involved with the conspiracy to kill him, also was serving time in Ray Brook.

★

Another individual I met was Lieutenant Cross of the prison SIS, who informed me that the reason why I was there was that there were no Gambinos at Ray Brook. I informed him my name was Gotti. I was taken to my cell block named Ausable. (It is a chasm in the Adirondacks.)

It was a four man cell, me and three kids from D.C. Bank robbers doing a long stretch.

Into the routine of prison. Up at 5:30 AM, breakfast at 6:00. As prison labor is cheap, and very profitable for the institution, we were assigned work. Not every labor sweatshop may be found in the third world. So, at 7:30 AM, we went to our assigned jobs.

My first gig was in the plumbing shop. Work was done by 2:30 PM. I was well paid at $8—per month. Looked like my filet mignon and Boodles days were over for a time. As time went on I changed jobs, and got a better assignment in the rec yard. Me and another guy called Fish worked at the outside weight pile in the yard, keeping it tidy.

Fish had done about seventeen years in prison. Two hundred pounds of East New York bodybuilder. A good guy. So from 7:30 AM to 2:30 PM, we had this walk in the sun job. But it was to get better for me, occupation wise.

Eventually, I was given an almost no show job. Myself, and two other inmates of my choosing, were in charge of maintaining the small room in the middle of the prison compound that housed vending machines. We called it the "7-11." Heck, I had legitimate vending machine experience on the outside. It was one of my businesses.

Weekends, we worked from 5:30–6:30 PM. We basically sat around drinking espresso. Myself, and Fat Larry Sessa and Raphael "Big Skee" Torres. Larry was doing twelve years due to his participation in the Colombo wars. Larry was a damn good cook. He prepared meals for our guys and the guys who were okay with us, even though not Italian.

We'd feed everybody at Christmas. The camaraderie of inmates and food replaced outside family and friends for a time.

I often tried to convince Sessa to leave the Life, but he was enamored with it.

Torres, was an enforcer for a Bronx drug gang, doing a fifteen year bid. He was what we call, *very capable*. (With respect to the ability to do violence.) I also hung out with Paul DeCologero and Brian Lindermann, who, at one time or another, were cellmates of mine.

Paul had been caught up with the Boston mob doing time for drug conspiracy. DeCologero had sued the FBI for $5 million dollars because the Feds had protected mob hitmen during the Boston wars of the late eighties and early nineties. Long time informants, like Whitey Bulger, were given a murder pass by the FBI.

The suit was dismissed in 2000.

Lindermann was a bank robber, who, at the age of seventeen, was bright enough to succeed in any legitimate endeavor. He fell in with the wrong crowd. He had been a member of what the media called the Giannini crew, named after a Queens cafe, which was their hangout. While in, Lindermann earned academic credits, and tutored fellow inmates, many of whom were learning disabled. He was doing a seventeen year stretch.

★

Now, some of you reading this may be saying "Aha! A summer camp. He (me) had this real cushy no show job."

So, you reading this…you have family? Get to talk to them for a total of 300 minutes a month on a monitored phone while they are 300 miles away from you? Want to visit them in a huge room filled with strange prisoners?

On one of the many government tapes made while I was in, I can be heard saying on September 5, 2003:

> The visiting room you can't even get up. You used to be able to get up and go outside. You can't even leave your chair now. This is the only visiting room in the whole system including penitentiaries, that you can't get out of your chair. This is the worst joint. How do you raise your kids on three hundred minutes a month?

Answer: you don't. For me the toughest thing about prison was isolation from my family, not the crap food, the confinement, the lack of privacy and the daily routine. Another tape revealed my state of mind.

> I've got five children too that I brought into this world and I have a responsibility my first responsibility is to my children and to my wife, You understand me? My father's dead and my first responsibility now is to my children and nobody else.

I couldn't live up to that job in jail. In 2002, about the same time as my father's death one of my children had been having trouble in school. I suppose my being away and all the publicity regarding my father in life and death began to take its toll.

I had made an arrangement with the school to have a weekly phone call with the school to check on the status of my child, and I had to make the BOP agree to this. First they said no, but after letters came from the school, they acquiesced. Reluctantly.

Thus, every Friday at 2:00 PM, I would be brought to the unit manager's office where the phone would be dialed for me to the school and I would be patched in. The faculty knew I was calling from a prison, I hoped that my child believed the story about me calling from a military base. My children had seen me in a uniform, and there were pictures of me in military like attire from my days at NYMA at our house and at my mother's house.

The calls went well for several weeks. Part of the problem my kids had was due to the reduction in phone privileges when I was in the hole. They were reduced to one fifteen minute call per month. This weekly phone call was a godsend.

I could spend up to thirty minutes on these Friday phone calls, sometimes my wife would listen in as well. The calls were beneficial to me, the children, the teachers and staff. Many who heard me, but had never met me, got a better insight into what I was really all about.

However, nothing good or bad lasts, so on one Friday call, when the prison staff was late bringing me to the phone, the hookup had been already made and all parties but myself were on line. The previous weeks I had been placed in the hole pending an investigation.

The usual routine was to have me in the unit manager's office before the call, when I was in population. Now, being in the hole, the procedure was I was cuffed up and belly chained, and I would always take care so that my children would not hear the movement of these chains, or them hitting something in the office. I did not want them to get an inkling of my actual conditions.

But on this particular Friday, the children and staff at the school get to hear the PA announcement regarding my transport from my cell, referring to me as "Inmate Gotti," to the strip search cell. They heard that. They heard steel doors clang, they heard chains. They heard the guards with me say, "Take the black box off of his hands, leave the belly chains on."

The guard asked the Lieutenant, "When's the hookup (to the school)?"

"I think we are already on," said the Lieutenant. He looked at the phone. "Yeah, the lights are on."

I began to feel sick to my stomach. I started to sweat, fearful that now my children would know where I really was, and the embarrassment this would cause them.

"Hello," I said into the phone.

"Yes, Mr. Gotti, we are all here."

I could tell from my children's voices that they were affected by what they heard. Their usual excited happy responses were now subdued, withdrawn. I continued talking, and told them how much I missed them. I thought about them every day.

They would normally respond with enthusiasm and thank the school staff for their time. Not this time however. I didn't hear anything. My children refused to attend any more calls. So, future sessions with the teachers went on without them.

In reviewing my initial decision to keep the reality of my situation from my children, I have some doubts that I acted correctly. I felt they were too young to tell them I was going to prison back in 1999. The oldest one had been nine. I felt that was correct. But should I have later told them of my true situation, so that they would not have found out from that unfortunate Friday phone call?

Twenty-twenty hindsight. But no doubt that call, that inadvertent discovery by them that Daddy was in chains, an inmate, left emotional scars.

★

I settled down to prison routine, and tried to do something constructive while in. I became a Certified Paralegal, which was to help me in later cases. I tried to get as much privacy as possible which in jail, especially if you are a Gotti, isn't much.

And I was put in an unwanted leadership role. The Italian boys looked up to me because of what I was (according to their way of thinking), and came to me with their problems, those in the prison, those in the street.

People's perceptions last, I guess. At least until enough evidence and enough time passes to allow them to change their minds—if they are open to that. So some of those that came to me with their street problems thought I was doing a Vinny the Chin act or something. Sure John, sure you ain't in the Life anymore, nudge-nudge, wink-wink.

So it wasn't only the agents and prosecutors that hated to think I left that world, that I was no longer mafia. What's the point of bagging an elephant with no tusks, a toothless tiger? No bragging rights.

The bad guys too. Those in the Life felt the same way, incapable of believing that I would walk away. I, who had been the son of the most famous gangster's gangster in modern history—since Al Capone. That guy would walk away from that? Walk away from being likely successor to the throne? Who would do that?

Me. But nobody believed it at the time. I was a Family man. But I also was a family man who had coached Little League when I was free. Neighbors had no problem leaving their kids in my care. I had worn a bad guy badge, but we all have seen over the years that those who wear Good Guy badges, a cop, a politician, a prosecutor, a judge—some of them are thieves, perverts, and even murderers. Worse than most mobsters.

★

I begged off from the street stuff. I was done with the Life. The prison stuff occasionally found me in the role of referee, between inmates, and sometimes between guards and inmates. I tried to quell problems before they became violent or deadly. If I, or one of my friends, would have been threatened, I would not have been hesitant to hit the yard with a knife in my pants, and, if necessary, use it.

When not engaged in the above, I even wrote a children's book. *Children of Shaolin Forest*. Yet to be published, but perhaps one day.

Then there was another routine prison event for me.

The hole.

My first time was for an alleged escape attempt. I had been in the prison law library with Paul DeCologero and we were listening to the ranting and raving of a guy called Rodney, a Montana Freemen radical militia type. He was lecturing on radical lawyering methods: how to stand up for our rights, how the government used the constitution's interstate commerce clause to oppress us—and such other bullshit.

The Montana Freemen did not recognize the authority of the US Government. They set up their own, the Justus Township. After an eighty-one day standoff with Federal Marshals in 1996, a lot of them got to recognize that part of the authority of the US Government that can keep your ass in jail for a very long time.

So Rodney is drawing some map explaining how the Constitutional Commerce Clause could be used by the Feds in criminal prosecutions. All of a sudden, guards burst into the library, seize the map, and lock me up for an attempted escape— or at least until the investigation thereof can be completed.

They can keep you in the hole for 90 days while whatever trumped up charges against you are being investigated. If nothing is found, well, too bad.

One time in the hole, they gave me a cellmate who was

a convicted child pornographer. I just learned, several days after the fact, that my wife had given birth to our fifth child, Gianna. I don't tolerate "short eyes" types of guys, and being with this one right after the birth of my fifth, made me even less tolerant.

On one occasion, I was choking him by the door of the cell, and told the guards shame on them for bringing this garbage pail into my cell. He was transferred.

Prison does not contain the cream of society. But it is in itself a society, and the lowest form of scum in that society are the rapists, and the child molester/child pornographer types. Would I have further hurt my former cell mate if he hadn't been transferred?

Yes.

Sometimes I was given gentlemen cellmates in the hole. One was Johnny Eng, a major heroin dealer doing twenty-four years, and leader for the Flying Dragons gang. Let me tell you about him.

Gambling in prison causes problems. Somebody owes and doesn't pay, they get hurt. Now the Italians pretty much agreed to avoid gambling, but not everybody. One Anthony Ciampi, a Boston street guy and a co-defendant with my cell-mate, Paulie DeCologero, was in debt to the Chinese gangs. Many thousands he wasn't paying. The Chinese wanted to take him out.

I met with Eng and diffused the situation. The debt was reduced as a favor to me, and a payout arrangement was made. SIS got word of what almost happened and threw us both in the hole. Together.

Eng was from Manhattan. Little Italy, where the Chinese and Italians were right next to each other, sometimes stepping on each other's toes. Eng, with the Flying Dragons, controlled heroin distribution in Chinatown. The Dragons were hooked up with a major Tong organization, the Hip Sings.

Eng had been subject to multiple arrests and was accused

of being one of the five biggest H dealers in New York in the eighties. Gerald Shargel had represented him in his 1992 trial. He was convicted.

Eng, despite his drug dealing, was an educated man, a highly intelligent person. He was guilty of nothing more than the same thing the CIA had done in the Golden Triangle. The CIA that tolerates and supports drug dealing organizations when they are useful information sources. The hypocrisy is obvious.

★

One of the most beneficial things for an inmate is to maintain contact with family and friends on the outside. It can help keep him sane. Denied this, he suffers more.

I have already alluded to the fact that the BOP only allowed three hundred minutes a month for phone time for an inmate. Imagine the effect when that is taken away. I don't have to imagine, it happened to me. Here's how:

It is a violation of phone privileges to make a three way call. In other words, you call Joe, but then Joe connects you to Jack. The security reasons for this are to minimize an inmate from communicating with those engaged in criminal activity on the outside. I understand that, but what I don't get is why they took my privileges away, under the circumstances of my third party call. (Actually I do get it, but I don't get the just part about it, the fair part about it because there is none.)

Around Thanksgiving, 1999, I called my house to speak to my wife. My young daughter, Nicolette answered. She was eight. Now, on inmate calls there is a recording played when the line is picked up by the other party to the conversation. It informs that party that, if they want to reject this particular call, they should hang up, and if they want to accept it, they push 5. If they want to block the number altogether, they are to push 77.

My eight year old hit 77 by mistake. I was blocked from calling home. So I called my sister Victoria, who then called my wife relaying my love to her. Nope. Violation of the phone rules. Off to the Lieutenant's office to find out what my punishment would be.

Phone privileges taken for six months. I had committed the sin of telling my sister to relay my love to my wife. That's it. Six months. Now phone contact is extremely important when you are three hundred miles from your family. Too bad for me.

For outside contact, I had one of my attorneys place a weekly "legal" call to me. It was my only sanctioned way of communicating via phone. My attorney would see to it that my family was informed of how I was doing, and he would inform me as to their welfare.

★

In prison there were some Hell's Angels. One at Ray Brook was a man named "Doc" Prosciutti. He was a senior Angel. Late fifties. Nice guy, class act, and his fiancée, Debbie, who came to visit him, was a real sweetheart who got around in a wheelchair. Doc was on the same cell block as me.

Debbie would always give me a holiday card or just the "thinking of you" type of card. (She would send similar cards to other Hell's Angels.) One time, she sent me a card with $25 in the form of a money order. "A little something to buy some sweets," the card said, or words to that effect. It was a Halloween card. Which, like all of my non-attorney mail is monitored, opened before I get it. Read before I get it. (Sometimes that happened with legal mail too.)

Alarms go off. I'm now shaking down the Hell's Angels. Off to the hole I go, while the matter is under investigation. They want to deprive Doc of 45 days of visits and phone calls, loss of commissary privileges for the same amount of time. They wanted to yank my commissary privileges for forty five days, and terminate visits and phone calls for six months; possible loss of good time too.

The Disciplinary Hearing Officer at the prison thought the

disparity of treatment abusive, and I got the same punishment Doc did. We both appealed the sentence, and on the 44th day of our 45 day punishment, we were told that we had won the appeal.

Hell's Angels are anti-authority, so was I in certain respects. So when guys like us are in prison, those in authority are going to have, what they believe is, their due. They are going to screw with us, put us in the hole for no good reason, just because they can.

Another event which illustrates the above was a time when Ray Brook was planning on installing a fourth security fence of barbed wire. Myself, the President of the Hell's Angels New England chapters, Greg Domey, and one of his top enforcers, Tony Ikes, were called in and asked to take part in the construction of this fence, as this would make it more likely to have other inmates participate. Domey turned to me and asked my position on this, and I told him I would refuse. "So will we," he said on behalf of himself and Ikes.

We all wound up being put in the hole for our refusal. However, when the warden found out, we were quickly removed from the hole, as prisoners are not allowed to be ordered to construct or repair security measures in the prison. The reason, of course, is that it would create hostility among those participating and true convicts.

★

In an environment when you have very little personal property, what you do have can become special. Important. You might have a favorite pillow, or a fork, or bowl. I had a pillow. Whenever I went to the hole, I had someone keep it for me so it would be there when I got back to general population.

You keep your stuff in your cell. When you go to the hole, no more cell, and your stuff is put in storage, bagged and tagged. Provided it hasn't been glommed by someone else before hand.

When you get out of the hole, you are put in a dormitory with up to another dozen prisoners, and you stay there until another cell opens up. Your property is still in storage.

Putting someone in the hole is beautiful psychological torture, if those words can be put in the same sentence. You minimize social interaction, you practically eliminate inmate outside contact, you remove such property as he has. You have made him homeless.

He who dwells in the hole now gets only one hour of rec a day, and that in a rec cage, which is a larger cage than the one he bunks in. Maybe ten feet long, and you get to look at the sky through the cage. Cages are lined up, spaced a few feet apart for the others in the hole. You pace like an animal. You can chin yourself on some of the bars on the top of the cage. But you at least can breathe fresh air.

★

I did get to get away from Ray Brook though. Not on any furlough, but diesel therapy. I will explain.

In November 1999, a 97 page indictment came down from the US Attorney's office in Atlanta, Georgia, regarding a fancy strip club down there, The Gold Club. The indictment said that a friend of mine, Stephen Kaplan (what the government called a *long time associate* of mine), was running a mobbed up strip club. Prostitution and credit card fraud were claimed.

Profits were skimmed and bumped up to the Gambino Family for protection, they said. Kaplan was facing twenty years, if convicted. I wasn't accused personally, but it was alleged that Kaplan had meetings with, and had been controlled by, us since 1988. Kaplan was, they alleged, handing over $2,000 bundles of twenties to a Gambino capo, "M.D." (Michael DiLeonardo.)

Even though he was acquitted by an Atlanta jury, it was DiLeonardo who was getting $500 a week from the Gold Club. No money was kicked upstairs.

Kaplan was out on $2 million bail. The government claimed he had made millions and wanted to seize his home in Oyster Bay Cove. You see, only the government is entitled to profit from crime—they call it forfeiture.

Government allegations spoke of strippers being flown down from South Carolina to stage lesbian acts for some of the team members of the Knicks. They also engaged in "team huddles" with the players. Each girl, supposedly, received one thousand dollars. Basketball stars Patrick Ewing, Charles Oakley, and others were getting free drinks, food, and female companionship. Celebrities were a good thing for the club, good press.

The government called an impressive list of witnesses. Ewing, Atlanta Hawks' Dikembe Mutombo, Atlanta Falcon's Jamal Anderson, Denver Bronco's Terrel Davis, and even Dennis Rodman. All had been supposed beneficiaries at the Gold Club.

The deal was: get the celebs laid, and they hang out at the club, which causes regular Joes to hang out where the celebs hang out. The motivation, according to a quote supposedly made by Kaplan, "Sit a fucking guy down like a jackass and get his money."

A lot of thousand dollar champagne bottles got sold at the Gold Club. Georgia was one of the few places in the U.S., at the time, that allowed full nudity at a bar. Some of the strippers there earned $5,000 a night.

I had never been in the club.

Now, the government wanted me to testify in Atlanta. On April 24, 2000, two guards at Ray Brook wake me up at 4:00 AM. Dress and cuff up. I was brought to Receiving and Delivery. I didn't know why, what was up, or where I was going.

Five marshals in full body armor appear, heavily armed. I get driven from Ray Brook to Albany. I am in a van, shackled up, with SUV escorts. Then I get sent by a small U.S. Marshals plane to Atlanta. Five armed federal agents as company. Flack jackets, shotguns, assault rifles.

I figure out where the Hell I am when I see a "Welcome

to Atlanta" sign at the airport. I am placed in an unmarked car along with two marshals, followed by another car with another two marshals.

They delivered me to a high security prison in Atlanta. The United States Penitentiary in Atlanta. Jimmy Burke, the Irish mobster, had done time there, Al Capone had been there, Thomas Silverstein, of the Aryan Brotherhood, had been there.

Now I was at the Receiving and Delivery when I am greeted by Warden Willie Scott. Big man. Small on charm. He had been the warden at MCC when my father was there in 1991. He had placed him in the hole there.

We don't exactly hit it off. This was his house, and I was going to live by his rules.

I told him that on the outside the roles would be reversed. But I didn't get sent to the SHU. He sends me to what serves as the hole. In the abandoned portion of the prison. The former psychiatric wing.

It was where the worst conditions in the prison existed. I was stripped, given an overly large and filthy pair of boxer shorts to wear, and chains. Belly chains; handcuffs.

I was put in a six by ten cage. Two inch foam mattress on the bed, just a sheet. A toilet and a sink that probably would have worked if there had been any running water. There wasn't. My urine and feces accumulated in the toilet.

I was under video surveillance constantly. When I used the bathroom facilities, I would wet some toilet paper and put it over the camera lens, so I would have at least some modicum of privacy.

I had to bang on the cage that separated me from the cell door to get drinking water from the guards.

There were two temperatures in the hole. Blazing hot during the day in that steel cell in Georgia, freezing during the night when they turned on the air conditioning full blast. Lights on 24/7. A continually buzzing noise from a light outside of the cell to keep me company. If you are thinking sleep deprivation, right you are. Another attempt to break me.

The above conditions, worse than we treat terrorists in Guantanamo, existed for a week.

I had suffered such sleep deprivation that I began to hallucinate. I saw, as clearly as you see whatever you might be looking at now, my deceased brother, Frankie. He stood there, staring at me, and I told him, "I'm cold." He walked over to me, sat on the bed, and then vanished.

★

At one point, I was taken from the cage, shackled up, and given a thirty second "physical exam." On the way back from that cursory examination, I was told by a Lieutenant, "Just answer the subpoena."

If I cooperated, the implication was I'd be sent right back to Ray Brook. So the conditions they put me under in Georgia were designed to do one thing: break me into testifying. It didn't work of course.

My lawyers find out where I am, and how I am being housed. My attorney, Richard Rehbock, had found out my location and contacted a local attorney, Linda Sheffield, an expert in prisoner's rights and federal litigation against the prison system.

She paid me a visit, and was appalled at my appearance, and the conditions under which I was being held. As she stared at me from the other side of the non-contact booth where the visit took place, she exclaimed, "What the Hell happened to you!"

Linda had known me for years. I had taken her to dinner when discussing my father's situation several times. Now, staring at the unshaven, unshowered mess on the other side of the glass, she could see what the government was trying to do. I tried to make light of my situation.

Sheffield called over a guard. "I want to see somebody

right now." Pointing to me, she said, "He needs a shower, he needs a shave, I am leaving right now, and when I come back tomorrow to visit him, I want to see him showered and shaved."

She turned to me and said, "I'm leaving, I'll be back tomorrow morning."

I told her, "Don't worry about me, I'll be fine. Stop complaining you're embarrassing me."

"Bullshit!" she said, and left.

★

I got my shower. Six guards came into my cell, told me I was getting a shower, then shackled me up again. I was brought to the shower in a cage, and when they took me out, they belly chained me with my hands in the front.

Obviously, with such limited range of motion, it was rather difficult to adequately make one's ablutions. I mentioned this to the guards watching, and they said, "That's the rules. You want a shower this is how you're getting it."

I could tell they weren't comfortable with this. When I went back to the cell, I was given a razor. They watched me shave, and took back the razor when I was done. One of the guards turned to me and said, "Mr. G, it's not us."

I knew that, and told them so. "I know who it is, no problem. Don't worry, I got a lot of game in me."

So did Rehbock. Sheffield made it clear that I was not going to respond to the subpoena. After several weeks, she got me transferred from that cell from Hell. Judge Hunt, who was presiding over the Gold Club case, required my presence in the court.

He also demanded that I be moved from my cell in the abandoned psychiatric wing. I was moved to the hole. Isolated. Locked in all day, no rec, one phone call a week. Shower twice a week. Not great, but better than where I had just come from.

Then, before my court appearance before Judge Hunt, I

was moved to a regular cell, alternate day showers, but still locked up all the time. Still once a week phone call.

AUSA Arthur Leach served my lawyers with papers demanding I testify at the Gold trial. Richard Rehbock, said, "It is not his intention to testify in the case, and he will exercise his right not to speak. He really has no business being there."

We knew the government was trying to set a trap for me. They forced me on the stand, but all I quoted was my rights under the Fifth Amendment. The government didn't like that at all. There was a secret hearing on the 17th floor of the Federal courthouse, Judge Willis Hunt presiding. I was there to answer four questions about my alleged involvement with the Gold Club. The prosecutors said I had no right to refuse to testify, my attorneys said they were trying to set a perjury trap, ergo the hearing. AUSA Leach was not even allowed to attend the hearing.

All of my answers were "Fifth Amendment." In his decision, Judge Hunt, after determining that I was still the target of several investigations, said I did have the right to invoke my Fifth Amendment rights.

The subpoena was quashed, and I was ordered back to my cell forthwith.

Ewing did testify. Received oral sex from the dancers. So much for a role model sports figure who was married with children. Kaplan eventually took a plea deal with the government. On August 2, 2001, he pled guilty to racketeering charges involving fraudulently inflating credit card bills and using strippers as hookers. He was looking at three years. He was sentenced to sixteen months, 400 hours of community service, a $5 million dollar forfeiture, restitution of a quarter million to 100 credit card fraud victims, and $50,000 to Delta Airlines for scamming tickets.

"I'm like a cancerous person, nobody wants to be with me anymore except my friends. Everybody's afraid of me, everybody points to me," said Kaplan after his sentencing. For the measly $500 we got from him he was a cancer, way too much trouble for us. He lied about the club as far as we were concerned—to me, in his running of his operation, he acted like nothing more than a pimp.

The judge said the government was relatively unsuccessful in proving Kaplan's mob ties. Leach, the prosecutor, said, "We did our job."

★

I had been housed under horrific conditions, but I came back ready to go at it with the government. Maybe it's the influence my father had on me, maybe the support of friends and family helped me, and definitely, it was the fact that I had learned my lesson since 1998—I would fight the government every step of the way from then on.

But not everyone is so resilient. Craig DePalma had also been called as a witness in the Gold case. DePalma had been a soldier in my crew. As you have already read, I was there when he was straightened out. He had been in jail related to the Scores case.

Now, DePalma was being housed in the hole. His time in there ruined him. He was deeply depressed. This man, who was superbly built, who was so well groomed he might have been a metrosexual, had lost significant amounts of weight; his appearance had gone to shit.

They brought him to the courtroom after the trial had commenced. He broke down in the courtroom and kept saying, "I just want to leave." The judge instructed that DePalma be sent back to his low security prison.

But the government left DePalma in his cell to rot for several weeks longer. He found a way out. In October of 2002, he hung himself with a bed sheet from a bunk bed. When they found him, he was still alive, but basically brain dead.

Eight plus years later, in 2011, at the age of 44, he died in a nursing home, never regaining consciousness from his coma. I had cried when I learned of his hanging, and was remorsefully relieved when he passed.

Craig was a fellow that I had cared for deeply. A good kid. I never felt comfortable bringing him into the Life. He wanted it, and his father (for whom I had gradually lost respect) pushed it. Once, I had taken Craig to dinner, along with Jackie Cavallo, a long-time friend. I tried my hardest to dissuade him from joining.

He would hear none of it, so I green-lighted his entry. Reluctantly.

I am reviewing files while I write this, and one document I am looking at is a card that Craig sent me before they had taken him to Atlanta. He mailed it to a prison post office box and then either his brother or girlfriend forwarded it to me.

There is a cute little cartoon rabbit on the card cover, with the words "There's nothing worse than a close friend..." and the inside punch line is "far away! Miss you."

On the blank part of the card, Craig had written:

John-Hey Pal! How are things with you? I heard that you are in great shape. Glad to hear that. How are your mom and dad doing? I hope well. How are your wife and children doing? Hope that everyone is well and healthy. Well, pal, from the inside, (heart) I miss you and always think about you. I saw a special on the NY Jets. Joe Namath was hosting it and showing his camp on TV. We'll see if the Jets can beat my team, the Dolphins this year. Well, pal, just a little note to say hello and miss you. Love always, Your Friend, Paul Crew.

That's how Craig signed the card, and how he signed all the cards he sent me. You see, Paul Crew was the quarterback on the prison team in the movie *The Longest Yard*.

You cannot have a prisoner directly corresponding with another prisoner. That's why Craig had to mail the card to a box, and then someone else had to pick it up and get it to me.

He couldn't sign Craig DePalma on the card, so he used the alias, Paul Crew.

Craig, wherever you are, I miss you too pal.

★

Now it was time for the government to do a number on me for not testifying at the Gold Trial. Diesel therapy. I was flown down to Atlanta pretty quickly. The journey back to Ray Brook took somewhat longer. Back to Atlanta airport in the dark. Loads of prisoners lined up awaiting transport. Marshals dressed for war. Me, some Aryan Brotherhood types and a D.C. bank robber are the last to board the plane. In the back of a Con Air 747 Jet. I am shackled again, black-box manacled, it is very difficult to move.

From Atlanta, I was bussed to a privately run prison somewhere in Georgia, back to Atlanta, on to North Carolina, then I wound up in New Hampshire. A short stay. Then to Stewart Air Force Base in upstate New York. Then to MDC in Brooklyn. In the hole. I got to hear government star witness, Sammy Gravano, who was in a cell not too far from mine. He was crying and complaining about everything, according to what an orderly, named Joseph "Baldy" Pistone,* had told me. Not very bull like at all. But Hell, my room at the MDC has a shower, things aren't so bad. I'm close to family and my lawyers.

I just get to sleep at MDC after my long journey, and I hear a voice calling me. "John?" It's me, Carmine." I got a surprise visit in the hole from my brother-in-law. Carmine Agnello who also was doing time at MDC. He got himself thrown in the hole on a make believe offense, just to talk to me, tell me he loves me. The word had spread like wildfire around the jail that I had arrived. Carmine had heard from other inmates I was being held in the hole.

We were looking forward to seeing each other at recreation the next day. It had been years. Unfortunately, the guards

---

* Not to be mistaken with FBI agent Joseph Pistone, aka Donnie Brasco.

got wise and the next day, the captain of the guards came and Carmine was taken out of the hole. Personally escorted.

So Carmine, naturally wanting to see me, comes calling. Nothing dangerous, nothing nefarious, just camaraderie. The result? Well, it is the first time I heard of the guards throwing an inmate *out* of the hole.

★

I don't stay long at MDC Brooklyn. I am carted off to Philadelphia MDC for a short stay. As soon as I am comfortable there, I am taken out.

Then sent to Lewisburg Penitentiary. This Pennsylvania Federal Prison was constructed in 1931, and opened in 1932, prior to completion. Despite its purpose as a modern dungeon, it is actually based on an Italian Renaissance Palazzo.

There have been some famous inmates at Lewisburg. Clifford Irving, the author of the bogus Howard Hughes biography, Jimmy Hoffa, and my father. As I have mentioned before, my father was sentenced to Lewisburg, after pleading guilty to hijacking back in 1968. He did three years there.

So here I was, more than thirty years later, entering Lewisburg for what turned out for less than two months. I am reminded of my visits with my father. A little kid going through iron gates, gaping opened mouthed at large forbidding walls. Staring up at the large tower as though it were a castle. Seeing my father in this prison with pretensions of being a palazzo.

Only now, the childish illusions are gone, and the shackles are reminders of where I am and how I am to be treated.

The first guard who greets me is obviously an old timer at the prison. A veteran. He's polite though, a decent guy. Tells me how much I look like my father, and that he was first starting out in Lewisburg when my father was an inmate there from '69–72. Half a lifetime spent working amongst misery, violence, and pointless routine.

"Sorry to hear that," I joke with him.

"Yeah, me too," he agrees.

The pleasantries don't last very long, for the captain of the guards appears and hurries me off to the next station at receiving and deliveries. Processing. About a hundred guys stripped naked waiting to be bunched up to get a jumpsuit, and move on to the next station at this assembly line, where names are processed into prison numbers.

Normally, an incoming prisoner goes to what is called I-block. It is a reception block. That's normally. For whatever reasons, I am thrown immediately into the hole.

The hole consisted of two man cells which were probably the filthiest Special Housing Unit I had ever been in. Two inch high water from flooded out toilets overtook the tier. You had to stuff whatever pieces of sheet that you had under the door so to stop the water from flowing into cell. The stench of piss and shit was everywhere.

At 6:00 AM, they would come escort you to the rec cages which were numerous, 15 x 15 foot, cages, side by side and across from each other. You would be individually placed in your cage, you could do pushups, burpees (a combination of pushup, toe touch and arm raises), or just pace back and forth.

After several weeks, I was moved to I-block. I-block is split into two sides. One medium to high security and the other for low security inmates. The higher security side housed between 150–180 inmates, the low security side between 60–80.

That's almost two hundred inmates in high security that share three toilets, three showers, and two pairs of shower shoes.

Lewisburg had an infestation of mice. The cells had three man bunks, instead of the usual two levels. Not knowing about the mice problem, I grabbed the lowest of the three man bunk beds in my cell. It was about six inches from the floor. Food trays get brought into the block and the prisoners eat in their cell. I saved a piece of fruit from the dinner tray for later. I placed it at the foot of my bed. In the middle of the night I feel a nibbling at my feet where the fruit was. Several mice. I rip off the blanket and they high tail it out of the cell.

The next day I slept in the middle bunk.

The showers were breeding grounds for disease. There was filthy brackish water, inches deep, that the prisoners must wade through. Human waste and other "products" float by. The Ganges is a crystalline lake compared to the showers at Lewisburg.

★

Eventually back to Ray Brook. Home sweet home, finally. So much for diesel therapy. (Prison buses are diesel.) More like cruel and unusual punishment for an inmate that was not charged with anything with respect to the Atlanta Gold case.

Back in my bunk at Ray Brook, I reflect on the fact that while it had taken me three hours to get down to Atlanta, when the government wanted my testimony, it took me several months to get back when they didn't get it.

★

I'm in the shower. I feel a hard bump on my left buttocks. Soon one became many. Some had grown to the size of walnuts, hard and oozing. So I had submitted a cop-out to see medical. Several days later I was put on the call-out sheet, (prison schedule for the next day), to see a physician's assistant

After he saw me, I was given a cream to put on my bumps, which had no effect. At this point I was running a low grade fever for several days and the infection had spread from my left buttock down to past my left knee. I put in another cop-out in several days.

The physician's assistant saw me, and admitted he didn't know what to do. He would have to get back to me. Two more weeks pass.

While on a visit with my family, my visit is terminated and I am escorted to the medical unit. I was locked down in medical for security reasons. I was about to travel outside of the prison, and they didn't want me to tell anyone.

At five in the morning I am loaded into a prison van, and brought to Saranac Lake Hospital, where I am seen by a real doctor. I told him that back at Ray Brook I was told my infection was likely a bite from a brown recluse spider. It was in their report.

The Doctor laughed. He said it was a staph infection (bad). I needed to come back in the next few days for treatment and some of the buboes that had formed needed to be drained. He wrote a request to Ray Brook, and said he would see me in a couple of days.

His request was ignored. Finally, six weeks later, the same drill of security procedures, then back to Saranac hospital. I had protested that I no longer needed medical treatment, but I was sent anyway The Doctor, upon seeing me, was furious with the prison escorts, and yelled, "I told Ray Brook I wanted to see him in days, not weeks!"

"Security did not permit it," they said. The doctor then checked me out and miraculously my body had cleared most of the infections. All that were left were scabs and dead skin, for the most part. I was issued some stronger topical medicine to help clear the remaining infections.

It would not be the last time I would be medically neglected by BOP.

CHAPTER TWENTY-ONE

The Last Days of John J. Gotti

An avidity to punish is always dangerous to liberty. It leads men to stretch, to misinterpret, and to misapply even the best of laws. He that would make his own liberty secure must guard even his enemy from oppression; for if he violates this duty he establishes a precedent that will reach to himself. —Thomas Paine (1795)

The caravan of black hummers pulled up to the well guarded building. From the vehicles, heavily armed men in camouflage spilled out, forming a protective perimeter. From one of the vehicles, a man, heavily manacled, emerged, held by some of the men.

The guards were ready in case of an escape attempt, in case of a rescue being tried to free their captive. Their automatic weapons were locked and loaded. Their eyes searching for trouble.

Who was the chained man? An international terrorist? A convicted spy?

No. It was John J. Gotti, my father. A convicted criminal yes, but one who not only never attempted a prison escape in the times he was incarcerated, but never even missed a court appearance.

There was an inmate witness to this Federally sponsored theatrical production:

> I was personally present to witness the actions that took place upon the arrival of Mr. Gotti...While being situated in the receiving and discharge unit where I had a clear view of what appeared to be a military action environment with guards dressed in camouflage with automatic machine guns in the woods and buses to secure the area for the arrival of Mr. Gotti. During this time period in which Mr. Gotti was brought into the Springfield facility it appeared that the whole institution was under a lock down status. [affidavit of Mr. Brown]

★

I was incarcerated in Ray Brook while my father was dying. Obviously, my knowledge of what took place during those times is secondhand from my conversations with my brother Peter, his journal notes, and talks with other family members. Peter was on hand during the final months, on site, until the end. He watched my father die slowly, denied the doctors he needed, forbidden necessary treatment, while the government got it all on tape. John J. Gotti was treated worse than a Guantanamo terrorist. They at least get decent medical care. John J. Gotti, an American Citizen, tortured by Government employees, who were only following orders.

> I observed that another high profile inmate by the name of Manuel Noriega was situated in a cell that appeared to be a suite when to my knowledge Mr. Gotti was in an isolated cell in the hole. [affidavit of Mr. Fagon]

Noriega's attorney at the time, Frank Rubio, disclosed that the Panamanian Dictator and Drug Dealer had a bad case of the flu. He got the suite. My father, who had from neglect in prison contracted stage four cancer, got the hole.

Those of you reading this only learned about this period in my father's life from the media. The media is a fact filter that does not purify, but soils and distorts truth. I will try and set the record straight in this chapter, and have the truth be finally told.

In the course of doing so, I will mix narrative with the actual journal entries of my brother, and affidavits and documents from others, as I feel this will be most effective in conveying the cowardly torture by the government of a man's man.

I will also add the views of history's great men, with respect to the nature of government, so that the reader will not think that I am spinning a story only as a fact filter equal to the media.

★

From my observations of what I heard through conversations between the staff and other inmates, it was stated that Mr. Gotti was being placed in isolation and being denied any of the privileges afforded myself and other inmates. From the view that I had gotten when I saw Mr. Gotti arrive it appeared that he was in very poor health. [affidavit of Mr. Fagon]

May this chapter reveal the intentional maltreatment and medical neglect by the prison system of a man who was perhaps the last of the old time gangsters: he lived according to a code, and he died according to one.

When governments commit crimes of violence, then there is no law to respect except that of survival, that of the jungle. My father was familiar with those statutes.

You might not like what he stood for, but remember, John J. Gotti was standing up all of his life, not kneeling down. The good guys of the Federal Government might have helped destroy the body of John J. Gotti, but they never put a dent in his spirit, and although he might have died in a cage, there was never any lion tamer in there with him.

> The only power any government has is the power to crack down on criminals. Well, when there aren't enough criminals, one makes them. One declares so many things to be a crime that it becomes impossible to live without breaking laws. [Ayn Rand, *Atlas Shrugged*]

★

Federal Prison is not usually known for the quality of its inmate health care. After all, the prison inhabitants, the unwilling ones, are the convicted, the condemned, society's outcasts or rebels. Those who did not tow the line, fit in, or play straight.

They are there to be punished. That is the reality. As to the concept of rehabilitation, that is purely a myth. Behavior modification—that there is. Within these type of boundaries, within these parameters, it is to be expected that those who administer the prisons are not very interested in the quality of life of the prisoners, until violations of human rights become public, either via the media, dedicated organizations, or via the court system.

Bureaucracy is a giant mechanism operated by pygmies.
—Honore de Balzac

Prison reform comes only after enough voices have screamed sufficiently long and loud for politicians to hear. On issues of prisoner rights, politicians are rather deaf. My father never screamed. He never sought the courts or the media to redress his treatment. He took the torture, never complained. He died without complaint. Perhaps it could be said that his character was a contributing cause to his untimely death. It was the foundation of his honor, in life or in death.

The news media were there on the death watch, the countdown to the death of the man they called the Teflon Don—but where were the investigative reporters when it concerned the violation of my father's human rights?

Where were the glaring headlines about intentionally substandard medical treatment for a high profile inmate.

Where were the voices on the six o'clock news with promises of *"film at eleven?"*

That particular silence was deafening.

I have already mentioned in a previous chapter how I almost lost a leg due to prison medical neglect. I recovered thanks only to the healing ministrations of time, and a young and resilient immune system.

What I went through was nothing compared to the suffering of my father. Cancer wasn't tougher than he was, merely more deadly, because the weapons needed to fight it were not forthcoming. When it came to cancer, the government denied him his fighting chance.

I can never be persuaded that this denial was other than intentional.

There is a unit at the Springfield facility in Section 1–4 entitled the Terminally Ill Unit. This is where people like Mr. Gotti, who are suffering with a terminal illness are put to make them comfortable while serving out their last days of life. I heard (Guards) P_____ and S_____ state that under the direct orders of the Warden...You will never make it to that unit... assuring him that they wanted him to die alone and miserable. The ill treatment towards Mr. Gotti went on everyday while I was there, and since Officers P_____ and S_____ did not rotate areas of the prison like the other officers did (I witnessed two rotations while I was there and these same two officers remained). They were able to continue their actions uninterrupted and unmonitored even though you could tell that the Supervisor(s) of greater authority knew what was going on. When superiors were around they would tend to show off how bad they treated Mr. Gotti. . . .

I could see that Mr. Gotti was not feeling or looking well and should have not been treated in such a degrading manner. There was no justifiable reason why he could not have been taken to the terminally ill area of the prison, since through the staff's own comments he met the requirements to be housed there.

Mr. Gotti did not present any danger to the staff or inmates nor did he commit any disciplinary violations that I was aware of. To me he conducted himself like a perfect gentleman, considering the conditions he was forced to live under and endure on a day by day hour by hour basis, that was inflicted on him by the administration and staff.

I only hope that someone of authority will have the power and decency to correct the inhumane punishment of a man who is even too weak with cancer to defend himself. I don't know exactly what type of sentence he was given, but his current treatment is nothing different than the medieval days of being whipped, starved and severely tortured in a dungeon. [affidavit of Mr. Brown]

★

My father had dental implants in 1990. He was told by his dentist that they would require regular care and maintenance. He entered Marion in 1992. No regular dental care and maintenance there. It was a supermax prison. It didn't get any tougher than Marion.

But there was plenty of time at Marion. Time to be locked up in isolation 23.5 hours a day. Time to be fed a survival diet in your cell. Chained up when you took a shower. Chained to a concrete slab in your cell, spreadeagled and naked, if you act up or even if the guards were having a bad day, and wanted you to pay for it.

The conversations between the staff was that the Warden who was previously in control of Marion when Mr. Gotti was there, had a strong personal dislike of Mr. Gotti, and was determined to make his life as miserable as possible... [affidavit of Mr. Fagon]

There wasn't much time for visits or phone calls for my father. Any visits were through plate glass. No human contact. Any non-lawyer phone calls were monitored. You got one fifteen minute phone call every ten days. (Now prisoners get 300 minutes per month.)

No time for visits from a private dentist. Not allowed. No time for visits from a private physician. Against regulations.

Plenty of prison regulations. Everything designed to crush a man's spirit, reduce him to a mere caged animal. Didn't work in John J. Gotti's case, however. He had his pride. He also had his hatred for those who hid behind a government good guy badge. But there was one trick they still had up their sleeve, this government of the people, by the people, and for the people.

Marion had its own medical staff. .

My father developed severe gum disease in prison, about two years after he entered. For years he did not receive proper treatment. Technically, there was a dental treatment program in Marion. You would fill out a "cop out" form, a request, wait for someone to get around to responding, and get a date to be seen by a dental *assistant*, which on that day, could take you sometime between 5:30 AM and 3:00 PM to get seen. You'd go to this appointment chained up and escorted by guards. What did you get? A mouth rinse.

My father, knowing this routine, and its futility, refused this treatment. Finally, he took matters into his own hands—literally. He pulled the agonizing implants from his own mouth, and blood and pus issued forth.

Denied proper medical attention, he resorted to the old

ways. For the infection—garlic. He rubbed it regularly on his open wounds. It helped to some degree, since garlic does have both antiviral and antibacterial properties. He was able to get garlic in prison, until they took his commissary away from him. I believe, had the authorities known the uses to which its government issued garlic was put, they would have denied my father this sooner.

But the old ways can only do so much. Modern medicine is sometimes required. By the time some professional attention was paid to my father's gum condition, it was discovered that most of the lower jaw bone had rotted.

It had to be filed down, partially removed, and replaced with titanium.

They gave him a titanium jaw. That they did. They just forgot to give him dentures for about a year. Oh they promised dentures, and they finally gave him some that didn't fit, but they never got around to giving him a proper set while he was alive. My father ate what he could with his gums.

All but nine of Mr. Gotti's teeth were removed in January 1997, but he has not yet received his false teeth. [letter by Linda Sheffield Esq. to Warden Bill R. Hedrick, Marion, 10/28/97].

He has been physically well enough for false teeth for many months, he has been fitted twice for new teeth, yet none have been provided. Inquiries to Warden Bill R. Hedrick have gone unanswered...[letter by Linda Sheffield Esq. to Director Federal Bureau of Prisons, 11/17/97]

Marion taught me to enjoy every meal, and to be thankful for the meal, and the company you are blessed with, for my father ate 6,000 meals alone in his cell, half of them without his teeth. [journal of Peter J. Gotti, undated]

So much for the Eighth Amendment.

There was more in store for my father after they replaced his jaw. They sent him directly back to Marion.

June '98 Marion Penitentiary
I vividly recall a particular visit as if it were yesterday. It's Uncle Pete, myself and family. My father is a bit agitated. Half way through the visit he excuses my family and I, and asked to speak with my Uncle Pete alone. Dad explains in explicit detail that he has a sensation and lump in his throat like he never had before, and explains that he has had a sore throat for weeks. His repeated requests to have his throat checked go unanswered. He explains to my uncle that he feels it is cancer. [journal of Peter J. Gotti]

Several months later, when the prison medical staff finally checked out my father's condition, they diagnosed stage four head and neck cancer.

For those who are not familiar with the stages of cancer, stage four often means—get your affairs in order—the cancer is inoperable and has spread to other parts of the body.

It is a miracle, a testament to my father's will and strength that he survived as long as he did.

Regular dental care could have diagnosed the problem early. Regular dental care could have checked the gum infections before they ate into my father's jaw, before they helped cause the cancer that killed him.

But this was Marion. This was John Gotti.

Now it is true that people who use alcohol and tobacco products have a higher risk of cancer. It is true that my father smoked and drank, but he had quit long before his prison sentence. It had been 27 years since his last cigarette, eight years since his last drink, at the time of his diagnosis. Bureau of Prisons blamed alcohol and tobacco for the cancer. Not surprising.

It is also true that unchecked gum infections can, among

other serious consequences, lead to cancer. Dental care at Marion? At Marion, even brushing your teeth could be hazardous to your health. Read well the following:

> On September 28, 1990, a report issued by the Agency for Toxic Substances and Disease Registry (ATSDR) (U.S. Dept. of Health Services) confirms that the Marion water supply is toxic and presents a health threat to prisoners. The reports states that the most immediate concern is the high levels of Trihalomethanes (THM's), including chloroform, in the water. Some of the tested water samples contain more than twice the amount of THM's established as an acceptable level by the Environmental Protection Agency (EPA). ["Prison Legal News," https://www.prisonlegalnews.org]

When my father's commissary privileges were rescinded, it also terminated his access to bottled water for drinking. The only alternative then was the carcinogenic water being pumped into the prison.

Guards and visitors had the benefit of posted warning signs stating that the water in Marion was not potable. Prisoners did not.

Marion has been notorious with human rights organizations, and those who believe that prisoners still remain human beings. Here are some relevant facts:

The 1987 John Howard Association Report concluded that Marion:

> is not a normal maximum-security prison on lockdown status but rather a firmly established, fully functioning behavior modification program...the Marion program seems to be designed to break the defiant spirit and behavior...through a year or more of sensory and psychological deprivation [in which] prisoners are stripped of their individual identities...

Prisoners normally stayed no longer than two years at Marion. Many left insane. My father holds the record for an inmate who did not commit a BOP infraction in lockdown at Marion. He stayed mentally fit until he died.

The 1987 Report of Amnesty International stated that:

> within Marion, violations of the [United Nations] Standard Minimum Rules [for the Treatment of Prisoners] are common... There is hardly a rule in the Standard Minimum Rules that is not infringed in some way or other." ["Supermax Prisons" by Erica Thompson and Jan Susler in *Criminal Injustice* 1996]

Independent findings; not my opinions. Findings made prior to my father ever being imprisoned at Marion. So this chapter is not propaganda, not a vendetta. It is merely a recitation of the record—the true record.

Marion is an embarrassment to a country that calls itself "the land of the free." Marion is the supermax superstar government prison showpiece chock full of Eighth Amendment violations. It was the first security Level Six prison in the country. A depository for the prison system's worst. Those who tried to escape, those who killed other prisoners and/ or guards—that's what was normally sent to Marion. The government, acting on its own, after a judicial commitment of my father to a maximum security facility (level 5), sent him to Marion, a Level Six Supermax prison.

> Please note that he [Gotti] is classified as a Separation [sic] from numerous individuals. He is also classified as a Special Supervision and Broad Publicity case. [memo by Warden Willie Scott regarding the commitment of my father to Marion, 4/3/91]

(You will remember the name Willie Scott as the warden who "greeted" me at the penitentiary at Atlanta in 2001.)

Cruel and unusual punishment at Marion was not only

extant, it was a daily occurrence. It was routine, it was standard operating procedure.

> *The illegal we do immediately. The unconstitutional takes a bit longer.*—Henry Kissinger

Marion is what you find when you pick up the rock of the Federal Prison System, and look under it. It is a crawling testimony to the real truth about government, our government, any government.

Those who rule, rule by intimidation, oppression, and deceit. Get out of line, and sooner or later it's lockdown. Become enough of a public challenge to authority, and you are sooner or later placed in a publicly financed hell like Marion. As the John Howard Association report had said, *"The Marion program seems to be designed to break the defiant spirit and behavior…"* [emphasis added]

Couldn't say it better myself.

There are dangerous inmates, those who can't be controlled, that require a Marion (or now ADX Colorado) that have the highest security conditions, level six.

Sometimes I think the only difference between the United States and a Third World dictatorship is that we have more consumer goods, better plumbing, and more television channels. I am not making an attempt at humor, I am deadly serious.

Come to think of it, whatever Fidel Castro did against human rights, he greatly improved the education and health care standards of the average Cuban. Castro, the enemy of our government for almost fifty years. The longest lasting dictator in modern history.

But Cuba has good health care for all, and many people in the United States do not. Such is our government.

You might not believe the opinions of John A. Gotti. I understand.

How about the father of our country?

Government is not reason; it is not eloquence; it is force.
Like fire, it is a dangerous servant and a fearful master.
—George Washington

The life sentence my father had received was becoming more of a death sentence, due to medical neglect by prison authorities.

September '98
Our family was granted a couple of visits behind glass after the diagnosis. My father's surgery was scheduled, but for so called security reasons we were not told when, or where, or how. We were only informed that he has a 20% chance of not coming off the table. [journal of Peter J. Gotti]

Prison physicians. How do they do it? How can they forget that portion of the Hippocratic oath which states, "Whatever houses I may visit, I will come for the benefit of the sick, remaining free of all intentional injustice, of all mischief..."

The reality of prison medical care is that it is conducted for the most part by physician assistants and those under them. An actual medical doctor might come in once a week.

If you treated a dog with the medical neglect with which my father was subject to, you would find yourself imprisoned. But dogs don't defeat Federal Cases, dogs don't publicly celebrate their victories. Dogs don't wink at the camera while thumbing their nose at what passes for "authority." As I write this, I feel the anger rising in me. I want to do violence to somebody or something. But how do you strike a blow with a fist at a procedural construct? How do you kick a perception? There is only one way. Through exposure. Through this book, for example. Through reports of organizations made up of people who care about human rights. Perhaps, one fine day, through legislation. (We should be so lucky.)

Human rights violations need the weapon of the pen, prior to the use of the sword. I am holding on tight to my pen, and I have a lifetime supply of ink.

After 30+ radiation treatments, my father was clear of cancer in March '99 ... Post surgery and radiation treatments removed nearly 60 pounds from his frame...

Upon one of the last monthly visits from his doctor, he was told that he was clear of cancer and did not need to be checked so often. [journal of Peter J. Gotti, undated]

This was according to prison physicians. My father's personal physician, after reading my father's files, and consulting with his partner who was an oncologist, knew that this type of cancer that my father had could reappear at any minute, and wrote a letter containing the following advice:

In my medical opinion I believe that Mr. Gotti should be cared for in a facility which has access to this [fiberoptic laryngoscopy equipment] and other procedure or treatment that he requires...Stage IV A Squamous cell carcinoma of the right tonsil has a relatively high degree of local recurrence and a reasonably high degree of distant metastases. [letter by Dr. F. Santi DiFranco MD, 3/11/99]

Advice that was intentionally ignored. As a result:

Shortly afterwards in September, 2000, squamous cell head and neck cancer returned with a vengeance. My dad, who spent his entire life defying odds was given one year to live, and shipped back to Springfield to slowly die in a completely isolated steel door enclosed hospital cell ... [journal of Peter Gotti]

But in this tragedy was one blessing. Contact visits with immediate family were allowed in a conference room at the

Springfield medical facility. As my brother notes:

> For people that were starved of contact with him for so many years even this bare minimal improvement in conditions was magical. Our children were able to sit next to him. It required his dying for the government to allow him the simple pleasure of touching his grandchildren. [journal of Peter J. Gotti, undated]

But the considerate Warden at Springfield, who allowed contact visits, was quickly replaced by the Warden of Marion, Bill Hedrick, who had not only a special hatred for my father, but constructed at Springfield, a special booth for non-contact visits for my father, while other inmates at the prison hospital had contact visits, and much greater freedom of movement.

I was not letting this go unchallenged. In a letter dated November 28, 2000, I wrote to Hedrick, the following:

> I am sending you this letter to give you formal notice that I have notarized affidavits from individuals that have direct knowledge of the treatment of my father in your facility and under your supervision.
>
> Additionally I have conclusive evidence from a person that was part of your medical staff that confirms the ill treatment of my father on your watch, that initiated in Marion and has spilled over to your present command in Springfield. Establishing that you do in fact have a culpable mental state as to any and all ill treatment towards my father in an unjustified retaliatory manner.
>
> This formal notice comes to you to make you aware that you will be subject in your individual as well as official capacity to a civil action.
>
> Although my father has put stringent restraints on the execution of this civil litigation, I must let you know that if and when he does pass away that I will proceed to the fullest

extent of the law in this litigation against you and other officials of the BOP including specific members of your staff, Officers P_____ and S_____."

I had sent a private investigator to talk to a former physician's assistant at Marion prior to sending the letter. He had left Marion, among various reasons, due to his frustration with the care of my father, or the lack thereof.

I had wanted to sue Hedrick and the government for my father's ill treatment, but my father, proud soldier that he was, refused to permit it.

★

It so often happens that in the midst of human misery, there are lighter moments, points of time where the comedy of the human condition takes center stage in the tragedy. My brother's journal notes one such time:

> In the next year we watched the prison doctors' predictions of death come and go. My father set small goals in regards to his health and tackled them one at a time. He drank plenty of Ensure, and took down anything soft that contained a high caloric content to give him the strength and energy to fight...We were able to purchase soft food items from the vending room. One day he came to realize that sometimes these machines carried Lasagna. My father was a world class eater. Loved his food. But by this time he could no longer take down any solid food, so he commented, "one way or another I'll force it down, (he loved Lasagna) If I can't eat it the normal way, I'll shove it up my ass." [journal of Peter J. Gotti, undated]

I wasn't around for that light moment. I knew my father was dying, and he was being neglected. Out of frustration and desperation, I even wrote Janet Reno, Attorney General:

I respectfully request your intervention and consideration for some measure of compassion for my family. Solitary confinement is no place for anyone to suffer a virulent and painful disease. He (John J. Gotti) does not ask for any relaxation of his custody, it is my family and I who ask for this consideration. I ask this as his son, and as one of many who are concerned about his very poor health. I respectfully request that you respond, to my attention, your views on this situation. Thank you for your consideration. [my letter to Reno, dated 10/12/99]

In that letter, I even suggested they lock *me* up in Springfield, under the much stricter conditions there than that I would have in Ray Brook. I would take solitary, if I could at least care for my dying father:

I am requesting that I be able to be assigned to the same facility. I am only requesting that I be able to have minimal contact with him each day, such as his one hour out of solitary time...Even though my custody status is far below a solitary confinement inmate, I am perfectly willing to be housed similarly with him or in the same unit.

Janet Reno (whom you may remember as having ordered the actions which resulted in the deaths of many children during the Waco incident at the Branch Davidians compound) gave me all the consideration one could expect from the government to a Gotti. She ignored my letter.

In October of 2000, I had written Amnesty International, the human rights organization, as my father's torture at Marion continued.

I am sending you this letter in great sincerity primarily (1) to thank you for investing your valuable time and concern into the grave situation involving my father as well as (2) your visit made to the Springfield Bureau of Prisons "BOP" facility on or about the first week of October 2000.

Please accept my apology, in that I do not feel that my father meant to insult anyone in refusing to see any of the caring representatives from your foundation when they arrived at the BOP facility in Springfield, MO. My father is just a person with old time "old fashioned" beliefs which prevent him from asking for help from anyone; nor will he accept assistance if it is thrust upon him. However, he would never refuse to help someone himself.

I strongly believe that the powers that be are keenly aware of the fact that my father will not complain about the sad conditions which he is compelled to endure, and that they are certainly imposed as a retaliatory punishment by the government in response to my father standing up for what he believes in and his resultant refusal to back down.

As I am sure that you are aware my father has spent the last one hundred and one months on lockdown status at the USP in Marion, Illinois without justifiable reason whatsoever to support the cruel and unusual conditions of his confinement. This seems especially egregious when taken into consideration that his was not a court ordered committal to a supermax, nor was he committed to isolation for the rest of his life.

Most if not all of the people having been compelled to isolation have committed an offense or violated rules within the prison system and were at least (we hope) afforded rights to due process concerning why they were placed into isolation. However, even these people are allowed the benefits of a "step down" program which will eventually allow the prisoner to be reintegrated back into the population.

The length of isolation that my father has been subjected to is unprecedented in the 17 years that Marion USP has been a lockdown facility. In fact, I don't believe that there has been another situation like this which would remotely compare to that of my father's, if one scoured the Gulags of the entire

BOP. You could not find one comparable instance of such harsh conditions of confinement without first having had them implemented upon the order of a court at sentencing. Even the similar situations which may exist or might have existed have been overturned by the Supreme Court as being an infliction of cruel and unusual punishment of a constitutional magnitude violating the Eighth Amendment.

I feel that the reason these conditions have been allowed to go on for so long a period of time is due to the fact that the BOP psychologist created a profile of my father that led the administration to believe they could subject him to whatever madness they could concoct, since his beliefs precluded him from asserting any administrative remedies on his own behalf. Thus, without outside intervention by myself, my family and the support of organizations such as yourselves, this mistreatment will likely continue throughout his entire sentence.

My contention is that the government is of the belief that by getting away with such actions (Note: I firmly believe they have a culpable mental state and awareness of the entire situation) they are defeating him. However, under his interpretation of values, he believes that he is the victor, for being able to endure such torment for so long without complaint evinces more than an attitude but a statement—"It is not those that can inflict the most, but those who can suffer the most that will conquer." (MacSwiney)

Existing factors have revealed that the psychological intake profile of my father is accurate—that he will not complain. Thus the administration is aware that any challenge at all to this sick punishment will not come from him. As his son, enough is enough.

This country of ours imposes hardships and embargos upon other countries who inflict similar cruel and unusual punishment in violation of basic human rights. How can we condone this within our own borders?

In closing this letter, I ask you to continue to pursue the matter—despite his lack of direct involvement. Please do this for the sake of his family and loved ones who are concerned that he be afforded the same decency as any other similarly situated inmate would deserve, i.e. to be treated as a human being.

Myself, in addition to the rest of his children and thirteen grandchildren, would like to see that he be allowed the same rights as any other inmate sentenced to an identical sentence, i.e. (1) contact visits with his family, (2) release into the general population as he has never done anything within the system to warrant being permanently removed from population, (3) the privilege of being able to eat the same food that is sold in the commissary to other inmates in the general population but which has been denied him while he has been stranded in perpetual isolation.

Thank you in advance for your time, consideration and cooperation in this urgent matter. In short, thanks for caring. The world is a much better place under your watch.

Amnesty International was to criticize Marion as a violator of human rights—the only United States prison they so accused.

★

Cancer is an equal opportunity killer. It was taking its time with my father, who was putting up a Herculean struggle against it. The battle, however, was coming to a close. The long slide towards eternity was picking up speed. There would be less than a year left of life.

My brother writes:

August '01
I received an emergency phone call from my sister Angel. She needed to be rushed to Winthrop Hospital [Mineola, New York] because of excruciating pain in her side. The doctors soon realized when she was screaming in the examination

room, that her gallstones had traveled to her pancreas, leading to an attack of pancreatitis. As my sister lay in pain, I received a call from my father's prison counselor. He put my father on the phone, who said, in a raspy voice, "Get our here now, I'm getting ready to roll a seven." [journal of Peter J. Gotti]

My father was rushed to the hospital with a severe blood clot and various heart ailments. Peter, my brother, called the prison every half hour from our sister's hospital room. No information was forthcoming for three hours. Then...

They confirmed he was alive, but they couldn't guarantee tomorrow. I caught the first flight out next day. I arrived at the prison early afternoon, they guided me to the hospital. We arrived to find two armed guards outside and a command headquarters set up on the first floor. We checked in and two more guards brought us to the intensive care unit. Five more guards, two with shotguns, and bullet proof vests at the door to his room. [journal of Peter J. Gotti]

Shotguns? Bullet proof vests? Necessary for what? Protection from an unarmed imprisoned man in intensive care, dying from cancer? Big brother was not only watching, he was armed to the teeth.

If you want a picture of the future, imagine a boot stamping on a human face—forever.—George Orwell

Orwell said it in his classic novel, *1984*. As far as the Federal Prison system went, it was an accurate prediction. The boot is government issue.

★

October '01

My father collapsed in his cell. A guard making a chance visit found him in a pool of his own blood. He was hemorrhaging from his neck wound. Doctors and nurses were pouring blood into him as it was pouring out. All and all he temporarily lost six pints of blood. Once again he was rushed to St. Johns Hospital. Springfield Medical Prison openly acknowledged that they cannot handle his condition...Under normal conditions and circumstances, an inmate would immediately be remanded to a local hospital to receive proper medical attention, but John Gotti need not apply. [journal of Peter J. Gotti]

The following came from handwritten notes by my *father*, these never having been seen by the public or the press before. He was unable to speak, and could only communicate by writing on a pad. His penmanship was parochial school perfect, but as the disease weakened him, his writing became more constricted.

They had to cut all my clothes and everything off me, everything. The lead dr. said I was in a 3 inch puddle behind my head and neck.

When my brother questioned him further about his condition, he wrote

6 pints of blood lost. 3 pints body fluid. Too much pressure on heart and lungs.

When my brother asked what the doctors said at the time, my father replied, "'We're losing him.'"

My father then wrote, "Did I call that shot that the tumor would bust?"

There are many tape recordings of my father's voice available to the public. They are on the Internet. They record a strong voiced man, a tough man. As I write this, and look at some of the last written words of my father, while he was dying, I remember his toughness. He took it with him. They never could take it, the government. They got his blood, they even took his life with their neglect. His spirit—never.

★

The fall of 2001 turned to Christmas time. Outside the walls of prison, America put on its happy face. People eagerly anticipated gathering with family and friends. Travel. Warmth of celebration, good times remembered, good times to be shared. The exchange of gifts. The joy of children at Christmas. The sharing of special food and drink.

We have been trained to forget that Christmas time coincides with the darkest days of the year, that it is the last celebration of a dying year, that it is a time when people also go deeply into debt to buy others things they neither need nor want.

This is not the place to engage in a diatribe about the hypocrisy of the holiday. However, the contrast from the grinning commercialization of Christmas, this enforced gaiety, with what was happening to my father behind prison walls, makes for bitter remembrance.

It was not easy reading the following passage in my brother's journal.

December '01

Our final visit before Christmas was a highly emotional one, as we were just excited that Dad lived to see Christmas, a goal he had set with the nurses. The excitement was short lived. As we said our goodbyes, Dad smiled, sat down across the visiting table, and proceeded to cough heavily. As we were being escorted out of the visiting room, I had to watch as my father coughed up a large glob of blood and rotted tissue on the table. I put my head down, and he slammed the table in disgust, asking himself why it couldn't have waited until we were gone. By December '01 he had a nine inch bandage taped over his neck, and another under his chin, to cover up the wounds caused by tumors eating through his neck.

Of all 36 ways to get out of trouble, the best way is—leave.
—Chinese Proverb

New Year. Resolutions made. Fresh promises. (Soon to be broken.) Fresh starts. But what is it really? It is an arbitrary fixing of time. The Chinese celebrate New Year in February. The Jews in September. Who's right?

In reality, there is no such thing as New Year. It is a fiction. It is an illusion. An arbitrary division of time, not even based on seasonal occurrences. But we cling to it, because it brings us hope. Hope for a better future, hope for a better life.

That "new lease" on life.

It is no coincidence that many of those who shout, "Happy New Year!" at midnight on January first are drunk. Drunk not only with what must, of necessity, be last year's booze, but drunk with hope. Hope for that brighter tomorrow—a day which never comes.

But as it often happens, he who breakfasts on hope, dines on hunger.

New Year 2001 didn't bring much hope for our father.

January '02
A couple of days after New Year's Day, I received a call from my father's counselor informing me that my dad is in grave condition, and I must fly out ASAP. On the 4th or the 5th, I touched down in Springfield for what would be a three week stay. [journal of Peter J. Gotti]

Things got worse.

February '02
I returned to New York, said goodbye to my friends, my new business, and my wife and three children. I finally moved to Springfield intent on not returning home without my father. By the first week of February, my father had already lost his

power of speech...the tumors had suffocated his esophagus and voice box. Not even any water would make it down the passage without exiting the gaping wound in my father's neck. He had started to grow a goatee because the tumors were tearing through his chin, therefore hindering nurses from shaving him. For this very reason, I will wear a goatee for the rest of my life in honor of what this man endured. My father was no longer able to speak, so he had to write on a legal pad, and we had to respond verbally for the cameras and guard. After one last trip to St. John's, where I once again tried to have him remain, to die like a human, he was immediately shipped back to Springfield, without his glasses or proper medicines, to die like a dog. [journal of Peter J. Gotti]

I was to learn from my brother that my father refused pain medication.

Dad is in agonizing pain, he is beet red, veins popping in his forehead, staring at the ceiling. A doctor and nurse came into the hospital room, and spoke as if he were not even present. "We can make all his pain go away, we can numb his senses. He won't feel a thing." Before I can even ponder my answer, my father slams the bed, and demands his pad. He wrote exactly as follows:

"No truth serum for me." The tripod camera never missed a beat. The same camera that the Bureau of Prisons denies existed.

★

Spring was coming. New life to the world outside. But, while it is true that green leaves will come forth in Spring, it is equally true that this is the season when the old ones fall to the ground to be swept away.

March '02

The pain was so excruciating that he hardly wrote. Most visits were spent watching him cough blood, or having to summon the nurse to suction out the blood and mucus that clogged his tracheotomy tube. Even at this point he never wavered, and maintained his amazing sense of humor. He constantly joked with the nurses, still picked losers, and always found ways to "talk" food.

A short time later, the chaplain came to my father's bedside to inquire if he wished to make his peace with the Lord. As I spoke with the chaplain, my father became aware of his presence, and stared at him. The chaplain said, "Mr. Gotti, you will soon be seeing your maker and I'm going to say a prayer for you." With that my father waved the chaplain away with a flick of his wrist, and turned his head the other way. I apologized to the chaplain, as he left he said, "Mr. Gotti, I will pray for you anyway."

As the chaplain was escorted away from my father, my father turned his head towards me, and winked, then laid his head back down on the pillow. I felt it was his way of saying, I am what I am, accept me if you want, I ask for no forgiveness. I believe once my brother Frankie Boy died, any religious belief in my father died too.

By mid March dad spent most visits sleeping, but sometimes even as distraught as he was he had moments. March 15th, my father looked deep in my eyes, and scribbled on his pad, "You will never know how much I love you." He then went to sleep for two weeks. [journal of Peter J. Gotti]

★

For some reason, the public treats its celebrities, or imagined celebrities, in ways that are rude beyond comprehension.

The famous are interrupted at times that an unknown person would be left quite alone. They are asked questions that are the height of impertinence, when an average citizen would never be so queried. It is as if the public owned the public personage, and could do with him and his, what they will.

As to the media? These paparazzi with a press pass? They are beyond all decorum, beyond all civility. *The people have a right to know*, they cry, when they shove a microphone in your face, or photograph you at your worst moments.

April '02
I stood steadfast as the prison, government, and media all started their John Gotti death clock. Many a night I chased reporters out of restaurants who actually had the gall to ask, "So how long does he have?" [journal of Peter J. Gotti]

As I write this, I notice a correlation of sorts between the times of the year, and the events which overtook my father and my family. It is an odd synchronicity, or perhaps I am merely seeking the symbolic to somehow soften an otherwise diamond-hard tragedy. I find another incidence of symbolic coincidence in the following journal entry by my brother:

April 2, '02
Nurses at St. Johns who used to give me glowing hello's now look at the floor when I enter the room. Mysteriously, Inspector Javert (the warden) has all his troops in full battle regalia. Are they expecting a breakout or an invasion. Well you know that dad is very well capable of wheeling himself, 25 machines, and ten tubes right out the door. Took my routine walk to Glenstone Blvd., and was saddened to see the rabbit that used to greet me almost daily, under the tire of a car. [journal of Peter J. Gotti]

It was Easter time, 2002. A time of resurrection for the Christians. "*In sure and certain hope of the resurrection,*" I believe is the language used at funerals. If it is sure and certain, how could it then be called hope? If true, then why do tears follow funerals like night follows day?

> Easter Eve '02
> I put my mother on a flight home after she said her last farewell to my father. It was my father's wish that only I be present for his death...Most times if he was awake, he would throw a playful punch at me, or grab my nose just to let me know he was still fighting. Often I wonder if he kept going just for me...One morning I arrived, and had a guard explain that I must remove all his personal belongings from the prison grounds. Obviously, I protested that it seemed like an insult, the man was alive, and occasionally awake...I refused help, and carried each box fifty yards to the car. [journal of Peter J. Gotti]

My father made my mother promise in February, after their Valentine's Day visit, that she would not come back. In his written note to my mother, he wanted to die with dignity. He didn't want my mother and sisters to see his end.

She still came back two more times, until my brother, Peter, enforced my father's wishes.

Most of May, my father was in a medically induced coma. Arrangements had been agreed upon, that upon my father's death, Peter would be the first to be notified. All tapes and notes would be turned over to him. An autopsy was waived. It was agreed that government issued clothes would not touch his body.

Right.

Even a professor of Law at Harvard wrote concerning my father's tapes. He wrote to then Attorney General John Ashcroft, perhaps one of the stupidest men ever to fill that position. Here is an excerpt from the letter of Charles J. Ogletree Jr., Professor of Law.

May 13, 2002

Dear Attorney General Ashcroft:

...Mr Gotti currently suffers from a form of cancer that is its advanced stages. As a result of the medical treatment he has received over the past few months, he is clearly unable to speak or write or communicate with the outside world. Nevertheless, it is reported by his family members that their private visits with him are videotaped and monitored. In light of Mr. Gotti's declining medical condition and his family's hope to spend some private moments with him, this form of videotaping is unconscionable and unnecessary.

Ashcroft did not respond.

★

Never forget that everything Hitler did in Germany was legal.
—Martin Luther King Jr.

Now, I am reading my brother's journal for June '02, and it's tough going. The sadness and the anger is welling up in me, as I read. Maybe, by now, you are feeling something too, something other than what the government would like you to feel about my father. I hope so.

June 10th '02

I was escorted to his cell; the guard set the tripod camera up, and sat to the right side of the room. I sat to my dad's right side. He looked up at me and lay his head down. I grabbed hold of his hand and put my head on his stomach. I fell asleep. For an hour.

"Times up!" bellowed the guard. I gave my dad a kiss on his hand and head, and exited, always looking at him. It was 10 AM when I left, 10:30 when I started a nap in my room. I was awakened by the phone ringing. I picked up the phone, and heard my sister Angel screaming, "Is it true?" I asked, "Is what true?" Needless to say, CNN and my sister were kind enough to inform me that my dad had passed away. I was not given the courtesy of a call by the government, as promised. It took me two hours to find out my father choked on his own blood and bile. [journal of Peter J. Gotti]

★

That day I awoke in Ray Brook, with an unusual feeling. I walked to the rec yard, in deep thought. I paced. At 10:20 AM the loud speakers announced recall. Back in my cell, I took a nap, unusual for me at 11:00 AM, but this was an unusual day. I dreamed.

I was sitting on my bunk reading. My father walked in, sharp as ever in the blue suit, white shirt, red tie, and polished blue shoes. Gleaming white gold pinkie ring and matching watch. Perfect hair—of course, it was John J. Gotti.

"What are you doing here?" I asked.

"I wanted to see you once more."

I commented on how well he looked, for a man who was dying.

"I will always be me, no matter what. Nobody and nothing can change that. Always remember that."

He nodded his head approvingly at me. Fixed his tie. Disappeared.

I awoke, knowing the significance of my dream. My father was dead. I walked out to the rec yard again. Several guards were waiting to escort me to the prison chapel to confirm what I already knew.

> *Fire, water, and government know nothing of mercy.*
> —Albanian Proverb

The king of the volcano was dead. The Teflon Don had passed. John J. Gotti, my father, had choked on his own blood. But he lived the Life, drinking the finest champagne, and whether it was blood or champagne, he was always a man's man, a true believer, old school. A gangster yes—but even criminals had a code of conduct, once. He lived that code. Died with it intact. He is perhaps the last one that did.

I knew that my father was, at least in his mind, the victor in the battle of Springfield and Marion. As I quoted Irish patriot Terence MacSwiney (1879–1920) in my letter to Amnesty International, "It is not those who can inflict the most, but those that can suffer the most who will conquer."

The government didn't turn over the video tapes. It took several lawyers to get the notes. And the rest of the deal, the rest of the government promises? Let Peter tell the story.

June 10th 2002 Continued

I raced to the prison to view my dad's body. To make certain that his dignity was intact. I was denied entry, and I was informed there would be an autopsy against my wishes. I was also informed that it is Missouri State Law, that a body is to be embalmed before leaving. I wanted to choose the funeral home to embalm him. I was refused and informed that the outfit that has the prison contract has to do it. The next morning, I demanded entry to the funeral home that held my father. Two armed correction officers denied me entry. I explained to them as hostile as possible, that he is not Bureau of Prison property any longer, he belongs to my family. I was still denied entry. Only after I threatened to fly an army of protesters and reporters to the funeral parlor did they finally allow me a visit with my dead father. I entered this old empty ragged parlor—the undertaker was the only man present. As expected, I figured I would be ushered into the back towards the embalming room. I was wrong once again. Much to my surprise, my father was in a government issued suit in a government issued casket on display in a viewing room completely set up with chairs and candles. The undertaker told me that in over twenty years, he had the prison contract, he had never seen an open wound like my father had on his neck. [journal of Peter J. Gotti]

It was another 48 hours before the government released my father's body to Peter's custody. The vultures, disguised as media, were circling.

June 12, 2002
A lifelong family friend Angelo, was kind enough to fly to my side and assist me in my efforts to return my dad to New York soil. To accomplish this without a treacherous four-teen hour media car chase, meant chartering a small jet...I pulled up at the funeral parlor, to a criss-cross of reporters with little regard for my father, or compassion for my loss. It was at the parlor that I posed myself a more disturbing question—How can I give my father the dignity in death that he so dramatically earned, if I can't even get past the media? My thoughts immediately focused on the two tint-ed window hearses that were parked outside of the funeral parlor. I reached the conclusion that common sense would place me in the hearse with my dad, and the media would follow whatever hearse I was in. Needless to say, I went in the other hearse, and headed for a different airport as a diversion, while the marshals quietly slipped away to the airport my father from where my father's body was to be transported. As predicted, the bait was taken, but media was staked out like carrion crows at the fence of the other airport. To add macabre insult to injury, it turned out that the charter jet's cabin was too small to hold my father's casket. The body bag was loaded in the plane. I tried to block the media view as best as I could. The photographers laughed as they snapped away. [journal of Peter J. Gotti]

I am now thankful that I was not there that day.

A street sweeper can maintain dignity at his job. A gar-bage man can have the same soul as a Bishop. But some in the media? The closest thing they have to a soul is a dead-line. The closest thing they have to dignity is a byline. I once thought the worst thing any of my children could become was a gangster like I once was. On reflection, it might only be the second worst.

June 12, 2002 [continued]
The two hour flight to New York was a silent one. An eerie comfort, a dark serenity entered my mind, my soul, if you will, as I flew home with my father's head in my lap. I had unzipped the body bag so I could finally hold my father outside of prison walls. [journal of Peter J. Gotti]

★

The right most valued by all civilized men is the right to be left alone. —Justice Louis Brandeis

Besides the newspaper accounts, friends had informed me of my father's wake, and his funeral. The wake brought forth a massive enclave of journalists, photographers, and FBI agents, trying to blend in, I'm sure. Let's take a look at some of the press coverage.

'Dapper Don' John Gotti Dead Brought Down by the Bull—CNN

. . . Gotti was a classic gangster straight out of central casting, with a larger-than-life appeal that sprouted from a contradictory mix of violent outbursts and an uncanny ability to win the admiration of his Queens neighborhood, where he was known for organizing picnics and giving handouts.

He was not brought down by "the bull" Sammy Gravano. He was betrayed by him, a turncoat serial killer, a man who cried in prison, and would swear to anything to get out of there. A man who after telling a federal judge he wanted a different life for his family, when free, quickly turned to dealing ecstasy, and was caught, along with his wife, daughter and son, and put back into prison. My father was never brought down by a man like that.

But someone who wrote that headline thought it was clever. It serves as an example how the media will sacrifice sanity for a sound byte, torture truth for a turn of phrase.

Here is another.

'Dapper Don' John Gotti Dies—Chicago Sun Times

He "was a gangster and proud of it," said J. Bruce Mouw, who pursued Gotti for more than 18 years as head of the FBI's Gambino crime family squad. "He was an old-fashioned La Cosa Nostra mobster

At least Mouw got it right. Of course, I am not a fan of Mouw, but he does have my respect. He was true to *his* code (for the most part), and respected his enemy, as should any warrior. Mouw had done service as a submariner in the Navy before joining the FBI and exploring another underworld.

One time, on a visit with my father at Marion, Illinois, I had referred to Mouw and another agent who had arrested my father, George Gabriel, as "cocksuckers." My father corrected me. "Why are they cocksuckers?" my father asked.

I was taken aback. "What do you mean?"

"John," he told me, "a guy is not a cocksucker for doing his job, as long as he does it right. Rats and liars are cocksuckers."

Mob Boss John Gotti Dead At 61 Ex-Head Of Gambino Crime Family
Dies Of Cancer At Prison Hospital—CBS News

. . . Gotti reigned for six years as the nation's most high-profile mobster, passing himself off as a plumbing supply salesman while strutting about in $2,000 Brioni suits and sneering at law enforcers who kept trying to put him behind bars. Some crime chroniclers called him the most important gangster since Al Capone, a comparison Gotti did not discourage.

That's pretty accurate for media. My father was born out of his time, too late for a life as an old time gangster. Capone reigned before RICO, and the government had to use its weapon of last resort to rein him in—tax evasion.

★

My father, had he been alive in ancient Rome, would have been a Caesar. He had the intelligence, the courage, and the leadership capabilities. Roman History was his favorite reading. That being so, I am reminded of the beginning of the funeral speech of Marc Antony in Shakespeare's *Julius Caesar*—I think it applies. *The evil that men do lives after them, The good is oft interred with their bones, So let it be with Caesar … The noble Brutus Hath told you Caesar was ambitious: If it were so, it was a grievous fault, And grievously hath Caesar answered it …*

I believe it is fitting to end this chapter with the words of the man himself, courtesy of the FBI. A famous tape, recorded in the apartment on Mulberry Street above the Ravenite Club.

GOTTI: I'm not in the mood for the toys, or games, or kidding . I'm not in the mood for clans. I'm not in the mood for gangs. I'm not in the mood for none of that stuff there. This is gonna be a Cosa Nostra 'til I die. Be it an hour from now, or be it tonight, or a hundred years from now when I'm in jail. It's gonna be a Cosa Nostra.

My Brother Frankie's Baptism
L-R: Danny Fatico, Margie Fatico, my mother and father

Lewisburg 1969
L-R: unknown, Frankie DeCicco, my father,
Angelo Ruggiero, unknown, unknown

Lewisburg 1970
L-R: unknown, Frankie DeCicco, George Remini,
my father, unknown, Mickey Boy Paradiso

Lewisburg 1970
L-R: father, mother, brother Frankie, and I

Lewisburg 1970
L-R: Sal Ruggiero, my father, Gene Gotti,
Angelo Ruggiero

Bergin Club 1972
Danny Fatico (second from left), Willie Boy (in plaid
sport coat), Angelo Ruggiero (in sunglasses and track suit)

Bergin Club 1971
Gene Gotti (third from left, sitting on top of car), "Skinny Louie" behind him, Joey Scopo next to Gene, "Foxie" behind Joey, Sallie Ruggiero next to Joey, Willie "Chisel Chin" in front of Sallie.

Lewisburg 1971 Visit
John Ruggiero, myself, brother Frankie,
Anna Marie Ruggiero

Function 1972
Far left: Mark. On right: Jimmy "Butch," Richard "Red
Bird" Gomes, my father, behind him Joey "Nerves," Gene
Gotti, Bob, Sallie Ruggiero, and Willie Boy (seated next to
my father)

Greenhaven 1976
L-R: Sonny "Black" Napolitano, my father, "Peanuts,"
unknown

Greenhaven 1975

NYMA 1980
My father, brother Frankie, and myself

Surveillance Photo 1989

My Wedding 1990

My Wedding 1990
L-R: my father-in-law, myself, Carmine Agnello,
Jackie D'Amico, and my bother Peter

My Wedding 1990
Above: Me and Bobby Boriello

Opposite Top: Jay Black singing
Opposite Bottom: Jimmy Roselli singing

Fourth of July at the Bergin Club

GOVERNMENT
EXHIBIT
121D
S1 04 Cr. 690 (SAS)**(ID)**

Surveillance 1991, at the Bergin
Myself, Jimmy "Brown" Failla, and Joe "Butch" Corrao

Surveillance at Bergin 1994

Ray Brook

Ray Brook 2002

Ray Brook 2002
My nephew, son, daughter and myself

Ray Brook 2000
My son and daughter

My daughter and I

Bobby Boriello Jr., myself, my daughter, my son

My Sister Angel's Wedding

My Father's Funeral
Flower car procession

My Father's Funeral
Residents of Ozone Park press against my father's hearse

My Daughter Nicolette's Communion

My Daughter Gianna's Communion

CHAPTER TWENTY-TWO

Post Mortem Regis

He was larger than life, and at his final exit from this life, he was larger than... death? The Don was dead, and the media feeding frenzy at the wake and funeral would now begin. The King of the Volcano was to have a send-off of epic proportions.

Farewell John Joseph Gotti. 1940–2002.

Of course, not everybody at the wake with a video or a still camera was a bona fide journalist. Some were law enforcement, taking pictures for their who's who at the wake. Even one of my attorneys, who attended the wake at Papavero Funeral Home in Maspeth, wound up on the evening news television in his double breasted pin striped suit. And he wasn't even my criminal attorney. I'm sure the FBI had footage of him also. (At the 2009 trial, when he testified on my behalf, there were plenty of still photos courtesy of the government.)

Of course, I could not attend my father's funeral, I was incarcerated at Ray Brook Federal Correction Institute. I didn't even bother petitioning the court to attend, because I didn't want to give the government another mini-victory against me by saying "no."

But I read about the proceedings. Later I conversed with my brother, my attorneys and friends, and got a pretty good idea of what went on at my father's funeral.

★

When it is a mob funeral, florists are raking it in—the expenditure is incredible. Imagine when it is a mob funeral for the head of the most powerful crime family in America.

There were nineteen flower cars. Dozens of floral displays the size of a full grown man. Countless smaller arrangements. There was a giant martini glass made from flowers, a racehorse, a huge Royal Flush, and even a massive Cuban Cigar. Even in death, my father was surrounded by symbols of his life's pleasures—almost as if he were a Pharaoh.

Perhaps in some sense he was.

When my father was moved from the wake site to the cemetery, crews of men followed behind just to sweep up the fallen flowers from the limousines. At the wake, the public could attend. And they did in droves. All races colors and creeds. In fact, one of my attorneys told me that there were a number of Hasidic Jews who came to pay their respects.

Our family had strict crowd control at the wake. It was a rainy day on one of the wake days, but nobody was allowed to bring their umbrella in the funeral home. Potential weapons, or potential screens for surveillance equipment. Plus, etiquette alone demanded there be no mourners with umbrellas in their hands inside.

There were some large individuals at the wake to make sure everybody was being polite. There weren't any incidents however. I was told that even strangers who came to see my father off out of curiosity were respectful, solemn even.

Of course, members from all Families involved in the Life attended my father's wake. Those that couldn't attend in person for various "reasons" sent their emissaries. Every day, of the three, saw a packed house at Papavero's.

Each day during the wake I would call from Ray Brook to speak to my brother and sisters at the funeral home, to make sure everything was just so. I heard that the smell of flowers permeated the air at the wake, and eventually there were so many that the excess were donated to local hospitals.

It was a closed casket wake. Cancer had ravaged my father's face, and it would have been wrong to expose his present appearance to family, friends, and admirers who remembered the immaculate movie star looks that my father sported while free.

But on top of the coffin was a large photographic portrait of my father with his penetrating gaze and his Broadway smile. Speaking of photographic portraits, I learned from Joe Arcuri, an old timer in the Life, that surveillance at the wake exceeded that which was present at Carlo Gambino's funeral, and Castellano's also.

Law enforcement agencies had come to pay their respects. Local DA offices, DEA, OCTF, ATF, and of course the FBI. Snapping pictures, rolling video, gathering intelligence, and of course being intrusive as only they know how.

★

There was a eulogy, written by my brother, Peter. Words of wisdom, sentiments profound. Unfortunately, it was not my brother who gave the eulogy, but a turncoat by the name of Lewis Kasman. He had come to praise the Caesar, he had, *sub rosa,* been trying for years to bury.

Kasman said that it wouldn't come across right to the fellows if my brother delivered the eulogy. So the self proclaimed "adopted son" of John J. Gotti gave the speech. Kasman was promoting Kasman on the corpse of my father to an audience of those who thought my father a god. He was a CI working his targets, even at the funeral.

A two faced informant giving the eulogy to the King of the Streets. The press made note that Kasman was visibly shaken while giving the speech. Perhaps a milligram of conscience was still in his possession. Maybe the immense disloyalty and hypocrisy in his making the speech at my father's funeral affected even him. Maybe. I have my doubts. In any event, after the eulogy, there wasn't a dry eye in the funeral home.

Kasman gave "The Long Journey Home" speech. It was eight forty-five in the evening.

He said, "Finally, after ten years of being separated, you were allowed to be next to me on the plane the other day to complete your long journey home. I live by your words, keep smiling and stay strong. Rest in peace with Frankie Boy now. We love you. I love you."

(Remember, he was reading my brother's words. I am still angry at my brother, Peter, for not reading the eulogy he had written. He told me later that he was too emotionally distraught to do it.)

Then Kasman read a letter from my sister Victoria. He quoted her,

I have never been prouder of the man responsible for giving me life than watching him fight the toughest battle of his life with every ounce of courage only a warrior can muster. Despite desperate attempts (by prison officials) to break him, he acted with dignity intact until the end. He will forever live inside me, until I draw my last breath. His legacy which is his legend will be passed onto my children, his grandchildren, so that they too will learn the lessons. A great man with a generous heart, that touched the world and passed on a piece of himself in each of his children. His roar will never go unheard. His courage never measured. And each time you hear the name John Gotti, you will think strength loyalty and dedication. He'll be remembered as a man's man in whom dignity prevailed. To the man that is my hero, you will always be the wind beneath my wings, I love you daddy—Victoria.

After reading the letter, the people at the wake shared

their feelings, openly displayed their tears. Most of them were heartfelt. One set however was made of pure crocodile—those belonging to Kasman.

Then Kasman read a letter from my sister Angel.

> Daddy, no matter what I ever did you shook your head and laughed. You always told me how proud you were of me. I adored the ground you walked on. I miss you so very much. I love you daddy. Thank you for being an amazing father and grandfather. Forever, Angel.

As I write this, I grow furious once again, that the heartfelt words of my beloved siblings were mouthed by this traitorous scum at my father's funeral. Kasman—the adopted confidential informant of the FBI. Tear stained handkerchief in one pocket, tape recorder in the other.

My father was overly charitable and generous to certain people, and would refuse to believe negative things about them. If he loved you, he loved you to a fault. Kasman was one of the favored for a time. Maybe it was his heart, maybe partly his ego, but my father had a hard time "showing people to the door," as he used to say.

But Kasman never should have been let in the door. Who was one of those responsible for my father's permanent stay in solitary? We believe it was Kasman. He told the Feds in a 3/12/97 report that my father was passing messages to the Family through his attorneys on visits. They were acting as his gofers. This was documented in an FBI memo. Meanwhile, in the press, Kasman was decrying the injustice of my father being kept in solitary.

This turncoat was a paid FBI informant, earning his money betraying my father, and also spying on me.

At a later date, Kasman, ever the gentleman, was recording his visit with my mother while she was recovering from a stroke. She had just had brain surgery, maybe two days out of the hospital. Kasman was wired for sound as he expressed his sympathetic feelings.

As the Don was dead, and beyond the betrayal of Kasman, I was up next.

He publicly denounced me in the way I chose to defend myself, stating my father would not have approved of my defense in the courtroom—while he, Kasman, was sitting in the courtroom with a wire on.

I doubt Kasman would have been so critically candid in my presence.

This traitor was a CI since 1996 or 1997, depending on the source of the information. I was indifferent to him, I could take him or leave him, but I never quite understood why my father liked him. Most of the Family tolerated this guy out of respect to my father.

I wonder when, many years from now, it is Kasman's funeral, how many people will be lined up to say good things about him. I think they might be counted on one hand of a man with no fingers.

He deserves a little more background here.

He "borrowed" $277,000 from his kids' college fund. He admitted to lying in his divorce affidavits. He tried to get back his legal fees via lawsuits against several of his attorneys.

Barry Levin, well known attorney, said of Kasman, "That this subhuman waste product is allowed to be in society…is a sad example of what cooperating witnesses can get away with under the guise of government protection."

In 2008, he was charged with stealing $90,000 while still working for the government. According to FBI agent testimony in 2009, Kasman was paid $12,000 a month from 2005 to 2007.

So what does this perjurer, thief and traitor have to say about himself? Well, in a July, 2012, *NY Post* article, he said, "I can look in the mirror. My children can be proud of me."

You'll hear more about Kasman later.

★

Ten thirty in the morning my father's casket was carried out by the pallbearers who included my brother Peter, Joseph Corozzo the attorney, and my Uncle Richie. The public applauded as the casket went by, and the religious amongst them crossed themselves.

Even in death, my father dressed sharp. My brother Peter had seen to it. Blue Brioni suit, matching tie and handkerchief. Red, blue, white, and a little yellow in the tie. It had been one of my father's favorite ensembles, and I told Peter to dress him this way.

Due to the ravages of cancer, that left my father weighing a skeletal 120 pounds, the suit had to be altered. Along with the suit, was a bottle of Petrus Bordeaux placed in the coffin, a Cuban cigar, some "walking around money," and some gold coins for luck.

★

The coffin was respectfully installed in the back of the hearse and the procession headed east on Grand Avenue away from 72nd Place. The procession passed my father's home on 85th Street in Howard Beach and swept by his old club, The Bergin on 101st Ave., in Ozone Park.

The people of Queens were out in force, gazing from their windows, out on the streets, holding candles, photos, "We Love You John" signs. Blowing kisses at the coffin, shedding tears at the loss of my father. Stores were closed in respect.

At times the progress of the hearse was halted by the multitudes saying farewell to the Don. All the time the media and law enforcement were recording it.

Obviously, the funeral itself was a family affair. No public. My mother observed at the funeral, "He lived fast and flamboyant, and his final day on earth reflected his style of living. He was the last of his kind."

Amen mother.

Even she was shocked at the number of people that were amassed in the streets, swarming the hearse that carried my father as it passed by them in Ozone Park. Tears in their eyes, they kissed the hearse. They didn't want it out of their sight, and my uncles had to clear a path to allow the hearse to progress to its destination.

In a phone conversation that I had with my wife after the funeral, she related how she couldn't believe the outpouring of love from not only friends, but the people of Howard Beach and Ozone Park who didn't know him; although they certainly knew of him.

I agreed that my father was a good man, and a man's man. But what was in my mind at the time, were the words Capo Ralphie Bones and his son, Petey, "He is a hoodlum's hoodlum and a very likable guy."

This came from an early eighties government bug.

★

St. John's Cemetery in Queens County is the burial place of many mob superstars. Carlo Gambino, Carmine Galante, Vito Genovese, Lucky Luciano.

It is also the place where my dear departed brother, Frank, dead at twelve, is interred. Now my father rests beside his son. Peace be upon both of them. They are missed, and in my thoughts every day of my life.

He also joined up once again with Neil Dellacroce and Angelo Ruggiero who were buried at St. John's. Due to Angelo's indiscretions, there was a time that my father had to avoid his friend, but now they are hanging together for eternity.

★

I said my father was buried in St. Johns, but not with a Catholic Mass. "Reverend" Andrew Vaccari, chancellor of the Brooklyn Diocese, gave a thumbs down on a mass for my father. He didn't want a mass said for a murderer.

How many murders have been committed in the name of religion? Ever hear of the Inquisition or the Crusades, Father Vaccari?

In true Christian Charity, Vaccari allowed that "there can be a mass for the dead sometime after the burial of John Gotti."

Well maybe the church wasn't interested in the formalities, but the media certainly was. Helicopters flew above the cemetery. Four of them filled with newsmen.

There has always been a parasitic relationship between the media and the name Gotti. Mention the name, sell more papers, get more viewers. But at least at the funeral itself, the public and the press were excluded.

★

My father had been buried. Three hundred miles away my life continued at Ray Brook. After my father's death, there were several days of inmates expressing their condolences. I didn't watch any of the news coverage of the funeral. It was hard enough not being able to attend his funeral, watching the procession on television would have only made it worse.

I made a short call to my mother, to see how she was handling things, and to offer such comfort as I could. Like any prison phone call to ones you love, it was too short.

I went back to my cell after the call and perused the file I had kept in my dealings with my father's conditions of imprisonment. Letters to the Bureau of Prisons, to Amnesty International, lawyers, and doctors. Even to DOJ. I attempted to bring some relief to my father's suffering, but it was a futile attempt.

To the government, the sooner he died the better. They saw him only as mob boss and killer.

But my father did not appreciate my efforts, either. He had his pride and dignity, they were most important to him. He felt that writing letters on his behalf showed weakness. He would have none of it. He had refused to see representatives of Amnesty International, and I had written them an apology.

"I can take whatever they can give, and then some," my father had told me. "I would treat them far worse if the roles were reversed. So we accept our fate."

I can look at these files, these letters today, and once again feel the same anger and frustration. I also experienced medical neglect while in the "care" of the Bureau of Prisons. I also was subjected to frequent periods of solitary confinement without valid reason.

★

After my father's death, I soon went back to prison routine. Back to working out, back to my legal studies. Back to trying to raise a Long Island family as best as I could from a cage some eighty miles short of the Canadian border.

Back to the biting black flies of summer in Ray Brook that made it almost impossible to stay outside for rec. They got in your hair, your clothes, and bit up your ankles, and any other part of you that was exposed.

CHAPTER TWENTY-THREE

A Warden and a Warning

After several days of inmates expressing their condolences to me on the loss of my father, I went back to the regular prison routine. You eat, sleep, move, and get counted. All at scheduled times. In Ray Brook, even the flies had a routine. Every summer they would swarm in large evil black clouds over the rec area, and dine out on us.

Sometimes there is a break in routine—a fight, a stabbing, or someone going to the hole.

I had just finished a workout on the outdoor weight pile when suddenly the prison PA system barked out, "Compound closed! Compound closed!" That usually meant a problem. I noticed a guard approaching some twenty yards away, another on my left side. Across the yard, about 150 yards away, the front gate opened and several more guards poured into the yard.

"Some poor sucker is going to the hole tonight," I said to myself.

The guards came up to me and then I realized I was the poor sucker aforesaid. All of the inmates were ordered to either face the wall or hug the ground. They didn't want anybody interfering with what was happening. Sure enough, I heard, "Gotti cuff up. We have orders to take you to the hole."

I was surrounded, cuffed. The drill wasn't exactly new to me. I smiled and said, "Why the parade, it's not like I had plans to go anywhere." The humor failed.

I was not given any reason for the hole. Stripped down, searched, given a jump suit, and placed in isolation. It would be several days later that I was awakened at 5:30 AM and told to cuff up again.

This time no jokes. I refused to move until told where I was going first. The guard told me I was going to SIS, the special investigation service of the prison. The guys who enforced the rules and investigated inmates and guards, when necessary—and even when it turns out it was not necessary.

I was led into the SIS Lieutenant's office. I knew him, (Lieutenant Cross) and I knew another guard there. But there was also a stranger present seated at the table, and I refused to step any further. It can cause problems later. So, I refused to stay in the office, until this "third man" was identified. I would not give the impression that I would step into a room and converse with an agent.

Special Agent somebody, with the FBI. From their Plattsburgh office. I didn't like that, so I refused to stay in the office and stood by the door. "Whatever you have to say, you can say it with me standing at the door—with the door open." I told him.

They agreed, reluctantly. Special Agent told me that I would be held in the hole indefinitely. Something about me and my uncles Gene and Pete plotting to kill the warden at Marion and Springfield prisons.

That was a new one. It was also false crazy nonsense. Where did they get this from? Later I found out it came courtesy of my late father's self proclaimed *adopted son* Lewis Kasman. He had told this fairy tale to his federal masters, who apparently didn't care about its truth or falsity, because it created an opportunity to put me and my uncles in lockdown.

Now, I have served many months in isolation. Actually it

adds up to years. For whatever reason, luck, inner strength, my genetics, I don't know, but I handled it without any noticeable personality changes. Not everybody is so fortunate.

Studies show that, increasingly, isolation units house the mentally ill. An investigation in 2006 reported that as many as 64% of the prisoners in Special Housing Units—Isolation—were mentally ill. (American Friends Service Committee Study)

Therefore, it becomes clear why many inmates fear going to the hole. Chances are you will be housed with a bunch of nut jobs. Most of the isolation units in Ray Brook were two man cells. Isolation didn't always mean literal solitary confinement.

By most prison standards, the SHU in Ray Brook was clean. That is a major plus. But it wasn't comfortable. Steel bed with the usual a two inch non-flammable mattress, military blanket, and no pillows. The usual steel sink and toilet combination. A 12"x30" desk bolted down to the floor and a steel stool likewise affixed.

The guards control the lighting in the cell, and the flushing of the toilet. If they want to mess with you, they can. If they really want to mess with you, your lights are left on 24/7, and your toilet may not get flushed for several days. This was not always the case in different prison holes, as sometimes the guards did not have this level of control.

My first weeks in Ray Brook, I was moved right into the hole of the DS or the disciplinary segregation section. Lights stayed on for two days. My toilet remained unflushed for two days. I guess my celebrity prisoner status didn't impress everyone.

So you have to ask the guard to turn off the light, to flush the toilet. It is degrading, demeaning, and designed to be so: to show the inmate who has the power in the prison.

The toilet was right next to the steel door which had a 3"x18" window of non-breakable glass for the viewing pleasure of the guards. Thus, while answering nature's call, the inmate is as much on display as a monkey in the zoo. (Which is basically how BOP regards inmates.)

★

So while the "investigation" continued into the supposed warden plot, I remain in the hole. After way too long, they realized the plot was non-existent, and other than depriving me of my rights, nothing had been accomplished in the investigation. But that was probably sufficient for government purposes.

In a hearing to determine the sufficiency of the evidence to hold my Uncle Peter with respect to the alleged threat against the warden, the court found the government's "evidence" mere speculation and insufficient to hold him. Judge Frederick Block ordered the BOP to release my Uncle Peter from solitary confinement and into the general population.

Judge Block determined after the hearing that, "There was no real substantive reason to keep him detained."

My Uncle Peter was ordered released from solitary at MDC in Brooklyn, but the warden at first refused to obey the order. Judge Frederick Block sought to hold the warden in contempt of court, and then my uncle was released.

Of course, it took another thirty days for me to be released as well as my Uncle Gene. My uncle Peter was a pretrial detainee, and not having (yet) been convicted of the charges he was facing, had more rights than myself and my uncle Gene, who were convicts.

Ergo, it took longer to release me and my Uncle Gene. I had used the findings of Judge Block, with respect to my Uncle Peter, to press the court to have us released, as these allegations of a plot to kill Warden William Hedrick of the Springfield Prison, were found by the court to be spurious.

My Uncle Gene, being somewhat more old school, sat back and did not actively participate—he felt it was a weakness to use the legal system to protect his rights. I understood the concept; I was just diametrically opposed to doing nothing when faced with the blatant violation of my constitutional rights.

★

Understand something. A convict has limited constitutional rights. The Special Investigative Service of the prison, the SIS, can throw an inmate in the hole for 90 days pending the investigation of charges that may be purely imaginative.

Worse, they can continue to reinstate these 90 day periods. In practice, we are often talking six months or more of being confined in solitary—for nothing.

In the United States of America, that holds itself as the light to the world when it comes to human rights, this happens all over the country in the prison system. This is the reality of our country that has the highest percentage per capita of incarcerated people in the world, that its correctional system routinely engages in cruel and unusual punishment, that routinely medically neglects sick inmates; all while making a tidy profit off of prison labor. UNICOR is the profit maker in the prisons.

Even after being released from solitary, I was still, in a sense, suffering from this unwarranted segregation from the general population. When you come out of solitary, you are put into an overcrowded dormitory setting, while you await an opening for a two man cell.

The conditions in the dormitory are often worse than confinement in solitary, because you are often dealing with newly incarcerated inmates who don't yet know the ropes, some of whom are hygienically challenged to say the least.

You might have a twelve man dormitory and one toilet.

I have said before, when you are stripped of almost every material possession those that remain—a favorite pillow for example—grow in importance. When in solitary, you lose these items, they are put in storage. When in the dormitory situation post solitary, you don't have access to them.

Fortunately for me, between inmates who respected me, prison unit managers, and counselors who were enlightened enough to realize they still were overseeing human beings, my few items of "favorites" were often preserved for me while awaiting reassignment to a cell, and often, I was reassigned to my old cell, with my former cell mates.

That too is important, for in an environment when "alone time" is non-existent, if you can work a deal with your cell mate that certain in cell time is yours while they are absent, and certain time is theirs while you are absent, it makes for a semblance of privacy in an otherwise sardine-can environment.

The "choice" of cellmate is also important for sleeping purposes. I recall many decent guys who I had to have look elsewhere for a cell because they snored loudly, and I was a light sleeper. They were instructed to do what was necessary to have themselves transferred to another cell, when requesting a transfer from the BOP. They understood.

It is a crucial psychological benefit to have the ability to sleep, to have certain personal items that become important in a deprived environment, to have compatible cellmates. It is of major assistance in keeping one's personality and identity intact in the prison environment.

★

So I had been released from the SHU in the fall of 2002, and then came the Christmas season.

A rough one this Christmas, because it was the first one I experienced when I no longer had a father living. I fondly remembered the Christmases in the past, when both my father and my little brother Frankie were alive to enjoy the season.

Still, we in prison did what we could do to enjoy the holidays. I made sure the Italian guys were fed, and any other inmates who didn't have access to the "cuisine" we were enabled to have—due to certain kitchen personnel favors and certain acquisition of available comestibles.

But while I might have spent long periods in solitary confinement, now, I was not alone. Surveillance of my visits took place—including legal visits, thanks to the implementation of the Patriot Act.

Tapes began to spin March of 2003, as I met with friends and lawyers. Tapes that were to clearly reveal that I had abandoned the Life, and that I strongly encouraged my friends who sought to be made, to abandon those false hopes and stay far away from formal relations with the mob.

But it wasn't just audio surveillance. SIS and other entities began watching me in the yard. Pictures were taken of me. The wolves were once again gathering, and I began to realize what my father had told me was true.

Once they had me in, if they could see to it, they would never let me out. Speaking of which, as my time was getting shorter, I was fully eligible for a halfway house—a reduced security custody arrangement wherein I would be able to work outside of the prison, and work my way out of prison altogether.

I was a certified paralegal by this time, I had opportunities to work for several attorneys in the city, and I looked forward to such arrangements for which I was eligible.

No. Didn't happen. It seems my paperwork kept getting lost. I'd fill it out again, and it got lost again. Obvious to me, this was because there would shortly be another indictment coming down, and they wanted to keep me just where I was.

I went through the various BOP ropes of complaining at different administrative levels about my not getting into the halfway house program, where I was bureaucratically delayed for about six months, until I could file a pro se lawsuit.

I filed one.

Dismissed. Shortly afterwards I was indicted again.

★

Just prior to my being indicted, it was clear that something was up. As I said before, I had been photographed in the yard repeatedly, and now my mail was being tampered with. While non-legal mail is read by prison authorities, correspondence with attorneys is not to be read, it is to be opened in front of the inmate to insure that there is no contraband contained inside, and then given to him.

Not in my case. Legal mail was repeatedly opened and looked at, on the excuse that the outside of the envelope did not have the exact language the BOP required, indicating it was privileged correspondence.

A ruse.

In fact, of many boxes of material that I had sent to one of my attorneys, several disappeared. Later on, several personal letters that were contained in the missing boxes came back to me at the prison.

I registered a complaint about this, and was told that the boxes must have broken up en route, and were improperly wrapped.

A lie. When an inmate ships boxes, he gets an appointment at the mailing facility next to the Receiving and Departing department of the prison, where he is assisted by personnel in the proper wrapping of a box to be shipped. The boxes were properly wrapped and improperly intercepted by either an individual, or a representative of an agency.

At later trials, certain legal correspondence which had "disappeared" manifested itself in the hands of the government. They claimed it had been photocopied by the prison, but the prison isn't supposed to do that with legal mail.

So in reality, the boxes of my legal mail that didn't get to my attorneys were not improperly wrapped. They did not break open. What was improper was the violation of attorney client privilege by the government, and the breakup of established rules.

But if you think that the government ever plays by the rules, think again.

★

So, at this time, I had mixed feelings. I was getting closer to my supposed release date and looked forward to being free again, but the other part of my mind was expecting another indictment

On phone calls with my family, I had to repeatedly warn my wife (sometimes rather loudly), not to get her hopes up, not to tell the children that daddy was coming home, because daddy wasn't all that sure that he was going home. I didn't want the children to have their hopes and hearts shattered again.

The other inmates would come by and wish me luck, saying "pretty soon G." They all assumed that I would be released shortly. I even started to give some of the stuff I had accumulated in prison to some of the other inmates.

I started believing that maybe after all I was wrong, and paranoia was getting the better of me.

If I were leaving, I'd be leaving behind some good men, and I wanted them to have my belongings. In retrospect, I had assumed too much, and the optimistic part of me caused me to take certain actions that, for my own interest, I shouldn't have.

So, I guess I should congratulate the government for the psychological warfare they engaged in. They knew that I was at least partly believing that the prison gates were going to open soon, and they, by their inaction, fed that belief.

Until they destroyed it.

CHAPTER TWENTY-FOUR

Headed South

I was in the gym on the July date that the government unsealed the indictment against me, and was working out with my friend, Rafael Torres, former drug enforcer, among other things. I had positioned myself on the weight bench, and was about to do my first set.

"G," said Torres, "look at the television."

There was my face up there on the small screen. The sound was off, so I had to go to that portion of the recreation area where the televisions had the sound on. I didn't like what I saw.

On CNN, at the bottom of the file pictures of me, it read, "Gotti Jr. indicted."

I smiled, not wishing to indicate what was going on inside my head at this moment. I said out loud, "You were right, Dad."

Torres asked me what I had said, but I replied, "Nothing."

According to the report, I would be facing one hundred and ten years if convicted. There was mention of the kidnapping of Curtis Sliwa and other charges. I was soon to be headed South, to the Southern District of New York, in Manhattan.

I contacted my attorney, Richard Rehbock, who felt sure that I would receive bail. He was making arrangements with my friends and family for sureties. I knew I would soon be downstate, but of course, for security reasons, the prison never tells you in advance when you are being transported.

Fast forward a couple of weeks. Three in the morning, the guards enter my cell and cuff me up. Shackles, handcuffs. My cellmate hugged me goodbye. "Don't worry about me, I'll be fine, I got this," I told him.

I wasn't all that sure that I did have it. Once again, the unlimited resources of the government would be used to try to put me in jail—this time for the rest of my life. As I was led to R&D for my departure, other inmates that had been awakened by the proceedings were banging on their cell doors, wishing me luck.

I wait. Two big Suburbans with blacked out windows pull up, and out of them comes five of the biggest marshals I had ever seen. The shortest among them was probably six foot two. Full assault gear, automatic weapons.

I am wearing belly chains and shackled hands and feet. Placed in one of the vans. Behind the two vehicles, a third vehicle followed as we drove from upstate New York down to the Metropolitan Correctional Center in Manhattan.

The marshals turned me over to the authorities at MCC. One of them wished me luck. I thanked him, because I knew I was going to need it. Around eight guards at the MCC took charge of me.

I was supposed to be taken to nine south, which is the hole at MCC. High security. I was to stay there until a bed became available. But the phone rang, and the Lieutenant came back and told me there would be a change of plans.

I would be housed in ten south.

The terrorist wing. Locked up 24/7, my lights and toilet controlled by the guards. Blacked out window so you couldn't see outside—you couldn't tell if it was day or night. No contact visits. No phone calls to family. Fireproof mattress with a built in bump serving as a pillow. Restricted access to pen and paper.

The 10 South Unit was built after the World Trade Center

bombing of February, 1993. It was to accommodate those responsible who were caught. Only six cells in the unit.

Five times a day, the other inmates, who were all Muslims accused of terrorist acts, would chant the call to prayer. I could set my watch to it, if I had a watch. I didn't. It wasn't allowed.

The government once again, was seeing to it that I got special treatment. They knew from taped conversations at Ray Brook that I was out of the mob, that I now hated the Life, that I was going straight.

What a perfect opportunity to turn me, they thought. To get me as a cooperating witness would be the largest feather in the Federal cap imaginable. I guess the government thought they could accomplish this by putting me in the worst hole of all the holes in the prison system.

Right away, my lawyers petitioned the court to get me transferred out of 10 South. It was impossible to adequately represent me when attorney visits occurred in a place where there was a metal screen between them and the inmate, where no papers could be exchanged, or even read by the inmate, because of the screen. No physical contact between the inmate and his attorney was allowed.

Every time you leave ten south for a legal visit, or any other purpose, you are stripped naked, cavity searched, shackled up, taken to another area and given a jump suit. Then, accompanied by an officer and one or more guards, you are moved to where you have to go.

★

It was obvious that there was no legitimate reason to house me in the terrorist wing, with five inmates who were held there for trying to destroy our country. I was a reputed mobster, not a member of Al Qaeda or any such thing.

But I was a trophy that the government badly wanted to own, and so I spent several months at 10 South, until finally, after repeated petitions, after numerous court appearances, after numerous times of the prosecution, assuring the court that they were taking care of the situation, the judge finally ordered that I be moved out of 10 South.

But the Bureau of Prisons is not controlled by the judge's order, they answer to the Department of Justice. However, when it becomes a question of whether or not an inmate can get a fair trial, when the government's case itself might be put in jeopardy, then the gates open up.

So I was transferred. To a unit called Five North.

I ran into a bunch of guys from the DeCavalcante crime family that is based in New Jersey. They were the basis for the well known show, *The Sopranos*. There was Louie "Eggs," and Steve Vitabile, long term consigliere to the Family.

Steve had told me, while we were playing cards one day, that he had been surprised by the news of my leaving. He had been in a meeting with my Uncle Pete, regarding resolution of an outstanding issue, when I got home.

Pete had told him, "My nephew is not involved with anything anymore."

Steve understood, and supported my decision. He was glad that I, who was a guy with a young family, was going to move on with his life. He correctly observed, "The days of the Gottis, when it comes to this government, they'll rip your family apart, and tear down every brick of every building to get you."

★

While at MCC, I met several other interesting individuals.

Alberto Vilar, a wealthy investor and patron of the arts, who got a ten year bid for securities fraud and money laundering, among other charges. Then there was the "Dino Gyno" Niels Lauersen, gynecologist to the stars, who indirectly was responsible for me getting a goddaughter. He was in for millions of dollars in billing fraud. He had received payment from insurance companies for uncovered fertility treatments for the poor. Seven years in prison was what he received.

While these men were at MCC, they had been placed on a tier with gang members, who, of course, were going to shake these guys down. I instructed them to sit at my table, so the powers that be would know that Vilar and Lauersen were "with me," and not to be trifled with.

Both gentlemen were very grateful. Lauersen, upon learning that my friend, Steve Dobies' wife, was having a hard time conceiving a child, wrote to them with full instructions of what to do, where to go, and who to see.

The advice proved effective, and I, shortly afterwards, had a new god child.

CHAPTER TWENTY-FIVE

Trial One

The audio surveillance lasted from the beginning of 2003 until the end of May 2004. Shortly afterwards, July 21, 2004, the new indictment came down. It was unsealed a short time later. I had learned about the surveillance from my attorney, Richard Rehbock.

Lawyer visits were monitored too, totally violating traditional rules of attorney client privilege.

The government had alleged in the pretrial that they had a "treasure trove" of taped conversations to use at trial. I couldn't figure that out, because I know what I talked about, and it all reflected the truth: that I had nothing but disdain for the street life, I was done with it, and I didn't want my friends involved.

The government was to realize however, that in the present indictment's time range of allegations, the door was open to the defense to use my Ray Brook tapes to support my withdrawal defense—that I had not been involved in mob activities for five years prior to the indictment. (Later on, the government would challenge my use of these tapes at trial.)

Some critics out there, including the government at later trials, accused me of staging my tapes, intentionally talking about being out to bolster my withdrawal defense.

Nonsense, because during the recording of much of the tapes, I had no awareness that I was being monitored. It wasn't being routinely done at the time. I certainly never dreamed *a lawyer visit* would be taped, as it would have been a flagrant violation of privilege.

Additionally, given the acoustics of the personal visits, in crowded rooms where multiple conversations were being carried on, what could the listener's even hear? I have had tape transcription experts listen to tapes which were made in visiting rooms, and *they* had a very difficult time making out what was being said.

Monitors are supposed to engage in "minimization" as a part of wiretapping protocol. In English, that means when conversations are not related to the investigation, after a few seconds, they stop listening, and then periodically check back to see if related materials are being discussed.

Not in my case. Everything was listened to and recorded. Everything except a visit I received from my Uncle Richie who came to tell me that as far as "they" (Pete and Richie) were concerned, I was still a captain in the family.

I tossed him from the visit and reiterated that I was done, through, and that they should learn to live with it. My father accepted it, they should. "When I get back home, I'm going fishing," I told him. "Don't fucking come back here ever again, I don't want to see you."

One particular tape with Ruggiero would show that, even with my father's passing, the Family wanted me in a position of leadership. I was told that when I got out, I could have what I wanted.

In reading this transcript, JR is John Ruggiero, JAG is John A. Gotti. This conversation was recorded on October 5, 2003, in Ray Brook Federal Correction Institution. U/I means what was said was not understood by the transcriber of the tape recordings, "Unintelligible."

JR: Remember when you graduated school, and there was two, two of your father's friends that came, remember them?

JAG: Yeah.

JR: They send their love.

JAG: Always cared for them.

JR: Yeah, they're doing well.

JAG: Good.

We were referring to Arnold Squitieri and Alfonse Sisca. Ted Otto and Michael DiLeonardo testified that Squitieri was acting boss of the Gambino family. DiLeonardo also said Sisca was a captain.

JR: (Whispering) For you, [Ruggiero then rubbed his face] for me[Ruggiero pulled his shirt]

[The face rubbing meant to be the boss, the shirt pulling meant Ruggiero getting made.]

JAG: Not interested.

JR: You got that John, you gotta think, you gotta think.

JAG: I don't want it.

JR: I'm not gonna lose your friendship, John. I'm not gonna, I'm not ever in my life...

JAG: Listen to me...

JR: Just think of this decision you're making.

JAG: Listen to me and understand what I'm saying.

JR: I understand.

JAG: I am saving your life.

JR: Think the way you're thinking.

JAG: You have no idea.

JR: Alright, no problem.

JAG: No idea.

JR: No problem. You know, I'm not like you. [Ruggiero tapped his forehead.]

JAG: You ain't.

JR: U/I never want me to see you. U/I

JAG: You ain't half of me. You ain't half of what I was. You ain't half of what I used to be. John, look at how they fuckin' turned on me. Are you crazy? Are you crazy? I'd rather be hangin' out with U/I. I'd rather be a Latin King. Are you crazy, John? With all due respect, due respect, there's some guys out there, John, that I got a good soft spot in my heart for. I think about my father, I think about them and vice versa, I really do. The question is what happened to me over the last five or six years should not have. What was done here, I'm bitter. I'm very bitter.

JR: I know and they know.

JAG: No you don't know and they don't know.

JR: I spoke to them.

JAG: John, you should only know how bitter I am right now.

JR: That's why you need to listen to me.

. . .

JAG: I don't care, John. Your welfare is what I care about. You are a legitimate guy, stay that way. Me, John, if I'm fortunate enough to make it home, I'm going fishing. I don't want to be bothered, John. Those guys are nice guys, there's a lot of good people that, they were my uncles growing up, a lot of good old timers that were my uncles growing up, John. You gotta understand something, you and I were born around that.

JR: Yeah, yeah, yeah.

JAG: We used to go with our fathers, our fathers never really spent time with us. When they did, they drove us by the club, dropped us off at the club, and that was it. We were 10.11.12 years old in a club full of men.

JR: Yup.

JAG: You're almost forced to emulate these people. OK, you're almost forced to emulate them. So now...

JR: There are some nice, there are some...

JAG: John, there were some guys...

JR: Very few.

JAG: There were some guys that I genuinely loved.

JR: Yeah, those two fellas.

JAG: Danny, Danny Wagons, Carmine Fatico. I loved these guys.

JR: John, John...

JAG: They were our uncles.

JR: U/I.

JAG: My point, my point, my point is this: you grow up around these guys, you fall in love with these guys and they're good people. Some of them are really good people. But it just seems that most of the people out there, John, today are real garbage pails. For six years, six years, I got the ass. It didn't bother me for six years, going on January, it will be six years I haven't bothered with them for six years. I like it that way. John, believe me, I sleep better, I sleep better. I don't owe anybody anything and nobody owes me anything. They owe my father a lot. They, me nothing, nobody owes me a thing. I just want to do my time, and go home, and go fishing. I don't want to bother nobody, I don't want anything from anybody.

JR: U/I. When your father died, I looked at one of them and one of them started crying. Unbelievable.

JAG: U/I.

JR: He told me, nobody can ever come to them, never, never, and you, number one. Very important, and your father. They love you, they're for you, love you dearly.

What I wanted—and this is crystal clear from the government tapes of my visits—was to never have anything to do with the Life again. The Hell with the money on the streets, the Hell with the power and the illusion of respect, I had quit, and I was never coming back.

A New Indictment

In July, 2004, the government indicted me along with several others. The most serious charge dealt with the alleged kidnapping and attempted murder of Guardian Angel founder, Curtis Sliwa. Let's look at that portion of the indictment:

> More specifically, GOTTI, D'ANGELO and YANNOTTI are charged with conspiring to kidnap and murder, kidnapping, and then attempting to murder Curtis Sliwa, the founder of the Guardian Angels, who sustained multiple gunshots wounds during an attack on June 19, 1992.
>
> According to press reports, in the early morning of June 19, 1992, Sliwa, who had been publicly outspoken in his criticism of organized crime figures generally, and of John J. Gotti, GOTTI's father, specifically, hailed a cab to drive him to work. Shortly after the cab driver pulled away from Sliwa's block, Sliwa looked up to see a second man pop up from the front seat. This man, who was wearing a cap and had covered much of his face with a bandanna, was pointing a handgun at Sliwa. According to press reports, the gunman shot Sliwa multiple times in the torso and legs before Sliwa was able to escape from the cab.

According to the DOJ press release, I was facing 130 years in jail if convicted of this and the rest of the charges in the unsealed indictment. Yannotti was facing the death penalty, and another co-defendant, Joseph D'Angelo was facing life.

So I did what I always did—I got to work and commenced strategizing with my attorney and the attorneys for the co-defendants. I did not share all of the allegations with the other defendants, but I was interested in assisting the accused, not only in jointly shared charges, but in all the charges that faced all of us.

I had the most experience in fighting Federal cases, and I was a certified paralegal. So I led the fight.

Unity was the goal, an all encompassing defense strategy. But it was not to be, because not everybody had the will to resist government pressure to cooperate.

★

The task would be monumental. The government had hundreds of hours of audio surveillance tapes. As an opening gambit, I moved to have the indictment dismissed, as I was in the '98 case and subsequent plea bargain, supposed to plea in satisfaction of everything they could charge me with past and then present.

But the words of my father were an accurate prediction. The government had no intention of ever letting me out of jail, and the motion to dismiss was denied.

Joint defense agreements were executed, so that the co-defendants could share information and strategies while still being protected by attorney client privilege. It was difficult to arrange meetings with the parties in both the MCC and the MDC, and since it was determined I was a greater transport risk than the others, when meetings were held, the other fellows came to see me at the MCC.

For the prisoners, meetings could be an all day affair, starting at 5:00 AM, with a variety of cavity searches and chains on and chains off. My co-defendants in the indictment, even though some faced different charges than others, were Mike Yannotti, Joseph D'Angelo, and Louie "Black" Mariani.

Mariani, who was then represented by my future lead counsel, Charles Carnesi, was charged only with securities fraud and construction extortion, and made bail. The rest of us were charged with violent crimes.

The separation of the co-defendants in different prisons, one in Brooklyn, one in Manhattan, served not only to make joint defense meetings very inconvenient to arrange, but further, it kept us from emotionally supporting each other, keeping each other strong. It was a form of divide and conquer.

★

The visiting room became a temporary "war" room. We had a white board set up with the charges enumerated in order to help strategize defenses, we had access to boxes of materials, documents, tapes, etc.

I made sure that all co-defendants and their attorneys were informed of what was going on in my situation, what my plans for defense were. I did not want anyone to think they were going to be left in the lurch, or that I was only concerned with my own welfare. If any motion was to be made, I instructed my attorneys to furnish the other lawyers with copies for the comments before filing them.

In preparation for one of the legal visits, I run into Frankie Fappiano, on the other side of the window of the room I was waiting in. Fappiano, who I knew well, and who was about to become a government cooperator. Fappiano had been a member of the same crew as Joseph D'Angelo, but then eventually wound up with his brother-in-law—Michael DiLeonardo. Fappiano's older cousin was Frank DeCicco.

He saw me, and tears came to his eyes. His entire family had been in the Life, and here he was now on the road to rat. I asked him, "You alright pal, you okay?" The guard hushed me up, because I wasn't supposed to be talking to him, but through gesture, I indicated he should stay strong. Keep his head up.

"I'm trying to take twenty years, but they won't let me," he said.

"Stay in the fight, Frankie, you'll be good," I told him.

Over the next days he flipped. I was told he was taken out of the building. I now figured D'Angelo would be the next one to go government witness. With Fappiano turning witness on the murder charges they were facing, it put a big dent in any defense D'Angelo could muster.

D'Angelo probably wanted to turn well before he did, but the government wanted him on at least one of the joint defense meetings. A mole in our field.

I never worried about Yannotti flipping. He was a torpedo, tough kid. So now, it was he, Mariani, and I, together to fight the charges, especially related to Sliwa.

★

So who was Sliwa? His version, in 1977, when he was twenty-three, he created the, supposed, crime fighting organization known as the Guardian Angels; and their red berets started becoming visible on city streets and subways.

They were not sanctioned by law enforcement, they had no authority, but they sure had publicity. Sliwa was a media hound, seeking press coverage regardless of the truth of the incidents he addressed.

Around Thanksgiving 1992, the Transit Police Union decided to file suit against Sliwa for damage to their reputation. Sliwa had previously admitted that many of the Angels' supposed crime fighting exploits were bogus—they never happened.

In 1980, he claimed he was kidnapped by off duty Transit Police Officers. Supposedly, it was an attempt to thwart Guardian Angels activities. Again this event never happened. In an attempt to avoid a lawsuit, Sliwa offered to apologize to those affected by his false claims.

When testifying at the 2005 trial, under cross examination by my attorney Jeff Lichtman, Sliwa admitted to having lied about multiple incidents that he claimed had occurred. He admitted that his claim to have personally fought off a would be rapist was false. He acknowledged that the 1980 transit police kidnapping was false.

After testifying, Sliwa told reporters, "Frankly, some of the things I did in the past, I deserved that line of questioning," referring to the destruction of his credibility during Lichtman's cross.

When testifying against me in the 2006 trial, Sliwa again admitted under cross-examination that he had faked multiple incidents in his "history" for public relations purposes.

My attorney, Charles Carnesi asked him, "That's something that you did quite often, interacting with the media?" Sliwa replied, "Yes sir, to try to generate at the beginning for the group positive publicity, because we weren't getting any."

On June 19, 1992, it appears in reality that persons did get him into a cab, briefly kept him there, and shot him, wounding him. If one is going to be a controversial media personality, it is often the case that you will attract certain crazies who may try to do you harm. It has happened before Sliwa's incident, and it will no doubt happen again to other media.

Ray Brook Transcript, Session 53

In reading this transcript, JAG stands for John A. Gotti, JR stands for John Ruggiero, and SK stands for Steven Kaplan. "U/I" means unintelligible, which means the transcriber couldn't understand what was being said.

JAG: I made the choices in my life. I chose to walk away. Nobody made that choice for me. From day one when I got arrested I saw how this life was phony. They're important my daughters and my wife U/I.

JAG: Tell me my son is involved in the street and I'll go hang myself, I couldn't do another day in jail. I could do all the time they give me, John, but if you were to tell me my son got involved with this life . . .

JR: John, forget about it.

JAG: I couldn't do another day in jail.

JR. Forget about it, John.

JAG: If you told me my brother got involved in this life, I would disown him, on my father and brother's grave, for life and I swear to god, I would never hello him again, ever, he won't be allowed in my house anymore. I'll tell my wife that my kids don't have to respect him.

SK: I don't think you have to worry about that.

JAG: Learn from me, Learn from me. Let me be the sacrificial lamb, learn from me, go on with your lives.

Ray Brook Transcript 10-05-03

In reading this transcript, JR is John Ruggiero, JG is John A. Gotti. This conversation was recorded on October 5, 2003, in Ray Brook Federal Correction Institution. U/I means unintelligible.

JG: They don't care about you. I don't wanna see you get proposed. You understand me? That's why I don't want you being involved with these people. Just stay away from them. They send for you, ignore them. Stay away from these people. I'm telling you be legitimate, I'm...

JR: You don't understand.

JG: I'm telling you to be legitimate, I'm telling you to stay away from these people.

JG: John, I want you listen, I want you to be a hardworking citizen, like you are. A responsible husband to your wife, a responsible father to your children, as I want him, and you want to know what, John, you're gonna live a long and fruitful life, you really will, you really will. You're gonna amount to nothing in life. At the end of the day they're gonna use you, abuse you...

JG: They know people are bitter here, John, and I don't want people to feel I'm bitter with them. I made a choice, are you listening to me, I made a choice, I made a choice that when I'm going home, my father's dead, my responsibility is to my mother, my sisters, my brother, my wife, and all my nephews and nieces, and my children, that's my responsibility, and to my dear friends, you, Steven, nobody else. I don't owe anyone else anything, John, I gave everything I had. I, I, I helped whoever I could help in life. That's it. I'm moving on with my life, with my head held high, with my self-respect, you understand me?

JG: It's not real, John. It's just not real, don't you understand? What's real is your wife, what's real is your children. That's what's real. Your brothers, they're real. These are things you gotta protect, you gotta fight to protect. Never mind getting caught up in any of that horseshit. Never mind that, John. Never mind it. Listen to me. Believe me.

JG: NO, what I'm trying to say to you is this: You're either a legitimate guy, a happy family man U/I not. If you're not, plead your case now or we'll stop seeing each other. If you are then please, it's my pleasure to see you John. If you're a street guy, leave and you shouldn't ever come see me. I don't want your troubles. I'm trying, I'm fighting with every ounce of my being to go home to my children. I think my family suffered enough. My mother suffered enough, my family. We suffered enough, I believe.

Gotti—Trial 2005

In August, 2005, my trial was to commence. First, however, there was the issue of bail.

Bail is a crucial issue for a defendant, not only for the comfort and enjoyment of being released from prison, for the psychological and emotional benefits of being with family and friends once again; but, more importantly, for the strategic and tactical reasons that an accused, free from the time and space constraints of prison, is much more able to assist his attorneys and investigators in the preparation and conduct of a trial.

In other words, he has a better shot at obtaining an acquittal.

My bail eligibility would begin at the termination of my sentence for the '98 case, which was September 7, 2004. I would then be permitted a bail hearing. My lawyers were confident I would be granted bail. It would most likely be a substantial bail package, but one would likely be granted.

I had eventually received bail in the '98 case, and now circumstances were different. I was out of the Life. We had the Ray Brook tapes made by the government as supporting evidence. Plus, I had never, in the past, been considered a flight risk. Up to the time of the consideration of this bail application, I had never been in warrant status. I had always showed up to court.

As far as being a threat to the community, the government would likely bring up the Sliwa charge, a violent act of which I was accused. But we were confident we could surmount those arguments at a bail hearing.

Wrong. The judge felt that the amount of time I was risking at this trial was a factor in my becoming a potential flight risk. Bail denied. The first battle, in what was to be a very long war, went to the government.

★

I was now under a significant defense disadvantage; forced to prepare for battle while in the confines of prison—limited access to lawyers, investigators, legal research materials, and needed documents.

But my idea of defense is attack, and the first target on my radar was the indictment itself.

I had entered into a plea in '99 with the stated (on the record) purpose of that plea being in full satisfaction of anything of which I might be accused, from that time going back. This was the foundation of our plea negotiations, and the *raison d'être* of our plea.

Now, I was being prosecuted by the same office with whom I had made that deal. The Southern District of New York in Manhattan.

My challenge to the indictment was denied by the Second Circuit Court of Appeals. So now on to the preparation of the defense for the trial itself. But the government had a significant advantage. They had listened to my thoughts expressed in jail and taped them.

In my meetings with my friend and then attorney, Richard Rehbock, we had discussed strategies, and what the government might do. There were fourteen months of tapes in the government's hands. It was clear that I wanted no part of the Life anymore, but I remember that Rehbock had said, "They don't give a shit, they have an agenda here. and you, my friend, are it."

Knowing he was correct, even while in jail, I began laying out a defensive strategy against a possible subsequent indictment. Tapes whirled on while I discussed my plans, government ears listened and remembered.

Two sided coin for me, these tapes. On the one hand, there was a clear demonstration of my having left the Life, of wanting no further part of it. But the tapes also revealed my expressed contempt for some of those in the Life. Tapes recorded my numerous complaints also, about friends and family. (When I love someone, I love them dearly, but not without occasional complaint or criticism.)

I had said that people had taken advantage of the fact of my father's demise. I had also admitted to walking away from large sums of money I had "on the street," but qualified that admission with the truth that I did not seek to recover them—I had abandoned the Life, and the money that went with it.

Those out on the streets were happy to cooperate with my abandonment of cash and property, and began circling around like sharks—or perhaps better said, piranhas, eager to feed themselves on what was left behind by the big fish who no longer cared to feed.

The government had been tuning in to my expressed anger and disappointment. They deemed it to be a weakness, and to further weaken me, as I said earlier, I was placed for a time in 10 South.

"I was angry with my friend and I told my wrath, my wrath did end. I was angry with my foe, I told my wrath, and my wrath did grow."—William Blake.

Many overtures were made by the government to me to cooperate. I stood fast in my refusal. They continued, and somehow the thought entered my mind to *seem* to possibly entertain the idea. The appearance, if not the reality. I could use this to destroy some of my enemies who had sought to destroy me. There was, I must admit, a certain attraction to the irony of using the government as my "hit men" against my mob enemies.

I met with the government. The financial pressures on me were crushing, assets seized, couldn't pay bills unless the government would allow me access to funds to do so. Hell, the government had forfeited 1.5 Million of my assets the last time around. If convicted, my home and other property would be seized, and my family rendered homeless. Additionally, I was facing the rest of my life in prison, away from my family—forever. If I were to cooperate, the prior forfeiture of the money and my property would be restored to me, was the message I received.

The restoration of my forfeited assets were of minor consideration. Revenge against two enemies was the major motivator here.

So I met with them. In a proffer session, what is called a "King for a day session." I had in mind two specific enemies of mine, if I were going to partially cooperate. I believed one had been a cooperator against my father and I. Now, the information divulged at these sessions cannot be used by the government, or used against you, without your cooperation.

I had spoken to the government about the bar fight in 1983. I ended my limited narrative with details about how my trucking company had engaged in illegal dumping in the Bronx.

The session probably lasted around forty minutes. Prior to the meeting, I waited for my attorney for more than two hours, because he had the notes we had scripted for the proffer session. Notes were taken by my attorney during the proffer session, which is standard practice. I had asked to tape the session, but the government wasn't going for it.

I spoke to an agent; my attorney took notes. We wanted our own record of what was said, to later analyze and compare with the notes we brought with us, to contradict any government embellishments, if necessary.

When I was done, it was back to my cell, and time to reflect.

I must admit to being somewhat disgusted with myself for having attended this proffer meeting. Truth to tell, I was sick to my stomach. I couldn't let the government use what I had spoken about in the session. As much as on the street, it would be kill or be killed with respect to those two enemies of mine in the Life, as much as this was to be my last act of treachery, I couldn't do it via being a cooperator.

What right did I have to bring my sons into my former world, my former scams? I had given them the name of Gotti, and would I then become a government witness and have them bury their heads in shame for the rest of their lives? I knew in my heart I would never testify against anybody—I couldn't, and for that I would pay a price.

I believed that, when I entered into the proffer session, I would be only telling the government a lot of what they had already learned from government documents, trial transcripts from the early nineties, listening to my tapes and those of Greg DePalma's; no matter what spin they put on it. Nothing came of it; nothing could come of it without me, except for message after message from the government to try and get me to flip. They were like sharks at a feeding frenzy, or rabid dogs.

I would be notified by the guard I had a visitor. I told them if it isn't my lawyer, send them away. So the government tried to get cute.

One time, I was told that I had a legal visit. It was a Sunday, and I thought it might be Seth Ginsberg, one of the lawyers defending me. I had expected him about two hours later on this Sunday, so maybe he showed up early.

I wasn't happy about this off schedule visit, so cursing, I jumped in the shower, and awaited to be transported to the normal site for a legal visit. When I arrived, I was directed to go "all the way in the back."

I thought this odd, because they always put me in the front visiting room where they could see me, make sure I wasn't passing or getting papers I shouldn't give or get. I walked towards the back, on this very quite Sunday, in the visiting area. All the available rooms were empty, except that one "all the way in the back." Now, normally the only reason I would be sent to the back rooms, would be if all the other rooms were taken by inmates in the SHU getting legal visits. But the place was empty.

What was up? I reached the back room and a casually dressed individual was seated there. As I entered the door, he rose as if to speak to me. I didn't know this guy, but I knew who sent him.

"Don't say a word," I told him. "Not a fucking word."

I turn to walk away, and yell for the guard to call transport and escort me back to my cell. I told the guard, "Tell the Lieutenant, if youse pull that shit again, I'm going to go hard."

I was loaded on the elevator and taken back to my cell. That night, around midnight, I hear chains rattling, feet moving rapidly. The noise was getting closer to my cell. I hear the gate on my tier open up.

I knew. I jumped up from my lower bunk, and told my cellmate, a Mexican busted on a drug charge, who spoke little English, so, in the Spanish that I had, "They're here for me. Make sure you pack my stuff, and nobody else, understand?"

"Si."

The door was unlocked, the light went on, and I heard that familiar, "Gotti, cuff up!" I threw on my jumper and cuffed up. I was then led away to the hole by four guards—no explanation as to why, no nothing.

This was March and we were in the middle of trial preparation. So my lawyers made a beef about me being in the hole, and about ten days later, I was released, again without any explanation as to why I had been there in the first place.

I guess the government was trying to show me the way, to see the light. But it wasn't going to happen—regardless of what they did or might do. My mind was made up.

★

Now, it was time to focus on the upcoming trial. The government had produced a bevy of witnesses that would be up against me and my co-defendants. The most serious charges in the indictment were against Michael Yannotti and me. Unfortunately, one of the indicted, Joe "Little Joe" D'Angelo, had flipped, and now would be telling the government all that was said in the co-defendant meetings.

I didn't really know Yannotti, maybe met him one time before. He wasn't a Queens guy. I didn't grow up with him. I was a bit leery. But we were now together in this indictment. Every morning at 5:00 AM, Yannotti (housed on a different floor) and myself were taken from our cells and brought down to R&D—Receiving and Departing, in the prison. We were placed in the bullpen with other detainees, and waited to have our names called, and then be strip searched, and handed our clothes to wear in the courtroom.

Then came the belly chains and the ankle chains, and then back to the holding area to await transport to the courthouse. There was a series of tunnels that connected the Metropolitan Correctional Center to the courthouse, about two blocks away.

As Yannotti and I were in civilian dress, we were separated from the other detainees in the bullpen at the courthouse, and placed in our own bullpen equipped with non-working metal sink, toilet, and wall-length steel benches.

So in this environment, Yannotti and I started to bond. From about 7:00 AM until the opening of court, somewhere between 9:30 and 10:00 AM, Yannotti and I would speak of our wives, our children, but little about the case. We were mindful that the marshals might hear us from the intercom system which was positioned throughout the corridor of the bullpen. We were guarding against saying anything which might impact on the case—give away strategy

★

Usually, about fifteen minutes before court would start, we would hear the banging of chains and metal handcuffs which the marshals brought to cuff us up and bring us upstairs to court. Once upstairs, we would be placed in a small cell (smaller than the bullpens downstairs). two doors down from the court-room.

From this cell you could somewhat hear the proceedings in the court.

★

Before the jury selection process began, we had filed a motion *in limine*, putting the government on notice regarding evidence we sought to introduce at trial. They were also required to file such a motion.

We sought to use the Ray Brook tapes in support of my

withdrawal defense—that I had not been involved in mob activities for at least five years. Amazingly, the government opposed the introduction of these tapes that had been made under their direction, supervision, and control.

Fourteen months of government tapes, paid for by taxpayers, and yet the introduction of these tapes by the defense was vigorously challenged by the government that made them. It was obvious why. It was, or would be, of tremendous value to the defense.

The judge, ruling on our motion, said that charges in the indictment covered activities until 2004. Therefore, tapes made up until and prior to that time, of course, *were* admissible.

But the prosecution was to do an end run around that decision. They go back to the grand jury, and amend the indictment to include only those activities made prior to the commencement of the taping by the government of my visits. (2002—the taping commenced in 2003). Ergo, tapes would not be relevant, since they bore no impact on the amended crimes charged, being prior in time to the tapes.

★

We were led from the small court holding cell to our places at the defense table. We were greeted by family, friends and well-wishers, and then the judge came out and we began jury selection. The jury pool consisted of some three hundred individuals.

The selection of "fair and impartial" jurors is an art, not a science. Jurors can be removed for cause, for example, prejudice, some conflict, some knowledge of the parties or the facts. Or, if they cannot be removed for cause, the prosecution and the defense have what are called peremptory challenges—a certain number of times they may remove a juror for no articulated reason, but these are limited. Ergo, a good attorney will try to get a juror excused for cause and preserve his peremptory challenges as much as possible.

After almost a week, a jury was selected, and on August 8, 2005, the trial began.

The government opened with the traditional litany about the Gambino crime family, and their activities, and the control over said family that was exercised by my father, and later by me. The government promised to "walk the jury" through the whole history, and to show how I had arranged, pursuant to my father's orders, the "kidnapping and attempted murder" of Curtis Sliwa in retaliation for his constant harangue against my father in the media.

They would also prove the violent acts of Mike Yannotti—assault, attempted murders, murders. But they were no longer seeking the death penalty.

Then there were the less dramatic charges the government would prove, construction extortion, loan sharking, stock fraud. Louis Mariani was the guy charged with the stock fraud. He was represented by Charles Carnesi (who was later to become my attorney in subsequent trials, and a very dear friend). Yannotti was represented by Diarmuid White. Jeff Lichtman was my attorney.

During his opening statement, Lichtman said to the jury, "This trial is about fathers and sons. John, loyal to his father, followed him in to the Life, but at some point became disenchanted and would fight to extricate himself from the world of which he had been a part."

Lichtman went on to say:

Unlike the witnesses that you will see paraded before you very shortly, John changed as a man when he realized that is children might very well grow up without him if he didn't change. John didn't change for any of the reasons that the cooperating witnesses changed in this case. He didn't change because of reasons like revenge, like Mike DiLeonardo who is going to come in here and tell you why he decided to cooperate. He is not going to tell you that he changed because he missed his money or that he wanted a reduction in his sentence. As the evidence will show he changed due to the fact that he had a wife and five small babies. One of them, the youngest, Gianna, was born while he was in prison. It took him five days to learn he even had a daughter."

The government cooperating witnesses were deridingly referred to by Lichtman as the "Sons of Sammy." Michael DiLeonardo, Frank Fappiano and the flipped co-defendant, Joe D'Angelo. They all had been close to Gravano. (It seems that those whose lives I had saved back in the warehouse meeting of '92 were now following their former crew leader Gravano, into WitSec.)

It was hard to understand. I had damaged my relations with people in the Life to save these guys, and now they were ready to hang me out to dry in a maximum security prison for the rest of my life. (I guess my adversaries that day in the warehouse had been right, after all.)

★

Fappiano was the first government witness called on August 11, 2005. His origins lie deep within the Life. Like me, he had many of his family in the Life. His older cousin was Frankie DeCicco. His father and several of his uncles were part of the Life.

I saw that Fappiano was very uncomfortable in his new role as turncoat for the government. He couldn't look at me, and labored with difficulty through every question posed by the prosecutor. (I had seen him before in the MCC bullpen and he couldn't look at me then either. It was then I knew he had turned.)

I actually felt sorry for him. Unlike the other cooperators, he told the truth about his reason for turning. "I don't want to do any more time." I respected his honesty. The others, they took my money, they were going to kill me, do it to me before I did it to them, etc. Fappiano answered honestly.

Fappiano did not prove to be an effective witness for the government.

★

Next up was Anthony Rotondo of the DeCavalcante family in New Jersey. (Not a son of Sammy.) The crime family that served as the basis for the show, *The Sopranos.* He was a capo. His father also had been part of the Life. Vincent "Jimmy" Rotondo. He had been a powerful capo, shot dead as a result of a power struggle in the family during the late '80s. January 4, 1988, to be exact.

Fresh out of college, Anthony became involved. He was testifying as to my pedigree, and a meeting we had as made men, regarding a contractor in the carting business. He struck me as intelligent, Anthony, but I still didn't really understand his utility as a witness in this case, except possibly for the jury to make a father and son comparative with me.

★

On August 17, 2005, Joey D'Angelo took the stand. I didn't know him that well, maybe met him a dozen times. He was being forgiven charges of assault, conspiracy ,and three murders in exchange for trying to get me for the government.

Joey had been a likable kid. Not too bright though. I believe the jury liked him in spite of the fact that his memory of the supposed events involving Sliwa was questionable at best. D'Angelo's father, Joseph "Stymie" D'Angelo, had been in the Life, and had been shotgunned to death when his son was a teenager. His father's closest friend and partner was Gravano. Gravano took the teenager under his wing and directed him straight into the Life.

So Gravano had been the role model for young Joey.

During his direct examination, D'Angelo testified about

a meeting that he said took place with me, Nicky Corozzo, Mike Yannotti and a guy named Sal. In a basement in a Jamaica Queens building, we met at midnight, D'Angelo said, and plotted the beating of Curtis Sliwa for his continued bad mouthing of my father and the Family.

In his testimony, D'Angelo claimed to have been provided with the necessary tools to complete the job, along with a specially rigged cab that would not permit Sliwa to exit once he had entered. Sliwa's residence, newsstand where he bought his morning paper and the location where he hailed his daily cab to the radio station were provided D'Angelo.

During his direct he spoke of the problems he had on June 19, 1992, while waiting for Sliwa to appear. An innocent couple tried to get into the cab with Yannotti hiding in the front under a black cloth. "Off duty," D'Angelo told them, and the couple exited. A short time later, a traffic cop in his three wheeler pulls up and tells them to move as the cab is parked illegally. They move the cab.

Just as they were thinking about aborting the mission, Sliwa shows up and enters the cab. They drive off. Here are some segments from his direct:

> Then he (Sliwa) said, "Hey buddy, you're going the wrong way."... Mike Yannotti jumped up. He was crouched under the seat and he jumps up with a gun and a mask on... Mike Shot him... Then Mike was wrestling with him... Then we are driving. Curtis is jumping around in the back. Couple more shots. Curtis starts calling out, Curtis is halfway out the window and Mike has got him. He jumped over Mike's shoulder and out the window and Mike is holding him. Then I just said "throw him out the fucking window." He went out the window.

After his direct, our defense team was able to poke some holes in D'Angelo's Sliwa story.

Also during the cross of D'Angelo, the defense tried to bring out his involvement in the racially motivated killing of Yusuf Hawkins, but the judge ruled against this line of questioning as being more prejudicial than probative of anything. (Hawkins had been killed in Bensonhurst at the age of sixteen by a mob of kids who thought he had been dating a local girl. He hadn't, but was still shot to death.)

Our feeling was that D'Angelo may have provided the gun that killed Hawkins. If true, it was likely that the gun was involved in other murders perpetrated by D'Angelo, which certainly would have been relevant on cross-examination as to character and credibility.

But it was not to be.

As a corroborating witness to D'Angelo, the government then called "Fat Sal" Mangiavillano. Instead of helping, he opened the door to inquiry regarding misconduct by the main FBI agent assigned to the case.

In 2002, FBI agent Ted Otto interviewed Fat Sal; it came out that Sliwa was shot for bad mouthing my father. Yannotti and D'Angelo were primarily involved. They were the shooters. Further, that Sammy Gravano was trying to get D'Angelo "straightened out," in other words to become a made man in the mob. Gravano sanctioned it. Supposedly, my father sanctioned the attempted hit on Sliwa.

Sounds good? Problem though. In 1992, Gravano was already in WitSec for about a year, and not in a position to sanction anything regarding the mob.

Fat Sal was confronted with this on the stand and then denied ever having made the statement to Otto. This was the beginning of what my lawyers and I referred to as the Ted Otto "Specials." An agent who never let inaccuracy stand in the way of a recorded statement, who courageously would parade them as Federal Bureau of Investigation "fact." (More on him later, and his attempts to have me killed by those in the Life.)

★

Curtis Sliwa took the stand on August 22, 2005. While I believe the jury believed he had been shot, his long history of fabricating incidents did not stand him well in the realm of testimonial credibility.

My attorney cross-examined him concerning the many lies he had publicly told. Staged acts, false incident reports. A boy with a red beret that liked to cry wolf—too many times.

★

The star witness of the government was Michael "Mikey Scars" DiLeonardo. Brother-in-law to Frankie Fappiano. He took the stand, and I felt a wave of disappointment come over me. I had hoped it wasn't true that he was going to testify, but here it was right in front of me.

He made reference to a time he had tried to kill himself, and that he had hoped that his "Brother John," appreciated what he was about to do. He had swallowed a handful of pills. He and I both became emotional during that testimony.

He went on to testify about the workings of the Gambino crime family. Here is a small excerpt from his testimony given in a subsequent trial (February 22, 2006), but similar to what he said at the 2005 trial:

Q. What kind of family is the Gambino family?
A. Mafia or Cosa Nostra family.
Q. You used that term "cosa nostra." What does that mean in English?
A. It means "our thing" or "this thing of ours."
Q. You say that the Gambino family is part of Cosa Nostra.
A. Yes.
Q. Are there other families that make up Cosa Nostra in the New York area?
A. Yes. There's four more in New York and one in New Jersey.

Q. And can you name for us the ones that are resident principally in the New York area?

A. Yes. There's the Genovese family, Colombo family, the Bonanno family, and the Lucchese family.

Q. You say there's an additional, or sixth, family that's principally based in New Jersey?

A. Yes. The DeCavalcantes.

★

He further testified as to Gotti control over the family and other organized crime matters.

On cross-examination, it came to light that, after a fake bail hearing, he was released and wore a wire when speaking to his friends. Even at his dying mother's bedside, when his friends had gathered in support, the tape recorder was running.

He tried to kill himself because he felt guilty over this behavior. But his girlfriend found him and called the ambulance. He was brought to the hospital, had his stomach pumped, and was released several days later—back to jail. Not in the general population, but in 10 South.

Inedible food. Lights on 24/7. Video surveillance. Foul smelling, filthy. And you stayed there, in that cell, for every hour of the day.

DiLeonardo lost fifty pounds. But as there was no mirror in the cell, he couldn't see himself. That was the worst, he said. Great government work. Already an attempted suicide, thrown in to the worst possible conditions of confinement.

Why? To turn him and keep him turned. Keep him loyal to his captors in true "Stockholm Syndrome" mode.

★

One month of testimony was given. A dozen government witnesses testified. Closing arguments were to begin on September 8, 2005. Both sides replayed the case, the testimony, the evidence before the jury during summation.

On the 9th of September, jury deliberation began. Yannotti and I were waiting in the bullpen. When the jury sent a note to the judge, we were brought back to the courtroom. On the way up, we wondered? Just a request for an evidence read-back, a request for more time for lunch, or was it a verdict? You can imagine how we felt during deliberations—or maybe, if you've never been in this situation, you can't.

September 21, Mike and I were in the bullpen. Suddenly the sound of chains and cuffs were heard. A note had been received from the jury. We stopped talking. The steel door of the pen opened, and more than the usual amount of marshals appeared. Six instead of four.

"What's the story?" I asked.

"Verdict's in," they said.

Mike and I nodded to each other. This was it. We were silent on the way up to the courtroom. It seemed so quiet, you could hear a mouse piss on a cotton ball.

The benches in the audience were full. Agents on one side, press and family on the other.

The judge entered and confirmed that, indeed, there was a verdict that had been determined.

"Bring in the jury," the judge instructed the marshal.

They walked in stoically. Judge Scheindlin asked for the verdict sheet. She read it and appeared confused.

"It appears we have a mixed verdict," she said.

She began to go through the counts. Gotti, not guilty as to stock fraud. Jury hung on all other counts. Yannotti, not guilty of all murder and attempted murder charges. Hung jury regarding Sliwa. Guilty of loansharking. Guilty of racketeering conspiracy.

We had done very well. Louis Mariani was not guilty of extortion or loan sharking, but was found guilty of stock fraud.

Judge Scheindlin thanked the jury for its service and gave them the option to leave, or return to the jury room for questions by the attorneys on the case.

She then addressed our attorneys. "Counselors, I'm sure you are going to want to make a motion regarding bail?

Yes we did want to do that.

Then it hit me. I might be going home. A tear rolled down my face.

CHAPTER TWENTY-SIX

Retrial Awaits

The government did not get their trophy in 2005, and now, awaiting a retrial, there would be the question of bail. At first, they indicated they would oppose bail. Judge Scheindlin, however, after hearing the case that the government said it would offer, was inclined to grant it.

The haggling would now begin regarding the bail package that would be acceptable. Finally it was agreed, there would be bail in the amount of $7,000,000, secured by properties and ten signatures of qualified guarantors. Once again, an electronic ankle bracelet would be on me.

I was to be under "house arrest" status. I was restricted to no more than fifteen feet from my property, unless it was a legal or medically related visit. Were I to violate this restriction, an alarm would go off. I believe the bracelet was monitored through a central monitoring office in Omaha, Nebraska.

Any other off property activities had to be approved by the court and what was referred to as Pretrial Services. (I would put in requests to attend school functions of my children, or some other family related purpose, and of course, the prosecution would oppose. More often than not, the judge would grant my application. I believe that Judge Scheindlin recognized the petty vindictiveness of the US Attorney and the FBI agents assigned to the case.)

On September 28, 2005, I was released on bail, subject to the aforesaid conditions. As a parting gesture, the government insisted that the marshals drive me home in belly chains and cuffed up.

My lawyers were outraged, and insisted that *they* be allowed to drive me home. The prosecution said no way. So, they got their way, because I wanted to get out of there, and instructed my lawyers to agree, and not waste anymore time.

The morning of my release, just like when court was in session, I was brought over to the courthouse and placed in a bullpen, to await the marshals who would be transporting me back home this time.

Several hours later, I was cuffed up, reprinted, photographed again, and led to a waiting marshal's car. Three marshals escorting me. One of them, said, regarding the cuffs, "You don't need these," and removed them. But this was spotted by the marshal supervisor, who ran towards the car and flagged us down.

"Prosecution orders," he said, "Gotti is to be secured properly."

Back in belly chains and cuffs. The marshals were even shocked at this. After all, I was being released to my home, not being escorted back to prison. I just smiled. We drove through the security post, and I was on my way home to my family. I felt guilty leaving Mike Yannotti behind, but thought to myself it will only be a few years and he will be home with his wife and children. Me, I have to do this again. (Unfortunately, those "few years" were not to be, Yannotti received a twenty year sentence.)

"Don't worry, John," one of the marshals told me. "Before you get home and see your kids, we'll take the chains and cuffs off."

I was relieved and grateful for that courtesy. I did not want my children seeing their father in chains. I felt euphoric, but kept silent on the journey home. That word "home" takes on a whole new meaning when you haven't been there for years, and the only home you had was often the "hole."

This night, I said to myself, this night I will sleep in my own bed. I will be among my children and my wife. There will be no physical bars. There will be no count ups. There will be a damn sight better food too. More privacy.

Well maybe not privacy, because when I approached my home, the media feeding frenzy was in full swing. A number of those damn helicopters hovered over my property again, but at least this time it wasn't a prelude to my incarceration. It belonged to the news, not the government. Representatives of Channels 4, 7 and 11 were there, I remember.

Police barricades were set up to contain the reporters. So you understand, where I was living was a small road, perpendicular to another small road. There wasn't a lot of room to move when there wasn't a crowd of news hungry journalists, and now, it was a packed house.

Screams, flash bulbs popping, as the car turned into my street. My entire family was coming out of the house, coming to the car. I tapped the marshal on the shoulder, and reminded him of his promise. Take off the cuffs. Gentleman that he was, he did, and I expressed my gratitude.

Unchained, I leapt from the car and ran to embrace my family. From the corner of my eye, I spotted the yellow balloons that had been hung all around the property. My kids had done that, my wife informed me.

I tossed a wave and a few sound bites to the reporters, hoping that the morsels would keep them happy (and away from me) for a while. The next door I walked through was not a prison gate, was not a courtroom door. It was my door—the door to my house. The door that led to my family *home*.

I was feeling incredible, joy doesn't even begin to cover it—and then one of the family dogs bit me on the ass.

"Beauty." A good looking, intelligent, out-of-her-mind, canine. Giant black shepherd. She had been purchased while I was at Ray Brook.

The dog didn't know me, and only saw my wife shoving me into the house. So being the protective pooch that it was, it got behind me and chomped down. I was so damn happy to be home, I didn't care. The dog could have eaten my leg off, and I wouldn't have cared or felt it.

★

That night—all night—the whole family played catch up. There was a lot to catch up. Outside the media were still circling, getting it all down on videotape. They even followed our family as we went to the local church, and the photo made it into front page news.

For the first time in many years, with special permission from my judge, I got to see my son John, a star athlete, play football for his high school, St. Anthony's. Sitting next to me by chance, was football legend Vinny Testaverde, who was also my neighbor. The media ignored him that day, and focused their lenses on me. He and I laughed about it.

The *Daily News* had another front page photo of my son and I walking off the field together.

But as the media has a very short attention span, eventually they went away. Home again, but all wasn't fun and games. It was time to focus and prepare for the next trial. My attorneys at the time and I had different opinions on strategy, so my attorneys at the time went their way, and I went to seek new counsel.

I wanted to put on a strong defense case, this time with witnesses on my behalf, and not just engage in what has at times been referred to as a Constitutional defense.

For those who are not familiar with the term, a Constitutional defense is where you render (or try to render) the government unable to prove its case beyond a reasonable doubt, which is their obligation in accordance with the requisites of the US Constitution.

But you don't offer up evidence yourself. You mainly rely upon cross examination to weaken the prosecution witnesses to increase the quantum of doubt so that the prosecution cannot meet its burden. It worked the last time for me, because the result was a hung jury.

Not this time for that type of battle. They would have their witnesses, and I would now have mine. I wanted an attorney who would get on board with that, and I found one in Charles Carnesi.

Carnesi had "made his bones" as a long time prosecutor—assistant District Attorney in the Brooklyn office. Invaluable experience for any defense attorney. He, like many criminal defense attorneys, learned his craft as a prosecutor, and then went private to *defend* the accused.

I got to know Charlie on the previous trial as he was representing one of the co-defendants. I thoroughly enjoyed his wit, his charm, and his eternal optimism, which for any attorney is a very rare quality. We hit it off.

With one of his big smiles, Carnesi agreed with my idea of putting on a vigorous defense. He knew it wouldn't be easy, however. We were both aware that much more often than not, a retrial of a case results in a conviction, or more likely a plea deal to avoid a post trial conviction and the greater sentence that would accompany it.

★

Carnesi and I met regularly. We had taken some space in the building where he had his office. We reviewed the government case, witness by witness, exhibit by exhibit, finding numerous inconsistencies in the statements of government cooperators. We must have reviewed thousands of FBI 302s.

★

Given the inconsistencies we found, it made more and more sense to gather and present witnesses for the defense. We would not just "hide" beyond reasonable doubt we would attack, and affirmatively prove that what the government said was not the truth.

We began to compile a list of potential defense witnesses. We were going through our case files, and some of the prospective witness addresses were very old, and this would greatly burden our investigators in locating them.

During our search for defense witnesses, we received a call from an unidentified caller. He would not tell us his name. In his call to Charlie Carnesi, he said, "I'm sick of what the government is trying to do to this kid. I know first hand that he is no longer part of that Life. He had told me so, and I relayed that to the government."

Now this caller had Charlie's attention. With further questioning on the phone, Charlie felt the caller was being very evasive. The man went on to say that he had been with me in Valhalla and had asked me to intervene on his behalf regarding a problem he was involved with in the streets. He told Charlie that I responded to him that I had removed myself from that world, and would not be able to help him. He had been shocked by my answer at the time, but it was later confirmed by Greg DePalma.

Charlie has requested a meeting, but the caller said, "No. No name, no meeting." He then told Charlie he would get back to him. After Charlie told me the details of the call, I knew exactly who it was.

"Joe Fusaro," I said. He was a friend of Greg DePalma and Louis "Louie" Brazziole, Greg DePalma's captain. I had only met him a handful of times, but I was sure this was the identity of the caller.

"Well, what's his story?" Charlie asked me. "He told me he said this stuff to the government, and why would he, unless he was a cooperator."

"In my '98 case, he had been brought in, already doing fifteen years, and had a falling out with his Bronx friends, which is why he approached me for help."

Some point later on, he flipped. In the end he wound up not testifying in the '98 case, because all of the defendants had entered into plea bargains before trial. Nevertheless, the government still cut his time down to approximately five years.

So now we had a problem. How to find this guy if he didn't call back.

Several weeks later, as we were approaching the time when we would put on the defense case, Charlie received a call, once again from this individual. "I won't be able to live with myself, if I just sit by and don't do anything to help this kid," the voice on the phone said. "What they're doing to him is wrong."

"You can help," Charlie responded, "by first giving me your name."

After a ten second pause, the voice said, "Joe Fusaro."

Charlie thought to himself, he later told me, John was right.

"Let me send an investigator to talk to you in person," Charlie said.

Fusaro agreed. He gave his present address and he received a visit from one of my attorneys and our investigator. He repeated the same story he told Charlie, but admitted he was afraid of government retaliation if he were called to testify.

He was told that his information was only useful if he testified. It was useless otherwise because it couldn't serve as evidence.

"Do you really think my testifying would make a difference?" he asked.

"Absolutely," said the attorney who was on the visit.

Joe Fusaro did come forward and testify despite warnings from government agents not to do so. He displayed great courage, for the threats could come not only from the government, but from the streets as well.

CHAPTER TWENTY-SEVEN

Trial Two

Jury selection in the case was to begin on February 14, 2006, which coincidentally was my forty second birthday. We had about ten weeks until then, and we doubled up on our preparations.

Trial prep was not my only obligation, and I had—and wanted to—attend to my family's needs. Think about what they had to contend with. I lose at trial, and no husband John for my wife—ever again. No father for my children—ever again. Their home would be forfeited to the government, and they would be rendered homeless. The commercial property I owned that provided the income for the family would be seized by the government.

Additionally, there was the constant presence of agents outside our gates. My wife had become used to it, but now my children were old enough to know what was going on.

Nicolette, my eldest daughter approached me once and said, "I thought this was all behind us. I thought by you going away and giving up all that money this would be over."

"So did I sweetheart," I replied. Failure was not an option in this defense.

One of the tactics of the government—and I grudgingly

admit it's a great one—is to impoverish or at least attempt to impoverish a defendant before he goes to trial. Cut off the money for investigators and attorneys, and you choke the life out of a defendant's case. So my bank accounts, my property rents were frozen.

I wasn't even allowed to apply for a second mortgage to help fund my defense, unless the court would grant it. I hated to, but having no other choice, I had to liquidate my children's college accounts—it was either that or sell off the property that produced the income the family needed to survive.

Several hundred thousand was thereby freed up to fund my war with the government. I figured if I beat the government, I could mortgage the properties and refund the college accounts with the borrowed money. If I had to, I'd sell the property to get those kids through college. But to do any of that, I couldn't get convicted.

This government imposed pretrial impoverishment made me doubt myself as a father, a husband, and a man. With all the trouble my being in the Life had brought my family, at least I wanted to compensate them with creature comforts, with financial security.

Not to be. Street life didn't end at the corner, it often crept into the doorway of one's family home. You couldn't tell your kids about the reality of the street, what you did, what might be done to you one day. You wouldn't want them to know.

The family and financial situation added to the already significant pressures on me. In order to bring some normalcy, some good times and memories to the family, I made sure that the Holidays would be special. Thanksgiving, Christmas, New Years.

Thanksgiving was always at my sister Victoria's house. An immense amount of food and drink for the guests, that year by year increased in numbers, as children grew and acquired new friends, new romantic interests. No wine glass was ever long found empty.

But for me, it was all about Christmas. Believe it or not, I am a kid at heart, and that rings true especially when I hear the bells of Christmas time. I always play host at home. I enjoyed decorating the property, inside and out, decorating the tree, with the songs of the season playing in the background.

Like my father had done, I had an open house policy for Christmas. If I knew you, and you had no place to go, you came to me. Nobody I was friends with would spend the holiday alone. If you didn't come to see me, you might have a slight problem with me.

The celebration would remind me of the days with my father. Friends and family gathered to enjoy the festivities. Then, as the crowd would thin out after midnight, the card table would be set up and we'd play Continental. About half a dozen of us around the table, playing until the morning. Late morning.

Good memories of good times had. But when the holidays were over, it was back to the battle, back to the preparations and strategy sessions for our defense of the upcoming trial.

Most of January 2006, was spent in the researching and drafting of pretrial motions and what would be motions *in limine*, as we were pro-actively defending this time, seeking to put on evidence in chief on my own behalf.

The week before the scheduled trial would normally be reserved for the determination of these motions by the court. Motions decided, Judge Scheindlin (she was again assigned), would bring the attorneys in to explain her expectations for the conduct of the trial.

★

I turn forty two this day, and *voir dire* begins in my trial. Jury selection. Questioning the strangers assembled—some of whom will be deciding my fate. At the end of this long day of jury selection, Charlie said he wanted to drive me home, because there were some items we needed to discuss—alone.

Charlie talked on the way home. A lot of it made sense to me, some of it sounded like bullshit. I knew this crafty streetwise lawyer had something up his sleeve. What would be pulled out of it?

I played along. The car pulled into the parking lot of a North Shore Long Island Chinese Restaurant, Hunan Taste. Why? What we were doing . . . oh. I remembered what day it was. I also remembered that according to my bail conditions, I couldn't be stopping here on my way home. I could violate the conditions of my bail, and then it would be back to jail.

"Don't worry," Charlie told me in his raspy voice, "I cleared it."

This would give us some alone time to discuss the case—and of course, eat the rather excellent cuisine of this place.

"Charlie, let's make it quick. My wife's got a cake at home for me, and . . ."

They were all there, my family, my legal team. Both beautiful and sad. None of my friends on the "no contact" list were there—it wasn't allowed. But still, a great time was had by all, food, drink, laughter.

But I kept my head clear. One or two martinis and that was it. I would be in court the next day, and I wanted to be ready physically and mentally. Within the ten o'clock curfew time, I headed home with my family, and went to sleep. (As much as one could sleep under the circumstances.)

★

On the 17th of February, the jury which had been selected were seated in the box, and the trial was ready to begin. Opening statements would be heard.

On the 21st, the government called John Carillo as their first witness. He was a former NYPD intelligence guy who was used in organized crime cases. He was an expert on organized crime. He provided background information and a "who's who." He also testified to having surveilled me from 1994–1997.

He testified that as boss, John Gotti's power was absolute. (My father, not me.)

Another witness called was Michael DiLeonardo. They brought him on third, and he was their big gun. His testimony was pretty much a replay of what he had said at the previous trial. The same with Joey D'Angelo's testimony—although there were some "corrections" of his testimony from trial one.

The government carefully tweaked D'Angelo's testimony regarding the alleged kidnapping and attempted murder of Curtis Sliwa. Over time while giving testimony, D'Angelo's sworn words seemed to mirror police reports and eyewitness accounts.

The tenth witness that the government called was Agent Robert Vendette, who had executed the search warrant on my Queens office back in the nineties. He, like the previous agent witness, gave the pedigree of the family, the who's who and what's what.

He even managed to bring some laughter into the courtroom. He told the story about how one time when he and another agent had me under surveillance, someone called the cops on them, and they wound up spread-eagled on the ground, until they showed the locals their Federal Bureau of Investigation ID.

He also testified that once my father was incarcerated, FBI attention to me increased. He made reference to subpoenas which had been served on me with respect to my business interests.

Next up on the government's case was the former head of the C-16 Squad, the FBI detachment dedicated to bringing down the Gottis, Bruce Mouw. Once again a litany about the Life before and after John J. Gotti. He testified as to his task to get my father and how he had become a top priority target, how he was responsible for the Ravenite bugs, and those in the Cirelli apartment above the club, and how with the help of turncoat Gravano, my father had been brought down on April 2, 1992, by his conviction.

Another agent took the stand, Special Agent Gill. He was the "money guy" for the FBI, an expert on money laundering techniques. He was a forensic accountant. He testified as to my business finances, separating the good money from the bad money, and making it look like it was all bad money.

Like many other accountants I've met (not all), he was boring. His testimony was monotonous. I don't think the jurors followed it, or if they did, they weren't paying much attention.

More prosecution witnesses came on, including Sliwa, who was no more credible than he was at the first trial, and on March 2, 2006, they rested.

★

I remember at the beginning of this trial, the sarcastic prosecutor, AUSA McGovern, would inquire of the court that we disclose the estimated time of our "vigorous defense" that we would be putting on. Seems like we had the last laugh the last time around, McGovern didn't get his conviction, and we didn't put on any witnesses on behalf of the defense.

This time it was different. But McGovern at the second trial asked of the court, "Your Honor, can we estimate how long this vigorous defense will take?"

(The government, this time around, had put on fifteen witnesses, wisely reducing the number of bad guy turned co-operator witnesses to two, to limit the damage to credibility that could be accomplished by cross-examination.)

McGovern was to find out about our vigorous defense.

Our first witness was the former wife of Michael DiLeonardo. Toni Marie Ricci nee' Fappiano. (Frankie Fappiano's sister.)

Her testimony came after much prior soul searching. First, Mikey Scars, her ex, had become a government cooperator, tearing her family unit apart. He was scheduled to testify against Fappiano her brother, until Frankie flipped.

The turning of her husband and her brother into cooperators made for total chaos in her family. Further, the fact that I had left the Life, and by street rules no loyalty or assistance would be due me, added to the outside pressure on Toni not to testify.

But she decided to follow her heart instead of the rules. Her Uncle George DeCicco (who we spoke of in the warehouse showdown earlier) told her "If by you telling the truth, it helps John, then fuck those guys in the streets. You have to look in the mirror and feel right about what you are doing."

And she did. She testified.

She effectively countered much of Michael's testimony, especially as it related to a visit his son had made to me while I was at Ray Brook. It was claimed I had ordered his son to appear after learning about DiLeonardo's defection, that it was some act of either intimidation, or an attempt to get his son to talk sense to the father.

Toni testified that I was like a second father to the boy. That the boy found great comfort in visiting me, and that the visit had been planned for over a year. (The visit took place only two months after DiLeonardo turned cooperator.)

I am grateful for the courage Toni demonstrated in taking the stand and telling the truth, regardless of the personal conflicts and consequences she might suffer.

★

We put on witness after witness to counter the government's case. Former NYPD officers, attorneys, private investigators, family and friends. Even my brother Peter, and of course, Joe Fusaro who we mentioned before. We called fourteen witnesses to the government's fifteen. They never expected such a "vigorous defense." We refuted the Sliwa accusations, supported the facts of my having left the Life, and countered loan sharking accusations.

And our witnesses had been at a disadvantage. They had to give a proffer to the government before testifying in open court—without immunity. They lie, they face perjury charges. Government witnesses did not. Lies could be cleaned up, (and later on, I will show you exactly how).

One of our better known witnesses was Civil Rights attorney Ron Kuby, who was also partnered up with Sliwa on his talk show. I had known Kuby since his days as protégé to Bill Kunstler, and I liked him.

He had represented a co-defendant in my '98 case. His client was ex-cop Sigmond the Sea Monster (who was briefly mentioned before in the Scores matter, and was the son of Mike Sergio, whose ass I saved in jail, and who later turned cooperator against me in the '98 case).

Kuby, with whom I had had frequent discussion about having left the Life, took the stand to testify as to that fact.

★

On March 7, 2006, closing arguments took place. Each summation lasted several hours. The next day jury deliberation began. I felt confident. Unlike the last time, I was surrounded by my family and friends during deliberation—immense moral support. I was also free to enjoy small comforts like going to the courthouse cafeteria, or out to lunch, or make a phone call home. (I didn't have my wife come to court.)

This time there was no bullpen, no marshals no chains.

What worried me most was the possibility that the jury would wind up deliberating on a weekend. Often that is not good for a defendant, because in reality, when it's the weekend, people are more inclined to get a case "over with," and get home. That isn't good when you are on the defense side.

Another reason I was afraid of a weekend deliberation, was the Saturday to come was the 18th of March, the anniversary of the day my young brother Frankie was killed in an accident on the streets of Howard Beach. Maybe I was being superstitious, but that's how I felt.

But on March 9, 2006, a note came back from the jury to the judge. They were hopelessly deadlocked. The judge was surprised to get this type of note so soon. She brought the jury back in and told them to try again. They left to deliberate.

Another note came in to the court. Was this the verdict? I was understandably tense before I learned that once again, the jury was hopelessly deadlocked. They could not agree as to my being guilty beyond a reasonable doubt or not.

The judge read an *Allen Charge* to the jury, which basically is a direction to the jury and a pat on the shoulder to get back and deliberate and come back with a verdict. Judges do not like hung juries, one way or another they want a verdict.

An Allen Charge should only be given once in a trial. (Although it was improperly given twice in my last trial in 2009—more on that later.)

So you better understand what was said to the jury by the judge, here is approved language for an Allen charge:

Members of the Jury:

I'm going to ask that you continue your deliberations in an effort to reach agreement upon a verdict and dispose of this case; and I have a few additional comments I would like for you to consider as you do so.

This is an important case. The trial has been expensive in time, effort, money and emotional strain to both the defense and the prosecution. If you should fail to agree upon a verdict, the case will be left open and may have to be tried again. Obviously, another trial would only serve to increase the cost to both sides, and there is no reason to believe that the case can be tried again by either side any better or more exhaustively than it has been tried before you.

Any future jury must be selected in the same manner and from the same source as you were chosen, and there is no reason to believe that the case could ever be submitted to twelve men and women more conscientious, more impartial, or more competent to decide it, or that more or clearer evidence could be produced.

If a substantial majority of your number are in favor of a conviction, those of you who disagree should reconsider whether your doubt is a reasonable one since it appears to make no effective impression upon the minds of the others. On the other hand, if a majority or even a lesser number of you are in favor of an acquittal, the rest of you should ask yourselves again, and most thoughtfully, whether you should accept the weight and sufficiency of evidence which fails to convince your fellow jurors beyond a reasonable doubt.

Remember at all times that no juror is expected to give up an honest belief he or she may have as to the weight or effect of the evidence; but, after full deliberation and consideration of the evidence in the case, it is your duty to agree upon a verdict if you can do so.

You must also remember that if the evidence in the case fails to establish guilt beyond a reasonable doubt the Defendant should have your unanimous verdict of Not Guilty.

You may be as leisurely in your deliberations as the occasion may require and should take all the time which you may feel is necessary.

I will ask now that you retire once again and continue your deliberations with these additional comments in mind to be applied, of course, in conjunction with all of the other instructions I have previously given to you.

The jurors returned to their deliberation room. No verdict by day's end. I got no sleep that night. The rest of my life hung in the balance. Freedom? USP confinement for the rest of my life?

Now there is a maxim that the longer a jury is out, the more likely they will return a favorable verdict to the defendant, or at least won't return a guilty verdict. Not always true, and I felt like I was hanging by a thread between eternity and the inferno.

The next morning before leaving for court, I made sure to kiss my kids. (Hopefully not goodbye.) I kissed my wife. I held them all longer than usual. I knew that it might be my last time I would do so without the confines of being in prison.

So here it was March 10, 2006, and my fate would be decided by "twelve tried and true." The media swarm tried to get a sound bite out of me before the reckoning. I smiled, admitting to being somewhat nervous and anxious to get this behind me.

I was in the courthouse cafeteria with my family and lawyer, when Charlie Carnesi's phone rang. The judge wants us in the courtroom. In ten minutes. I would like to know what my blood pressure reading was at that moment. My pulse was beating faster than normal, that's for sure.

Charlie's phone rang again. It was my wife. She had heard on the television that a verdict was in. Ever the optimist, Charlie told her all would be well. We went up to the courtroom and settled in at the defense bench.

Judge Scheindlin entered. We got up, she sat down, we sat down.

"We have a note," she said, "But we will wait to bring the jury in."

We waited. The jury came in. But they came in as they had gone out several times before—hopelessly deadlocked. They wanted out.

Judge Scheindlin said, "I feel it now appropriate to order a mistrial."

The applause that erupted in the courtroom was music to my ears. It drowned out the protests from the prosecution. I hugged Charlie.

"C'mon kid," he said to me. "You're going home."

★

After the trial, most of the jurors hung around to be questioned by the lawyers for both sides. The jury foreman told us that it was 9-3 and 8-4 for acquittal. It also came to light that two of the jurors had made up their minds for conviction prior to the commencement of the trial.

Well you can't please everyone, but I had pleased enough people on this day, and once again I was free.

The question now was, "Would there be a third trial?"

CHAPTER TWENTY-EIGHT

Trial Three Pre-Game Show

So the government had its do over. Their retrial. What they didn't get was a conviction for the second time, and to paraphrase Matthew 3:17, I was the son (of John J. Gotti), in whom they were *not* well pleased.

Charlie and I were, however very well pleased with the mistrial. We doubted that the government would try for a third time, as that would be a rarity, and doubted that Judge Scheindlin would let them.

Charlie Carnesi had been speaking to the jurors in the jury room with the judge present. I was waiting for him downstairs. We then joined up to face the reporters we knew would be waiting. Out of the court and in to the frenzied arms of the media. Questions instead of fangs tore into us, so we decided to feed them some answers.

I glanced at Charlie, and instead of looking happy now, he looked pissed off.

"What's wrong?" I asked.

"You know what that agent Otto said?"

"No."

"This ain't over."

"You're kidding me," I said.

"No," Charlie said, "Ask Seth, others heard him say it too."

I just looked at Charlie, incredulously.

"The balls on him," said Charlie, "like we did something to him."

"Fuck him," I said. "Fuck him."

At the time, I did not know that it was going to be "fuck me," because they were coming up for a third time at bat. I shrugged it off at the time. The day I walked out of that court-house in lower Manhattan a free man—that was a day when the world was my oyster. I was going home again.

★

My respite didn't last long. Three weeks after I walked out of 500 Pearl Street, it was clear that the government would indeed bring me to trial a third time. We fought this by a motion in front of Judge Scheindlin, but she reluctantly, after much thought on the matter, approved a third trial.

I couldn't believe it, Charlie couldn't believe it, but it was true. (I was reminded of the movie *Brian's Song*, when the protagonist is told he requires an additional operation to save his life from cancer, after he is barely recovered from the previous operation.)

I was deflated. Charlie, ever the optimist, said he was not concerned. No way could the government beat us. (I looked at him and saw a terrier that thought he was a mastiff.) Of course how I felt was irrelevant to the situation, and for the next four months we would prepare for trial again.

And raise the money to fight.

★

We had to review the entire recent case, shore up our weaknesses, predict the likely tactics of the government, and figure out how to counteract them. Would they paint more violent overtones on us, or this time go for a technical money crimes oriented case?

Or would they just re-up with the same old song that they did the last time. This possibility we ruled out. After all, the split on the jury in the government's last case, 8-4, gave them a signal that it was time for a change, if they were going to convict me.

We received an answer soon. This time around, Victor Hou, who had been the USA's money expert in previous trials, was taking lead role in the prosecution. Unlike AUSA McGovern, Hou was a likable guy, which means a juror would in all likelihood—like him.

Not good. So now that we knew, our strategy was to change, and we were to concentrate more on technicalities, than on "blood and guts." But even though the charges might be "drier" the situation would be as usual with the government—no rules.

As an analogy, perhaps in the first go round against me, the government fought by Marquess of Queensberry rules. Pretty fair fight. But after being pummeled in the second trial, it was time to fight dirty, kicking, biting, and eye gouging allowed—metaphorically.

But nothing had prepared me for the coming onslaught in both the courts and the streets.

Opening government salvos in the media prior to trial were fired. Agent Otto performed his dirty tricks on the street and in the press—especially the *New York Post*, which never evinced a great fondness for me.

The FBI was now issuing subpoenas to some of our witnesses to intimidate them from giving testimony. They even threatened through my attorney to serve my sister, Victoria with a subpoena. They also engaged in serving subpoenas on my enemies in the Life, to maybe have them save the government the trouble of a trial.

Otto had served my enemies Danny Marino and Joe Watts with a subpoena, and told them, "You could thank John and Charlie for this." Now the government knew, via surveillance and cooperator reports that Marino and Watts hated me (and I hated them as well), and that Marino and Watts, according to the government, were not adverse to killing people. Marino, according to Press reports, was also on the ruling panel of the Gambino family.

They knew that Marino and Joe Watts were very interested in me being hit (Borghese 302). And a Federal Agent pulls what Otto pulled. The good guys wanted the bad guys to kill me. They didn't care how they got me, either in court, or on the street, they just wanted my head for a trophy.

Fortunately, Marino was a very close friend of Charlie Carnesi. He tipped Charlie off about Agent Otto's dirty tricks. "What are they trying to do, stir shit up between me and John?"

Charlie was pissed off to say the least. But he would be given even more reason for anger. On April 13, 2006, an article appeared in the *Post* about how my potential defense witnesses had been subpoenaed, and that several of them, including Toni Marie Fappiano (as if she hadn't already been through enough), and Joe Fusaro were being very closely looked at by the government.

Fusaro, who had helped the government in the '98 case against me, was now being threatened with perjury charges by them, because this time around, he had testified for me, and in essence against them.

On April 17, 2006, we were in front of the judge requesting a hearing about this pretrial smear campaign and worse, and seeking to have the government enjoined from further dirty tricks.

Judge Scheindlin asked lead prosecutor, Victor Hou if he thought the actions of the government was proper in trying de facto to get me killed with the serving of subpoenas, he replied, "It is intemperate," answered Hou angrily, "but probably not illegal."

Scheindlin responded, "Saying to the witness, you know

who to blame for this, *who!* That's almost the government sending out, as I said, an attack dog." (The subpoenas were nonsense, nobody was ever called.)

It was shortly afterwards, that AUSA Joon Kim contacted my attorney Charlie Carnesi, telling him that they had credible evidence there was a plot afoot to kill me. He wanted to know if under the circumstances I would come in from the cold and turn cooperator.

Charlie knew what the answer would be, but bound by the law of agency and as my defense attorney he had to relay the message. As I was sitting next to him when Kim had called, it was easy to obtain my response.

"He can go fuck himself," I responded loud enough for Mr. Kim to understand that I would not in fact be coming in.

"Who brought you the info on the death threat?" Carnesi asked Kim before he could hang up.

"Agent Ted Otto," Kim said. Surprise, surprise.

★

The government was not worried about Judge Scheindlin, and stepped up their terror tactics against me.

Now, they wanted to put me in a rat costume, and on June 15, 2006, an article appeared in that unofficial spokesman for the government vs. Gotti, the *New York Post,* saying in a headline:

Junior had Singing Tryout— Turned Canary in Futile Bid to Stay out of Prosecutor's Cage

I was accused of being a mob rat. My former attorney, Jeff Lichtman, interviewed within that article, stated,

Two trials later, the government has been brought to its knees and has responded in the only way it can—through a disgraceful whisper campaign designed to embarrass John and pressure him into taking a plea.

This article made reference to a proffer session that had taken place (of which we had spoken earlier), totally mischaracterized what had been discussed, and never should have been printed in the first place.

This kind of assault on a defendant in the press has been ably commented on by noted Civil Rights Attorney, William Kunstler.

To counter prosecutors trying defendants in the court of public opinion, before they actually go to trial, defense attorneys must use the same forum, but in a different manner. We have to counter a presumption of guilt with a presumption of innocence. Since winning a case depends in part, on a jury's perception of who a defendant is, and since jurors are members of the public, the public must truly comprehend a defendant's humanity—that he is not a devil or evil incarnate, but a man or a woman like you and me with a job, a family, problems, and emotions.

But we could not use that forum. The defense was under a gag order, and to speak to the press would be contempt of court on my part. The prosecution's improper actions were protected by the columnist invoking the Shield Law to protect her source, although she did admit that such source was to be found within law enforcement.

Somebody had leaked all over me. Either to have me flip or have me killed. The government, which includes Special Agent Ted Otto, knew from 302s in their possession, knew from tapes that had been made at their direction that I was, and had been out of the Life since 1998. Apparently, they didn't care, as long as one way or another they got me.

The people in the Life didn't give a damn about me, as I had left, which was something that you weren't supposed to be able to do. The people in the government only saw me as a trophy—someone to convict, or turn or have disposed of by unofficial means.

So wouldn't a man in that position join Team America to save his ass? Or wouldn't the mob whack him out—what was wrong with gangsters today? Wouldn't Gotti go away soon, one way or the other?

No, he wouldn't. So the government stepped up their campaign another notch.

Once again to the *New York Post* the government did go. August 25, 2006, an article appeared with the usual lurid headline:

Squeal 'N' Deal Junior is a Rat— Fingered Father's Cohorts: Report

There was a picture of my head superimposed on a rat's body. There was also a very interesting line in the article: "Gotti is now on trial for a third time after two previous juries failed to reach a verdict."

What responsible party would plant that story while a trial is ongoing?

The government? The smear campaign was launched prior to trial, and continued throughout. This type of behavior is nothing but invective, injustice, and infidelity to what the justice system and law enforcement is *supposed* to be about.

But it is conclusive evidence of what those entities are *really* all about.

Personal vendetta may be a frequent occurrence for the people in the Life, but it should *never* be a factor in law enforcement and the administration of justice. Yet, it was in the case of the Gotti family.

The *Post* was the trumpet through which the government blew its notes. Coincidentally, Paul Carlucci, the publisher of the *Post*, was the godfather to Curtis Sliwa's son, and was also the Chairman of the Guardian Angels Board of Trustees. He was one of Sliwa's close friends. If you go to the Internet, you can see all of the social functions at which these two are seen together.

Obviously, the publisher didn't like me very much. So when it came to the *Post*, it was a case of "All the news that fits we print."

(*Post* invective against me was to continue for many years after this trial. They were my own personal jeering section.)

★

Let's take a closer look at this supposed rat session in which I participated, let's look at the reality of the proffer session I had, not the hype and inaccuracy as reported by the *Post*.

I met with the government on January 18, 2005. Yet the government 302 report of this meeting was not issued until thirteen months later. This report, which was a greatly expanded version of what had been said—expanded with inaccuracies and impossibilities—shows the dangers inherent in these 302 procedures.

As had been mentioned before, there is a definite reason why the FBI has a policy of not recording 302 sessions. They wouldn't want the truth of what was said to get out, they wouldn't want the truth messing up their strategies and standard operating procedure of mucking up the actualities of what was said, of painting their own colors on information relayed so that they could put a frame around the facts and the interviewee. (Don't get me wrong, when I went in I had manipulation on my mind as well.)

Right away you should see a problem. A recorder is a mechanical instrument, it does not shade meaning or misinterpret. (It can of course have its recording media altered, but such alterations are subject to being discovered by an expert.) An FBI agent is not a mechanical instrument, and can—and often does—shade meaning, interpret for the benefit of the government what is being said by the interviewee.

Now the risk to the interviewee in contesting the accuracy of the 302? He might be prosecuted for lying to the government. These government interview forms can be very useful tools in a prosecution, and are also quite capable of being tools that warped and bent to the advantage of the prosecution—in violation of truth and justice, and a defendant's rights.

In a *Forbes* article, July 27, 2011, author and criminal defense attorney, Harvey Silvergate wrote about the inherent wrongs with the FBI 302 system, and stated in regards to the 302 procedures, "Hence, a potential witness' script is written—and not necessarily by the witness himself—the moment he opens his mouth in the presence of an agent."

Silvergate also made mention of a former US Attorney in Arizona, Paul K. Charlton who instituted a policy of recording all statements from investigative targets in his office. He was fired shortly after that.

★

The notes that had been taken by my attorney at the proffer session, varied greatly from the notes that were in the agent's 302. Numerous mistakes (?) had been made. Somehow 347 words of a statement became five pages long in a 302.

Where did the other information come from? FBI. What about those inaccuracies?

One example was the 302 had me talking about corrupt politicians and their link to dumps in the late 1980s over which I reportedly exercised control.

Oak Point Landfill in the Bronx (purchased in 1988 by a David Norkin and another landfill in Matamoras, Pennsylvania, which was purchased by others afterwards).

Reportedly I had used a capo named Joseph Zingaro as a conduit to bribe a Bronx politician to obtain needed construction permits.

So said the 302. Problem was, Joseph Zingaro was a capo during the Castellano administration, who my father, in early 1986, removed, and put on the shelf. FBI surveillance records and mob hierarchy charts confirm the absence of Zingaro from our family since early 1986.

Further, Zingaro, from 1986 until 1991 (well after the closing of the dump in Oak Point in 1990 after multiple legal proceedings), was under government monitored home confinement while he was indicted, tried, convicted, sentenced to five years, reversed his conviction on appeal, remanded back to the court and resentenced to home confinement again.

Ergo, he couldn't be used to pass anything to anybody without getting a Judge's okay for the trip. Further, the bribe, according to the 302, took place in a Bronx catering hall, Alex and Henry's, a place I've never been to.

I don't believe I ever met Zingaro, but I did meet Norkin after being straightened out in December, 1988, through my maternal grandfather who was a long time friend of his.

Additionally, government cooperator Al D'Arco in 302s and testimony in 1991 and 1992 regarding Oak Point and Matamoras implicated a John Joseph Zagari as being involved with at least the Matamoras land fill. This trial testimony resulted in a 1993, 60 count indictment, in the case of *United States v. Zagari et. al.*)

Here's a portion of the transcript of D'Arco's cross examination at a 1992 Federal trial:

Q. You made sure Zagari got paid?
A. Yes if—yeah I made sure he got paid, yes.
Q. By the way, at one point you sat down with John Gotti to discuss this dump, didn't you?
A. No.
Q. Did you sit down with the Sammy the Bull Gravano?
A. Yes I did.
Q. –to talk about this dump?

A. Yes, I did.

Q. Did you meet with John Gotti Jr. and talk to him about this dump?

A. Yes I did.

Q. Was he a made member of the Gambino crime family?

A. Yes, he was.

Q. Did you talk about selling this dump to them, meaning the Gottis?

A. I was in the discussion. I didn't talk to them about selling it. That was brought up to them by Pat Maselli so we were—we sat there and discussed the pros and cons of it.

Q. Pros and cons meaning you wanted $500,000 for this, right?

A. I didn't want $500,000 for anything. I didn't even own it.

Q. Who was at the meeting?

A. There was Anthony Casso, Sammy Gravano, Pete Gotti, Big Louie, John Gotti Jr., Pat Maselli and myself.

Q. You didn't say a word in this meeting?

A. Yes, I did.

Q. Did you say anything about $500,000?

A. We were discussing, they were asking for the price of $5 million.... There were two figures there. One of the figures was $5 million. The other figure was $500,000. If they would work the dump estimated on the amount of landfill that was going to be removed from Oak Point in the Bronx to be brought up there, it would be $10 a yard.

I never met Zagari, and I don't know if he was convicted.

D'Arco was scheduled to testify against me in my 1999 trial, which never took place because of my plea deal. The government's failure to review the D'Arco materials as well as thousands of hours of DePalma tapes contributed to their numberous inaccuracies in the 302.

From the above, it is obvious that what was reported in the 302 was wrong.

In the area of discussing the bar fight which took place at the

Silver Fox, the FBI has in their 302 reference to an individual who was stabbed—that never was stabbed. Another guy stated as having been in that fight, doesn't exist. Another man, stated to be alongside me in the fight, had died three years previous to the incident. Another individual was also mentioned, who was not on the scene, but might have been dead prior to the occurrence at the Silver Fox.

DD5s which are NYPD reports, would verify from over a dozen witness statements, that the above referenced individuals couldn't have been in the Silver Fox that night.

An individual, who had committed suicide about a year afterwards, may not have actually killed himself, according to rumors which had been going around in the neighborhood. He might have had "help."

In my proffer session with the government I had used this rumor to my own advantage, and spun a tale about three individuals who I *suggested* were involved in the death of the suicide. Of those three, two were dead (one of whom was a nineteen year cooperator with the government), and a living one who was a suspected cooperator. Joe Watts, who according to stories planted in the press, was a government cooperator going back to 1994.

It was reported that Watts had been the informant whose first memo in 1994, as we have previously referenced, was responsible for the continued incarceration of my father in solitary at Marion. The second memo, in 1997, we have already spoken about.

Supposedly at first, Watts was targeting my father and myself, but later had a change of heart according to the press. The government hearing my Ray Brook tapes discussing this issue didn't feel the need to verify my claims. Here's a segment of the taped conversation:

> JG: I'm a victim. I should go with the big shirt that says V on it. That's what a victim is. A victim. Dom Borghese

$330,000 This one for $170,000 and which also I got a beef. U/I Dom Borghese he says in his transcripts. That $100,000 of our money went to Joe Watts. And Joe Watts was gonna pay it back, but he doesn't pay it back. I got it in the transcripts. U/I Piece of shit. He robbed millions from everybody. U/I millions. U/I Never got pinched though. I'm reading the transcripts, John (talking to John Ruggiero) so far about the body count. So far ten bodies are rotting. Ten, I'm counting right now. I'm reading all the transcripts, so far ten bodies, reports are saying. How? How? Borghese ratted on 'em, like seven of them? How? That's like you ratting on me. What shot do I got? Borghese was Joe Watt's best friend. That's like you ratting on me John. What shot do I got, I'm dead. I need out. If the government thinks I'm not going to subpoena Joe Watts if I get pinched, and expose what he's doing.

(If he were doing it—I would later have my doubts.) So, as I said, I had made claims in a proffer session suggesting that Watts and two deceased fellows "helped" a guy hang himself who had been a supposed witness at the Silver Fox incident. Did the government check this out to see if it rang true?

They had access to police and Medical Examiner reports, after all, they are the FBI. What might they have found out, had they bothered to check? What were the circumstances surrounding the death of John Cennamo, the man who had hung himself?

Let's take a look.

The 5/27/84 police report by Detective Houlihan of the 113th precinct made reference to the fact that the deceased, "had been depressed lately because of the fact that he had recently lost his job and recently broken up with his girlfriend."

In said report, reference was made to another officer, Police

Officer Mary Stoecker who had "seen the deceased crossing the street and coming away from the telephones."

The deceased was found across the street hanging from a tree by a garage. No mention in the above report by Stoecker of anything suspicious, nor any person accompanying the deceased prior to his hanging himself.

In a note to the ME Detective Siry of the 113th stated, "Deceased was seen approximately 15 minutes before by friends. Deceased was depressed and had talked suicide. Deceased was recently fired from his job. Nothing suspicious."

Not infrequent motivations for self murder. The report further states that the ME at the scene stated, "No signs of a struggle and nothing other than hanging marks on the body."

It isn't easy to kill someone who doesn't want to hang himself. There *will* be signs of a struggle, and there *would* logically be additional "marks" on the body. But perhaps an on the scene investigation wouldn't reveal the medical details that an autopsy would.

So let's take a look at the ME report. One line is very significant, regarding an analysis of the deceased's muscular skeletal system: "Palpitation of the upper and lower extremities, spine, ribs, pelvic bones fail to reveal any trauma."

If someone is trying to kill somebody and make it look like a hanging, they are going to have to get real physical with the guy who doesn't want to hang. There is going to be trauma to other parts of the body besides the location of the ligature around his neck. But in this case there weren't any signs of such trauma.

Beginning to look like a legitimate suicide, no? That's what the ME report said: "Asphyxia by hanging...Suicide."

The point? The government who basically creates the 302 out of the interviewee's statements and whatever thin air they like to add, doesn't feel compelled to verify the information they are given, as long as it serves *their* needs. It happened with my 302, and it certainly happened with the government running rampant with the 302s of witnesses against me. (You will read more about this later.)

★

One of the advantages to a defendant like me, of agent "creativity" in reporting these 302s, was that by nature of the process, and by nature of the different interviewees, inconsistencies regarding salient facts would often appear, and these inconsistencies were to prove very useful at trial—to me.

One would think that federally funded investigators would do some fact checking in regards to the stories woven by various interviewees. As I have clearly demonstrated, one would often be wrong.

So, from the above, it is apparent that the 302 process can be susceptible to inaccuracies from both parties involved.

★

What the government had tried to do to me with their 302s, they had similarly tried to do to Joe Watts. In a letter dated June 24, 2009, to Eric Holder, then Attorney General, in my protesting government misconduct, I wrote about the subpoenas that were served on my enemies by the government "thanks to me," and that with respect to Joe Watts:

> In 1996, law enforcement through the *New York Daily News*, released information regarding Mr. Watts informing on my father and I. In my own personal opinion, truth or not, I feel that this was done in order to either drive him in or to have him killed...

When I had sent this letter to Holder, my realization was crystallized that perhaps I had misjudged Watts, perhaps he was not a cooperator, but like myself, was being set up by the government to become, if not a cooperator, a corpse.

Dirty Pool

Press leaks to damage me, intimidation of potential defense witnesses via subpoena, and then the government went further. They attacked my finances.

My family had banked at HSBC for a dozen years, suddenly we were "asked" to leave. I met with bank officials, bringing along the family attorney, and requested a reason why, that after all this time I was being told to take my banking elsewhere.

I was told that some mysterious "team leader" had decided that I was persona non grata when it came to bank accounts at HSBC, but I wasn't given any reason. They were sorry to see us go, but orders had come down from on high.

Then another bank did the same thing.

I found out from other sources, however, that it might have in part been because of Federal subpoenas that the bank was served with regarding my finances. Soon to follow, State Bank of Long Island was to do likewise and tell me to please go.

Loan applications I had made, that initially were to be granted, were suddenly denied. The name Gotti on a loan application seemed to be a guaranteed thumbs down. My family attorney, who had experience in mortgage brokering, contacted long time loan brokers he knew. Initially the financials passed muster. But the name game was played, and my application was "regretfully" declined. A decision from someone upstairs telling downstairs no loan.

So the government conducted a brilliant pretrial tactical campaign against me. Psychological warfare in the press, financial warfare in the cloistered halls of banking and lending. Demoralize the troops, then take away their bullets.

Except we didn't demoralize easily. I managed to put together the funds for my defense of the upcoming third trial. I kept Charlie Carnesi as lead counsel, and Seth Ginsberg as his assistant, but this time, due to money laundering charges in the indictment, we added a brilliant attorney, experienced in mob cases, and very knowledgeable about the kind of financial crimes the government was alleging.

Sarita Kedia. She had been working with Gerald Shargel, and was involved with my '98 case. She would be handling what Agent Gill (remember him from trial two) would be dishing out about money matters.

Charlie and I worked out of offices in Garden City, New York. Sarita was in Manhattan. To assist, I had hired on a few law students to deal with what would no doubt be voluminous discovery materials. (Of course, the government was to dump a large pile of it on us at the last minute.)

The provided documents and other items? Materials that had been subpoenaed from the banks, documents going back to the 1980s, many thousands of pieces of paper that needed review and analysis.

Important also, were the Ray Brook tapes, as this time around, they would be of much greater use, due to the dates of the alleged crimes charged against me. Tapes made on visits with my father in Marion were also involved, along with certain tapes made of Greg DePalma, Ravenite recordings, Bergin recordings, my office, my cars, etc.

DePalma's tapes alone made up seven thousand hours of recordings. So there I was with my small team, pouring over pages of documents, glued to tape recorders, listening to tapes. I wished that I had the monetary resources that the government was expending to get me.

When you don't have a lot of workers, those you do have are doing overtime. Sometimes we'd work sixteen, eighteen hour days. Additionally there was the preparation of defense *in limine* motions and the opposition to government *in limine* motions.

We moved against the government charges of money laundering. I'll get back to that in a moment, but first I want to make you aware of the government's dirty tactics in dealing not only with me, but any defendant that they don't happen to take a shine to.

The government, as we have already seen, in all trials had sought to forfeit as much of my property as possible, and the prime target was the commercial property in Queens, that was the main source of my income to support my family. In 1998, it cost me 1.5 million cash plus an additional property in forfeiture to keep two Queens properties and keep the rents from it. I was also to keep another property.

There were times in '98 that the government was collecting my rents, and not distributing them to me, and charging me for the privilege. The receivers of the government did not pay property taxes from the rents collected, nor were they concerned with seeing that rents were paid current.

Eventually, after paying the aforesaid tribute, I got my property back, got the rents back, and got back the disaster that the government had caused me due to their neglect of properly managing the property for which I was paying them a significant fee.

I received a letter in 1998, regarding the above, from AUSA Bart Van De Weghe granting me the property back and permission to use the rents.

Yet, after 1998, they would still seize this property in subsequent actions against me, deny me the rents, all with the purpose of starving my family and starving my ability to defend against the government charges.

In the days you may be reading this, you have no doubt learned about Islamic terrorist groups that charge a tax to those who do not convert to Islam, and/or to those whose lives they spare. How is what the government did all that different? Remember we are talking about *pretrial* forfeitures, financial penalties *prior* to any adjudication as to my guilt or innocence.

It was unjust—it was outrageously unjust.

When I did get the right back to my rents, the government,

now in trial three brought the money laundering charges against me for collecting the rents which *they* had allowed me to collect. It was straight out of a Kafka novel.

Pursuant to Rule 29 of the Federal Criminal Procedure Law, we moved to dismiss the money laundering charges. Under Rule 29, the judge can dismiss outright, or reserve decision and revisit the issue after the trial is over but before jury deliberations are held.

Judge Scheindlin agreed to hear our motion to dismiss the money laundering charges. She was incredulous that the government would be engaged in such chicanery. After reviewing the moving papers, the judge was inclined to dismiss the case.

But AUSA Victor Hou dragged in his supervisors to the courtroom and bellowed that such a dismissal would gut his case, which would cause him to withdraw the present indictment, and return with a new indictment. (Which without saying it, meant seeking a new judge.)

The judge reserved decision on the motion, and ultimately let the counts remain. However, she noted in her decision that prior to a jury determination after a trial, the issue could be revisited.

I felt a combination of disappointment and anger. No way should these charges be allowed to remain. My attorney felt differently, however. I couldn't understand it.

"She's aware these counts are absurd, and she's pissed off at what Hou pulled in the courtroom. She's going to stick it up his ass at trial," Charlie told me.

Okay, now I understood. I agreed with him. But I was amazed at the balls of the prosecution. The government tells me to go ahead and collect my rents, then charges me with money laundering for doing so. If you look at what had transpired, we had an agreement reduced to a writing with the government for me to regain my rents, and the government took affirmative steps so that would happen.

You know what that means in legal terms? The *government* conspired with me to launder money. Agreement plus overt act does a conspiracy make.

An entrapment argument could also be made.

CHAPTER TWENTY-NINE

Trial Three

Jury selection started in the third trial on August 11, 2006. But a phone call we received changed that. I was awaiting the birth of my sixth child, and put the court on notice about this. Judge Scheindlin would daily ask for a progress report on the pending birth, and my attorney Charlie Carnesi would reply, "Nothing yet, Your Honor."

So now, in the beginning of the jury selection process, the call comes. It's time. We let Judge Scheindlin know, and she dismissed court early. The labor lasted longer than we originally thought, but eleven hours after court was dismissed, at 2:17 AM, my son, Joe, came into the world.

It would be a short celebration, for on Monday the 14th of August, jury selection continued.

By now both sides had gotten rather efficient at jury selection. The pool was over three hundred people. In three days the jury had been selected, and opening statements would be given.

After opening statements, the government put on its first witness. Diego Cruz, an officer with the Organized Crime Task Force. He detailed the evidence obtained from subpoenas served in 1997, and the search warrant. He referenced the several years long investigation of Greg DePalma. (He held the record for hours of tapes generated by anybody in organized crime—like I said before—seven thousand hours worth.)

A running joke with us in the 90s had been, you pass any phone, dial any seven numbers, and there's a fifty-fifty chance Greg DePalma will pick up. He was running his mouth about me, about others in the Life, politicians from the Bronx-Westchester area, and even about his son. This led to a bunch of problems in the nineties, and now he was doing it again in the new millennium. (He had done it in the seventies also and continued to do so until his death.)

DePalma had a reputation on the street as an embellisher, a bullshit artist. Nobody who knew him took him seriously. But he was very generous with the government when it came to information.

After Cruz's testimony, the government brought in more law enforcement types to detail the crime scene regarding the Sliwa kidnapping attempted murder charges. Then, up came Joey D'Angelo.

After all his practice, D'Angelo's testimony was getting a little better. Nothing different, more of the same, just a little better at spouting what the government wanted him to spout. Some "corrections" to previous testimony, some adjustments to dovetail with the government's theory of the case.

The next witness after D'Angelo was totally unexpected. An Aryan Brotherhood member, Glen Allen West. He was the more presentable of the two AB witnesses the government had on their list.

So there he sat on the stand. Fresh from the penitentiary with his cheap polyester suit, matched with high top basketball sneakers. Dirty, and missing teeth—all of them. This specimen of human garbage had done twenty seven years of his life in various prisons.

His resume included bank robbery, escape, kidnapping (he had taken hostages when he was caught), attempted murder. Doing a life bid, he then again attempted an escape from a federal prison, and again took two hostages. He was in possession of a homemade bomb at the time. Received two more life sentences, with another twenty six years thrown in for good measure.

While in prison he had become a member of the Aryan Brotherhood, a group involved with drug dealing, gambling, extortion, assaults and murder. A bit more about this gang:

Formed in 1964 by white inmates in California state prisons to oppose the black power types, they are rabid racists. In the seventies they grew into the Federal prison system. They are involved with drug trafficking, gambling and extortion in prison and outside of it, strictly enforced by violence. Those brothers on the outside have to use some of their criminal proceeds to support those inside. According to the FBI in 1982, "The rule of thumb is that once on the streets one must take care of his brothers that are still inside. The penalty for failure to do so is death."

What did Mr. West have to say on the stand? While he was housed at Marion, he informed the court my father supposedly told him that I was the boss of the Gambino family. Further, he testified that needing money for a prison drug deal he had gone to my father who had arranged to make him an interest free $2,500 loan. Supposedly, on my next visit to my father, I was to bring the money.

My sister and I visited my father, and of course, we were under video and audio surveillance on the visit. Cameras could zoom in on anything occurring in the visiting room. Our voices could be amplified.

Is there a tape or a recording of one of us giving him cash? Anybody heard saying, "Hey, Dad, I took care of the twenty-five hundred?" These Marion visits weren't contact visits, we spoke to my father through a thick glass. How could the money have been transferred to him?

Glen Allen West was a crack smuggling heroin dealing AB member. He was basically sentenced to die in prison, and then some, who was now up there testifying as a free man. Could there be any greater indicia of credibility than that possessed by this Federal witness?

West went on to testify that the AB protected my father at the Marion prison, as well as Nicky Scarfo, boss of the Philadelphia mob.

What West must have forgotten was who he was discussing. Unlike Scarfo, my father held on to power until his death. If AB or anyone else disrespected my father, I'm sure he would have had no problem hitting a target close to that person on the street, to send the appropriate message.

By way of example, there was the incident at Marion with Walter Johnson.

It had been front page news complete with a picture of my father, his face injured. My father had an altercation with Johnson, a bank robber serving time in Marion. Johnson had sucker punched my father, allegedly because my father had made a racial slur.

Nonsense. My father was no racist. His beef with Johnson involved the sound level of rap music that Johnson was singing in his cell. In Marion, it's old school—no steel doors on the cell—it's bars. My father, in his unique style suggested to Johnson that the volume should be lowered, or my father was going to shove Johnson's head up his ass.

Johnson took umbrage at this and sucker punched my father in the prison rec yard as they were being prepared to be escorted back to their cells. (Inmates in Marion in my father's cell block were allowed forty five minutes a day recreation—the rest of the time they were locked up.)

Both Johnson and my father were ordered down to the ground. They were then told to rise slowly. When my father turned to be cuffed, Johnson ran over and threw a few more punches. Cheap shots, that's all.

The press had a field day with this, talking of my father being *bruised, bleeding, and bent on revenge.*

Not so.

Let's take material right from the actual incident report. According to the report Johnson waited until the CO came to move the men back to the range. At this time the CO observed Johnson throw a punch, hitting my father in the head. (In prison everybody knows this is a coward move: you are in a rec cage for forty five minutes, and you wait until the guard comes to throw a punch?)

The CO dialed "deuces," the alarm the guard wears on his hip. Guards gave inmates a direct order to stop fighting, and all inmates then went to the fences. Then inmates Gotti and Johnson walked to the center of the rec cage (to be secured), and then Johnson in the presence of the guards, then struck Gotti again. The guards then ordered both inmates to lie face down. Gotti and Johnson laid face down on the ground.

Within 24 hours of the incident, I had a prison visit with my father. My father was pissed off, but his face unmarked, which is clear from the video of the visit. From a recording made of our conversation, he expressed disappointment in himself for allowing a mutt like Johnson, less than half his age and much larger than my father, to sucker punch him. "The bitch waited for the guards," my father told me.

According to the inaccurate reports of the media, my father made a deal with two Aryan Brotherhood chiefs, to have Johnson killed. But in reality my father refused all offers from not only Aryan Brotherhood, but La Eme (known as the Mexican mafia) to have Johnson killed. Both groups had a tremendous amount of respect for my father and made offers to kill Johnson (one unauthorized attempt had been made); but my father didn't want his group to look weak, and said he would deal with it himself.

Johnson only had three or four years left on his bid and if an Italian prisoner couldn't hit him, it would have to wait until Johnson hit the streets. This was confirmed when I met up with AB associates M.G. Stein and Little Terry while we were in the bullpen awaiting transfer at USP Atlanta.

I had asked Stein what was the story with the Johnson incident, and he said from his understanding the dog (Johnson) stole a punch when the guards were present and your pops (my father) sent out word not to deal with it—he would.

(Later, my recounting to John Ruggiero on a visit to me in Ray Brook about having spoken with Stein and Little Terry was recorded by the government who put the recording into evidence in my third trial.)

This was also confirmed by another associate of the AB who was housed with me in Ray Brook—Jimmy Hazelton.

Word was sent to him by his people that John (my father), wanted to deal with it. Even if someone wanted to get to Johnson they couldn't because he finished up his bid in protective custody.

On a visit that I had received from John Ruggiero, he relayed to me as soon as this guy (Johnson) hits the streets, he's gone. I had instructed Ruggiero to mind his own business.

A few weeks after Johnson's release, while he was traveling to try and kill a girl he felt betrayed him, he had killed a Washington D.C. police officer and was sentenced to life plus a hundred years. My father died a short time later, and his orders regarding Johnson died with him.

But prior to that, two inmates from the D.C. area had rolled in to Marion. Housed there with my father at the time was Vito Guzzo, a solid tough kid from Queens, whose (now deceased) father was friends with my father in the seventies. One of the two D.C. inmates was a friend of Walter Johnson's. In a confrontation between the two and my father and Guzzo, the friend of Johnson caught a beating. This was during the time my father was in the advanced stages of cancer.

★

Back to West's testimony. Was any of what he said true? Well, he was at Marion. He was a drug dealer. But the rest?

No. Neither my father nor myself when in prison had any dealings with West or any of the Aryan Brotherhood. A respectful distance was kept. No fights, no loans, no protection, and nothing that could serve as a factual basis for manufactured FBI testimony. This was just a cheap shot at my father.

Under cross examination, West was asked how it was that, during visits which were video and audio taped, there was never a mention of any loan, of any money being brought in. He responded that hand signals and lip reading and eye blinking were used.

Charlie went on to ask him, "So my client's father would blink his eyes twenty five hundred times to represent twenty five hundred dollars?" (It's comical, considering the fact that the prison video would zoom in on my father's face on a constant basis. What might the viewers have thought about all of this supposed eye blinking? That my father was having an epileptic fit?)

Video surveillance would have picked that up. It didn't because it didn't happen. West was committing perjury. If it were true, why didn't the government introduce any video or audio tapes of this supposed money bringing visit? Because it *wasn't* true. They had introduced into evidence other Marion tapes, but none concerning this allegation.

It goes to show the lengths the government went to, to try to convict a Gotti, whether it be me, my father, or any other member of our family. The amazing thing is that these prosecutors and the "Special" agents that furnish them with their witnesses don't even seem concerned with assessing the value of their witnesses—or the potential harm they can do the *prosecution* case.

At least DiLeonardo, when he was testifying was clean and well groomed, and had some air of credibility. He looked the part, and didn't embarrass his handlers. But West? The opposite was true.

A trial, especially a high profile criminal trial is a *gestalt*. Every part of it, everything that goes on, not only on the stand, but at the prosecution and defense tables, anything that might be in the view or hearing of the jury *matters*.

Psychological research has determined that we form first impressions based on someone's face in not sixty seconds, or thirty seconds, but in ⅒ of a second. A series of experiments by Princeton psychologists Janine Willis and Alexander Todorov reveal that all it takes is a tenth of a second to form an impression of a stranger from their face, and that longer exposures don't significantly alter those impressions. (Association for Psychological Science, *Observer* Vol.19, No.7 July, 2006.)

So if you produce for the jurors a dirty, cheap looking witness with no teeth, before he utters a word, you have greatly reduced his credibility in the eyes of those jurors. West was useless to the prosecution before he ever opened up his toothless mouth.

I had respect for AUSA Victor Hou. At times I thought he was brilliant. When he put Glen Allen West on the stand, it was not one of those times.

After West got off the stand, the government brought on Special Agent Cindy Peil. It was an antidote to West. She was soft spoken, attractive, likable. She provided background information on organized crime, in general, and specifically to this case.

She had been teamed up with Ted Otto, and you could certainly say she was the better half.

Next up was an officer from the SIS of Ray Brook—the Special Investigation Service. He testified about my visits, and phone calls. He displayed surveillance photos of me taken at the rec yard at Ray Brook, and spoke of the "power" that I wielded in the prison. Over the Italian inmates at least.

He also expressed his belief that I was manipulating the

audio surveillance of my visits, to bolster a future claim (if needed) that I was out of the Life, in support of a withdrawal defense. That certainly was objectionable testimony, because it basically put this SIS man in the position of a mind reader. How could he testify as to my state of mind when I was talking on visits?

Interesting that when I spoke in such tapes that were useful to the government's case (especially a legal visit tape made with my attorney Richard Rehbock), I was not engaged in deceit, in any pre-planned perjury. But when there was an overabundance of government recorded evidence that my state of mind was I never wanted to have anything to do with the Life again? That was when I was cleverly setting up my defense for future trials—before I even knew there would be future trials. (Remember, the government started taping my visits in 2003.)

★

Charlie Carnesi and I were wondering when Sliwa was going to take the stand. He wasn't even on their witness list. But being as though this was a money laundering case, the government brought in someone who knew about my financial affairs.

Paul Tong, my accountant. He had done my books since the early '80s. Working for a firm Kahn and Associates, he started with me when he was a rookie. We had hit it off, and became friends—dining out together, inviting each other to respective holiday parties. He was a close enough friend, that I had invited him to my home—and I am very protective about that.

Tong was looking to send his son to New York Military Academy, and I advised him about that. But then things changed.

In 1997, FBI and OCTF raided Tong's office in Orange, New York—during tax season. They did their best to intimidate him, and succeeded. His files, his hard drives to his computers were seized. On these were the financial stories of many people, not just me.

For good measure, they threatened him with arrest. That was a joke, because with Tong as my accountant, I would regularly overpay taxes due, that's how conservative, how square this guy was. A regular "t" crosser and "i" dotter was Paul Tong, CPA.

When he had his whole business seized by the government, he was in tears. The practice he had toiled for many years to build, was now going to be lying around in boxes in some government evidence locker.

He filed complaints. Nothing. His clients now could not get their taxes filed on time, and could not get their records back. Tong was losing his clients. To assist Paul Tong in having his practice eviscerated, the FBI was "kind" enough to inform some of his clients that Paul Tong worked for the mob.

A civilian with no background, with no involvement in crime. Yet the government was financially destroying Paul Tong for no other reason than he was my accountant. (They knew better than to try this with my attorneys.)

Wait, I said that nothing happened when Paul complained, I was wrong. His office was raided again. But Tong and I remained friends, and I remained his client. He had even come to visit me in prison.

Now, on August 24, 2006, Paul Tong sat in the witness box. I felt sorry for him, and almost a little guilty. Even though I had not done anything to him, my being his client had brought him to this. He was asked about me and my finances.

Calling him as a witness did nothing to help the government's case, but it worked wonders in causing a significant decline in Paul's accounting practice. (It didn't help any of my businesses in which Tong was my accountant, having lost access to many records and files.)

After his testimony, during a recess in the proceedings, I went up to Paul in the hallway, and gave him a hug and a pat on the back. His attorney wasn't overjoyed about that.

★

There was some wrestling about the use of Ray Brook tapes, as they related to Sliwa. It had been agreed that a portion of the tapes would not be played to the jury. The transcript dealing with the segment not to be played would be redacted. The prosecution said, no need to bother the judge with this.

So in keeping with their normal ethics, during the trial, the tape portion got played, and the transcript was not redacted. (Had the judge ruled on that, we would have known in advance what would be used, and what wouldn't.)

The damage was done, but we had to do what we could to mitigate those damages. The judge saw to it that the agreement we had with the prosecution was kept—after the breach. At least for the record, which is useful in case there was going to be an appeal necessary.

On September 5, 2006, the government brought in their big gun—their main case agent, Special Agent Ted Otto.

Once more he gave a background about the Gambino family. He testified as to the taping of visits with my father at Marion between March 3, 2001, and March 26, 2001, and also on April 1, 2001. (There was also a Ray Brook tape he spoke about from August 8, 2003.)

Testifying about the April 1, 2001 tape, Otto said he had listened to it dozens of times. The significance of the tape, according to Otto, was its recording the passing of the scepter from my father to me and the other three men that made up a ruling panel. Nicky Corozzo and Jackie D'Amico were mentioned, and in an earlier part of the tape, Jimmy Brown Failla's name came up. It was a small segment of the recording. Otto was obviously proud of it having been made. I said to my attorney, Charlie, that there was no way they could have my father on tape saying that. I explained why, and color started coming back into Charlie's face.

Then Otto went on about the August 8, 2003, Ray Brook tape. In this tape, according to Otto, I am telling my sister Angela that I am a capo. Otto claimed to have listened to this tape some 70-100 times.

Otto is on the stand saying I admitted to being a Captain in 2003. He had a transcript that has this. So the jury sees it in print, and hears it from the mouth of a special agent. It was funny, but in our copies of the recording, we never heard that.

Quick lesson in court reality. According to discovery rules, the government has to give you copies of tapes that they intend to introduce into the trial. But they don't have to give you *good* copies. What you get could be multi generational recordings—in other words, a recording of a recording of a recording of the tape. Makes life difficult for the defense.

Often the transcripts you get from the government are loaded with U/I notations—where the words spoken were unintelligible. Many times, when defense tape experts listen to the tapes, those U/I words miraculously become understandable, and for some strange reason, most of these are helpful to the defense.

This sort of prosecution dirty trick is a travesty. This is a viewpoint of a trial being a game, of justice being a contest, instead of a search for truth in furtherance of the administration of justice. Defendants should be presented with the same quality of recordings as is the government, to somewhat level what in reality is a very slanted playing field.

But they often aren't.

In order to counteract Ted Otto's mischaracterization of what the tape recorded, my attorney, Carnesi told him, "I'm gonna play the tape five times. Every time you hear John say the word 'Captain' raise your hand."

Otto, of course, raised his hand at the appropriate word that he said was "captain."

By using this cross-examination technique, my attorney obtained the reaction he wanted from the jury, who now, without the aid of the government tape transcript, showed incredulity as to Otto's claim regarding hearing the word "captain." Several, in fact had shaken their heads in disbelief.

★

On September 6, 2006, after the government had rested, we began to put on our defense case. We brought in our witnesses to counter the testimony of each government witness. One of the people we called—whom the government didn't bother to call—was Curtis Sliwa.

He was one of the first witnesses that we called. We walked him through the labyrinth of his prior trial testimony, and when finished with this documented liar, we handed him over to the government for cross.

On cross, the government was able to resurrect Sliwa's testimony, in fact with the help of the prosecutor, he actually had improved as a witness compared to the last two trials.

At this point, my attorney and I thought calling Sliwa as a defense witness subject to our direct examination might have been a colossal mistake. Giving the prosecution the opportunity to cross Sliwa, gave them the ability to significantly polish off the tarnish we exposed on direct.

So we put on more witnesses, including a gentleman who had been Sliwa's number two man in the Guardian Angels. William "Swan" Diaz. On cross, Victor Hou asked Diaz if he believed that Sliwa shot himself. Diaz said, yes, he did believe that.

Hou wisely said, "No further questions," but the judge asked Diaz, "Why do you think he shot himself?"

Diaz gave a detailed answer. He told the judge:

> He had fabricated a lot of situations, your Honor. And the story that he was saying—we had already had a big falling out—the

story that he was saying just didn't jive with me. We were trained as Guardian Angels. We used to train a lot of women in self-defense training and we always trained women before they went into cabs or any strange car that wasn't theirs, to look in the front seat. I just found it strange that Curtis got in a cab and didn't look in the front seat the way we trained so many women to do.

Mr. Hou had paid the prosecutorial price of having asked one too many questions on cross examination, and the judge had unwittingly magnified the damage to the government, but I was quite pleased with what had happened.

★

We put on distinguished attorney and Harvard Law Professor, Charles Ogletree, who had been part of the plea negotiations in the '98 case. He was to reiterate what he and I had discussed about putting my previous life behind me, and how that plea in that case was all about closure. (Professor Ogletree was actually advising to go to trial in the '98 case, being both distrustful of the government, and confident that we had an ability to win at trial.)

We put on Michael DiLeonardo Jr. (the cooperator's son, aged twenty one, who like his mother, later changed his last name). He was a brave kid and I was touched by his testimony. He testified to his relationship with me, and his wanting to visit me. He wanted to see me after he and his mother were abandoned by his father.

Having heard his testimony, and the obvious sincerity in his voice, I had no doubt but that his mother had done a wonderful job raising him.

On September 11, 2006, the fifth anniversary of the World Trade Center attack, we put on Tom Owen, our tape expert.

Some background on him. Tom Owen runs Owl Investigations. He enhances audio tapes, authenticates tapes (determining whether or not they were altered), does voice identification, and also enhances video tapes. He has been qualified as a tape expert in trials in more than forty states, and is a member of the American Academy of Forensic Sciences.

He has worked with the FBI, the DEA, NSA and the CIA.

Owen addressed the April 1, 2001, tape made at Marion. The conversation was between my father and attorney Joseph Corozzo. His transcript and analysis of what was said on the tape differed from what the government had placed into evidence.

What Otto had claimed were words of appointment—selecting me to serve on the ruling panel—were actually words of disappointment. My father was letting out a barrage of verbal abuse at Jimmy Brown, Jackie D'Amico and Nicky Corozzo and me. He was furious with our having taken pleas in previous cases. It was not true to his code. You fight cases, you take the government to task.

One would think that an experienced agent like Ted Otto who had served in the FBI for twenty years, knew this could not be my father passing the scepter, for one of the men discussed had been dead for two years prior to the conversation taped—Jimmy Brown Failla.

Otto is a highly intelligent man, whatever else he might be. He had long been involved with the investigation and prosecution of members of organized crime. Yet he came up with the testimony that my father in April 1, 2001, when speaking about appointing an administration, was discussing a dead man.

Otto also previously testified that at this time, in April 2001, my uncle Peter was the official boss, Arnold Squitieri underboss, JoJo Corozzo consigliere. So where did everyone else mentioned in the conversation fit in? Otto should have known his testimony was inaccurate.

Well, maybe it was April Fool's Day that caused the misunderstanding, or maybe it was just the fact that Otto was playing fast and loose and was obsessed with bringing me down at any cost.

Otto then moved on to the August, 2003, Ray Brook tape. In this tape, according to Otto, I am telling my sister, Angela, that I am a Captain. I would never discuss business with my sister, or any non-made member of the mob. I would not be telling my sister, "By the way, Angela, I'm a Captain."

But Otto said I basically did that. Owen had listened to the tape. What Otto said was "Captain" was my actually asking, "What Happened?"—after hearing something about one of my uncles.

But in Otto's case, who heard only what he wanted, his hearing was to be proven wrong. The tape was played on a radio show—Sliwa's show (along with co-host Ron Kuby the famous attorney), and it was clear that what was said on the tape was, "What happened?" Otto went to the producer of the show, Frank Morano's superiors and complained about what Morano had done, and used his position as an agent to put pressure on them, which almost caused Morano to be fired.

Otto's testimony went like this:

Q. Approximately how many times have you listened to this? [Referring to tape]

A. I have listened to this session, in whole or in part, I would say 70-100 times.

Q. (THE COURT) Why do you listen to it 70-100 times?

A. Your Honor, it's going through it the first and second and third time it—there are portions in here that seem to speak to some of the most crucial elements of this indictment.

Q. (THE COURT) I see.

A. And each and every time we went through it, the acclimation to the voices, and also we were—with improvements to the software we able to step up these conversations back from 100 percent as we are speaking now, in increments of 1 percent, and we found that when we listened to these at 85 percent...

Q. (THE COURT) Speed? You mean 85 percent speed?

A. 85 percent speed yes. And they—the recordings that you hear have been duplicated at 85 percent.

Q. Oh.

A. So we found—we just, to use the term we were combing through it and each time we went through it there seemed to be more and more that we were able to pick up.

So agent Otto had the benefit of listening to the tape numerous times, of slowing it down, of enhancing it with software. He *knew* what was on the tape.

★

After Owen's testimony, Otto was brought back on the stand as a rebuttal witness on September 14, 2006. Then both sides rested.

AUSA Miriam Roach did the summation for the government. She commenced in the afternoon and continued on the next morning. Then it was Charlie Carnesi's turn. In several hours of summation, Charlie walked the jury through the case witness by witness. We also put on a power point presentation to refresh juror memories, as the government always did this.

With tears in his eyes, Charlie went through the relationship between me and my father, and how it had impacted my life in the Life, and my eventually leaving it. Charlie appealed to the jury to keep me out, keep me with my wife and kids.

Prior to the jury deliberation, the issue of the motion to dismiss the money laundering charges was finally heard again by the Judge (outside of the hearing of the jurors of course). Judge Scheindlin decided to dismiss these charges. Such absurdity would not stand in her court.

★

On September 19, 2006, the jury began to deliberate. During the next week of deliberations, a few notes were brought in from them, but nothing of any great significance. On September 26, 2006, Charlie gets the call on his cell phone. "Report to the courtroom in ten minutes."

Was this a verdict? We felt so. We waited for the judge, she finally came in, we rose, she sat, we sat.

"I have a note to read to you," she said. The jury was deadlocked and need guidance. Soon afterwards, an Allen Charge was read to the jury. They went back to deliberate, but the next day, I was on the courthouse terrace on the eleventh floor with my attorney and family members, and once again Charlie's phone rang.

His faced tensed as he heard the words, "Report to the courtroom in ten minutes."

I remember every step I took back to that courtroom. I remember the feeling I had, focused, yet in somewhat of a dissociative state. The press was streaming into the courtroom. Every seat in the place was occupied. No standing room.

In about five minutes the judge comes in, we rise, she sits, we sit. There was another note from the jury, *Deadlocked*.

She declared a mistrial—for the third time.

Once again, I would be free to go home to my family.

CHAPTER THIRTY

Parole Evidence

Free again. I woke in my own bed, in my family home. At the time I felt this freedom would be enduring. Free from the Life, free from the dangers of the three previous trials. It was the first time in twenty years I felt this way.

The members of my former existence had accepted my withdrawal, hopefully after three failed attempts to convict me the government would accept it and acknowledge it. I was alive, despite FBI efforts to correct that situation. I was at liberty, despite DOJ efforts to put an end to that status forever.

Now what was I going to do with myself?

I wanted to shake the dust off my feet and leave New York. But my family had their roots here, they wanted to stay. I was thinking the Carolinas somewhere, they weren't thinking of moving.

But while I wasn't the boss of the Gambino family, I was (I thought at the time) the boss of the John A. Gotti family, and one night at Sunday dinner, I put my foot down and told the family, we are moving, that's it.

I had enemies on both sides of the law, from the streets and from the government. The former would have me killed, the latter if their efforts to have me killed failed, would imprison me for the rest of my life. I was still bumping into members of my former life in various places, which was awkward to say the least, and I would wave them off. The chances of that happening down South were minimal, I explained to my family. It would be better for all of us if the fish that got away swam South.

My family pointed out that it wouldn't matter where I went. It was the Federal government, and they are in all fifty states. Could I be sure there would be no more prosecutions—either in New York or elsewhere? Would I want to be facing a trial in a different state than New York, where friends and extended family would not be around to help me, or help my family?

The family where it was, enjoyed the acceptance of many people, they weren't freak show curiosities. Would that be the case in some Southern conservative state? How would the children fare? Nobody was going to change their name, or deny their father.

There was pride in who my father was, pride in the street life, for it was an accepted thing in New York. We believed in certain things. We acted in a certain way. Would that be accepted or even tolerated in the Carolinas?

They were good arguments against moving. Now, Oyster Bay wasn't Howard Beach, but it also wasn't Raleigh, or Fayetteville, either. My kids had friends here, they were doing well in school. If I got arrested and imprisoned again, would I want my family isolated in an unfamiliar area, with people of a different culture?

No, I decided. I would stay. But back to the original question, "Now what do I do?"

A trip with the family would be a good idea, to get my head together, but that required permission from my parole officer. I was on supervised release. For three years. Supervised release of federal convicts came about in 1984, and was ramped up after 1986. It was basically a way to control the life of a convict after release from prison, and would last in my case until

September 7, 2007—three years from the date I would have been released from Ray Brook.

I was given permission, and we were off to Disney World. Great time with the wife and the kids, my first trip with them in ten years.

A joyful week had passed, and now it was time to get down to business. How was I going to make my living? My parole officer became interested in the very same thing, and suddenly was demanding all of my financial information. I got along well with him, but now it was let's see your tax returns going back to '99, let's see your financial statements.

Somebody up there didn't like me again, and I could see the government was starting to manipulate my PO. What was it this time?

A month later, the answer came. I had to check in weekly with my PO at first, then twice a month. On one of those visits, my PO said, "Some gentlemen are here, and they would like a word with you."

Attitude change on that. No more smiles. "What gentlemen might we be talking about?"

"They're sitting at my desk, waiting for you," my PO said.

Surprise, surprise, the FBI. Two of them. One named Robert Herbst, (who turned out to be Kasman's control agent), and the other was William Johnson. (No relation to Willie Boy, of course.)

They stood up to shake hands. I shook them (unlike my father). "Come in," they said, and motioned me into the office. The door closed.

"No," I said, "leave the door open, and say what you have to say. I'm only still standing here, because otherwise this fellow (pointing to my PO) will violate me. What can I do for you?"

"We want you to know," they said, "that trouble is coming your way and we are here to help you if you choose."

"Forget it," I said, "never going to happen. Whatever is coming I will deal with it, like I did in the past."

I turned to my PO, "Let me call my attorney." Turning back to the agents, I said, "You people just won't let it go, will ya?"

The agents got up, shrugged their shoulders, and politely made their way out. They were respectful, but I was still steaming. Especially at my PO for setting me up in that trap. I called Charlie Carnesi and told him what had just transpired. He advised me.

"Any future visit here," I told my PO, "I'm coming with a lawyer."

On my next visit, I returned with family attorney and friend, W. Adam Mandelbaum. No agents were present. After the second visit, with my attorney, I was informed it was no longer necessary for me to come to the PO's office. That was a clue.

Within the week, Charlie was notified to bring me up to White Plains to answer accusations of having violated parole. Something to do with my taxes. I was arraigned on the violation on September 12, 2007.

White Plains. That's where the '98 case started. We were given an adjourned date of November 27, 2007. (Rather close to the Thanksgiving Holiday.) The AUSA involved with this matter was David Massey.

In between court appearances, I was booted out of another bank. Additionally, potential mortgage lenders had just informed my attorney Mandelbaum, that they were unable to lend—wish we could help, but sorry we can't. It was obvious that any potential bank or lender was being harassed by the FBI.

So much for enduring freedom. There was wisdom in what my wife and kids had said—would I be left alone from now on, was I sure? Now I was sure I wouldn't. It happened in New York, and it could very well have happened in the Carolinas, where my family would be at a significant disadvantage.

Now considering what I had already been through, these tax allegations were lightweight contenders, but still something to be concerned about. So I had to pull out all the documents, all the old case files, and it was time to prepare once again for battle.

I looked at the financial information I had initially provided Pretrial Services, I reviewed the exact text of Judge Barrington Parker's direction regarding the payment of taxes in my judgment of commitment, while I was on parole. I reviewed the sentencing minutes.

Charlie, Seth Ginsberg, and I reviewed everything and coordinated efforts with my new accountant. Tong was of course no longer in my employ. I wanted to spare him future government harassment.

So it was time to address the accusations that I had violated Judge Parker's directions regarding payment of taxes. From the prosecution viewpoint, this meant up to and including 2007 taxes. From our point of view, it meant from '99 and back.

I had filed amended returns concerning the returns Tong had filed previously, as he had me overpaying—out of caution. Additionally, and with the support of well established case law, we believed we were entitled to significant deductions in defending myself and my property from the forfeiture actions of the government, because these were indeed expenditures incurred for the preservation of income.

★

November 27, 2007. I was up at White Plains with Charlie, Seth, my accountant Tony Perrone, ready to testify, and my family attorney who handled my business affairs, W. Adam Mandelbaum, again, ready to testify. (Mandelbaum could also testify about parole visits, in case it was needed, and he had actively engaged with my PO in the supplying of all requested financial documents.)

Previously, we had sent the judge two letters regarding what had happened with my banks. Judge Parker had been elevated to the Second Circuit Court of Appeals (they hear appeals from lower Federal Courts in the New York metropolitan area), and Judge Stephen C. Robinson had been assigned to this parole violation proceeding.

Robinson had previously (9/12/07) instructed the Parole Office to give them a full report to aid in his assessment of the case. This case would be decided via bench trial, no jury. The government also wanted to review the documentation that had been supplied to Parole.

The report he had received demonstrated the tremendous debt that I had incurred in defending the past three trials. It further showed the expenditures incurred in defending the properties I had. The figure was in the millions.

The government didn't care. They were alleging that my being behind in the payment of income taxes and *real estate* taxes, were tax violations, and a violations of Judge Parker's orders. This was utter nonsense of course, with respect to the real estate taxes, as they are a county, town and perhaps village level matter and have nothing to do with income taxes which are state and Federal matters.

But the government didn't mind overreaching into the ridiculous if they thought it could hurt me.

Or hurt my mother, who due to the prosecution her son was suffering, suffered a stroke. She is a very strong woman, but she is not immortal. She had been through Hell, bearing witness to what the government had done to my father, who was twice the man I was. He always told her, "Butch, they can't beat me because I will show them how a man dies, and motherfuck them all—all the way to the gate."

But in the end, his body had been destroyed with the cancer that was medically neglected by the government. Perhaps she believed the government had beaten him. In any event, the strain on her had been terrific.

She had seen me in prison, she had seen all of the previous attempts to put me away in a federal penitentiary to die. It was taking its toll on her, as she also saw it was beginning to overwhelm me. Her "little cowboy" as she used to call me, was once again surrounded by the Indians.

I was determined to beat this, to heal my family, to regain the new life I had thought I had won back on the first morning of my freedom after the third trial. I spent more time with my family than I had ever done before. "Soon you guys will be sick of seeing me," I had joked.

What was the government after? A parting shot to give me a couple of years more prison for a parole violation? Or something more sinister, to have me put away, and then bring on a new trial when I would be at a severe disadvantage in defending myself.

Didn't have to wait long for the likely answer. I had learned that Lewis Kasman, the self proclaimed "adopted son" of my father, had been walking around with a federal wire on him.

I was on an overnight trip with my wife, my daughter, Gianna, and my baby son, Joe, when I found this out. So that was why he had told my family members that he desperately wanted to see me. This guy—whom I never really trusted, but tolerated out of respect to my father. I had ignored his requests and letters for an audience.

I remember Kasman coming in on a Ray Brook visit. He was wearing a government tape recorder in his watch, while the government was already recording me via an FBI agent Conrad. (I didn't know at the time that he had been a CI for several years.) This double taping reminded me of the fiasco of the search warrants at my Sutphin Boulevard offices in 1997.

On the visit, I told Kasman that his watch was beautiful, and joked it would be a nice gift if I make it home. He agreed. (The FBI would have loved that.)

What had infuriated me about Kasman, was not the Ray Brook nonsense, but the fact that he had recorded my mother on a visit with her, shortly after her stroke. She was recovering from brain surgery, and had been sedated. As directed by the

FBI, are there no limits to what these low lives will do at the behest of their government masters? No.

Let me give you another example of Kasman's duplicity. On August 7, 2002, Kasman sent me a card entitled, "Thinking of You." It had leaves on the cover. On the inside flap he wrote

> Just to let you know, I am thinking of you. Summer moving along. Hope you're feeling good. Kids are in camp. Be home in a few weeks. Before too long you will be home. Going to Florida for the winter (5 months). Eileen and the girls are looking forward to that and so am I. One of these weekends I'll pay a visit to Ray Brook. Look forward to seeing you and telling you "I'm here." But I'm sure you already know that. I'll close for now, stay strong and keep smiling.

Several days later, I was placed in the hole because of information—false information—Kasman had supplied to the government, prior to his sending that card. You will remember this was about a supposed death threat to the warden of Marion and Springfield prisons.

Here is another example, shortly before I left the hole, I received a card dated November 20, 2002—again with leaves on the cover, which said "You're a special brother–A Special Friend."

On the printed inside of the card was:

> A wonderful brother, a special friend… That's what you've always been, and so this wishes joy to you on Thanksgiving Day and all year through. Have a Wonderful Holiday, Love, Lewis.

This from the man who was *responsible* for my being in the hole on Thanksgiving.

★

I was also getting wind of the possibility that Alite, whom I had mentioned earlier, was in the government's employ as a cooperator. It seemed that once again the wolves were gathering.

Kasman, Alite, Otto, the alleged parole violation. Obviously the government had grander plans for me that trying to get me incarcerated for a few years more on a violation of parole. I knew they were going to come at me again.

But the immediate target to shoot at was the parole violation hearing. We argued that in the '98 case, I had forfeited 1.5 million dollars, a property in upstate New York, and restitution of $339,000. Plus the three years of supervised release. Plus taxes due and owing were to be paid.

Note the language, *due and owing*. The only possible interpretation of that would be taxes that had been determined due and owing, which meant from the time of Judge Parker's direction going backwards.

Of course, the government didn't let logic or fact stand in the way of getting what they want—which in this case was revenge for their failure to get a conviction in several trials.

In an October 15, 2007, letter to Judge Robinson, we had pointed out regarding the government's desire to get its hands on my financials that had been supplied to Parole that Parole

> had not indicated that it required the U.S. Attorney's assistance to ensure that Mr. Gotti has complied with the terms of his supervised release.

Further we argued that even had Parole needed assistance, they would be the ones to:

> make an application for permission to disclose Mr. Gotti's financial documents. . . . [They had] done nothing of the kind. . . . [Also] Probation recently reported to the Court that with the exception of the matter currently being litigated, Mr.

Gotti has been cooperative and compliant. . . . [It was further noted, that I] subsequently complied with the order to produce financial records to the Probation Department's satisfaction.

[It was further pointed out to the judge that I] entered into a payment agreement with the Internal Revenue Service under which [I] will soon satisfy [my] tax obligations. More to the point however, is the fact that the U.S. Attorney knows full well that it created the situation that made it virtually impossible for Mr. Gotti to satisfy his tax obligations during the pendency of his three trials.

The letter went on about how the government liened my properties to disable me from using them to defend myself, and it wasn't until an application for federal monetary assistance to conduct my trials, that the government backed off on one of the liens. (I sold that one to pay for my defense.)

The Probation department (in charge of my parole) issued a report to the Judge two days before my court appearance in November.

The government wanted to put me in jail for several years on this supposed violation. The probation department recommended as follows:

The probation department stands by our original recommendation that the term of supervised release be revoked and the release be sentenced to a custodial term of one day, to be followed by a new term of supervised release . . .

(I would have taken that day if need be, but lo and behold, a short time after the November appearance, the government said it conceded and agreed with our position. They had sent a letter saying so.)

There was no hearing on the 27 of November, so I left the courthouse with my attorneys and accountant, and bumped into reporter Pablo Guzman on the courthouse steps.

(I previously talked about the Ted Otto dirty tricks of making me appear to be a rat. I said I would take a lie detector test, if Otto would take the same test regarding his service of subpoenas with "Thank John for this," and his complicity in leaking the story about my proffer to the government. More specifically the content of the 302 that had been written up. He would be connected to the machine and say what I said, then I would be connected to the machine and say what I had said, and we would let the machine make the determination who the liar was. Charlie had been called by the *Post* one day, and said they had the polygrapher standing by. I asked if they had Otto also standing by. No. He wasn't there. Was I coming in? No.

So Guzman fired a question at me about my willingness to take a polygraph.

"When youse can bring him up on charges (Otto) for what he did to me and my family, I'll go on national TV, I'll be on the polygraph hooked to me, and you can ask me any questions you want about where I've been. Not where other people have been—where I've been."

"You still stand by that," said Guzman. "You would do that?"

"Would I do that? In a heartbeat."

My attorney Charlie joined in with, "But they have to fulfill the second part, they have to have the agent come forward and take the test about what he's done."

That of course didn't and would never happen.

★

As I said, several days after the court appearance the issue about the parole violation was over, the government had acknowledged it was wrong. The case was dismissed.

So here I was free again, but wiser this time. I knew there would be more to come. My family gathered and we celebrated, but part of my mind wasn't there, it was focused on the battle that I knew would be coming sooner or later.

So the kids continued their running around and tearing up the house. I loved it. But I was on a mission, and at 6:45 AM one morning, I was up and about, tearing boxes from the basement of the house, and making arrangements to get my materials that were in storage in Queens. Other materials were with two Long Island lawyers. I would be getting that too.

My wife woke up and asked me what I was doing.

"Getting ready for the next trial."

She stared at me for a moment. "It's all over, let it go."

"Their coming."

"Get a grip," she said. "You're not your father, they will let it go, so should you."

I told her to go away and let me do my work.

"Your work?"

She walked away. She had put a call in to Charlie and told him to call me, which he did.

"You're like a war vet that can't let go," he told me. "They're done with you; the parole thing was a parting shot. At this point I'm sure they accepted that you have left the Life, so now is the time to create a new life for you and your family. Be happy and go enjoy your family."

You have to give it to Charlie. Ever the optimist. Fortunately, I wasn't. Each night in my own bed came the realization that it could be my last. Prison for life, or death. (A thought always on my mind in the Life and even more now.)

But I realized that the main threat was not from those in the Life, it had been ten years since I left. My nemesis was the government. They would be the ones to come a gunnin' for me again.

So I made sure I spent a lot of time with my family, making memories as my father had instructed me to do. I also spent a lot of time with my private investigators, putting together the material I needed for when.

I believed myself to be an automatic bail candidate, no history of missed appearances, never late for a court date, in compliance with previous bail conditions. Excellent reputation in the community and significant involvement in that community. I knew I was also able to garner numerous supporting letters, as I had done in the past.

I contacted Charlie and Seth requesting materials I needed. My brother was spending time at my guest house, sifting through boxes of material. I instructed him that if anything happens, my lawyers are to get all the material.

My brother (also an optimist) agreed with my wife that I was overreacting. "They're done with you man," he told me. "Let it go."

He no doubt changed his mind later on, when an agent was pointing a gun at his face when they came to arrest me on August 5, 2008.

CHAPTER THIRTY-ONE

Men in Black

I had been up the entire night with my baby son, Joseph. He was sick, and I, of course, was concerned. It was one week before his second birthday. I love all of my children, but I think any parent has a special fondness for the baby in the house.

I certainly did, especially that night.

The complete dependence, the innocence, the absence of any façade or falsity, leads directly to a father's heart, and when that baby is other than well, it also leads directly to a father's guts. Especially someone, who lost a brother that only lived to be twelve years old.

We are assured of nothing when it comes to the ones we love. They are all on loan to us, and we on loan to them. Sooner or later we shall all be taken away from each other. That is a thought I live with every day, especially in light of repeated governmental attempts to see that I would be taken away from my family and friends—for the rest of my life.

There are certain things I *have* grown to be sure of in my life, however. One of them is continuous well publicized government harassment. The other is a press feeding frenzy when my name is deemed "newsworthy."

So, I had spent the night with my baby son getting sick

on me. He had spent the night in bed with my wife and me, and being up all night, I was exhausted. I was in the bathroom cleaning up the mess that was on me early morning on the 5th of August 2008, when my dogs started to bark uncontrollably.

I was pissed off, thinking that the disturbance was caused by my brother, who had temporarily been staying at my guest house. I remember saying to myself that he gets home this late at night, I'm gonna tear him a new ass for sure.

Then it occurred to me that the dogs knew Peter, and there wouldn't have been a continuous barking once they recognized him. But there was a continuous barking. That was my first clue.

The next clue was a not so faint *wubba-wubba-wubba* that meant there were helicopters hovering above. None of my family or friends own helicopters, so that meant only one thing—and it was bad.

The FBI had come for me again with their helicopters. Or maybe it was just the news helicopters, couldn't be sure. And there would only be one reason why news helicopters were hovering. Which again meant the FBI had come for me again. I went to the bedroom.

"C'mon, Kim, get up, let's go, they're here," I said.

"Who?" She asked still groggy from sleep.

I looked through the window and saw them coming. She understood and started to cry.

"C'mon, there's no time for that. You know the drill," I told her.

Before I get into the gory details of this quite unnecessary waste of tax payer's money, and quite unnecessary traumatizing of my wife and young children, I would like to ask you, the person reading this, if you remember the stories about how the Gottis resisted Federal apprehension, about how we assaulted members of law enforcement, how we skipped bail?

You don't remember them? The reason is that such things never ever happened. There were never any such stories.

But every time the government came to arrest me, despite their knowing full well—their being told in advance—that I would voluntarily surrender, they had to come on like traditional "gangbusters" with guns, dressed in black fatigues, SWAT types in full tactical gear, black vans and helicopters. As if this was some sort of major anti-terrorist operation.

And of course, by some coincidence the Press just happened to be there to catch it all on video.

The searchlight from the helicopter harshly illuminated my property, as the army of agents poured through the gates and over the wall as if this were a raid on some enemy stronghold. It was a raid—on a family home in one of the nicest, and safest neighborhoods, not only in New York, but in all probability, the country.

My brother was at my home, and hearing the commotion, went outside when the raid came. The dogs were barking furiously, and the agents coming on to the property ordered my brother to restrain the dogs or they would be shot. Then he was pushed up against the wall of the guest house, with a government issue pistol shoved in his face, and told to shut up and not move.

I opened the window, and told the agents, "Relax. The door's getting opened right now."

My wife went downstairs and let them in.

"Offer them coffee," I said. "Let me get shaved and cleaned up."

They came into the bathroom and said I didn't have time to shave, and could do so later—in jail. I told them I was going to shave right where I was, and that the next move would be theirs. I take pride in my appearance, even if that appearance is on a perp walk in front of the voyeurs who call themselves journalists.

I was stripped search, and then dressed in casual clothes, which the agents first searched for any contraband or weapons. You may have seen, and depending upon when you read this, may still see both stills and video of my being led away by a male and female agent.

The one good thing was they were courteous enough not to handcuff me in front of my children, who by this time were crying as their father was being taken away.

No matter what else I am, I am also a gentleman, and while being carted away, while being videotaped, I cautioned the female agent to be careful where she walked, so that she didn't trip over some obstruction in the road. You can see that on the video also.

I have forgotten the name of the female agent, but William Johnson (who I have previously mentioned), the male special agent, was a gentleman, which is not always the case with law enforcement personnel. But both those arresting me that day acted professionally and were polite.

CHAPTER THIRTY-TWO

Diesel Therapy

I was arraigned in Manhattan, and then sent on a circuitous journey to Tampa Florida, because this time the government wanted a crack at me with a Southern jury. Now it takes about two hours to travel from New York to Tampa by air. It took the government rather longer to get me there.

From my Oyster Bay Cove home, I was taken to the FBI Melville, Long Island office. I was asked to join Team America. In other words, cooperate. I declined.

I was then arraigned in Manhattan at the Federal Court-house at 500 Pearl Street, and then housed in the SHU—the Special Housing Unit of the Metropolitan Detention Center in Brooklyn. Read that to be the hole—solitary confinement. Locked up 23 hours a day, and even the attorney visiting room was locked up behind bars and Plexiglas.

The attorney was locked in with me in the visiting room, and unless and until the guards let him out, he was a prisoner too. No access to a bathroom. Too bad. Often, after I was once again cuffed up and manacled up and taken away, it would take another 45 minutes to get the attorney out of there.

From MDC I was taken to Stewart Air Force Base in upstate

New York. I was put on a prison plane, in the company of Federal Marshals. I was seated in a special section, manacled, chains around ankles, waist, black-boxed, so movement was very restricted.

Are Oklahoma or Texas or Georgia on the flight plan from New York to Florida? It *was* on Con Air—the name given to air transport provided to convicts. Want to know why?

The purpose of this circuitous route, the many stop offs at out of the way prisons, was twofold. First, the physical and psychological harassment was meant to break one down—a softening up process. Second, the journey was a punishment for having been successful against the government several times already in previous proceedings.

The government's feeling was that a New York jury would be reluctant to convict me. They already failed to reach a verdict several times. They figured that the good old boys in Florida, when judging the innocence or guilt of an Italian from New York, might be more of a sure thing for a conviction.

In addition, the government was looking at the time for a death penalty, and since New York puts the kibosh on that—in fact if not in law—the government figured a Florida jury would be more likely to okay my execution.

When I finally arrived at the jail at Pinellas County Florida (there was no nearby Federal facility in which to keep me), I was soon to learn that the budget for food for prisoner per day was about one dollar, ergo, the terrible quality of the food. Also, I could not have contact visits with anyone, as visits were by TV screen, not in person.

When I was arraigned in Tampa, I had been escorted by two unmarked cars in a convoy. As I entered the courtroom, I saw my attorneys Charlie Carnesi and local counsel Henry Gonzalez, they smiled at me, and I at them.

At the prosecution table were several assistant US Attorneys, and two federal agents. Not unusual for one of my cases. However, also seated in the "well" (that part of the courtroom for the attorneys and the defendant) was New York FBI agent Ted Otto.

He had no business being in the well, this was a Florida case, he was a New York agent. He gave me a treacherous smile, and I returned it with half a smile, and a slight nod back, partly in acknowledgment of the dirty game he was playing against me. He had made good on his promise to me, "It's not over yet."

After pleading not guilty, I was denied bail, which was also not unusual in my cases.

At first, I was housed in what's called complete lockdown, but, eventually, the conditions of my confinement were somewhat more relaxed. I was moved to a four bed secure control "pod."

About two months into my Florida confinement, I began to experience significant pain to my left kidney area, radiating down to my penis. The pain increased, in the next week, to severe pain. I began to drip blood from my penis. Finally, I was taken to see a doctor at the prison medical unit (Pinellas County Jail houses some 4,000 detainees, and needs one) and given a sonogram.

I was diagnosed with kidney stones, and the one in my left kidney was large enough so that it would not pass normally. After several more days, the doctor said he would seek permission to schedule me for ultrasound treatments to break up the stone. In the interim, Tylenol was the only pain killer I was given.

Meanwhile, my attorneys were moving the court to get me back up to New York jurisdiction.

The doctors in the Florida jail finally approved my ultrasound treatment to address my kidney stones, thanks to the untiring efforts of my excellent Florida attorney, Henry Gonzalez.

Henry, who had litigated against the author of the RICO law, Notre Dame professor, Robert Blakey, was well known as one of the stars of Florida's criminal defense bar. He had been a friend of my father, and his client list included Santo

Trafficante and Neil Dellacroce. (He got an acquittal for Neil in a Miami case.)

So Henry was getting my medical needs addressed, but then my New York attorneys did too good a job in their application to the court.

★

They had moved to transfer my case to New York. It was submitted that the transfer of the case to Florida's jurisdiction was prejudicial to my defense. It impacted on my ability to obtain and produce defense witnesses, and prepare with attorneys and investigators, who were based in New York. (At the previous trial we had called twenty defense witnesses.)

Carnesi put it all on the record:

> They know it, Judge, because in those three trials, up in New York particularly in the last one, his financial status was put under a microscope, analyzed, reviewed and was in fact the subject matter of some counts in the indictment, counts which the judge threw out at the Rule 29 (hearing) which never even went to the jury. They know his financial position . . . It's not good. It's certainly not liquid. So this is a real problem in terms of this case.

In following up, Carnesi said:

> The strategy of separating an enemy from his homeland and cutting off the supplies that he needs to fight the fight, or the war, may very well be an excellent strategy in the art of war. It's not an acceptable strategy in a process that is supposed to be about the search for the truth.

Some of those witnesses we sought to use had been intimidated by the FBI serving subpoenas on them, and making veiled threats, but it didn't work. It was proposed that this attempt at a prosecution was an end run around the witness problem for the government.

My attorney, Carnesi, in addressing this issue, said:

> FBI agents tried to intimidate those witnesses into not testifying between trials number two and trials number three. They weren't able to do that.
> [He followed up with the reason for the government wanting a Florida venue for this case]
> In a final move to try and deprive Mr. Gotti of his opportunity to defend this case, "Let's isolate him from his witnesses."

Judge Merryday had inquired as to the timing of the prior New York proceedings. Carnesi, in speaking of the trials said, "It was within 24 months (from the first to the latest) Judge, in answer to your question, yes. It was actually a shorter period of time. The trials began in 2005, and were concluded during 2006. So it's really—the actual time would probably be closer to a year."

"And Judge Scheindlin tried them all?"

"Yes Your Honor."

"And none resulted in a verdict in whole or in part," asked Judge Merryday.

"That's correct, Your Honor."

"And the present defendant was the sole defendant in each trial?"

Carnesi answered, "Not in the first trial. There were two other co-defendants, Judge, each of whom were convicted of different crimes within the indictment."

Judge Merryday asked, "In the same trial?"

"Yes, Your Honor."

"So," inquired the judge, "the same jury that convicted them, did not convict the present defendant?"

"That's correct Your Honor."

Later Carnesi informed the court that the "Prosecutor's

office (in New York) stood up and said to the court, 'Judge, in essence we're moving—well not in essence, specifically— we're moving to dismiss this case at this point, we're not going forward.'"

Carnesi further explained, "They were unable to convince a jury of 12 unanimously that he had not in fact withdrawn from this conspiracy within five years. That's the status. Wasn't an acquittal. It was the government itself standing up and saying after three mistrials..."

Judge Merryday interrupted, "And you mean literally that the court was in session and..."

Carnesi finished for the judge, "Absolutely Judge. Yes Judge.

"The court was in session specifically for that motion. There had been a mistrial. Then calendared for a conference. In the interim, the judge had clearly signaled in all honesty, to the prosecution that she was not inclined having heard the case three times—that she was clearly not inclined to allow them to proceed to a fourth trial—but it never got to that issue."

Carnesi went on to address the allegations in the Florida indictment regarding murder charges. In speaking of a government witness at the last trial:

> He was Mr. Gotti's close contact or associate within the organization, there's never been any testimony about any of these murders. These murders, two of which have been the subject of prior trials in New York. Witnesses have come forward, cooperators, cooperators who were in much stronger or substantial positions within that enterprise than the people who are now suddenly cooperating here in Tampa, who testified against Mr. Gotti, completely and certainly as proffered by the government candidly....
>
> What you have here, Judge, the basis of this here, Judge, is that notwithstanding the so called hierarchy of this enterprise and their cooperation with law enforcement over the years and

their willingness to testify against Mr. Gotti, there was no such evidence, there were no such allegations including the drugs, the homicides and the drug dealing. Nobody's ever said that.

What you have here now is you have two or a number of low level individuals who aren't even technically members of the enterprise who've gotten themselves in trouble, who've been basically made to understand: 'You want to get out of trouble? The key is mention Mr. Gotti. Mention Mr. Gotti. That's what it is all about.

Also, it was an obvious attempt at forum shopping. Having been several times unsuccessful with New York juries in New York prosecutions, the government wanted a shot at me down South. Different culture and environment, maybe a good chance at a different outcome. Yet the offenses charged were basically mirror images of previous charges in indictments obtained in New York, involving New York, and being tried in New York.

The judge ruled:

The Florida indictment charges the same RICO conspiracy against which Gotti has defended himself three times in New York. The present indictment poses the troubling question whether after three unsuccessful prosecutions in New York of a RICO conspiracy, along with other charges against Gotti and charges against other defendants in the United States, (the government) can, so to speak just pull up the roots of the indictment the United States cultivated for years in New York, and summarily re-pot the whole operation in Florida, hoping for more favorable conditions and a more favorable result and dismissing as inconsequential the resulting expense and dislocation visited upon Gotti. Of course, the United States in this instance accompanies this re-potting by flavoring the allegations with the details of some events in Florida. But the RICO conspiracy charged in the Florida indictment is unmistakably the same RICO conspiracy charged in New York, the alleged local incidents notwithstanding.

Of course, the fact that the previous case's Judge, after a mistrial, intimated that there would be no fourth trial of these issues, made Florida very attractive as a venue to the government.

"The United States Attorney has chosen oddly to charge only a crime, specifically RICO conspiracy that by any measure occurred largely outside Florida and that has been repeatedly charged and tried before a jury elsewhere," Carnesi argued. Regarding the indictment, Carnesi pointed out, "The indictment instead alleges the single RICO conspiracy offense charged and tried repeatedly without success in New York."

Carnesi had also argued given the nationwide resources of the FBI and the US Attorney's Office, there would be no prejudice to the government in relocating the case back to New York. As Carnesi said,

> The fact of the matter is unlike my office, or Mr. Gotti's position, the prosecution, the US Attorney's Office, obviously is a national office. They can go anywhere to try a case. The FBI is a national operation. The resources available to prosecutors, whether it is here in Tampa or in New York, are nationally wide.

★

The judge determined the afternoon of December 2, 2008, that the government bringing the case to Florida created, "The unmistakable and disquieting impression of 'forum shopping' contrary to sound principles incorporated into Rule 21b [of the Federal Rules of Criminal Procedure]," Judge Merryday said. And he went on:

> Gotti is merely another defendant, presumed innocent in fact,

unsuccessfully prosecuted three times for the charged crime and unreservedly entitled to the protection of the principles codified in Rule 21 b... The interests of justice decisively comment both the transfer of this prosecution to New York, and the interruption of this attempt by the United States to pursue in Florida an indictment that results in material and unwarranted inconvenience and that stands athwart off the manifest interests of justice. Gotti motion to transfer is granted and this action is transferred to the Southern District of New York.

The judge granted the motion.

★

I was going back to New York.

After MDC, on my way to Tampa and then back to New York, I was a government "guest" at over sixteen prisons, some clean, some filthy, and all short stays. My mode of transportation left something to be desired.

You might have seen the smug Floridian prosecutors take full advantage of their photo op on the day of my arrest. I found it to be typical of the arrogance of Federal prosecutors. There pretrial "tribunal" held in the press was highly prejudicial to me, and with the later denial of my bail application, I was basically guilty before trial, and the presumption of innocence was nowhere to be found. However, the Florida prosecutors only enjoyed a rather short lived triumph.

Special Agent Stephen Ibison, in charge of the Tampa FBI office, told the press, "What should be noted today, is whether you violate the federal law today, tomorrow, or 20 years ago, the FBI and its law enforcement partners will pursue the matter to its logical conclusions."

Well there are several things wrong with that pronouncement.

While murder does not have a statute of limitations—a time

limit in which to be prosecuted—other charges do. One of my defenses was "withdrawal"—that is I had been out of the mob for more than five years. Twenty years were not required. (Actually at the time of these trumped up charges, it had been some ten years that I had left the Life.)

On some of the charges in the indictment, agent Ibison had inherent problems with even a technical defense based on the statute of limitations. It was not his only difficulty. The FBI knew that their "star" witness was a low level thug, a drug dealer and a murderer, ready to say anything against anyone to shorten his upcoming sentence. There was a distinct possibility that a jury would find him less than credible.

The "logical conclusion" of the FBI, however, was not to care, as long as the finger was pointed at me.

In every previous trial, no government cooperator (some 20 of them) made mention of my ever having dealt in drugs, or having participated in the murders of the individuals I supposedly had killed. Not a one.

But the government was more than happy to use these individuals, like Alite, who could be released from the rest of their sentences of imprisonment by testifying against me.

As is often the case, their testimony was nothing but self serving and government encouraged—and sponsored—perjury.

The 2008 bust was no surprise to me. I knew it was coming, but I just didn't know when.

We have already mentioned that, while I was on Federal Parole in 2006-2007, when I reported to the USPO (United States Parole Office) in the Federal courthouse in Central Islip, New York, there were times that FBI agents were there, assuring me that "it wasn't over," and they'd be back.

Unless, of course, I talked to them.

As I have already mentioned, it got so that when I went to see my parole officer, I brought with me my family friend who was also my family attorney, just in case. Early on, I had started to prepare for what I knew was coming, reviewing former trial transcripts, having experts transcribe existing tape recordings to have *accurate* transcripts of the tapes, instead of the garbage that the FBI produced and provided.

I was also served by the fact that in the early nineties, I had attended York College, and besides the credits I had obtained towards a degree, I received four paralegal certificates, and after testing, became a certified paralegal.

From my experience in 1998, I also knew the government was going to make a big production of my arrest. It would be a prime time treasure trove of viewers for the networks.

Let me give you some history.

Back in January '98, my attorney at the time, Richard Rehbock, received an anonymous phone call from some-body—obviously connected with law enforcement. The caller stated, "Something's going to happen, we're not responsible, we don't like the way this is going down."

At the time OCTF and the FBI were in competition hunting for my head. The Secret Service was also interested.

Rehbock placed a call to the "authorities" and informed them that if they wanted me to surrender before January 21, a Wednesday, I was ready willing and able to comply. But after that date, they would have to wait a bit, because I was going to see my father's Boston based appellate attorney to assist him on an appeal.

Rehbock did not receive a return call.

I was on my way to Boston, when all the beeps and buzzes started to go off. My wife informed me that the FBI, OCTF, and Federal Marshals *Blitzkrieg* team were at the gates with guns drawn, a news helicopter in the sky, black vans, black uniforms, and the press snapping and taping away outside of the gates to our home.

My father-in-law started to videotape the invasion, but was told to cease and desist by the agents, and his video re-corder was seized. After removing the tape, they returned the recorder to him.

The FBI informed me that if I didn't return to New York now, and surrender myself at Yonkers, they were going to issue a fugitive warrant. I went back to Queens first, got a haircut and shave, called Rehbock, and we went together to Yonkers.

Once again, a tremendous waste of time and *your* tax dollars, just so the FBI could get a nice photo op of my arrest. Except at that time, while they were all dressed up, I wasn't at the party.

When you add it up, after I pled guilty in 1998, and served the time I was supposed to serve, the government took five more shots at me. Four trials and a parole violation hearing that even they realized wasn't worth seeing through.

Some of you reading this have seen indictments before, some have helped create them, some defend them. But I am assuming that the majority of readers are not familiar with them. An indictment is only an accusation, it is not proof of anything.

In the Federal mob indictments, they like to tell stories. Here are some samples from the 2008 indictment against me, for your edification:

> Made members of the Gambino Crime Family, were aided in their criminal endeavors by other trusted individuals, known as 'associates,' who sometimes were referred to as 'connected' or identified as being 'with' or 'around' a certain member and who operated under the umbrella of the Gambino Crime Family. Associates participated in the various activities of the Gambino Crime Family Crews.

Now there are such things as associates. But in this persecution/prosecution of 2008-2009, who were some of the individuals that the government either directly claimed or implied were associates of the Family?

A friend of mine who did my landscaping, who had zero

criminal record, and was a hard working and honest individual and family man. Another friend of mine, who had no criminal record, had a Bachelor's degree in accounting, a wife, and young child.

Even my family attorney, who never even had a moving violation, who served in US Intelligence, who served honorably in the United States military, and was given a Top Secret Clearance by the same government that was prosecuting me, was put under the microscope.

I tell you this to show you the "logical conclusions" of the FBI.

Here is another part of the indictment:

> It was further part of the conspiracy that the GCF Enterprise members would and did travel from New York City and elsewhere to the Middle District of Florida, the Southern District of Florida, and elsewhere to commit various crimes involving the threatened and actual use of deadly force and violence....In this regard, the members of the GCF Enterprise would and did establish footholds in the city of Tampa Florida, in the Middle District of Florida, as well as other cities in the Southern District of Florida and elsewhere.

What I can tell you is that, if there was organized crime in Florida, in Tampa, the families in New York, the "capital" of underworld activities, didn't know about it. Other than the remnants of those affiliated with Santo Trafficante, in reality there was nobody left in Tampa—in the last fifteen to twenty years it had all vanished.

Tampa is up north. In Southern Florida, the situation was quite different. But Tampa was where Alite had wound up, after being chased from New York to Philadelphia, and from there, to Florida. There he could claim allegiance and support to our flag, and the nobodies down there wouldn't be able to call him on it.

But eventually it began to trickle back to us in New York, that this low life junkie, whom we had chased long ago, was flying our flag to make himself look like something he most certainly was not. So we sent word back to those in Florida, that we had chased this guy, he was nobody to us.

After that, things didn't go so well for Alite. He was given the short shrift, and treated like the refuse that he was. The flag was gone, and the wannabes in Florida knew now that Alite was all wrong.

They weren't the only ones to come to this conclusion.

★

I was elated when Henry Gonzalez told me we had won the motion to transfer me back to New York for trial. I received the news while I was in the medical unit awaiting treatment for my kidney stones. The irritation had caused an infection.

But I got tired of waiting for treatment, and filed a request to be moved back to my cell. All of my legal documents were there, and that was where I needed to be to prepare for the next battle. My request was granted.

Another week went by, and still no medical treatment. I filed a request to learn when I would actually be receiving treatment.

The answer I received, not reduced to a writing of course, was, "You're going back to New York; you are no longer our problem."

I couldn't believe it. I was suffering significantly from the kidney stone, I had an infection, and now I was no longer their problem? Henry contacted Charlie Carnesi to request that the Marshal Service expedite my removal to New York, so at least I could get treatment somewhere for my condition. Charlie promised to inquire.

Big mistake, I told Henry. Now that the government knows my condition, they will do what they can to cause me more pain. Henry stopped me, and told me I would be fine.

With all due respect to Henry, in my heart and mind I knew better.

★

A couple of weeks later, I was gathered up at 4:00 AM and brought down to R&D. I was held in a bullpen until marshals came to load me onto a bus for transport to Tampa airport. There were dozens of other inmates on that bus.

At 8:45 they began unloading us. I was last off, and put through the maze of security, searched, leg manacles, belly chains, black box, the whole program. I was about to be put in the plane in this condition.

But suddenly, I was removed from the plane, and placed on a large gray bus with blackened out windows. The bus had open seating, two on each side of the bus, but there were also three cages in this bus. Side by side. The first one was where they put me. It was about three feet by three feet. There was a bench.

The other inmates, although cuffed and chained, had free access to a restroom at the back of the bus. I didn't. If Henry were there at the time, I would have said, "I told you so." I heard the officer mention the time when the bus pulled out, 9:15 AM.

I stayed in that cage until the bus finally pulled into a prison in Denton, Georgia. Eighteen hours later. Unloaded from my cage, I was met by a large black lieutenant, some three hundred pounds and around six feet two.

He came over to me and asked me politely, "Mr. Gotti, do you mind if I take a picture with you?"

"No," I said, "but you gotta get me clean underwear and a tee shirt."

"Of course, we do that for everyone," he said.

"Let me change out, without being with the other inmates."

"Come with me," he said, and took me to the strip search and changing area. My chains and black box were removed. I could move my hands once again. As I disrobed, I saw a blood stain of approximately eight inches in diameter on my boxer shorts. The Lieutenant saw it also.

"What did you get cut?" he asked.

"No, kidney stone left kidney. The blood drips out of me."

He shook his head in disbelief.

"They locked me in that bus cage for eighteen hours, no restroom privilege."

"Do you need medical?"

"No," I said, "just rest."

I went through pics and prints, and was escorted by the Lieutenant and two other guards to the hole.

"Sorry," said the Lieutenant, "It's orders."

"No problem," I told him.

The chains on me were removed by my placing my hands through the food slot, and the Lieutenant said he would be back in fifteen minutes. He was, bearing toothpaste, toothbrush, soap, shampoo, a comb, clean towels, and a new pair of boxer shorts. (It was a kindness I will remember.)

The cell had a shower in it. Built into the wall. So, I thought to myself, not too terrible.

"Take your shower," said the Lieutenant, "and I will be back in fifteen minutes with the food tray."

I took the shower, and was feeling pretty good. The food tray opened up, and there was the food. Fresh scrambled eggs, sausage, and two biscuits with gravy. Apple and orange juice. Coffee and cake.

The best I had eaten in months, I thought. Hope I get to stay for awhile in this place.

I thanked the Lieutenant for his kindness. He winked and walked away. I tried out the prison bed. It had a real pillow. I rated it a ten at the time. There was a roll handle on the cell window, which you could open to get fresh air. I heard the rain falling. Also, what sounded like a flag banging against a flag pole. That rhythmic sounding put me to sleep and sweet dreams.

The dream ended abruptly, a short time later, as I was awakened by a fist pounding on the cell door. It was the Lieutenant, and this time he had a sad expression on his face. That did not bode well.

"Get ready," he told me, "there are some men here for you."

I shook my head in disbelief. I became a believer when four marshals were outside my cell. "Cuff up, Gotti," they commanded. I turned my back to the food slot which had opened, and I put my hands through behind my back. I was cuffed, and led back to R&D.

Strip searched, belly chained, black boxed once again. I glanced at the clock—6:10 AM. So much for a good night's rest. I was placed on a bus once again, this time alone, and transported to the United States Prison at Atlanta, Georgia.

Arrived. January, light snow, biting cold. The bus drove through electric gates, behind outer walls, and through another gate. Outside, I awaited the buzzer which would admit me to the prison.

As I waited to be buzzed in, I had a flashback to my beginning military school days, standing outside, freezing. I had come from Tampa, and was dressed in Khakis and a tee shirt. The three marshals that waited with me were dressed in coats and hats.

After what seemed an eternity in the cold, the buzzer sounded and I was admitted to the prison. I went to R&D, walking through a long corridor of windowless concrete and steel. The marshals handed me over to the BOP guards, and left.

Stripped down again, given a jumpsuit, and allowed to keep my boxer shorts. Escorted to the hole. There I stayed until my next abrupt move several weeks later.

I was taken by prison bus from Atlanta to the airport, and there loaded on Con Air, to go to Oklahoma. Once again in the hole in this prison. I remember, when I was brought there, a guard who was an older Native American. He was one of those that had stripped me out in the hole, gave me a jumpsuit, and a change of underwear.

"Are you related to Gene Gotti?" he asked me.

"Yes, he's my uncle."

"Nice man," the guard said, "he was here not too long ago."

"Great, let me have his cell." It was a joke.

"Let me see what I can do." I thought he was joking too.

The joke was taken seriously, however, and that's what I got, my Uncle Gene's cell.

The guard told me, while putting me in the cell, "This is where Gene was. He loved watching the planes land and take off." (The prison was attached to the Oklahoma City airport.)

At night you could see the bright blue lights of the runway from the cell. I too, enjoyed watching the planes land and take off. They enjoyed a freedom of movement denied me. The guard was a good guy, often coming by to greet me, tell me about my uncle, and being generally respectful.

After several weeks of watching arrivals and departures, I myself departed the Oklahoma prison, this time on to Texas. Quick stops in Amarillo then El Paso. From there to New Hampshire, then to Stewart Air Force Base, in Newburgh, New York.

A bit of irony there, for on Greg DePalma's tapes concerning political corruption, the family was alleged to have bribed officials to get favorable construction contracts on the base. From Stewart, I was taken via prison bus to MDC in Brooklyn. That's where this case started several months earlier.

CHAPTER THIRTY-THREE

New York State of Mind

At MDC, I had the opportunity to meet Vincent Basciano, known as "Vinny Gorgeous" in the press and on the street, as he was the owner of a Bronx hair cutting salon, "Hello Gorgeous." He was also a handsome, well groomed man—even in prison, his hair was perfect and he sported a tan.

Basciano was the alleged acting head of the Bonanno family, and in prison on several murder charges. One of those charges involved allegations that he had conspired to kill the judge and the prosecutor on his case. The charges were absurd, but now he was held in the Special Housing Unit, the SHU in MDC—in other words, the hole. In isolation.

I met him when I was in the hole while in a strip cell—where they strip us down and search us. "Hey Bo!" I heard a voice say.

"Who's that?"

"Me, Vinny. Vinny Basciano. From the Bronx."

I had met him in passing in the bullpen at MCC in Manhattan years ago. But this is the first time I actually conversed with him, never did on the streets.

"How you making out, pal?" I asked.

"Me? I'm doing great. This is like being in the Fontaine-bleau in Miami. I get room service and everything."

I had to laugh, the guy had a sense of humor that prison couldn't put a dent in.

"How you doing?" he asked me.

"Great, several months of diesel therapy, but no big deal."

"I know, Bo, I can only imagine. I'm rooting for you pal."

"As I am you," I said.

Then guards came to move him, and a second group came to strip me out. I was then moved to what is known as Range One. You walk through the hole, and at the end, there is a steel door. Beyond that door was where I was housed. Now I was alone.

Wrong. Once again I heard, "Hey Bo! Yeah, it's me Vinny. I'm four doors down. Just you and me pal."

"Couldn't hope for anything better," I responded.

"Nope, I'll try to send you some magazines."

"I appreciate it."

"Bo, your dad was, and is, my idol."

"I appreciate that even more."

Then the guards came in. Two of them went towards Vinny's cell and instructed him that we can't communicate with each other. They didn't want to get into trouble.

"No problem," Vinny said. Then, the next day, he was moved to Range 2, and in his place, two Mexican gangbangers were put in the cell. The SHU at MDC was probably the noisiest time I had in prison.

The guards rarely heard anything from me. Rarely. One of those rare times was when I inquired about getting my kidney problem addressed. On the 20th of January, 2009, I received a written response dated 1/15/09 from a D. Williams, the ISM manager. Here it is in its entirety:

Dear Mr. Gotti:

This is in response to your inmate request to Staff Member, wherein you requested to be seen by the Health Services Department for your kidney stone condition, and be provided Tylenol for your kidney stone pain.

I spoke with Mr. Ittayem, Assistant Health Services Administrator, and informed him you would like to be seen for your kidney stone condition, and be provided Tylenol for your kidney stone pain. Mr. Ittayem indicated he would have a member of the Health Services Department see you regarding your kidney stone condition, and review your chart to see if Tylenol was provided in the past.

I hope this information has satisfied your request.

Sincerely,
D. WILLIAMS
ISM MANAGER

As I review this, I note that five times in this letter, they make reference to a kidney stone condition. There was no question that I had this condition, and furthermore, the letter is complete bullshit as a response. The prison had been provided with the response from the Medical Unit at Pinellas County Jail regarding my condition. From the response it was clear what my situation was—it clearly says "On Tylenol":

11/21/08
REQUEST TO BE SEEN FOR: (BE SPECIFIC)
Severe pain comes and goes in left kidney when I have urine flow it's at 40% at best and other times nothing at all. [my reason]
On Tylenol—Renewed. [their response]

To this day, I am still trying to obtain my medical records from Pinellas County Jail. But MDC had the response paperwork weeks before I requested medical attention from the guards. Interesting to note, there was no record of my request to see a doctor. Obviously, after a diagnosis was obtained for kidney stones, I wanted competent medical advice.

Eventually, I was given Tylenol.

Some days were better than others. Some days I would feel relatively little pain, and some I would be doubled up in my bunk in agony, trying not to breathe too hard. I've been in a lot of fights. Took my share of kicks and punches, and have been stabbed a few times. So pain is not a stranger to me, but the pain I experienced with the kidney stones ranked top on the hurt list. Never before had I experienced anything like this.

★

Severe pain has its psychological effects beyond the purely physical. I remember a dream that I had one night while suffering from the stones. It was tough to sleep because of the pain, but eventually, I must have drifted off.

I was having a conversation with someone in my cell. I could hear him, but I didn't see him. "What about your metal?" the voice asked. "If we cut your father down the middle what you'd see on the outside, you'd see on the inside. How about you?"

I listened.

"If we cut you open, what would we see?"

I didn't respond.

"You always loved your dad's prison stories," said the voice. "Well, tough guy, you have any fun prison stories?"

Again, I wouldn't answer this stranger's questions.

"Not so much fun, eh tough guy? How much can you take, tough guy? Come on, speak up!"

In the dream, I looked into the cell mirror. The voice was coming from my reflection. I woke up.

★

I filed another request for medical attention, but this time I waited for the Thursday Walk Through, when the warden of the prison and his staff would walk through the hole. It served dual purposes. One, to demonstrate "concern" for the inmates, and two, to show that the prison administration was "hands on" and in control. It would serve to be useful in the event of a suit against the prison, alleging negligence, or intentional mistreatment of inmates. The inmate was given an opportunity to address his concerns, problems, etc. with the Warden and his Assistant Wardens, as well as the officers on the unit staff.

It gave an *impression* of accessibility.

The night before the Warden's walk through I made sure not to flush my toilet, to demonstrate the accumulation of blood in my urine. Normally I wouldn't acknowledge the Warden on his walk through, putting up the toilet sign, or pretending to be occupied with something else.

Warden and assistants would normally stop by my cell, as if I were some sort of special exhibit. Normally, I would ignore them, to show them they meant nothing to me. But this particular Thursday, I pounced on the opportunity to address the Warden.

"Good morning, Mr. Gotti," he said to me.

"Good morning to you," I responded. "Warden, can you look down and see my bowl?"

"Yes,"

"What color is it?"

"Looks red."

"Correct. It's blood. It comes from my urine, and has for the last several days. At what point do I get to see a doctor to address this condition?"

"I'll get right on it," he said, "meantime, file a cop-out."

So I did. I filled out the form notifying the Lieutenant in the SHU of my request for medical attention. (Used a two inch pencil we were given to write with.) I slid it out the door, as per normal procedure, and the night Lieutenant was supposed to pick it up and file it so I could get a response.

Several days later, no answer. I complained to the day Lieutenant. He said, "Let me get you a BP9." That is a form requesting an administrative remedy. I slid it under the door for later pickup.

Here was what was written on the BP9:

> Inmate Gotti requests to be seen for a kidney stone problem that he has had for over two months. I have been urinating blood on and off for the same number of months and had shown both the warden and his AW (Assistant Warden), the same on their Thursday walk through. I am in a tremendous amount of discomfort and request aid. I was seen by medical professionals while housed in Tampa at Pinellas County, and was given a diagnosis of an enlarged stone stuck in my left kidney. In advance, I thank you for your time on this matter. 1/26/09.

A response dated January 29, 2009, was received on 2/5/09. Here it is:

> For the reasons listed below this administrative remedy request is being rejected and returned to you. You should include a copy of this notice with any future correspondence regarding the rejection.
>
> REJECT REASON 1: You did not attempt informal resolution prior to submission of administrative remedy, or you did not provide the necessary evidence of your attempt at informal resolution.
>
> REJECT REASON 2: You may resubmit your request in proper form within 5 days of this rejection notice.

Here is the epitome of bureaucratic stupidity. An inmate, a human being that still has some constitutional rights, in this case with respect to the Eighth Amendment, makes it clear that he is suffering from an excruciatingly painful medical condition.

What does BOP do? Instead of doing the intelligent humane thing—get me to a doctor for treatment—they reject my request based on my not conforming to their administrative form, their bureaucratic rules of protocol and chain of command.

Of course, prison procedure clearly states that after a cop-out is filed, and there is not a satisfactory response, the B9 is the form to use. That's what I did. I followed procedure. It didn't work.

But court was coming up. I refused to go, figuring that this would bring some judicial attention to my medical condition and the BOP neglect thereof. When it was time to get ready for court, I refused to go. They came in—in force. I still refused.

Judge Castel questioned Charlie Carnesi regarding my non appearance.

"Does Your Honor remember the issue regarding the kidney stones? Well, it is still not resolved."

Judge Castel was not pleased, he didn't want to have his trial interfered with by this issue, and must have sent strong word to the prison authorities to remedy this situation. I say that, because, all of a sudden, the MDC authorities made sure I got to see a doctor. I got the treatment I badly needed—and had needed for months—and the problem was basically solved—I thought.

(Later, when I once again was free, and had access to medical help at will, I was told by my urologist at North Shore Hospital in Long Island, that, after a sonogram was taken, scarring to my kidney due to the neglect by the BOP, had caused a reduction in function in my left kidney.)

My morning pain with respect to this condition remains.

★

The medical condition finally having been addressed, it was time to focus on my serious legal condition. By BOP regulation, while in the hole, I was to get an hour a day of "recreation" which took place in a larger cage than the one I lived in. I was placed in a cage across from Basciano, and even with a wall between us, we could converse.

Several times this happened, and we would talk about New York restaurants we had visited, about our children, and other normal subjects when two guys get to take time out and bullshit. Vinny told me stories about the times he spotted my father in Manhattan, or with Frank LoCascio in the Bronx. He was star struck every time he saw my father.

"Pal," I told him. "I lived with him, and at times I got star struck too."

★

Soon, by administrative error or by chance, Vinny and I ended up in the same section of the hole. Maybe it was by design. Cameras outside the cell, inside the cell. I told the guards unless the warden could guarantee there were no female guards with video access to my cell, I would continue to use available means to block the camera while I was answering nature's call, or showering. (Available means was wet toilet paper, formed over the lens.)

I know Basciano did the same. I never got their guarantee, and I continued to obscure the view. We were breaking the rules, and that was going to be addressed.

It was addressed by housing an inmate next to us that was completely crazy—or close enough to it. R.D. I wondered who he had fucked with to wind up here. He was in for drug dealing and murder charges, but he wound up with us (I learned shortly after his placement), because he was accused of attempted murder of a guard at the MCC. He made a shank (prison slang for knife) out of metal from his bunk, and had repeatedly stabbed a guard in the head and the neck.

Fortunately for the guard, he survived. Unfortunately for us, they placed RD next to our cells. The first couple of days after he joined us, nothing much happened. He merely attempted to communicate with me through the vent, or under the door.

I wasn't there to make friends, and frankly I was short, and at times even curt with him. I had good reason.

RD would wait for a female guard to pass his cell and masturbate when they were in view. (We call these low lifes "Gunners.") Worse, he would flood the tier with his bodily waste by stuffing up the toilet. At least twice a week. He screamed loudly and repeatedly flushed the toilet.

I would tell Vinny, "Plug your door, this mutt is at it again."

"Got ya bo," he would say, and he'd plug up his door. This went on for weeks.

★

Vinny was again moved, as it was no doubt decided by BOP that we shouldn't be communicating. At least the warden did. As the escort came to move him to another Range, he shouted to me, "Bo—I feel horrible, like I'm bailing and leave you with this animal. You should worry about your case, and this mutt is a distraction. You have to be focused. I'm only sorry I never met you on the streets."

"Me too," I said. "Good luck."

So while most of the pain from my kidney stone was gone, I now had to deal with this maniac in the cell adjacent to mine. With his constant screaming and incoherent rants, I couldn't sleep, I couldn't read.

One morning, around six in the morning the CO came and asked if I wanted to take rec. It was cold, and I believe it was late February. Normally, I would have declined the offer, it being too cold, and too early in the morning. But this particular day, I wanted—I needed—something like fresh air in my lungs.

It had been about a month since my last rec period. I was brought to the rec cage and uncuffed. I began to do some pushups, then ten laps of the fifteen foot length of the rec cage, and then repeated the sequence.

Suddenly I hear keys and chains being moved, and the door to the rec cage next to me being unlocked. Good, I thought, some company. I looked at the cage next to me. Not good. It was RD the bug. Now I could see this loony face to face through the steel gate of the cage.

"My man," I addressed him, "what is your problem?"

He said nothing at first, and I continued, "People are fighting for their lives here, and you're causing all this ruckus."

"You don't understand," he replied. "The government tried to frame me, I didn't do nothing."

I cut him short. "Show some respect. You hate the government?"

"Yeah."

"Then quiet down and let me prepare for trial. By your outbursts you think your affecting these people? They go home at night and forget all about you. All you're doing is affecting my ability to defend myself. You did it with Basciano, and he's facing the death penalty."

"I know, Vinny," he said. "I love Vinny. I was with him at the MCC.

"You didn't show it."

"Alright brother," he said, "I'll be cool. I'll fall back man."

"Good," I said.

For the next week he behaved himself. He would always ask the CO to put him in the rec cage next to me. I didn't mind, I had patience with this guy. One day, from his cage, he is spewing about his cases. He started talking about how they lied about him stabbing the CO.

"Fella," I said, "if it happened in the legal visit room it has to be on tape." (I knew the layout at the MCC, I had been there.)

"Yeah," he said, "the BOP and Jason Randazzo fucked with the video tape."

That got my attention—I stopped my exercising. That name was familiar to me.

"Who's Jason Randazzo?" I asked.

"The liaison between FBI and BOP in New York."

I knew I had heard the name. I just didn't remember where I heard it. About fifteen minutes later, the CO came in and I was brought back to my cell. I began pulling out my legal files, and then it hit me. A private investigator, Larry Frost, had made numerous tapings of several interviews with Alite. I had the transcripts, and in those transcripts, Alite mentions Randazzo. He was confirming what Frost and others already knew. Alite had a relationship with an FBI agent. Now there was a name pinned to that agent. Randazzo.

Alite said he began meeting with Randazzo starting in the early 1990's. On at least seven occasions. So now, it was all making sense. My medical neglect, my legal mail being opened before I was to see it—a flagrant violation of my rights and prison policy. (Normally, correspondence marked as legal mail is opened in front of the inmate in the cell, to confirm there is no contraband contained therein, but the guard doesn't read it.)

While I have not been able to independently confirm this, I believe somehow Randazzo was involved, working with FBI agent Otto. Otto worked Alite, when he was in New York, having been handed him from Randazzo. The special treatment I had been receiving may have had a direct link back to agent Otto, or so I thought. I felt that because of his obsession with me, Otto may have used Randazzo, in his capacity as liaison between FBI and BOP, to screw around with me.

I am not some rabid conspiracy theorist, but neither am I deaf or blind. It was time to get more information. I obtained a copy of Randazzo's affidavit on the RD case.

Randazzo, in said affidavit, alluded to his being an agent

since 1990. (A short time before Tony Pep had said Alite was a cooperator.) He goes on to say he was liaison with BOP in the New York metropolitan area since 1992. Involved in investigations in BOP matters.

Alite, once he turned, officially was treated a bit differently than I was. From his prison in Brazil, a forty million dollar US government jet transported him back to Tampa. In a taped conversation between Alite and his mother via telephone, we hear in January '07:

> Alite: I mean did they explain to you? They picked me up in a private Gulf Stream 5, the direct FBI plane. They put just me and Mike Bradley [FBI agent] and two other agents. The plane was beautiful. Forty million dollar plane.

My mode of transportation was somewhat lower down on the ladder. Prison buses, black boxed in a cage, denied bathroom privileges. When I flew, there was a variety of aircraft, but what stayed consistent is my being manacled and black boxed during the flight, surrounded by marshals.

★

If you were in possession of every single recording made of me having prison visits, you wouldn't find me whining about my conditions of confinement. What about Alite? How did he handle his situation? Let's go to a phone conversation he had with his brother (BJ: Alite's brother; JA: Alite):

> BJ: You need to get a grip and like I said, stop being so fucking super focused on yourself. Forget about it. Think about having fun and get yourself out of the picture. Relax. Think about making money, think about coming out. Think about whatever you want that's going to make you happy.
>
> JA: I'm having a difficult time thinking about coming out and

having fun when I'm locked up 24 hours a day in a little fucking part that I'm locked down...

BJ: That's what you gotta do.

JA: Three quarters of the day.

BJ: Yeah, it sucks but we know everyone's got their own prisons. You'll be out of it and when you're out of it you'll make, you'll do what you have to do to have the fun and the life...

JA: Hey, let me ask you something.

BJ: what else are you going to do? Cry and be like...

JA: Jimmy.

BJ: Man up!

JA: Just shut up. I never complained.

BJ: No, man up. Man up!

★

From tapes of phone conversations of Alite with his mother, especially the one from January '07, it appears she was able to call the FBI, and make requests about his housing conditions. I have known some prisons and some prisoners in my time, and I am not familiar with any other inmate who can have his mother call the FBI and have an inmate's housing status changed.

Yet Alite did not admit to being a cooperator at these times. He goes from rotting in a Brazilian prison, flies via a Gulfstream 5 to Tampa, and has his mother calling the FBI when he has a problem with his accommodations. Not yet a cooperator? Really?

It seems this killer had a trouble doing time. This tough guy, six months later, again requested to be moved from his location, because he felt threatened by another inmate. Now a full-fledged cooperator, he was afforded multiple furloughs from prison: as was made clear from government tape recordings of Alite and the FBI, such as the one made on 2/28/08.

★

About a month or so before I was to be moved to MCC, I was in the legal cage, a four by four foot closet like structure where I would listen/watch tapes related to my case. I heard the gates opening and keys rattling. I paid it no mind until I heard, "Hey John, how you doing pal?"

I turned and saw Nicky Corozzo. He had been a fugitive for the past year or so, and had been indicted on a murder charge. The law had been unable to find him, so the government used its tool, the press, to put in an article about how they were looking to charge his daughter on some trumped up charge of harboring a fugitive.

No way would Nicky allow that to happen, so he turned himself in. Hadn't seen him in thirteen years, and he looked pretty good. We wished each other luck. He had it. He only remained in the hole for a few days, then was put in general population. I heard that he pled guilty for a thirteen year bid. Always liked him, and hope everything works out for him.

★

Given all of these interesting *coincidences* that were taking place around me, I became more interested in RD. But for the appearance of this low-life wackadoo in my confinement area, I would never have learned what I learned.

RD went back to his old habits, flooding the tier with his bodily waste, screaming. To protect my legal papers, I had to wedge a towel under the door so as not to have them fouled with RD's feces. The smell alone was overpowering—a significant distraction to concentration.

I threatened him to get him to quiet down. On occasion, he would scream out my and Basciano's name, and that the Mafia were contracted to kill him. He started refusing to eat. He would toss his food tray, along with his human waste, through the food slot. A prison psych outside of his cell door asked him about that. I wasn't really interested in whatever justification he had for that, I was however, very interested in getting the Hell away from this nut job.

I filed a cop-out. It read as follows:

Inmate Gotti had made a request to be moved from Range 1 to be separated from an inmate RD. The move was granted on 7/11/09. Inmate Gotti wants to establish a record to protect his fifth amendment rights to obtain a fair trial. If inmate RD is ever placed on the same range as I, it could only be for one of the following reasons:

1) To harass me by screaming out of his cell at all hours of the day to anybody who will listen, that the Mafia and the US government made a pack to kill or set him up. (Constantly).

2) To say I had threatened his life. (Which he has already said).

3) To set me up with a lie (laughable but why else would a guy who says his life and rights are in danger by the mob, the government, as well as myself, now want to move on the same range as me?)

For these reasons I request to be separated from inmate RD and for some reason if this is not possible, a letter from the warden that none of the above reasons are valid reasons to keep two inmates separated.

I want to establish a record to protect my Fifth amendment right. I thank you for your time in this matter.

J.A. Gotti.
P.S. If RD is placed on the same range as me, a least a letter of acknowledgment will afford me some protection in court.

★

I was notified that I would soon be moved to the MCC in Manhattan, to begin my trial. About a week and half later, at 4:30 AM, four COs and a Lieutenant came to get me and my belongings. Certain inmates required the presence of a Lieutenant—those deemed security risks. Like me.

About fifty yards from where I was housed, was Basciano's cell. As I commenced my journey through the first of the four doors that led me out of the hole, I saw Vinny standing by his cell door. He must have heard the tell tale sounds of being moved, keys jangling, feet stamping, etc. He wanted to say "Farewell."

The COs allowed me a short pause to say goodbye. "You'll be in my thoughts, pal."

"As you will be in mine," he said. He tapped his heart when he said that.

The COs moved me along. Although I had not known Basciano in the Life, I saw how he comported himself in prison, and developed a lot of respect for him.

Now I was placed in a strip cell. Stripped out for the second time. First time you strip is before you leave your cell. Then again in the strip cell. Then, when I went to R&D, once again strip searched.

Then the cuffs and chains and the prison bus transport from Brooklyn to lower Manhattan. Short ride. Then I was at the Federal Courthouse in Manhattan on Pearl Street. This is connected, via underground tunnels, to the Metropolitan Correction Center—the MCC. So from the bullpen at the courthouse, I made my underground journey, feeling somewhat like a 21st Century Dante, descending into the inferno.

Except this inferno was a lot better than what I had at MDC. I was housed in five north, in general population. I recognized several DeCavalcante fellas that I had been with at MCC back in 2004 and 2005. They were back at MCC while their cases were on appeal. They eventually did well on appeal, they overturned life sentences and plead out to fifteen year terms.

Besides these guys, were about a half a dozen other guys I had served time with. It was like homecoming week. I settled into my cell, but there wasn't much time to get comfortable. Trial was coming up, and I made requests to R&D for all of my legal files.

After MDC it felt great to have such relative freedom of movement. I could walk around the unit, watch TV, and use the phone. Not much of that in the hole. No walking around, no TV, and phone was a rare occurrence.

Housed in lower level security conditions than at MDC, I could now have family visits. I hadn't seen my kids in fourteen months—except once. My wife and mother, maybe two or three times. There was an adjustment period, and my family was shocked to see how much weight I had lost in prison.

Work to be done, motions *in limine* to be filed. Charlie Carnesi was with me again, but we had a new defense team otherwise. John Meringolo and Tony D'Aiuto were assisting Charlie. For the first time, I had an all Italian defense team.

I had briefly worked with Meringolo on trial number one. He was now Charlie's right hand man. Tony D'Aiuto, a brilliant guy with a sky high IQ, was to be the motions man and my constant contact with Charlie and John. Tony had successfully moved for a change of venue, in a Seattle, Washington case, so he was a veteran motions guy, and our Tampa motion was based upon his successful Seattle application.

The motions were made. But unlike the last three trials, whatever we moved for would get denied. The same kind of motions that had been granted in previous trials. What Judge Scheindlin had ruled in our favor, assigned Judge Castel ruled against us.

In limine motions that granted us the use of certain tapes in Scheindlin's courtroom, were denied by Castel, so that what we were able to use was totally eviscerated. Interesting, same court, same building, and only a few floors had separated the courtrooms from the past, and the one we were in now.

But while the physical location was basically the same, the position of this judge was very far from that of Judge Scheindlin. Scheindlin was a highly experienced judge in criminal matters, highly intelligent, and fundamentally fair.

Judge Castel? Perhaps not sharing in those qualities with our previous judge. Had he been handpicked? Was he to be another prosecutor in the room, but disguised in a black robe? When you are on trial for your life, you wonder about these things—but how much of it was paranoia and how much of it was prescience—I will leave that up to the reader to determine after reading this book.

It is important for the lay reader to understand that Judge Castel was on the same judicial level as Judge Scheindlin—he was not presiding over a higher level court. He was dealing with the same case law that Judge Scheindlin dealt with. But he wasn't making any favorable decisions for the defense, thus hampering us before opening statements even began.

CHAPTER THIRTY-FOUR

Trial Four

September 15, 2009, jury selection began. Again the pool of potential jurors was huge, about three hundred people. Three days later a jury was selected. The process had gone rather smoothly.

September 21, 2009, opening arguments began. Lead prosecutor was Elie Honig. He was highly intelligent and personable. I could see that he commanded the attention of the jurors throughout the several hours of his opening, as he previewed the government's case.

Once again details were given of the workings of the Gambino family. Then he previewed the tapestry of lies that had been concocted between John Alite and the government.

As I heard the garbage that was being told the jury, I felt almost physically sick. Charlie told me he was not surprised, and there would be more muddying of the waters. Basic tactics when you don't have either the facts or the law on your side. Appeal to prejudice, appeal to fear—as much as you can get away with.

Honig had finished, and Charlie was up for his opening. He attacked the government's position, and previewed for the jury our defense. He explained to them that, in the majority of instances, a defendant would attack the prosecution's case via cross-examination (what is sometimes called the "Constitutional Defense"), and not launch a counteroffensive by affirmatively putting in a defense case, with defense witnesses. He told the jury this time that is what we would do—we had our witnesses.

"In all my years as a prosecutor, then as a defense attorney, we will do something that I have never before seen done," Charlie told the jury. "We will go deep into WitSec and bring you their witnesses that the government doesn't want you to hear from. We, the defense, will call them to the stand."

The jurors seemed to be impressed with Charlie's presentation. "Now, understand that for the defendant to do this there are inherent risks, there is danger in doing this. These witnesses have agreements with the government to cooperate and an expectation of either a reduction or elimination of their jail sentences. They want to please their new masters.

"So any way they can screw up our case, and bolster the government case—they will. It's like asking the opposing baseball team to borrow one of their pitchers. Very risky. However," Charlie said, "we will be armed with prior statements, either through 302s or testimony. So even in protecting their position with the government, there is only so far they can go.

"It was always a belief that the government prosecutors were the best at cultivating and direct examining of witnesses. Because... that's what they primarily did. Defense attorneys were the best at cross-examination, because that is what they did.

"In my last three trials," Charlie told the jurors, "we had flipped that script."

Charlie sat down, and the government called its first witness. Joseph DeLuca testified to his relationship with Alite regarding bookmaking. DeLuca was an equipment manager for the New York Mets, and had a friendly relationship with former Mets player, Keith Hernandez.

He testified about using Keith's name in placing bets with

Alite, which allowed him to run up a bill of over thirty thousand dollars in the late 1980's. Alite began to call in the money. DeLuca had represented that the bets were those of Hernandez, but in reality, they were DeLucas'. He didn't have the money.

DeLuca went to Hernandez and said that he was in trouble and needed to borrow $32,000 to pay off a debt. Hernandez refused to lend him the money he asked for, but did give him $7,000 to help him out.

DeLuca then called Alite and told him he would meet him the next day, and that he had something for him. But DeLuca, being a degenerate gambler with $7,000 cash in his pocket, was getting anxious to turn it into more money, prior to meeting Alite.

He went to Atlantic City, where he turned the $7,000 into nothing. He met with Alite and told him that some of the bets he represented as being those of Hernandez, were his, and that he couldn't pay. At some point, DeLuca's parents stepped in to help him pay down the debt to Alite.

I told Charlie that the majority of DeLuca's testimony was true. On cross, Charlie asked a few questions, to challenge the parts of his testimony that DeLuca had "embellished" and then sat down.

So this was the government's opening shot—it showed that Alite was a low level bookmaker, one of many that we controlled.

Bonner Testimony

It will be shown in actuality, that Alite was a small time drug dealer. How many big bookmakers are in the business of selling drugs? How many drug dealers are in the bookmaking business? If you are making big bucks as a bookmaker, which is a much less severe bust if you get caught than drug dealing—why would you take the risk by taking to selling drugs? If you're making big bucks as a dealer, why bother with bookmaking? If, as Alite claimed during his testimony, he was making millions of dollars dealing drugs, why was he taking the risk for small change doing stickups and home invasions?

Alite was involved with a number of small crimes because he wasn't talented enough to do anything big. Other than being the kind of idiot you'd send out to hit some miscreant with a bat, Alite was not really up to par. He didn't have the brains to develop anything on a large scale.

So the witness, as far as I can figure out, was just to show an attachment between Alite and our crew.

The government continued with its witnesses, in what Charlie and I called the parade of the junkies. Next up was Kevin Bonner. A crack head from Jamaica, Queens, he was a boyhood friend of Alite and a guy named John Gebert, as well as Stratton.

Bonner testified that he had been at the Silver Fox in 1983, the night of the stabbing of which we spoke about in an earlier chapter. He testified that, on March 12, 1983, he had witnessed me stab the victim, Daniel Silva, who was the one fatality of that bar fight. Bonner also claimed to have left with me after the fight.

It would have been convenient, to say the least, if the federal agents, prior to having Bonner brought in as a witness to what he never saw, would have vetted him. They would have learned that from the over two dozen people that NYPD and FBI had interviewed who were at the Silver Fox the night of the stabbing, not a single one of them ever placed Bonner at the Silver Fox. Including me.

Bonner further testified that he had been at the Silver Fox before. He claimed he had been there numerous times. Further he said this was not the first time he saw a stabbing. Years earlier, he was present with Caputo in a bar fight, and had seen Caputo stab someone. So he knew who Caputo was, but could not place him in the bar with us.

Strange, all of that, because those aforesaid two dozen

witnesses saw Caputo at the bar, me at the bar, the Massa brothers, Anthony Amoroso, but no Bonner. He didn't receive any mention in any police reports. I don't believe he was at all involved in the '04-05 Grand Jury investigation of the stabbing; never called as a witness.

In the many years following the Silver Fox incident, in the ongoing investigation that took place, nobody charged me with anything related to that incident. But in the 2009 trial, this garbage was brought in to try and muddy the waters against me with an uncharged crime, completely unrelated to those offenses of which I was charged.

Judge Castel had no problem with this. Judge Scheindlin had, and didn't admit it. The government knew that, had they actually charged me with something arising out of the Silver Fox incident, the witnesses we had would decimate their case.

Even after having visited some of the witnesses who were serving prison time and offering them get out of jail free cards for testifying against me, they couldn't put a case together enough to bring charges against me. And these guys weren't my friends, they were friends of Silva, the deceased.

Let's focus on one witness, Thomas "Elfie" O'Neill. He was at the bar fight, and was one of the guys that I actually had fought with. He had been visited by Cold Case Detectives and FBI. Several times. They didn't like what they heard, because Elfie told them I did not kill Silva. He told them that while he was fighting with me, Silva was on the other side of the bar, nowhere near me. Elfie was man enough to tell them, while they wanted him to put this on me, he wasn't going to do it, and that the government knew I didn't do it.

"I'm not going to lie to get you a trophy," Elfie told them. "You and I both know that John Gotti didn't stab Silva." Even O'Neill, who had been fighting with me, wasn't stabbed. (Contrary to what appears in the FBI 302.) Two of his friends wound up being stabbed that night, one of them was Silva.

So did the FBI read law enforcement reports of the

investigation prior to placing Bonner on the stand? If they did, they ignored them. From the information garnered by my Private Investigator, Gerald Gardner, Elfie told him the FBI offered him the moon and the stars to have him testify against me.

"I don't like John, or his friends," Elfie said. "But I won't lie about him."

So, the logic of the government was, if you can't make this case hold water by charging me with the crime, you sprinkle it during my trial as an *uncharged* crime, hopefully to prejudice the jury into giving you a verdict you want on the crimes that I *was* charged with.

Mr. Bonner, the next government witness, however, was perfectly willing to help himself to a reduction or elimination of the multiple sentences he was facing. He was serving a twenty-five year bid for armed robbery. Bonner had done a series of gunpoint robberies of dry cleaners to feed his heroin habit. Once he had led the police on a high speed chase, involving dozens of police cars with news helicopters circling overhead. For this, he received the twenty-five year sentenced. He was about to be charged with additional crimes that would have virtually doubled his sentence.

Bonner dealt with an agent Gerard Conrad, the guy who had wiretapped me at Ray Brook. Conrad had first called Bonner then met with him. Bonner, facing close to fifty years, wasn't a tough sell.

Despite his bad intentions, Bonner's testimony was actually useful to my defense. He testified that he hadn't seen me since '90-91. That was just a "hello/goodbye." He further testified that, around this time, Alite told him that I had forbidden Alite to sell drugs. Alite further told him he was having financial problems and had borrowed money from me. Further, that the relationship between Alite and myself had soured.

Bonner said, about this time, that Alite was running to a fellow named Ronnie "One Arm" with his problems.

Bonner also testified that Alite had a problem with Carmine Agnello, my former brother-in-law, which he learned of by phone. He had denied waiting, with Alite, outside of Carmine's junkyard, to shoot him. They had never been near the yard. (Contrary to what Alite had testified to, that both he and Bonner were laying in wait outside of Carmine's yard, looking to shoot him.)

★

Bonner, prior to his testimony, in his 302s, made mention that Alite was trying to arrange fraudulent car accidents in Florida in 1990. Why would a, supposed, big-time drug dealer do this? Of course, Alite was not a big-time drug dealer. Further, Bonner, in his 302, referred to Alite answering to different crews—my crew, Trucchio and Corozzo.

Importantly, he also told agents, in his 302, about the murder of George Grosso—a killing of which I had been accused by Alite and that had been made part of the indictment. He reported that Alite killed Grosso because Grosso was getting high a lot and Alite thought Grosso would inform on him.

Michael Stratton

Next up for the People of the United States, as the government is referred to in cases, was another junkie—Michael Stratton. He had done time for killing someone with a knife. Also, dealing angel dust. He was as reliable as one could expect an angel dust user to be. He too, grew up with Gebert and Alite. Bonner too. They were part of what was called the 7&9 gang.

Stratton claimed he was paying shakedown money to me and the Howard Beach crew. He also put me down as responsible for the death of his brother-in-law, Bruce Gotterup. I, supposedly, protected Alite and a guy named John Burke, who Stratton identified as a member of my crew, who had killed Gotterup. Problem there, I never met Burke in my life. (He was right about the shakedown part though. These guys weren't our friends, as I said before, we preyed on them.)

Alite's drug dealing and the Gotterup murder were the deciding factors that got him chased from the neighborhood. Much later, the accusation made by Tony Pep that Alite was a cooperator would be confirmed.

Some of Stratton's testimony was true. Not when he spoke about knowing me, I had never met him, nor had any of my friends known him. But like I said, we did shakedown these mutts, via Gebert and Alite.

Was that correct thinking as I reflect on it? No. We were punks with strong opinions of self-worth, that's all.

★

As I write about this assembly of lowlifes and junkies, I recall a letter I received that had been delivered to me while I was on a different floor (than Burke), at Pinellas County Jail, by an orderly. Here it is:

> I know that you don't know me. The government has been trying to get me to lie about you since my arrest in 2001. But I'm not like everyone else. I won't lie to benefit myself, I have self-dignity and faith that God will deliver me from all of this. My mom is related to Tony Lee and I always pulled for you and your dad.
>
> The buzz in the prison is that you are suffering from kidney stones—painful and I hope you get well real soon. I will pray for you. May God bless you and your family.

There are some men who are not set up to be prostitutes to injustice, regardless of their having an opportunity to be free of long term confinement in prison. There are some in whom dignity rises above self-serving deceit. These are men in the true sense of the word—more on this later.

★

Stratton finished his testimony and sat down. Then the court broke for the Yom Kippur holiday. It is a time for the Jews to reflect, to engage in introspection, and atone for their sins. During the break, that's what I did too.

I looked back on the sheer idiocy of hanging with miscreants like Alite and Gebert. By associating with them, was I any better than they? I had opened the door to the outhouse, and the stench had stuck with me—for decades.

But the battle loomed, and reflection time was over, it was time to get back to the fight, and on September 29, 2009, we once again filed in the courtroom to continue with the trial.

★

Agent Gill came in to testify to financial matters, which were being eclipsed by the dirtier doings testified to.

Phil Baroni[*]

Then came former policeman Phil Baroni. He testified about his relationship with Alite and Alite's father in the bookmaking business. Baroni testified to me getting a skim of 25%, from 1990 to maybe 1992, from Alite's take—according to Alite. That's why nobody bothered them or extorted additional moneys from them.

He further testified about the murder of George Grosso, a drug dealer Alite killed in 1988, supposedly—according to Alite—with a gun supplied by me. Baroni contradicted this and said he was present in the car where Alite shot Grosso in the head, and it was another friend of Alite's, Tommy Crisci, who, Baroni had observed, gave Alite the gun earlier in the evening,

---

[*] Former NYPD policeman Phil Baroni's name appears in news stories two different ways: Phil Baroni and Phil Barrone.

Under cross-examination, Baroni had admitted to being a crooked ex-cop. He had done two years in Transit, and thirteen years at NYPD before retiring in 1986. He denied the claims of Alite that he had been receiving law enforcement information from a friend of his, Jimmy Arenella, and providing it to the Gambino family. He was asked about doing this in the same case involving my uncle. He denied it. He also mentioned that he was approached on the Gene Gotti case. The truth is that he was never given a dime.

Then Baroni was asked if law enforcement so called "mob expert" Joe Coffey had been on the take. You may remember Coffey as the detective who bragged about his tough guy talk to my father when he was busted (never happened), and also the expert that was unintentionally responsible for me making bail in my 1998 case.

Coffey crooked? No way. He made love to his badge every night. But that bastion of believability, Alite, had testified that Baroni and Coffey had regular dealings, and Coffey was dealing in confidential police information for the benefit of the bad guys.

On cross, Baroni denied knowing Coffey. He denied ever telling Alite that Coffey was providing any information. In regards to Alite's accusations, Coffey was to tell the press, "Absolutely unbelievable."

Bo Dietl, a famous highly decorated former NYPD detective, who had also been accused of being crooked by Alite, was a little less polite than Coffey when he said, referring to Alite, "He's a fuckin' liar."

Ergo, the government's own witness, Baroni, brought out contradictions to the tale told by the government's star witness, Alite. Baroni was testifying to avoid the consequences of his having been involved with the Grosso murder.

If he did right, he would be absolved from all sins.

But he didn't bolster Alite's credibility, he helped to destroy it. Interesting, how in his 302 (which is never subject to recording) he supposedly says he knew about Gebert and Grosso trying to kill Alite. Alite was angry and believed others were out to get him.

On the stand, he said he didn't know anything about Gebert and Grosso trying to kill Alite. On reviewing the 302 he said he didn't write it.

"I had no idea about these two guys shooting Alite," Baroni testified on cross. "He never told me."

The 302 also had in it that Baroni had a conversation with me about the murder. Supposedly I asked, "Do you think everybody involved will keep their mouth shut?" Supposedly he answered, "I think they will."

But nowhere in his testimony does this appear. Why? Because the conversation never happened, except in the 302 which had been prepared by Ted Otto.

★

Otto had always stood out to us as somewhat of a rogue agent. But it turned out, it wasn't just our opinion. He had been suspended by the FBI, and we wanted to know why. Prior to trial, on August 24, 2009, my attorney, Charlie Carnesi sent a letter to AUSA Elie Honig, lead prosecutor on my case,

> ...to make a formal demand for the personnel file of agent Theodore Otto, as well as the dates of his termination and subsequent suspension and reinstatement....Given Agent Otto's history and undeniable bias against Mr. Gotti, the Defense requests access to his file in order to determine any potential impact it may have on the pending case. Undeniably, the case agent who committed misconduct in the past and was fired, is the case agent, and as such a central figure in this prosecution and investigation.

The government never responded to this demand.

Michael Finnerty

Another government witness was a Michael Finnerty. A younger guy from Howard Beach that ran with some of the younger guys there. He hung around the Carneglias—mainly Charles Carneglia. He was a big Irish kid, whose father was with the Stage Handler's Union.

His testimony was used for background on Howard Beach and his association with those denizens in organized crime. (After all Howard Beach was a small tightly knit community, brimming with those who participated in the Life.)

The government attempted to prove his association with me by presenting a tape of the April, 1992, wedding of Michael Finnerty, that shows me at a table with a number of neighborhood guys. One guy you didn't see at that table was Alite, because I made it clear that I would not attend if he were there. Normally, he would have been at that wedding, as he was a close friend of Finnerty.

But he wasn't. Any photo you might see of me and my friends after 1991 will have Alite remarkably absent. He was gone. In surveillance video, in surveillance photos, in reports, on audio tape—no Alite after 1991.

While one of my visits was being recorded in Ray Brook, a tape was made that described the status of Alite with respect to myself. Here's a snippet:

(3/23/03 Law Enforcement Recording of Gotti visit from Steve Dobies)

JG: Tommy stopped by over there. What does he want? Alite? This other guy [Alite] I haven't seen in twelve years. What do they want? Tell him I don't want these people going over to my property. If he needs these people, tell him then, here's what he does, tell him move his tire shop someplace else. Take his tire shop somewhere else.

SD: I don't this U/I pop up on

JD: Tell U/I that's the case, John said, "he loves ya and all but take the clients out someplace else, because he don't know these people. Nor do I wanna know them."

★

This tape was part of the foundation used to show the fabrications of Alite and those who testified about any close relationship he might have had with me.

On another note, Michael Finnerty at his sentencing asked the judge, "Consider who I have become today, and not what I was many years ago." He also went on to thank his wife for being responsible for turning him around.

She failed to turn herself around, however, and Stephanie was charged in Nassau County, New York, in September, 2010, with statutory rape, having had sex with her daughter's underage high school boyfriend.

For his cooperation with the government, it was reported on May 14, 2010, that Finnerty did not get additional jail time, but three years' probation, and a $12,000 fine.

Before he testified against me, he was facing decades in jail for armed robberies and assaults.

Kasman is not Called to Testify

We were now expecting Lewis Kasman to testify, and frankly, we were chomping at the bit to get a shot at him on cross examination.

We were disappointed when it turned out that the government was not going to call Kasman after all. Instead, the government put on the stand the FBI handler who had been dealing with Kasman, Special Agent Robert Herbster. (He was one of the agents that approached me when I was on parole.)

I felt somewhat sympathetic towards Herbster, as he testified about Kasman and his dirty dealings. He truthfully answered questions about the numerous times that Kasman had committed crimes while a cooperator, and how the government, after learning of these, ripped up old agreements and entered into new ones with Kasman. Let's go to the trial transcript.

His cross examination went something like this:

"So you caught him in another lie, what did you do?"

"We tore up his agreement," answered Herbster.

"And then what?" Carnesi asked.

"We gave him another agreement."

"And then you caught him stealing, what did you do?"

Herbster looked at Carnesi and said, "Tore up his agreement and gave him another."

"Then you caught him extorting money, what did you do?"

"Tore up his agreement and gave him another."

It went on in the same vein.

Herbster appeared embarrassed, and I can't blame him.

Now the usual prosecutor move to encourage jury belief in the fantasy of cooperator agreements is to close its direct examination of their witness with this question: "Mr. Cooperator, what would happen if you were to lie to the government as a cooperator?"

The prescribed answer is: "My agreement gets torn up and I could get the maximum sentence."

The reality is this seldom or never happens. If they can still use you, they can excuse you—and they do, with the agreement intact.

When I think of Kasman, the movie, *Informant*, with Matt Damon, comes to mind. (Damon's character steals nine million dollars while wearing a wire and working as an informant for the FBI.)

So just who was this individual, Lewis Kasman? He has been previously briefly mentioned, but now let's take a closer look.

He was a bright kid. Nice Jewish boy. Went to law school, graduated, and got a good job with Armand D'Amato, brother of Senator Alphonse D'Amato. His parents threw him a big party—a catered affair, when he graduated. They even bought him a car. Everyone was proud of him.

There were just several minor obstacles to his career path as an attorney. He never graduated law school, it is doubtful if he ever even attended law school, and his greatest involvement with the law was his repeatedly violating it. When he was outed as a fraud by an employee of nightclub owner Phil Basile, who at one time employed Kasman, he no longer worked for D'Amato.

Lewis Kasman—the self proclaimed adopted son of John J. Gotti, my father. (The information in this chapter comes from trial transcripts, news articles, and interviews with relatives of Kasman.)

★

You would think that, when the government uses a cooperator, a person who by the very function of cooperator will likely one day find himself testifying in a judicial proceeding wherein his credibility is going to come under attack, they would select someone who could be trusted—someone who can follow their instructions, and not violate cooperator agreements.

When we speak of Lewis Kasman, think again.

Kasman's entire *modus vivendi* was one wrapped in fraud, covered in lies, and garnished with deceit. He claimed that when his father died, he was left seven million dollars. The reality was several hundred thousand. He was accused of stealing $10,000 of FBI money to be used against an attorney that Kasman tried to set up for the government. (Joe Bondy, who was my Uncle Pete's attorney. Bondy never got the money.) During my first trial, wearing a wire, he tried to set up my lawyer, Jeff Lichtman, in the courthouse restroom—Lichtman had none of it.

He robbed the payroll taxes from his uncle's garment center business—in excess of six figures. (In fact, due to Kasman's theft, the uncle had to go hunt up money to pay his payroll taxes.) He ripped off businessman and club owner Phil Basile and his family, somewhere in the neighborhood of one million dollars.

As we have already mentioned, he was accused of taking from his children's accounts $391,000. He admitted to "borrowing" $277,000 in cash earmarked for his kids, but it has been reported that the lawyer for his wife in the divorce action claimed he may have taken as much as half a million from his children (Gangland News, "*My Kids My Money*"). It was further reported that in divorce documents it was alleged that he removed these moneys by forging his wife's name on bank documents.

Perhaps the only time Kasman told the truth, was when, in a trial as a government witness against Vinny Artuso in Miami, Florida, he admitted to being a liar. Here's the segment:

Q. While you're cooperating with the FBI, while you have signed three separate documents agreeing to tell the truth, while the FBI is telling you you cannot lie, you kept lying, correct?

A. Correct.

Some of the moneys that Kasman had taken were used (according to some of his relatives and other sources) to buy luxury items for his male "friends." He also gave them large amounts of money to hold for him, which I am told they wound up embracing for their own benefit. (His preferences for friends are irrelevant, but the means in which he obtained money to take care of them indicate the level of honesty of Lewis Kasman—absolute zero.)

I said above that Kasman's preferences in relationships are irrelevant to me, but may have caused him problems in the prison environment. He reportedly had an inappropriate relationship with an Hispanic man in prison, and this did not sit well with inmate and Bonanno associate Randy Pizzolo, who told Kasman he was a disgrace to John Gotti. He punctuated the insult with a slap across Kasman's face.

Kasman, furious at his embarrassment in front of other inmates, hired Latin King members to give Pizzolo a severe beating in prison. Kasman didn't participate himself, of course.

The Bonanno family were looking to have Kasman hurt for this, but Jackie D'Amico and myself ran interference for Kasman, meeting with the consigliere for the Bonanno's, Anthony Spero, and that didn't happen. This was back in 1997, before we were aware of what Kasman was.

Both Jackie and I were embarrassed about Kasman's prison behavior, despite his denials.

What he was was a turncoat, who, from 1997 until 2008, was on the Federal payroll, getting $51,000 in cash and $338,000 in FBI expense money. From 2005 on, the government was paying Kasman twelve thousand per month—part of which was to go to paying his mortgage. The house wound up in foreclosure proceedings—Kasman wasn't paying the mortgage. His family wound up in the street.

At one time, again before we knew what Kasman was, he was holding millions of my father's money. That was the last time it was seen. He also wore a wire at my first trial, taping members of my family and my attorneys. While a trial was ongoing—and as an agent of law enforcement.

Kasman and his wire were everywhere. He'd badmouth me to those he thought would lend a sympathetic ear, but when there were good things to be said about me, the tape stopped running. He controlled the on/off switch of the recorder.

But one time he got hoisted on his own recording, and this was why the government arrested him for extorting $80,000 from businessman Harvey Shear.

He was taping a conversation with JoJo Corozzo, who used to be my father's driver. Corozzo was chastising Kasman for shaking down Shear, who was his friend. "I put you guys together to do a business deal, and you stole eighty thousand dollars from him."

Kasman denied it.

"Let's get him on the phone right now," Corozzo said.

Suddenly "it was a misunderstanding" that Kasman swore he would take care of.

The FBI heard that, and also became aware that Kasman was not only a "recording engineer," he was an editor too—turning the digital recorder on and off at his whim. (Besides the fact that such action was inherently dishonest, it was idiotic. An acoustic expert would be able to recognize "start-stops" on a recording, which, if it didn't preclude its admissibility, would certainly eviscerate its credibility.)

Kasman wasn't all pro law enforcement, however. He was busted in Nassau County, in 2006, for tipping off a suspect regarding a pending arrest.

Yet time after time (and crime after crime), the government ripped up old cooperator agreements with Kasman, and issued new ones, as we have seen from the Herbster testimony, above.

Kasman was a special case with the FBI, and was to wind up being a case that contained nothing but trouble and lies.

In July, 2011, there were news reports that Kasman had several publishing companies interested in a book in which he would "tell all" about the workings of the Gambino family. In his divorce proceedings, Kasman claimed to have been living off of the advance he got for this book, which was to be entitled, *The Last Son*.

As I write this, it is late September, 2014. Where is that book? Was the story of this book just another Kasman concoction to deceive a court—this time a divorce court? There is one thing of which we can all be sure: Kasman is the embodiment of the legal doctrine falsus *in unum falsus in omnia*, false in one, false in all.

So the government decided not to use him as a witness.

John Alite Testifies

Litigation is war with more rules—especially in the ultra high stakes of criminal litigation, which those in the Life often face.

While both prosecutors and defense attorneys will tell the jury in *voir dire* that a trial is a search for the truth, in my case it was more a skirmish, and at times a full scale battle. An almost violent clash between the offensive maneuvering of coerced and manufactured testimony by the government, and the counterattack by seventeen defense witnesses.

In this counterattack, seven of the defense witnesses were *government* witnesses in previous trials. An additional two were FBI agents. One other witness was an assistant US attorney. In part, we used the prosecution's own troops against them. The other witnesses were those who had nothing to gain by coming forward for the defense, and some, in fact, had much to lose.

The victors in that battle, the winners of that war of printed and spoken words under oath—the "truth"—will be determined by the deliberations of the jury.

It may well serve as a useful reminder that, before the jury system was instituted, guilt or innocence was determined by ordeal and trial by combat. The jury system is the best we have come up with so far, and a great deal of the time—it works. But believe me, a criminal trial is still an oppressive ordeal for a defendant and his supporting witnesses (if any). The conflict between prosecution and defense is still a trial by (more civilized) combat.

Before we go into the details of the testimony of John Alite, and the demolition of that testimony from cross-examination, by rebuttal witnesses, and by government documents, I am going to ask the reader to do what the trial attorneys often ask of jurors on *voir dire*. "Use your common sense."

In trial four, which took place in 2009, allegations were made in the indictment that brought me to trial, concerning drug dealing and murders which took place in the eighties and nineties. Allegations made which were never part of any indictment against me in the previous three trials.

The crucial allegations of trial four weren't part of any previous trial, and couldn't even make it past a Grand Jury (which as it is often said, "can indict a ham sandwich"), because these allegations were never even submitted to the grand juries that brought on trials one through three.

Does it make sense that the FBI, that has virtually unlimited investigative resources, unlimited prosecution funds (courtesy of the tax money that both citizens *and* the accused pay), and the ability to "overlook" the previous convictions (including multiple murders) of government cooperators, could not find evidence, could not find corroborating witnesses for the accusations made *only* in trial four, *before* trial four?

I respectfully submit, that no, it does not make sense.

What does make sense is that, in trial number four, a government "star" witness appears that is willing to testify—for the first time—as to these crimes. A witness that had been taken from a hell hole prison in Brazil where he was subject to attacks by guards and inmates, and was looking for his "get out of jail card" at any expense.

It was ironic, this Brazilian imprisonment. This man, in search of paradise, had abandoned his sick wife and his children (something I never did, or could ever do), and settled in Copacabana, with a new and younger "wife."

John Alite.

Alite had a long history as a government cooperator, but refused to testify in the past. This time around he had no problem testifying against me to save his own skin. At least Willie Boy Johnson, another long time government cooperator, had the stones to refuse to testify.

Again ironically, Alite, with respect to Willie Boy Johnson's murder, testified that I was on the scene, and involved with the killing in the summer of 1988.

But, Frank Gangi, who had pled guilty to five murders,

and was given government absolution for those five murders, had testified successfully against Bonanno family members and never mentioned me.

Neither did Gravano, when he testified, mention me. Sammy Gravano had testified against my father regarding Willie Boy Johnson's murder, and had said members and associates of the Bonanno Crime Family had carried out the murder. (Remember, Gravano was part of the administration of the Gambino Family at that time.)

★

Alite, while imprisoned in Brazil, was sending out letters trying to extort money from various people, and was already actively exploring with his lawyers his becoming a full fledged cooperator—in other words, now, he *would* testify for a deal.

In a phone conversation in December, 2007, between Alite and Ted Otto, the following was heard:

JA: Let me tell you something, I told him to get in touch with Jason [Randazzo]. I told him to get in touch with the district, your district. And I told him specifically get in touch with Jason, and he told me no one is talking to me.

TO: That's an absolute flat out lie.

JA: Yeah, that's what I'm saying, in arbitration I should be able to say you fuckin' lied, you lied to me, you, you, I retained you under false pretenses.

TO: It's probably just, he looked at it as just work, that would require coming up to New York and sitting through negotiating a separate cooperation agreement or a separate proffer agreement, and having to unfortunately sit through two or three proffers.

JA: Right. . . . That's one of the things that I wrote to him, that I wasn't happy from the outset, but then the new stuff that came to light in what he did. Actually I don't know what the ramifications are but he out and out lied to me.

He told me he got in touch with the Southern District
and you know he just lies. There's no other thing to say.
I mean why he lied to me like that could only be because
of financial.

TO: Yeah, I wish he had, you and I would have been acquainted
a year and a half ago.

A line from one of his letters in 2006 is clear, "I will give
their names and make a deal with the government to return
to the United States. Their move now!" (He was attempting to extort hundreds of thousands of dollars from several
individuals.)

Alite also went on to warn them that he would put them
on a murder charge and this would be the last warning that he
was going to give them. Failure to pay Alite would have them
spending the rest of their lives in jail, according to his letter.

Alite, during his trial testimony, would give evidence about
all the money he was making dealing drugs, how rich he was,
a multimillionaire, keeping at home several hundred thousand
dollars in cash hidden around the house. Alite estimated that
between 1986-1993 his drug business grossed seventy million
dollars.

Once again, his own words reveal him to be a liar. In a
circa 1993 letter to me, Alite says,

> I got another job part time building houses with this greaseball
> from Newark, nice guy though he pays me alright. . . . I can
> basically work when I want so it's not bad for a little extra cash.

Why would someone who had made millions as a drug
dealer need a little extra cash and work part time in construction? Obviously, he wouldn't, and once again, Alite comes up
short when it comes to telling the truth under oath.

Again, as to Alite's claim to wealth: When Tim Donovan
(who we shall meet later in this chapter in greater detail) testifies

as to his dealings in Florida with Alite, he speaks about being hit up for a ten thousand dollar loan by Alite in 1991 or 1992. He doesn't give it to him.

The multi-million dollar drug dealer needed ten thousand?

From trial transcripts, we can see Alite's under-oath-opinion of his *own* reputation for veracity.

"That was part of the Life. Treachery, lies, conning people." (transcript page 1949, Alite cross)

Now, if at the beginning of this book, I provided my *own* sworn testimony about my *own* lack of credibility that paralleled what Alite said about himself, would you believe anything that came afterwards?

I respectfully submit that you would not. Nor should you.

★

Another factor that is useful in the cross-examination of a witness, besides his credibility, is the opportunity that he had to observe the matters upon which he offers sworn testimony. In other words, was that witness in a position to personally observe the matters he is swearing to in open court in front of a jury that must determine whether or not the words that issue from his mouth are true?

To "refresh the recollection" of the reader of this book, I respectfully remind you that Alite was only a low level associate, a non-Italian who could never become a made man, and an individual that was "chased" from our people and our dealings back in 1991.

But our major defense focus was on Alite, because he had come to testify about things which were never mentioned—never even charged in the previous three trials. Additionally, we had an abundance of evidence and testimony to offer that would destroy his credibility, and in the destruction of the government's most important witness against me, would likely be found my salvation—either in an acquittal, or a hung jury as had happened three times before.

Does it stand to reason that this type of individual would be party to the inner doings of a criminal organization in which he only played the part of unimportant pawn? Does it make sense that someone like myself, who back in my days in the Life was the son of the head of the Gambino Family and heir apparent of that Family, would confide in a John Alite?

Isn't it revealing that, instead of calling a witness who had plead guilty to participating in the murder of an individual— one of the three which I was charged in this trial—a man who was actually on the scene, the government instead called Alite, who was never there. (More on this, in this chapter, when we analyze specifics of testimony by Alite, and contradictions offered in response.)

★

In addition to credibility assessment and the determination of a witness' opportunity to observe what he testifies to, there is the factor of witness bias; which can be brought out in cross-examination. In other words, does this witness have motivation to manufacture testimony—an ax to grind?

Alite testified to a souring of the relationship between us in 1993. (It was actually two years earlier that he had been chased.)

So I submit that the stage has been adequately set, constructed from the words of Alite and common sense, in which we can examine the value of testimony Alite gave at trial.

He admitted to being a liar, it defies common sense that he would have been party to any inner workings or business of the Family, and he testified to a souring of our relationship.

We have covered the broad strokes, let us go to specific charges, comparing Alite's testimony on direct, his responses to cross-examination, the testimony of rebuttal defense witnesses, and government documents.

The Murder Charges

In this trial, I had been accused of conspiracy to commit murder in the killings of George Grosso in 1988, Louis DiBono in 1990, and Bruce John Gotterup in 1991. Alite was the man the government was using to convict me on these charges.

The John Gotterup Killing

Alite spoke to the FBI about the Gotterup murder, and his information was recorded in an FBI 1023 written by agent Ted Otto, a Confidential Human Source document. According to this:

He made reference to his drug operations in Queens, and several tavern locations wherein cocaine sales were conducted. Gotterup was a neighborhood trouble maker, and had caused problems in the Jägermeister Bar, one of the Ozone Park locations where drugs were sold by Alite and his people.

Gotterup and his friends had started fights in the bar, and on one occasion shot up the bar, almost killing a nephew of Gambino soldier, Ronnie Trucchio. Then he tried to extort $500 per week protection money from the owner of the bar.

According to Alite, I put the bar "under my protection" for a weekly payment to the Gambino Family of $500. Also, according to Alite, who allegedly met with the owner of the bar at a diner to discuss the removal of Gotterup, our Family would take care of the matter in exchange for the owner buying liquor from a Gambino controlled supplier and placing our joker poker machines in his location. I was also to get an unspecified percentage of the price, in the event the bar was sold.

The owner agreed, according to Alite, and I ordered the hit on Gotterup. Alite said he was instructed to handle it, but not to be anywhere near the actual killing, as I didn't want my "right hand man," Alite, near a drug related murder.

Ronnie Trucchio, the soldier whose nephew was almost

shot at the bar, wanted Gotterup killed also, according to Alite's 1023 written by Ted Otto. Gotterup would be lured to the Rockaways on Trucchio's wish, and killed there. John Burke, previously mentioned, was to do the work, and Ronnie Trucchio was informed of this, by Alite, as per the 1023.

Alite said Gotterup was shot in the head while pissing on the boardwalk, and the next time he supposedly saw me, I was told that Gotterup was dead.

John Burke who was convicted of the murder, in a letter to me in jail, made reference to the fact that I didn't know him, never met him. He was already doing life, had refused government offers to testify against me, so why would he write this in an unsolicited letter? Because it was true.

In Alite's testimony 10/7/09 at my trial, he was asked about his statements to the FBI in the 1023. Alite made several references that the 1023 was not written accurately. The 1023 of which we speak was written by Agent Otto—so the question arises, "Who was lying?"

The defense called Steve Newell, a former drug associate of Alite's, who was involved in the drug sales at the Jägermeister bar. Newell was charged with the Gotterup murder in 1995 and was acquitted. He testified at my 2009 trial that Gotterup and his friends were terrorizing the Jägermeister Bar, and the fellow who controlled the drug sales there Guy Peden.

Peden received a bad beating from the Gotterup group. John Burke, who has been mentioned earlier, came home from prison and ran up a debt with Peden to the tune of fourteen thousand dollars. Peden knew he couldn't collect on this debt, so he used Burke to kill Gotterup, to satisfy the debt, and for Burke's involvement in future drug sales at the Jägermeister.

(Newell had testified at my trial that Burke had admitted this to him.) A short time later, when Peden got in trouble for drugs, Newell and Burke took over two kilos of cocaine and the drug spot. Newell also had testified that Peden, before the murder of Gotterup, had brought Newell to meet Ronnie

Trucchio regarding the incident with his nephew in the bar.

But, Peden already had the wheels in motion to kill Gotterup. Note: At one time, Newell once was a cooperator for law enforcement. He was one of many government cooperators that I called as defense witnesses in the 2009 trial.

The Murder of Louis DiBono

Alite, in a 1023, again written by Ted Otto, "detailed" conversations with Bobby Boriello and myself, concerning a hit on Louis DiBono, ordered by my father. According to Alite, the hit had been ordered by my father because DiBono ignored a summons to "come in," when he was called by my father.

Supposedly, I ordered Boriello and Charles Carneglia to do the work. Boriello was to be the driver, Alite and Carneglia were to be the shooters. I ordered them, according to the 1023, to leave DiBono in the street as a warning that, when called, a man should show up.

But, according to Alite, he was taken off the hit team, and replaced by Kevin McMahon. I also told him that my father was aware of the change in personnel.

Now let's take a look at the veracity of Alite's information to the government.

Louis DiBono was a made man. A low level low life like Alite would never be used on this type of work, and as far as my father knowing that an unauthorized man was involved with this? God forbid that should ever come to light, there would have been Hell to pay.

Alite initially thought I took him off to shield him from another murder, but told him also that there would be plenty of future work for him—again, this according to Alite. He also said that weeks after the hit, I told him "We got that guy DiBono, that piece of work's done. They got him in a parking garage, they left that piece of shit there."

Alite also said that Kevin McMahon had been the driver, and that he had run into McMahon at the Hernando County Jail, and confronted him with being on the DiBono hit. Supposedly McMahon asked, "How did you know that, I didn't do it, Bobby and Charles did it."

All of the above Alite statements were in the 1023 written by Ted Otto.

In his testimony, on cross, Alite contradicted something in his 1023. In the 1023, he stated that he, "Didn't learn of DiBono's murder for several weeks." In his cross, we see the following on transcript page 1908:

> Q. ... let's talk about your understanding as to who was actually at the scene [of DiBono's murder]. Charles Carneglia, Bobby Boriello and Kevin McMahon ?
> A. Correct.
> Q. OK, how do you know that?
> A. John Gotti Jr. told me.
> Q. And he told you that it was those three people who ended up killing Mr. DiBono, is that right?
> A. Yes.
> Q. And when was it that you and Mr. Gotti had this conversation?
> A. Right after DiBono got killed.

In his 1023, Alite had made reference to Boriello making a joke about McMahon being the driver and being so short, he couldn't see over the steering wheel—he had to look *through* it.

On cross, when asked about his saying this to the agent taking the 1023 (Ted Otto), Alite said, "No, I don't recall saying that, no."

So who was lying now? Alite? Or Agent Otto? We now have two contradictions between the 1023 and testimony. Did Alite even talk to Boriello about McMahon?

On cross, when asked about this, Alite said, "That's not how I remember it." (transcript page 1930, Alite cross)

In his testimony in a previous trial, against Charles Carneglia, Alite had testified that McMahon had been the driver on the DiBono hit. When asked the source of his information at that trial, he had responded that it came from me and Kevin McMahon.

Interesting that, in its effort to tie me in to the DiBono murder (as I briefly mentioned before), the government didn't call McMahon who was at the hit, and who pled guilty to being involved in it—they brought in John Alite, who was never anywhere near the DiBono murder.

Would it be because McMahon would not testify in a way that would be beneficial to the government, and might have been beneficial to me?

So Alite in his 1023, written many years after the DiBono killing, says DiBono was killed because he didn't come when called. However, in testimony at trial, he stated, DiBono was going to be killed, "Because he was having a problem with Sammy Gravano, Sammy the Bull, with money, something with construction."

Odd, how that didn't make it in the 1023.

Back to McMahon. He had testified at the Carneglia trial, that one of the participants in the DiBono hit was named "Harpo." This fact was never mentioned by Alite, who repeatedly claimed I told him everything. Harpo, whose real name was Anthony Vinciullo, was on the hit, because as a reward he would be made (and in fact was made), according to Gravano's testimony. Harpo was to plead guilty to the DiBono murder in 1994.

So Alite didn't mention any Harpo in his 1023, and he didn't mention Harpo on the stand. If he was so in the know, how come he didn't know that there was a Harpo on this job? McMahon testified that Harpo was the driver (transcript page 2584). McMahon had been there.

Alite, as we have said, claimed to have been told prior to the hit, that he had been replaced by Kevin McMahon. Common sense comes to bear again—in McMahon's testimony, he says:

> After we got out of the car, Bobby made a phone call and then gave me a speech about nobody knows I was there, don't tell nobody, you'll end up like Louis DiBono, just forget about it, don't tell nobody you were there, deny it… [transcript page 2603]

To have someone who was not authorized on the hit, for that to be found out, would have serious consequences—so is it likely Boriello made a joke to Alite about McMahon being so small he couldn't see over the steering wheel? Especially since McMahon was never the driver. Boriello had orchestrated the hit.

Would it be likely that someone would tell me about McMahon being on this piece of work? So how much more unlikely would it be for me to send him on it, and tell Alite about it?

Prior to McMahon's testimony (who was one of our defense witnesses called), Michael Finnerty, the government's witness, testified, on 10/13/09, that Boriello told him in no uncertain terms not to tell anybody that Kevin McMahon was on the DiBono hit. He was especially instructed not to let *me* know.

Finnerty coincidentally had shown up at Carneglia's house, as Carneglia and Boriello and McMahon were coming back from the hit. It was then that he realized it was the Dibono hit because of the guns the men had. It was here that he was instructed as above. At trial, he specified that the "John," that was not supposed to be told about McMahon's participation, was John Gotti Jr.—me.

I submit that this Alite story is incredible. I did not send anyone on this matter, because I was not involved with it. In fact, it was only at trial that I learned McMahon was on the hit.

What Boriello and Carneglia did in using McMahon was a breach of protocol. Gravano and my father had given explicit instructions (according to Gravano's testimony), to use specific people on the DiBono hit. Yet, Alite testifying about his knowledge of the DiBono hit, said, "John Gotti told me he (McMahon) was involved." (transcript page 1935, Alite cross)

Taken all together, the contradictions, the timing, the incredibility of what Alite testified to, what was written in his 1023 by Agent Otto, all lead to the conclusion that Alite was telling a story that his government puppet masters wanted him to tell, with absolutely no regard for the accuracy of what was testified to.

The Grosso Murder

A Queens drug dealer got killed five days before Christmas, 1988. It was long considered an unsolved homicide, and wound up in the cold case files. That is until it heated up as an indictment allegation against me in the 2009 trial.

Alite first testified to the Grosso killing in the Charles Carneglia trial of March, 2009. On the stand, at that proceeding, he said, that "He (Grosso) was running his mouth that he was dealing coke for the Gottis, which he was warned to stop doing, but he kept doing it anyway."

Alite had a personal motive to kill Grosso, without invoking his usual mantra of *Gotti made me do it*. As testified by several witnesses, Alite had a long standing feud with Grosso and his brother-in-law, Gebert. In fact, in 1988, he had been shot at by them.

Now, in his role as government witness, he was dressing this up as a Gotti sanctioned hit. Alite then testified that he put together a crew, including his buddy Joey DiCarali, and two ex-cops, he had threatened from Brazil, Nick Tobia and Phil Baroni.

(Baroni had testified that the killing of Grosso was not

planned, but spontaneous, when Grosso had walked into the bar where Alite and friends were watching Monday night football.)

At the bar, Alite, Grosso and several others were drinking vodka, except Alite maintained in his testimony that he was only drinking shots of water. He then went on to say he left the bar a short time later to go to another watering hole.

DiCarali was driving the car, with Alite and Baroni in the back seat. Grosso sat in the front seat passenger side. Nick Tobia was following in a "crash" car. As they traveled along the Grand Central Parkway in Queens, Alite shot Grosso in the head, according to his own trial testimony.

Later he testified that the body was pushed out of the car, as they drove past Flushing Meadow Park.

So this was the testimony of Alite at the Carneglia trial, just six months before mine began.

When he took the stand at my trial, he claimed I was particularly incensed with Grosso, as he was claiming in the streets to be operating under my father's flag. Alite said, that at a meeting he supposedly attended with Grosso and myself, I threatened Grosso, and told him to stop using my father's name.

"I'm not gonna warn you again," I said, at least according to Alite.

Keep in mind that with Grosso, Alite was admitting to murder, but he was never indicted by the government for it. He was merely charged with "participating." That's because the government had created the fiction that I was the "puppet master" pulling Alite's strings.

Alite, on the stand, said after the Grosso hit, he came to see me the next day at the Bergin, and I insisted on seeing the body to "verify that Grosso was dead." At the scene, where the body had been found by police who swarmed the area, according to Alite, I quipped, "He doesn't look that good."

It's time here for a reality check. I am going to place myself where a murdered man is dumped in a public park in a highly populated area, being investigated by the homicide squad? It strains credibility doesn't it? Largely because it is an incredible and ludicrous bit of fiction.

Phil Baroni had contradicted many of the details of the Grosso murder as relayed by Alite. He was there, and was convicted of the murder. (You have seen some of his testimony earlier on in this book.)

Drug Dealing

There was testimony from Kevin Bonner, who was involved with Alite in drug dealing, that around 1990-1991, Alite told Bonner that he was having financial difficulties, because I had specifically ordered Alite not to deal in drugs.

We have already discussed the Grosso murder, and how it was used to tie me in with drug operations. In reality, George Grosso had been a competitor with Alite in the cocaine business. Small time stuff.

So eighteen years or so before my last trial, I was telling Alite to stay away from dealing drugs, yet now, Alite was testifying to my involvement with cocaine distribution in Queens.

My crew wasn't drug dealing, but *had* we wished to go into that filthy business, we had no desire, and certainly no need, to become involved with a low level street dealing garbage pail like Alite, or any of his competitors.

According to the testimony of DiLeonardo and Gravano, during the time of the Castellano Regime, the Gambino Family had access to the two largest dealers of drugs in the country. Had my father wished to become a drug trafficker, we could have activated these men, and not be bothered with bottom feeders.

On the issue of Alite's drug dealing activities, we will hear more from his former close friend and drug partner Joe O'Kane, who was to testify as a defense witness in our case.

Jury Tampering

One of the other charges of which I was accused was conspiracy with respect to jury tampering. Alite testified that he was on scene at the courthouse, observing the jurors as they came out, with me, Kevin McMahon and Michael Finnerty, and Mark Caputo.

Finnerty and McMahon had pled guilty to jury tampering. Finnerty testified at my trial as follows:

> Q. While you were doing this, [jury surveillance] while you were engaged in this activity, did you see John Alite on the scene?
>
> A. No. I don't recall him being there.

As for McMahon, he named numerous people that *were* involved, but not Alite.

In their testimony, neither Finnerty nor McMahon mentioned me being there, or Mark Caputo.

My Supposed Involvement in Florida Doings

One of the "reasons" I was initially charged in Florida, in order to try and justify that venue, was that I had business dealings down there. This, of course, came from Alite, who we will show, was once again fabricating testimonial evidence at the behest of his government handlers.

Alite testified about a relationship with a Timmy Donovan, whom he had known while both were attending college in Tampa. He had reconnected with him in 1989, and told him "I was making a lot of money and that I was with the Gottis."

Alite said that Donovan came down to Cancun, where Alite was vacationing, and discussed the Valet parking business. According to Alite, Donovan was very interested in those in the

Life. Alite testified that Donovan requested to be introduced to John Gotti Sr., myself, and Sammy the Bull (transcript page 1418, Alite direct).

Alite said he brought the valet parking idea to me (transcript page 1419). According to Alite, after speaking with me, he invested drug money in a valet business, Diamond Valet, that was owned by Donovan (transcript page 1421). He used the term "our money," when he spoke of the investment.

Q. When you say our money, whose money?
A. John Gotti Jr. and myself. . . .
Q. When you put it in the business, how did you pay Mr. Donovan? How did this transaction occur?
A. It wasn't a big amount of money. It was like $25,000 cash.
[transcript page 1422, Alite direct]

Let's stop here for a moment. Alite supposedly paid Donovan $25,000 of drug money that he said belonged to me and Alite. What did Donovan have to say about this when he testified?

Donovan, on his direct, was asked:

Q. Have you ever had any business relationship with Mr. Gotti?
A. Never.
Q. Was there ever an occasion when Mr. Gotti met you in an airport at Tampa and gave you a bag of money?
A. Absolutely never.
Q. Was Mr. Gotti ever involved to your knowledge in either any valet parking business that you operated in Tampa or any other business that you operated?
A. Absolutely never.
[transcript page 4360, Donovan direct]

On cross examination by AUSA Trezivant, Donovan was asked:

Q. Sir, you went back to Tampa and ultimately you walked
   away from your valet business, correct?
A. Yes sir.
Q. All the lots?
A. Yes sir.
Q. How much money did John Alite give you for those?
A. Nothing.
[transcript page 4386, Donovan cross]

★

Alite also testified on direct about an interest "we" had in a Florida glass shop.

Q. Who was going to purchase it?
A. Myself, John Gotti Jr. and Timmy Donovan.
Q. Did you all purchase it?
A. Yes.
Q. How much money did it take to acquire—what exactly
   did you acquire there?
A. The initial down payment we were giving Timmy, me
   and John Gotti Jr. flew down to Tampa and John Gotti
   Jr. handed Timmy Donovan $60,000. I believe it was in
   a bag in the airport.
[transcript page 1423, Alite]

Now, you can go back and take a look at Donovan's testimony above.

Alite admits in his direct that there was never any documentation showing the purchase of either the glass shop or the valet parking business.

Q. Any documents drawn up that showed your interest or
   the defendant's interest?
A. No.
[transcript page 1424, Alite]

Alite goes on to say (1425) that approximately $200,000 was invested in Donovan's businesses, and that he and I flew down to Tampa to give Donovan the money.

So what did Donovan have to say about all of this?

Q. Was Mr. Gotti ever involved in that business [the glass business]?
A. No sir.

Donovan also testified that he had not seen me with Alite since 1990 or 1991.

Winding up the direct of Donovan, my attorney Charles Carnesi asked:

Q. Did you ever discuss with anyone else, other people who were dealing with Alite, Mr. Alite's reputation for truthfulness?
A. Yes. He is incapable of telling the truth.
[transcript page 4372, Donovan]

But he *was* capable of exploiting his own children, while he was extorting people. Donovan testified about one of the face to face meetings he had with Alite, after Donovan had been receiving continual threats to get out of the valet business at the locations he had.

Mr. Alite says, to prove that you're going to be safe, he is going to bring his child with him to prove there is no danger, and there will be no gunplay, nothing like that. He said he was going to bring his child, which I thought was strange.

But OK so we meet.... I show up and he's standing in the parking lot with his son, probably at the time anywhere between six and ten years old. As soon as I walk up, the first thing he does is flash a gun, to show me he has a gun, which I didn't have a gun. [transcript page 4366, Donovan]

★

On the one hand you had Alite, trying to stay out of jail, testifying about my supposed involvement in Florida with Donovan's businesses. Involvement that was supposedly paid for with drug money.

On the other hand, you had Donovan, who was not going to benefit in any way from his testimony, stating that he never got a dime from Alite, or me, and that I had not participated in any of his businesses. He was a *victim* of Alite's criminal activity and not a violator of the law.

Credibility follows where there is no motivation to lie. You should be aware that Donovan had been a *government* witness in the trial *US v. Trucchio*. He had testified on these issues at that trial also.

In fact, AUSA Trezivant thanked him for his testimony at the trial. He wouldn't have thanked him for giving false testimony, would he?

Other Instances of the "Credibility" of Alite
The Magic Bullet

In a 1023 written by agent Ted Otto, Alite accuses me of shooting one Vinny Furci.

Supposedly, I shot Furci from a dispute arising out of cocaine dealing. Alite said he and Furci went to a house to do a six figure drug deal with some Colombians. Part of the payment (the larger part) they were tendering was in counterfeit money, and while the Colombians were counting out the money, Furci got nervous and excused himself from the scene, leaving Alite alone to face whatever might happen if the Colombians noticed the bogus bills. Quoting from the 1023:

> A short time later, GOTTI, Jr. told the source (Alite) he had arranged to meet with FURCI and was going to kill him during this meeting. On that occasion, FURCI picked up

Gotti Jr. and the source outside a restaurant on Cross Bay Boulevard. The source and GOTTI, Jr. drove through Howard Beach with FURCI to the vicinity of 164th Avenue near its intersection of 83rd and 84th Streets in Howard Beach. According to the source, after GOTTI Jr. told FURCI to slow down near an area of marshland, FURCI apparently sensed a problem and jumped out of the slowly moving car and tried to run away. The source stated GOTTI fired several shots at FURCI, hitting him at least once in his hip or lower back. According to the source, despite his wounds, FURCI managed to escape by running into the marshland area. The source never saw FURCI again, but learned from others that he had survived this attempt on his life."

However, Alite had testified in the Carneglia case, that Furci was shot *in* the car.

Q. You tried to kill someone named Vinny Furci?
A. John Gotti Junior shot him.
Q. While in the car?
A. That's right.
Q. He was to be killed before he jumped out the window, is that correct?
A. That's correct.
[transcript page 3639–3640, Alite at Carneglia trial]

Furci was six feet three over three hundred pounds, and he was in a Chrysler K Car according to Alite. At my trial, we see the following questions to and answers by Alite:

Q. How quickly did the defendant fire the first shot?
A. He only fired one shot.
Q. How quickly did he fire the shot?
A. About when he was like two feet away from the car. As he stepped out John fired the first shot.

Q. When he fired the shot, what did you observe as to Mr. Furci?

A. After he fired the shot, he yelped.

Could the testimony be any clearer? I shot Furci, and wounded him in the hip or the buttocks, according to government witness John Alite.

Except there was a problem with that.

Despite repeated assertions by Alite that Furci was hit by a bullet, when law enforcement acted pursuant to a search warrant against Furci some time after his supposed wounding, after pulling him off of the construction site where he was working, and conducting a strip search, there was no bullet wound found on the body.

Further Furci denied that this had ever happened.

If a man is struck by a bullet, there will be a wound where it strikes him (assuming he is not wearing protective armor of course). If there is no bullet wound on the man, he was not struck by a bullet, ergo Alite lied about the Furci incident.

The lies of Alite in FBI interview documents, scripted by Ted Otto, perhaps reveal as much about Agent Otto, as they do about Alite.

Let's refer back to the FBI 1023 form where Otto "took notes" from his Alite interview detailing his involvement with the DiBono killing. This single spaced two page memo entitled "The Murder of Louie DiBono," was written on August 17, 2009, less than a month before my fourth trial began with Alite as the lead government witness against me.

As it turned out, Otto's 1023 regarding the Furci incident, entitled "The Attempted Murder of Vinny Furci," was created by Otto on the same date as the DiBono memorandum, as were several others. It appeared that Otto was working overtime at the eleventh hour to bolster Alite's credibility.

So you have to ask which is worse: a gutter punk like Alite who is willing to say anything to escape from a Brazilian prison courtesy of the government, or a senior FBI agent who, with a magic wand for his pen, records Alite's fabrications into an official government document to be presented as evidence to the court deciding a murder trial?

It is important to understand that these 1023s and 302's were last minute government memorializations of interviews that had taken place years prior, the details being reduced to a writing.

Unfortunately for the government, when many of their witnesses were cross examined on these documents at my trials, they frequently would respond that they never made the statements found in the 302s and 1023s, or they did not remember making them.

If this was the case, and I believe it was, then the recording agent must have embellished or failed to accurately record the information provided. If an agent presents false evidence to a court, it is a fraud on a tribunal. It is also the height of hypocrisy, in light of the fact that lying to a federal agent is a felony punishable by up to five years in jail. (Martha Stewart served jail time for doing just that.)

What was even more infuriating at my fourth trial was the improper limitation by the judge of my attorneys' cross-examination of witnesses on these documents.

In the prior trials with Judge Scheindlin, she allowed detailed cross respecting these prior written statements of the witness being crossed, and their purported lack of memory of having made them.

Castel, in my fourth trial, unlike any other judge my attorneys or I have ever dealt with, only allowed the witness to be asked, if after looking at the statement, it refreshed their recollection of what they had said. Upon the witness saying "no," Castel would allow no further questioning regarding the statement, and abruptly told my attorneys to "move on."

Harrigan That's Not Me

Alite, in a 1023 written up by Ted Otto, stated he was summoned by Peter Gotti, to meet with him and me at a social club, where we said orders came from "The Chief" (my father) that a Dennis Harrigan was to be killed.

Supposedly, an attorney for one of Harrigan's co-defendants at this upcoming trial, Anthony Lombardino, met with Alite, me, and my Uncle Peter and told us that Harrigan was a cooperator. Harrigan, according to Alite, was murdered by Ronnie Trucchio and Iggy Alogna.

However, in an FBI 302 by Peter Zuccaro and his testimony, Peter Zuccaro said he was originally involved in the conspiracy to kill Harrigan, but was told by Angelo Ruggiero, to stay out of it and mind his own business.

He had later learned that Harrigan was shot to death in a phone booth by a man named Frankie Americanda. He was paid ten thousand dollars for the hit.

Peter Zuccaro's interpretation of the events was somewhat supported a decade earlier by Lucchese cooperating witness, Frank Gioia.

I was never mentioned, nor were any of the other men referred to in Alite's report.

Gym Destruction

Alite had also testified that around 1994 he was involved with a gym in South New Jersey. He testified that he had a problem with his partners, so he received permission from me to trash the place and burn it.

Then he testified that some time later I had set up a meeting with Ralph Natale, who at that time was the acting boss of the Philadelphia crime Family, to resolve the issue. I can tell you that I had never met, spoken to or sent any message to Ralph Natale, who, in the late '90s, like Alite had done earlier, became a cooperator.

The first time I had ever heard of the gym incident was in a letter from 1993-4 from Alite, which said:

> Anyway, I had more problems, someone wrecked that gym I used to be involved with, they broke in one night, and smashed all the windows and ruined all the equipment. So, naturally the owners blamed me. Detectives came over, and broke my balls. Then a week later the bomb squad, because someone called and threatened to blow up the place. I told them I don't even know how to light a fucking firecracker.

Alite then goes on in his letter to say how he's being harassed in the area, and he concludes by saying, in the letter, "So I think I've had it for this area."

When he was confronted with the fact that I had retained this letter all these years, you could see the look of shock on his face. His response to this was, "Well, I was telling John in code."

His letter started with, "Hi John, how's it going, I hope things are well, I've been in the area recently, but as usual, no one sees you."

So obviously, he has had no contact with me, or at least by his coming back into the neighborhood, people would tell him "John's not around, you can't see him."

The FBI certainly saw me, so did the Queens DA during trial preparation. I reviewed logs showing constant surveillance on me from the OCTF (showing logs of over 52 agents surveilling me and mine), then the FBI, Queens and Brooklyn DAs at the Bergin Club, or my Sutphin Boulevard office in Queens.

In fact, at that time period, journalist John Miller followed me every day for weeks to put together a one week special on me for television, at about the same time period as Alite's letter was written.

I could always be found. I was just not accessible to people such as Alite, with whom I wanted nothing to do. Alite went on to close the letter, "Have a great Father's Day, I miss ya, I'll always keep writing. I hope you at least read these before you throw them out. See ya, Johnny."

So this letter (which was found miraculously in an old office desk drawer, along with other attempted communications of Alite to me) was dated around Father's Day, 1994. At this point he was under nobody's flag. He had always moved between crews, but for the most part they were Gambino crews.

In reality, nobody had anything to do with Alite since November, 1991. He freelanced, used young kids, and would move in and out of Queens. To "Hello" me at this time he would have had to go through many people, because he was an outcast. In the world of dirty, this was dirt that even the mob didn't want.

Department of Justice is Blind

One thing that the government hates to have made public is how the FBI turns a blind eye to crimes perpetrated by those for whom they have use.

In a January 14, 2013, letter to the Justice Department, FBI officials admitted that its fifty-six field offices authorized its informants to break the law at least 5,939 times during the 2012 calendar year. (This had been obtained by the *Huffington Post* pursuant to a FOIA request.)

When Whitey Bulger was convicted of nineteen murders, many of those had been committed *while* he was a government informant.

So it would have been very inconvenient if John Alite had committed a murder while being an informant. The question is, did he?

Alite Testimony Continued

Charles Carnesi, on cross examination of Alite, was inquiring as to the murder of John Gebert, and a meeting Alite claimed to have with respect to the murder. What follows is a section of the Q&A.

Q. When Mr. Gebert—how long after that discussion was it that Mr. Gebert was killed?

A. What time are you talking about? I got a little confused what you are asking me here.

Q. After you had this discussion with these people about killing Mr. Gebert.

THE COURT: Let's fix a time on that discussion, When was that?"

THE WITNESS: 1996 Approximately.

Q. Mr. Gebert was not incarcerated at that time, right?

A. No.

Q. Nor were you?

A. No.

Q. Then following that, in the years after, did there come a time to your knowledge that Mr. Gebert was incarcerated?

A. Mr. Gebert wasn't incarcerated after 1996.

Q. When did you begin having a discussion with those individuals about killing Mr. Gebert?

A. I only had one discussion I believe with those individuals, 1996.

Q. Do you remember having a discussion about John Burke being run over by a car driven with, I am sorry, run over by a car driven by Brendan Gebert; do your remember that incident?

A. Do I remember the incident, yes.

Q. Did you ever remember discussing that incident with Peter Zucarro?

A. No, not really.

Q. Do you remember telling anybody that that was another reason why you wanted Johnny Gebert killed?

A. No, not at all.

Q. Do you remember having a meeting with peter Zuccaro about killing Johnny Gebert at the McDonald's on Atlantic Avenue?

A. Ask me that again.

Q. Did you meet with Peter Zuccaro to discuss killing Johnny Gebert at the McDonald's on Atlantic Avenue in Brooklyn?

A. The only meeting I had with Peter Zuccaro was after John Gotti Junior spoke to him, that was in 1989, I believe, 1988, somewhere around there, that's the only...

Q. I am going to ask if you would try to answer my question. Did you ever meet with him in Brooklyn at the McDonald's on Atlantic Avenue to discuss killing Johnny Gebert, yes or no?

A. I don't even know where McDonald's is in Brooklyn, so I guess.

THE COURT: No. Did you understand the question?

THE WITNESS: No, not really.

MR. CARNESI: I will try again?

Q. Did you ever meet with Peter Zuccaro at a McDonald's on Atlantic Avenue in Brooklyn to discuss killing John Gebert?

THE COURT: Mr. Alite, do you understand the question?

THE WITNESS: Yes.

THE COURT: Answer it please.

THE WITNESS: No.

Q. Did you ever discuss with Mr. Zuccaro the fact that Mr. Gebert hung out and sold drugs at Frankie & Johnny's Pub and that he would be found there?

A. Not that I remember, no.

Q. Do you remember having a discussion with Mr. Zuccaro about killing Johnny Gebert then going to meet Mr. Trucchio?

A. No.

Q. Did you ever have a discussion with Mr. Zuccaro as to who would be used to commit the murder of Johnny Gebert?

A. No.

Q. Did you ever discuss with him that Dave D'Arpino, Mike Malone, and Patsy Andriano should be the ones to kill Gebert?

A. Did I have a discussion with Peter Zuccaro about that?

Q. Yes.

A. No.

Q. Did you ever discuss with any of those individuals that Johnny Gebert should be killed when he was released from jail?

A. Not that I recall, no.

Q. Did you ever discuss with any of those individuals, that they should wait to kill Johnny Gebert until he came home and after you yourself had surrendered to go to jail?

A. I spoke to Patsy Michael and Dave D'Arpino in that car and I told them when I am in jail, that would be a good gift.

Q. Did you ever discuss that they would be doing this and would be supervised by Peter Zuccaro in committing the murder?

A. Did I ever discuss that with them?

Q. Yes.

A. No.

Q. By the way do you know if Mr. Zuccaro has also begun cooperating with the government, right?

A. Do I know that?

Q. Yes.

A. Yes, I heard he was cooperating.

Q. He begun cooperating in 2005, when you were still a fugitive, right?

A. Did Peter Zuccaro start cooperating in 2005; I don't know

Thus went Alite's testimony. What did Peter Zuccaro tell

law enforcement back in 2005? Let's take a look at his 302 dated 11/1/05.

Zuccaro's 302s

JOHN GEBERT was murdered as a result of a long standing disagreement over control of a drug area. John Gebert's drug operation was in the same area as the drug operation controlled by JOHN ALITE and RONNIE TRUCCHIO.

Gebert had fired a maching [sic] gun into the PM PUB, which was a location where Trucchio and Alite had control of selling. After this incident Alite approached INDIDIVID-UAL [sic] and told him that Gebert needs to be killed. A short time later a meeting took place between Alite, PATSY ANDRIANO, MIKE MALONE, DAVE DARPINO (ph) and STEPHEN ZUCCARRO [sic]. During the meeting Alite said that Gebert had threatened him and Alite instructed them to kill Gebert. However, Gebert was arrested on heroin charges went to jail to serve a prison term before they were able to kill him.

After Gebert completed serving his prison term, Alite told individual that Gebert is now out of jail and they should kill him.

Around this time JOHN BURKE was run over by car driven by BRENDAN GEBERT, (John Gebert's brother) in the parking lot of LaVilla in Lindenwood Queens. This further incidted [sic] the tensions towards Gebert.

Alite and individual had a meeting about killilng [sic] Gebert at the McDonald's on Atlantic Avenue. They discussed that Gebert hung out and sold drugs at FRANKIE AND JOHNNIE'S PUB, therefore he would be easy to find there. Individual advised that CARL CAPELLO and JOHNNY BANDANNA (LNU) sold drugs for Gebert at Frankie and Johnnies. Alite told invididual [sic] to use Patsy Andriano, Mike Malone and Dave Darpino (ph) because they need to make their bones. (After this meeting individual observed Alite meeting with Trucchio.)

Individual then attended several meetings about the planning of killing Gebert. During the meetings Alite told Individual to wait until after Alite surrendered and went to prison. At that time individual was to assemble Darpino (ph), Malone, and Andriano to kill Gebert.

After Alite surrendered individual instructed JOE LAMPA-SONA to steal a van. This was the van used during the shooting of Gebert. The assignments were Andriano and Darpino as the shooters and Malone as the driver. They all wore wool hats and scarves around their faces, and individual believed they all had guns. Individual was in a vehicle near Frankie and Johnnies to spot when Gebert was there. Walkie-talkies were used for individual to communicate from individual's vehicle to the van that Andriano, Malone and Darpino were in.

Individual radioed to them when Gebert was observed at Frankie and Johnnies. Malone drove the van to Frankie and Johnnies, Andriano departed the van and shot Carl Cappello outside Frankie and Johnnies. Gebert ran inside Frankie and Johnnies but Darpino followed Gebert and shot him under a pool table.

They then departed in the van and dumped it. Then they all went to the Rockaways and threw the guns into the Jamaica Bay. Individual then told them to depart and to burn the clothes that they were wearing.

Thus Zuccaro's 302 directly contradicts Alite's testimony given at my trial. Zuccaro, during testimony, revealed that he had killed one John Gebert. He had been brought in for the defense based upon his prior testimony at the Carneglia and Pizzonia trials. He testified that he never had discussions about Gebert's murder with me, John Carneglia, or my Uncle Gene. No meeting ever occurred at the Bergin or in a luncheon-ette.

Zuccaro was facing a death penalty for this crime, as Alite would have, because in the early nineties drug murder became a death eligible offense. As to Ronnie Trucchio, he never answered to me, he answered to JoJo Corozzo and Peter Gotti.

This killing was a personal vendetta for Alite, who was trying to impress people. Further, Grosso and Gebert had, in the past, shot at Alite. Let's got to Zuccaro's testimony:

Q. Who wanted John Gebert murdered?
A. John Alite. [page 899 of direct transcript]
Q. Did Alite ask you to get involved in the murder?
A. Yes.
Q. Why did he want Gebert dead?
A. He asked me to get involved in the murder way back in '88.
Q. Why did he want him dead in 1997?
A. Because John Gebert was a fearful force in the neighborhood who was chasing made men around with a machine gun, shooting up their bars. He was controlling drug dealing on Jamaica Avenue and he was a pretty treacherous fellow.
Q. John Alite also was a drug dealer on Jamaica Avenue?
A. Yes.
Q. You just mentioned a number of reasons why Alite wanted him dead, right?
A. I don't know all the reasons, but those are some of them. [900 and 901]

What did Alite have to say about all of this at trial?
Charlie Carnesi asked Alite on cross regarding the death of Gebert:

Q. And you directed the people who killed him to commit that murder, right? You told your guys to do it?
A. No. I told them it would be a nice gift if they killed him.
Q. It was just a suggestion?

A. Yes.

A few more questions, and Alite admitted to having pled guilty to conspiracy to kill Gebert, but not for killing him (transcript page 2007, Alite cross).

So Alite didn't order the killing of Gebert. Except at another trial, where Alite was testifying against Charles Carneglia, this happened:

Q. You said you also participated in the murder of Johnny Gebert. Is this the same Johnny Gebert who was your best friend in your late teens?
A. Yes.
Q. What role did you play in the murder?
A. I ordered it.
[transcript page 3385, Alite direct, Carneglia trial]

Now Alite during his cross-examination, testified that I approved a hit on Gebert back in 1988, 1989.

Q. Who ordered the murder?
A. John Gotti Jr.
[transcript page 1977, Alite cross]

Alite, at one point in his testimony, said that he discussed the matter of Gebert with me, Johnny Carneglia, Peter Zuccaro, and my Uncle Gene at the luncheonette across the street from the Bergin Hunt and Fish Club on 101st Ave., Queens (transcript page 1979, Alite cross).

Peter Zuccaro, who previously had been a witness for the government, in my trial testified that the meeting of which Alite spoke about, never took place. Zuccaro did confirm that a meeting had taken place between him and Alite only, at a *McDonald's* in Brooklyn, in the parking lot.

As further indication that Alite was manufacturing testimony, there were *no* government surveillance tapes, photos, or videos submitted with respect to this imaginary meeting. There couldn't have been.

Did Alite kill Gebert during the time he was an FBI cooperator? Did they care once they learned of it?

When questioned further on Gebert's killing Alite said it was ordered at that meeting (the one Zuccaro said never happened), and once it was stamped (ordered), it's done. On cross examination of Alite, Carnesi explored prior inconsistent statements.

Q. At the time, did you meet with Mr. Kaplan in New Jersey by the New Jersey Turnpike.

A. Yes.

Q. Did Mr. Kaplan inform you at that time that Mr. Gotti wanted you to leave Johnny Gebert alone, keep Johnny Burke away from Johnny Gebert and Johnny Gebert was not to be hurt, leave him alone?

A. Yes.

Q. Do you remember how you responded to Mr. Kaplan?

A. There was another part before that.

THE COURT: Keep your voice up. Turn to the mike.

Q. Did you tell Mr. Kaplan to tell Mr. Gotti, mind your own business?

A. I don't think so, but I could have said it if I was mad, yeah.

Q. At the time you saw Mr. Kaplan walk away, make a cell-phone call, and when he came back to you, you told him tell Gotti, Gebert would not last more than a few weeks. Do you remember telling him that?

A. I don't remember but I could have said it.

Q. Showing you 3506-10 beginning at the bottom of page 2, the first tow paragraphs on page 3.

THE COURT: Have you ever seen this document before, sir?

THE WITNESS: no.

Q. Have you had a chance to read it? (after a pause to allow witness to read document)

A. Yes.

Q. Does that refresh your recollection?

A. What's the question?

Q. Does it refresh your recollection?

A. Yes.

Q. That what you said is tell Gotti to mind his own business, Gebert is going to be dead in two weeks?

A. Yes, that's what I said.

Q. Do you remember being sworn at Carneglia's trial a couple of months ago and being asked about the murder of Johnny Gebert?

A. Not specifics but yes.

Q. Do you remember being asked this question and giving this answer:

> Q: You were going to kill this guy no matter what?
> A: You got that right.

A. Yes, I said that. I remember that.

Q. You ordered the murder of Johnny Gebert. You told them—you are shaking your head—you testified in Carneglia's trial, we went through that a while ago this morning, that you ordered. Is it that you did not order it now? Was that false, that testimony?

A. I told my guys to kill him, yes; he ordered the murder through me, yes.

Q. You directed the people who killed him to commit that murder right? You told your guys to do it?

A. No, I told them it would be a nice gift if they killed him.

Q. It was just a suggestion?

A. Basically, yes.

Q. Did you plead guilty to the murder?

A, Yes.

Q. You sure, you pled guilty to killing Johnny Gebert?

A. Conspiracy to kill Johnny Gebert.

Q. That is different. You pled guilty to conspiracy to kill

MR. TREZIVANT (AUSA): Objection, argumentative.

THE COURT: I am going to sustain the objection.

Q. Did you plead guilty to killing Johnny Gebert?

THE COURT: No. (meaning the question was improper)
Did you plead guilty to a charge in connection with the
killing of Mr. Gebert?

THE WITNESS: Yes.

THE COURT: What did you plead guilty to?

THE WITNESS I believe conspiracy to kill Johnny Gebert.

[transcript pages 2004-2005, Alite cross]

Alite was caught in a variety of lies and contradictions between his sessions with the FBI, and his prior testimony, and recordings that had been made. At one point in my trial, he is questioned about whether or not he testified at the Carneglia trial as to having seen government transcripts. He denies it, but under further cross, admitted it.

In fact, Investigator Larry Frost had spoken with Alite in 2006 by phone when he was imprisoned in Brazil, and Alite mentions having seen prior testimony and 302s from several witnesses. He was reading from notes made from the 302's and the testimony to Frost.

In short, this is a man that had no problem lying under oath. Did the government care?

Here's another example of Alite being divorced from the truth.

Alite had claimed, on direct, when he came home that he no longer wanted to be affiliated with the Gambino Family, and acting Lucchese boss Joe DeFede wanted him with his Family. Alite said he had communicated with DeFede, through a Lucchese associate named "Boopie." A meeting was set up, according to Alite, between Richie Gotti, my uncle, and Joe DeFede for this move.

What follows is Alite's testimony from my trial.

Q. So who did you—who interceded on your behalf in the Lucchese crime family?

A. Joe DeFede

Q. What if anything did Joe DeFede do for you?

A. Joe DeFede set a meeting when he was getting hip replacement, he set a meeting with Richie Gotti, John Gotti Jr.'s uncle.

Q. How did you know Joe DeFede?

A. I knew members of the Lucchese family, also from my neighborhood, and I interacted with them in different businesses. Shakedowns, robberies, all that. Grew up with them.

Q. There was a meeting?"

A. Yes.

Q. Between who and who?

A. Richie Gotti Sr. and Joe DeFede.

Q. Who was Richie Gotti to this defendant, if you can explain generally who Gotti Sr. was and the defendant, just explain the relationship to the jury so they will understand.

A. John Gotti Sr. was the boss, Gene Gotti at one time was captain that John Gotti Jr. answered to.

Q. Was that John Gotti Sr.'s brother?

A. Yes.

Q. Who went to the meeting for you?

MR. CARNESI: Judge, can we just know when the meeting took place?

THE COURT: Yes.

A. The meeting took place I believe around 2000, if I am correct, 2000, 2001.

Q. Sometime after you got out of prison?

A. Yes.

Q. Was it Richie Gotti Sr. who sat down for you sir?

A. Yes. Not for me, he was trying to keep me with the Gotti family.

Q. And Joe DeFede?

A. Joe DeFede wants them to release me to the Lucchese family. You have to be released from—John Gotti Jr. has to OK me to let me go and be under the umbrella of the Lucchese family.

Q. Did anybody report back to you the results of that meeting?

A. Richie Gotti Sr.

[transcript page 1668, Alite direct]

Great story, here's the problem. On cross, Carnesi began to walk Alite through the story. At the time Alite was testifying about, 2000-2001, Joe DeFede was in prison in Lexington Kentucky. (In fact, he had been imprisoned since 1998, spent some time with me in Valhalla, and a short time later he was moved to Kentucky.)

When confronted with this, Alite didn't even know that DeFede was in prison, and was unaware that "Joe D," as he was called, had joined the Federal Witness Protection Program in February '02.

Additionally, at no time during his cooperation with the government did Joe DeFede mention any such meeting with Richie Gotti, or anyone else. So Alite goes on in his testimony to conclude that the Gottis were not releasing him. On November 18, 1999, a tape made of my Uncle Gene in prison, recorded him discussing Alite with Charles Carneglia.

GOTTI: Let me tell you what she told me, Charles. Try to keep it in your head so youse get it straight fast. She's an open motherfucker. Here's why. It's got nothing to do with your brother, your brother I'm gonna love him until I die.

CARNEGLIA: Yeah, I know.

GOTTI: Here's she quoted—this kid Johnny Alite had him
    on the phone with her.
CARNEGLIA: Right.
GOTTI: I don't know how he got on the phone with her,
    this kid is a mysterious kid. With his three year bid with
    all these cases. I don't trust him a hundred ways. (Whis-
    pering) No good.

You also heard me on a tape March 23, 2003, in Ray
Brook, harshly lecturing a friend on even "Helloing" John
Alite. Nobody wanted anything to do with this miscreant.

An Affair not Remembered

Alite, in a 1023 written up by agent Ted Otto, went into
detail about his affair with my sister, Victoria, in the eighties.
He described how he had an ongoing relationship with her
prior to, and after, her marriage to Carmine Agnello, and how
one time he was confronted in a bar by Agnello and several
other individuals.

Carmine, according to Alite, pulled a gun on him, but
Ronnie "One Arm" Trucchio, who was present, cautioned
Carmine not to do anything in the bar. Agnello and Alite
argued outside of the bar, but the situation was calmed down
by the arrival of my sister and myself. Alite said, at the time,
that if Carmine threatened him again, Alite would shoot him.
So goes the 1023.

In testimony at both the Carneglia trial, and in my trial,
there are significant contradictions to this 1023. The number
of people pulling guns changes, the number of people present
changes, the names of people vary that were there, and the
actions outside of the bar are different.

Did any of this happen. My sister, besides vehemently
denying it, backed up her denials by taking a polygraph test.

During her test, she denied having sex with Alite, and she

denied being beaten by Carmine. The results of the polygraph indicated truthful responses.

Many state that a polygraph test is only as good as the operator, so what, in this case, were the polygrapher's credentials?

Judd Bank, who had administered the examination, was a former Detective Investigator with the Queens District Attorney's office. At the time of my sister's test, he had conducted over 7,000 examinations. He served as an expert witness, a lecturer to the Bar Association of the county of Queens, and was a polygrapher for the Legal Aid Society.

In other words, the man knew his business.

Alite never offered to take a polygraph. Further, an individual who Alite put at the scene of the incident, and became a cooperator; nothing found in his documentation, provided to us in discovery, indicated that the incident ever took place.

Alite Confidential

I mentioned that back in '91 Tony "Pep" had named Alite as a cooperator. It had come to light that Alite was meeting on a regular basis with an Agent Randazzo, whose background was mentioned in regards to my stay at MDC.

It was first exposed to John Alite that certain people were well aware that he had had a relationship with an agent, Randazzo, from a phone call made by Alite, via a smuggled in cell phone in the jail.

In late '05- early '06, in a untapped call between Alite and Joseph Corozzo, an attorney, the lawyer mentioned a relationship between the agent and Alite. He then revealed the agent's name to be Jason Randazzo.

In a later conversation between Alite and private investigator Larry Frost, hired by Corozzo, on behalf of his client Ronnie Trucchio, when Randazzo was mentioned, Alite said the following:

"Having problems with Ronnie," Alite said, "and I only meet him on my terms—I told the agents this in 1995. I don't trust him or anybody else from that neighborhood. I met agent Randazzo from the Eastern District at Victory Field, a park in Queens, New York. I told Corozzo this already."

He had also told Frost that he had mentioned to Randazzo that he believed Trucchio and Vito Guzzo (who we mentioned before) were trying to kill him. They were planning on luring him in with the promise of repayment of bookmaking money that was due Alite. Alite went on to mention that he told Randazzo he doesn't trust Ronnie, "so he can keep it" (the money).

He also admitted, in his conversation with Frost, that in 1999 he had been subpoenaed by a Grand Jury and told the prosecutor and the agent that he would tell them what they wanted to know, regarding me, but he wouldn't testify.

Once again we were to raise this issue. Charlie Carnesi had made a request for any notes or 302s agents or prosecutors may have regarding meetings between Alite and Randazzo. They said they hadn't any. (Reminiscent of the 1998 case and Agent Jack Karst.)

So at this point we decided to base our inquiries of Alite on the taped conversation of him and investigator Frost. On the stand Alite admitted that he had met with agent Randazzo a number of times, but he didn't remember how he would contact him. When he was pressed he said he had a contact number but didn't know how he got it.

When asked further, about where he would contact the agent, Alite said at the agent's home or the FBI office. He further went on to say that he didn't remember what was discussed—other than baseball.

He said he didn't remember discussing Ronnie Trucchio, but later would say he may have discussed him. Even later, he admitted that he might have discussed Trucchio with the prosecutor and the agent in the room adjoining where the Grand Jury was being held.

He also didn't remember if he had ever discussed me to agent Randazzo. But when pressed, he did think that he mentioned Carmine Agnello, my brother-in-law, and me trying to kill him. He then went on to say after numerous "I don't remember" responses to what might have been discussed with Randazzo, he would discuss some truth and some lies.

Alite confirmed that Randazzo knew about him, because Alite was all over the news. He didn't remember if he ever discussed his criminal doings with the agent.

(If one reviews the testimony of Alite, it appears that his memory is much better regarding supposed events of the eighties, whereas when it comes to an event a decade later in time his memory of conversations with an agent are not all that vivid.)

When questioned further by Charlie Carnesi regarding what Alite might have discussed with Randazzo after 1994 (Gebert had been killed in 1996), the following took place:

Q. Did you discuss any of the activities that you continued to be involved in with Randazzo after 1994?"

A. I don't think so.

Q. As far as—if I understand your testimony, as far as you can recall right now, the only contact you had with agent Randazzo after 1994 would be basically social conversations, how you doing. Remember, those brothers we used to play baseball with, things like that...

A. No, I didn't say that either.

Q. Well, then explain to me what kind of contact did you have?

A. What I said is, there is a movie called The Sting and everything you do you are conning people. That's what I did. So I don't know what the Hell I said to him. I could have been trying to con him, I don't remember. All I know is, I may have talked to him, I may not have I'm not sure. I don't know.

Charlie Carnesi then went on to question Alite about other contact he might have had with agents. There were several, but we will focus on those that related to the Grand Jury proceedings in 1999, to which he had been subpoenaed.

He said he didn't remember, again, being asked questions about Ronnie Trucchio. (Alite had testified earlier that he was godfather to Trucchio's only daughter.) Then Carnesi questioned Alite about his testimony that was given at the grand jury. What follows are grand jury questions:

Q. Did Ronnie Trucchio have a nickname?
A. A nickname?
Q. A street name.
A. Ronnie "one arm."

Carnesi went on to ask, "Does that refresh your recollection that you were asked questions about Trucchio?"

A. I guess I was, yes, I don't remember it, but yes.
Q. Now there comes a point when the assistant US attorney who is conducting the examination reminds you again, 'Mr. Alite, we had *a conversation outside, prior to your testifying, and you told us certain things.* Now, we are asking you those things, and if you lie to us, you could be indicted for perjury.' [emphasis added]

Alite went on to say that he lied and flim-flammed on the stand, but in light of the testimony above, it is apparent that when he was talking with the government *before* testifying he was giving them accurate information.

That means Alite told the prosecutor and the interviewing agent, Breslin, the truth outside, but was lying on the stand. (Remember the statement earlier that Alite made to Frost in the phone call from the jail in Brazil, regarding his cooperating but unwillingness to take the stand.)

Carnesi had further asked Alite if he remembered discussing his former business partner and close friend, Joe O'Kane at the grand jury proceedings. He didn't remember. (You will learn more about O'Kane when we discuss the defense witnesses.)

Alite also acknowledged in my trial as to having contact with at least two other agents besides Randazzo and Breslin. The reader will remember our discussion about Tommy Sparrow Spinelli who had been killed for his failure to report his contact with a Federal agent. Just what mob was Alite associated with in the nineties?

One might also ask what agency is Randazzo working with?

In the preparation of this book I had interviewed two retired federal agents, one a former FBI agent from the Western states, Dan Vogel, who gave me a lengthy phone interview, and the other a retired DEA agent, Jerry Laveroni.

(Laveroni had an extensive law enforcement and security background. He had been with the Los Angeles Sheriff's Office and was on the scene at the Tate/Labianca killings, and later was an undercover DEA agent. After that, he was with the New York Yankees for many years as head of team security.)

Both had stated that standard operating procedure would be (whether it was a CI or not) for any agent having contact with a known criminal or in this case an OC associate, especially on a constant basis, to memorialize that contact in writing on the appropriate agency form, or at least a memo to their supervisor.

"It is absolutely imperative," Vogel said, "particularly if the source is an organized crime figure."

Supposing agent Randazzo's meeting with Alite at night in a park, walked into an ongoing surveillance by a law enforcement agency. Those surveilling would be required to ID the person meeting with the target.

Were it to be confirmed that it was a law enforcement agent met with the target, and this was not put on record by that agent, the agent's supervisor, upon learning this from an outside agency, or even from his fellow agents conducting the surveillance, might imagine that the agent seen might have been compromised.

The above concept is crucial, especially in an atmosphere where law enforcement and organized crime figures had an unholy relationship, as had been revealed in both Boston and New York in the nineties.

So the fact that the government stated it had no 302s or notes regarding Alite's meeting with agents is inexcusable and incredible.

Alite, who had been involved with criminal activity including murder during his relationship with Randazzo in the nineties, would not have had his informant status documented as it could easily have been a source of embarrassment to law enforcement, and diminished significantly any value he would have as a witness at a jury trial. (Remember, agent Karst was demoted for shredding his notes of meetings with his CI, regarding the Scores case in '98, who was a pedophile.)

Alite Just Called to Say I Love You

At many times in this book we have spoken of how a cooperator facilitates government efforts with respect to organized crime matters. Now, I will tell you about how the government facilitated Alite in his aggravated harassment of his former wife, by supplying the "instrumentality of the crime."

You have read about the special treatment that was given to Alite—furloughs for the day out of jail, private planes for transport. Another perk given to Alite was the use of the private cell phone of Agent Otto.

This was brought to light after my attorney was put in contact with the former wife of Alite, Carol. At first she was interviewed regarding lies her former husband told about his financial situation and lifestyle, and for his abusive treatment of her and other women.

At this interview, she and her fiancée Don told Carnesi that they had received over twenty phone calls and text messages from unrecognized numbers, but most times from one particular number. These were threatening and harassing phone calls and texts from Carol's former husband, John Alite.

Don had had enough, and decided to call the phone number that had been the main source of the harassment and threats. The number was answered by Agent Ted Otto.

Remember, this was an FBI agent lending his private cell phone to a sociopath who was making *unmonitored* calls.

We subpoenaed Carol Alite to trial to testify not only to this incident, but with regard to the aforesaid financial fantasies spun by Alite about his wealth in the late eighties and early nineties. (They had been married since 1990; Ruggiero and I had been witnesses for the civil ceremony.) In reality, her finances were such that the house she lived in was foreclosed, and she was evicted. Alite had only been paying $137 per week for each of his children.

We were also going to ask her about an incident where Alite had hired someone to rob and stab her brother.

The day she was to testify Carol was late. The judge wouldn't wait for her, and said, "The train left the station." How callous can you be? I was fighting for my life, and the judge says this. Carol did show up, but was not permitted to testify.

She sat in the courtroom as a spectator.

Book 'Em Alite

While in jail, at the relatively comfortable Witness Protection Unit, a recording was made between Alite and his brother, Jimmy, on December 23, 2007. In this recording, Alite reveals literary ambitions, and talks about a potential book deal.

Here is a transcript of the conversation:

JIMMY: Don't be depressed my boy, think of the future. Think of getting out.

JOHN: I just talked to Denise about that guy, right, the one she met in the city.

JIMMY: Which guy?

JOHN: The guy for me. She met in the city that she was talking to.

JIMMY: Oh, oh, okay yeah.

JOHN: She said at first she was really optimistic, but now she is saying...

JIMMY: You know why? Because she talked to me. That's exactly why, she talked to me. You know why I said that?

JOHN: Why, watch what you say.

JIMMY: I know, because first of all he never did anything before ever, second of all he's not going to have any connections with anybody.

JOHN: Yeah but I thought he's got all kinds of connections.

JIMMY: Nah, nah, nah. You gotta have someone, I mean you really wanna get someone that...

JOHN: I thought he was a big time guy like in his field.

JIMMY: Nah. Never wrote anything, never did anything before. Never wrote anything. Never did anything in that capacity before. He did like other things, but not in the capacity that we're talking.

JOHN: But doesn't he know people?

JIMMY: It doesn't matter who he knows, he's got to be ... you wanna get someone who already did something that's on the charts. It's like that knows big production things and stuff like that. I'm gonna take care of that when the time is right. I mean, I'm not saying to disqualify him completely, I'm saying when the time is right, let me make connections and stuff like that, I'll do it.

This was not the only taped conversation about a book deal that was obtained. Alite had been warned numerous times by agents Otto and Bradley to watch what was discussed in jail phone calls (especially when the subject was recruiting cooperators, or prisoners on whom he was informing). Therefore, Alite would talk around a subject, be more oftentimes vague, than specific.

On the stand, he was asked about a book deal. He denied he was interested in a deal, said it wasn't even legal for him to write one. However, the reality is he has written one in concert with a crime journalist, according to a source who confirmed this.

I had sat through days of Alite's testimony, listening to him falsely call me everything from a drug dealer to a co-conspirator to murder. He didn't just go after me but my family, and the sheer audacity of his fairy tale was compounded by the fact that it was being presented as the truth by lawyers for the U.S. Department of Justice and veteran FBI agents whose presence in the courtroom gave weight to his lies.

My frustration at listening to Alite, knowing the real deal about what he was, and knowing that he was receiving government absolution for all of his sins, had me to boiling point.

He had boasted about torturing an electrician who had had sex with a girlfriend on Alite's bed. He had stripped the man down, broke his jaw and ribs, and threw him in a lake in freezing weather. He shot towards the man ordering him to stay under water.

"I tied him up naked, put him in my garage, so he couldn't leave, and I went to dinner," Alite told the shocked jury listening to his testimony.

Alite further had testified to a strangulation killing of a girl in a motel, in which he implicated others. Although I have no proof, after Alite was chased, people began to speak freely about him—having been removed from our protection. They, including the victim's brother, said they believed he was involved in this killing. Alite, however, has always denied any participation in this incident.

After breaking for lunch recess, as he climbed down from

the witness chair, he walked past me and smiled, like he could say and do whatever he wanted. I looked at him with disgust and he responded with, "You have something to say to me?" As I made a move to go around my lawyer to go after him, Charlie pushed me back. I began shouting to him, "You like strangling girls? You punk dog. You were a punk and a dog your whole life, that's all you ever were." The marshals escorted Alite from the courtroom, and Charlie Carnesi restrained me.

The situation was quickly defused. It didn't happen with the jury present and I later respectfully apologized to Judge Castel.

But after this account of the trial that you've read, I hope you can understand my frustration at that point. Don't forget I was facing life in prison and to escape jail for his own crimes, this sociopath was trying to put me there.

Right after the incident my mother Victoria told the press that Alite had tried to provoke me because my lawyer Charles Carnesi was getting too close to the truth. In fact, the *New York Daily News* described the confrontation this way:

"Carnesi had forced Alite to recount hundreds of lies he had made to the government, lawyers, family, and friends as he tried to worm his way out of a life sentence."

Michael DiLeonardo

The government decided to close its case with its polished cooperator, Mikey Scars. This would be the fourth time he testified against me in a trial. Unlike Alite, Scars testimony was more practiced.

He was certainly far more intelligent than Alite. His testimony was basically the same as in the previous three trials against me, with a few exceptions. The government was now attempting to prop up Alite via Scars' testimony.

Scars, in previous trials, never even mentioned Alite. There was only a small mention of him in 2002 FBI notes.

The notes referred to my having chased Alite. Now, however, Scars was trying to rehabilitate the credibility of Alite, his fellow cooperator.

At this point, it was too late.

What was even more telling, regarding testimony, was what Scars was to do next. He began to testify about my involvement in the DiBono killing. He said he had been told about DiBono from Eddie Garafola, whom we had referred to in the warehouse showdown meeting. Eddie was Gravano's brother-in-law.

Mikey Scars testified that, in a conversation he had with Eddie, Gravano had left me out of the DiBono killing, because it was a son for a son thing. Gravano would not implicate me, in order to assure that vengeance would not be taken out against his son.

Carnesi on cross, questioned Scars as to why there had never been any mention of my involvement in the DiBono killing at any previous proceeding, or 302 or any other document—other than a newly created 302 in 2008, which was obviously prepared for use in my trial in 2009.

Scars said on the stand that he had mentioned it before at previous trials. Carnesi stood at his full five feet four, and wheeled in all of the transcripts of Scars' previous trial testimony. The pile of scripts was so high, that Carnesi could not see over them.

"Tell me the trial in which you spoke about this before," said Carnesi, indicating the pile of transcripts in the courtroom. "Didn't I cross examine you in trial two?" Carnesi asked.

"Correct."

"Do you remember responding to a question I had asked you about fabricating evidence and your response was, 'Counselor if I wanted to lie about John I would have put him on murders.'"

Carnesi had him. We also accomplished letting the jurors know that this was not my first trial. Judge Castel issued a previous order that we were not to mention any of the numerous prior proceedings, in order not to prejudice the jury against the government.

As references were made during Carnesi's questioning of Mikey Scars to trials one, two and three, it hit home to the jury that this was not the first time I had faced the government in open court. However, it was the first time I was facing murder and drug charges, and more specifically the DiBono murder charges.

DiLeonardo (Scars) was a capo in the Gambino Family. He testified that we had been made in the same ceremony. Further, he regarded himself as not only my closest friend in the mob, and often times called me "brother," but called himself a "Gotti."

The use of DiLeonardo on the DiBono murder at trial to support Alite's testimony was a strategic error on the part of the government-especially in light of the aforesaid quote by DiLeonardo in the second trial.

According to the judge in this trial, this jury had been one of the most educated juries ever to sit in his courtroom. So, to have brought out Scars as a witness on DiBono was a major mistake in front of this jury who would quickly and easily see that this first time around testimony was likely manufactured and false.

Through attorneys, we had made contact with Sammy Gravano, one of those who had ordered the hit on DiBono, and in a letter, Gravano said no such "son for a son" deal existed. It was pure fabrication.

The government was to call several more witnesses.

D'Angelo was called regarding the Sliwa kidnapping and my trial strategies while he was still a co-defendant. With respect to this testimony, in all of the previous trials, Judge Scheindlin had ruled that any testimony regarding trial strategies would be inadmissible as it was protected by a joint defense agreement in place prior to D'Angelo deciding not to go to trial and instead cooperate with the government. Even D'Angelo's attorney,

Barry Levin, had testified to the existence and propriety of this joint defense agreement, which served to aid Scheindlin's holding.

Now once again, Castel ruled against us and permitted this testimony to be heard. Charles Carnesi was stunned. He went on to say to fellow attorneys and myself, and AUSA Honig, lead attorney for the prosecution, that in his thirty some odd years of practicing law and as a prosecutor as well, he had never seen anything like this—"not even in the (my) father's case."

It would have been one of many reversible errors (court mistaken rulings that could have overturned a guilty verdict on appeal) that would have been available to us had they been needed. The government rested on October 26, 2009.

Defense Witnesses

The government had rested. To say I was mentally exhausted would be an understatement. This trial was turning out, as far as I was concerned, to be the most psychologically difficult.

To listen to the swill that came from the cooperators on the stand—to think that this *was* my world. It was not the embellishments and the creations of some of the cooperators, but the fact that these people were part of the street world—a world that we ruled—that made me almost physically sick.

Don't get me wrong, I had the honor and pleasure of meeting some quality men in my former life. I made, as my father would say, "good memories." But, weighing that, against what had occurred on the stand, with these type of men, was one of the lowest points of my life; the loss of my younger brother, Frank, being the worst.

On reflection, however, I realized that I had put myself in this position by being a part of that Life. These profound realizations occurred to me as I was escorted through the tunnels from the court, back to the MCC.

When I had reached the MCC, I heard a voice that was

familiar to me from my Ray Brook days. I had also heard it in my previous trials.

"Hey, my pal," he said. It was Brian Lindemann, my former cellmate. It took me out of my thoughts. As I looked over towards him, next to him was Joe O'Kane, a fellow from the neighborhood who I had not seen in over fifteen years.

They both had arrived on the transport. Brian over from USP Lewisburg, and Joe from USP Canaan—two very violent penitentiaries in Pennsylvania. Along with Joe and Bryan was a young fellow, who I later learned was named Matthew Morris, from Florida. He was a former cellmate of Alite's in Tampa, and was now here to testify on my behalf. All three of them were there for me.

Seeing them in chains, being led to the R&D, smiling and telling me to keep my head up. "I love you bro," said Brian.

I smiled back, touched my heart, and nodded to them in acknowledgment. It was like being pinned down in a pitched battle, and then hearing the sound of the cavalry arriving.

My witnesses were now being moved into the MCC. I noticed that Joe O'Kane's jaw was wired—it was broken. I heard in prison that Joe was a rough kid, that wouldn't take a backward step from anyone. But, now, seeing his jaw wired, made me wonder.

Our witnesses weren't scheduled to go on the stand until the following week. I made sure to have one of my attorneys, Tony D'Aiuto, find out what had happened to Joe. My first thought was it was a torpedo sent by some of the guards to keep him from testifying on my behalf—or it might have been the guards themselves that had broken his jaw.

Joe had refused offers to receive his "get out of jail free" card, by Ted Otto. (You will hear more about that in his testimony.) I do know that when Charlie Carnesi had interviewed him, a short while before, at USP Canaan, Joe was fine.

So, my mind wondered. Joe being a man's man had told Tony that he had broken his jaw playing football. Who knows?

That night it was difficult to sleep. I had many such nights, but now my mind was racing, mainly regarding our defense witnesses. One of our bold and dangerous moves was our use of WITSEC witnesses for the defense—cooperators that had been given government absolution to testify *against* me. These were people who were duty bound by their agreement with the government to give "substantial assistance in the prosecution of others for the government."

For this they would receive a letter, known as a 5K1, which would be presented to the judge by the prosecution to basically forgive them for their sins. The government did indeed do this for Peter Zuccaro for his testimony against accused Gambino captains, Dominick Pizzonia and Ronald Trucchio. McMahon also received absolution, along with other government witnesses.

We were calling them to have them, once again in front of a jury, tell the tale that they did in previous trials that had earned them their reward. We knew that they knew that their "truth" would now hurt their government masters in this trial. We would hold them to their previous statements given in government 302s and previous testimony.

Alite had told so many lies, and the government had so many cooperators which were used against me, now we would use them against the government. However, witnesses Joe O'Kane and Matthew Morris had never before testified. Lindemann, had, in two previous trials, as one of my defense witnesses.

They could only expect possible retribution from the system (BOP, Marshals, Law Enforcement). The government 5K1 witnesses were cowards taking the easy way out. People like O'Kane, Morris, and Lindemann were just there to do the right thing—to right a wrong, no matter the cost.

I was no longer a member of the Gambino Family, so people were sending them messages (just like I had mentioned in earlier trials), "Why help him? He's not a part of us."

So you can understand the courage it took to go on that

stand, against the wishes of both sides of the law, the government and the mob. Any mob guy worth his spit would still be rooting for me to defeat the government—the same machine that they felt had oppressed them.

I was asked at one point, why, after all I had been through, I just didn't cooperate. My answer was in three parts. One, I couldn't do to other families what had been done to mine; two, I wouldn't scar my sons with shame, and have them change their name (like Mikey Scars' son did); and three, whether this would be a factor or not, my dislike for the government far outweighed my disenchantment with the streets.

At some point that night, I did fall asleep.

Matthew Morris

One of our witnesses was Matthew Morris, at thirty six he had already been tagged as a career criminal. While in Tampa, facing bank robbery charges, Morris had shared a cell with John Alite.

He was convicted of the robbery charges and sentenced to years in prison. We had subpoenaed him from a federal penitentiary in West Virginia. A month before trial, we were contacted by an attorney on behalf of Mr. Morris stating that Mr. Morris had exculpatory information for your benefit regarding Alite.

My private investigator and one of my attorneys had conducted a phone interview with Mr. Morris. It was determined that the information Mr. Morris had was important, and we would subpoena him to New York for the trial.

We immediately notified the government of our intentions to call Mr. Morris, and had an order to produce him issued to the Marshals, to have him available in time for the trial.

Shortly after starting this process of bringing him to New York, we were notified by the government that they too were contacted regarding Morris' information.

When the government has knowledge of exculpatory information, it is required under the constitution and case law that they disclose it to the defendant. The fact that the attorney who notified us about this had notified the government, and that we knew this, precluded the government from failing to disclose this information.

Once Morris arrived in New York, my attorney Tony D'Aiuto interviewed him, and prepared him as a witness for the defense. Mr. Morris was to take the stand on 10/27/09, my father's birthday.

We had notified the government of our intent to call Morris on this date, several days before. As Morris was waiting downstairs to be called to the stand as our witness, he was notified by the government that he had been charged in a murder case, and was facing a death sentence.

Learning this on the day he was to be called delayed our case, while the court assigned an attorney to Mr. Morris to advise him of the problems he may face were he to testify.

We were certain that the timing of this was intentional, and that the government sought to intimidate him into not testifying. The charges he was now facing were from alleged events two years previously.

Now, Morris was facing a decision; testify, or not. His attorney advised him not to. Morris was a tough kid who seemed, according to his attorney, now more determined than ever to testify for me, because he thought this government move, "A bully tactic and I hate fucking bullies."

His attorney was unable to dissuade him from taking the stand. On 11/5/09, Matthew Morris testified. Charlie Carnesi, on direct, went through Morris' criminal history. This was an interesting kid.

He went on to tell how he wound up in a cell with Alite, while in Tampa facing his bank robbery charge. He testified that the two had become friends, "We talked a lot, we worked out together, we ate together, and we shared books together."

At some point, Alite had told him that he would be getting out soon.

Morris didn't understand this, because Alite was facing an "asshole full of charges." (As Morris said in his interview with D'Aiuto.) Alite went on to say that I was his key to get out of prison. He told Morris he would do whatever he had to do to get out of jail.

My attorney asked him about Alite, "Did he ever indicate to you his present feelings, his feelings at the time of the discussion, towards Mr. Gotti?"

"He hated his guts," Morris said.

Charlie also asked Morris, "With regard to this drug business he [Alite] was involved in, did he ever mention Mr. Gotti?"

"No, not really," Morris testified, "the only thing that he mentioned about Mr. Gotti was saying like, when he lived up in New York, those guys didn't want him coming around because of the drugs."

Just before he left the stand, Charlie asked him, "Do you expect to receive a reduction in any sentence as a result of your testifying here?"

"No, not at all," Morris said. Further he mentioned being contacted by an FBI agent upon his arrival.

Angelo Noviello

One of my defenses to the charges was my having withdrawn from the Life for more than five years, which was the statute of limitations for RICO prosecutions. Actually, at the time of trial, it was more like eleven years. So the government needed something to hang its hat on so they could destroy that defense.

Around the April before my trial started, Kevin McLaughlin received a visit from the government. McLaughlin was a hard working kid, a former Marine, without any criminal record. The FBI accused him of being a participant in a real estate deal where I was the supposed puppet master. After government intimidation, McLaughlin became a cooperating witness.

In the transaction between McLaughlin and Noviello—the real estate in question was the building that housed the old *Our Friends Social Club* in Ozone Park on 101st Avenue.

Noviello had purchased the building for a price much lower than the market price, according to the government, and they submitted that he was acting as a straw man for me.

Both my attorney, who represented him, and Noviello came to testify as to the *truth* of the matter.

The property had been condemned; there were high five-figure fines and assessments against it from the city EPA, the water department, and other agencies. Additionally, there was approximately $350,000 (retail) worth of remediation and renovation work required to make the place habitable—which it wasn't when Angelo bought it, except for the mold, rats, and roaches.

Noviello was born in Italy, came to the United States, worked hard as a landscaper and mason, never was arrested, raised a family, and even had an aunt that was a nun in the Vatican.

But this didn't stop the government from bugging his car and planting a GPS on it.

Let's look at some testimony:

> Q. Since you on occasion have driven Mr. Gotti around in your car, have you become aware of any government surveillance?
>
> A. Yes sir.
>
> Q. Have you become aware of any devices that were placed on your car?
>
> A. Yes sir. [Referring to the GPS device.] It kept falling out and I kept putting it back under there.

During his testimony government photos were shown with

Noviello and his attorney (who was also my family attorney), W. Adam Mandelbaum, walking around in the vicinity of Mandelbaum's office. I also appeared in some of these.

The government was trying to use these photos to show the collusion between me, Noviello, and Mandelbaum and see if a jury would accept the government version of things.

An ironic part of this is that Mandelbaum, in his military service for the government, had received a Top Secret Category Three Crypto clearance, the highest security clearance one can get in the area of electronic espionage, yet he was now being surveilled and scrutinized by that same government.

This reach by the government to try and use an innocent and irrelevant real estate deal to demolish my withdrawal defense showed how desperate they were. In New York, all you have to do is go down to the clerk of the county where the property is located, and you can learn the entire ownership history of a building, as well as many other things.

The FBI, the US Attorney's Office have extensive and expensive investigatory resources. They couldn't find out from public records that I never owned this building; that I was not a mortgage holder on the property; that I had no liens against the property, that as a matter of easily ascertained fact, I was not involved in any way shape or form with this building that Noviello purchased.

Joon Kim

Former U.S. Attorney Joon Kim had been the AUSA who prosecuted my first and second trials, and after losing the second, he had called Carnesi to warn him that there had been a threat on my life.

This time, rather than using trial transcript, I'm going to let Charlie recount his direct examination of Kim, who was now in private practice when we called him:

This alleged threat to John's life, reportedly came from John "Sonny" Franzese, who, at the time in 2006, was an underboss in the Colombo crime Family. He's considered the oldest acting member of the Mafia and one of the most famous. A legendary character. It's inconceivable that anyone who worked organized crime in New York, as an FBI agent or AUSA would not know of Sonny Franzese.

Anyway, when Joon Kim first called me back in '06 he mentioned only that there was a threat, but refused to say from who or under what circumstances it had become known to the government. But we later got hold an FBI 302 memo dated April 3, 2006, right around the time he called me.

It stated that Franzese "had recently met with the Howard Beach crew," who would have been John's former associates and who, by the way, had left him alone since he formally renounced the mob back in 1999.

Now according to this 302 per Franzese, the people in Howard Beach were "very upset about (John's) recent behavior and noted that there is no such thing as quitting the mob." This document fit perfectly into proving our withdrawal defense. John makes it known he left the Life, now there's people in it wanting to kill him.

[The government suppressed this 302, which they had prior to the *third* trial. Had Judge Scheindlin known about the existence of this 302 at the time of its drafting, there likely would not have been a third trial no less a fourth.]

Joon Kim and others unsuccessfully argued in the first three cases, that John had *not* left the Life. They said it couldn't be done. Further, it added fuel to the 'death threat' story leaked to *The New York Post* and that might have resulted in John's death if certain people in the mob had believed it.

But the kicker in the 302 was that Sonny Franzese had supposedly given "his consent to kill John Jr. if they thought it was necessary."

The government had been arguing this ridiculous theory that John could not be out of the mob, because if you're in, you're in for life. Well, according to that 302 and the call I'd received from Joon Kim, they wanted to kill him, so I put Kim on the stand.

I say to him, "You were an Assistant U.S. Attorney, experienced in organized crime. You called me about a death threat?" And he answers, "Yes." So I ask, "What was it about?" and he responds, "I don't really recall."

I say, "How did you hear about this death threat?" He answers, "My supervisor told me to call you."

"Well, what was the nature of the conversation with your supervisor?" He responds, "I don't remember." So I ask, "Where did the death threat come from?" and he says "I don't remember." "Now remember, we're talking about the highest profile case in New York in many years, and the son of John Gotti, and you don't remember?"

Now, I tell him I have the 302 from the agent that had to have gone to him, based on what he was calling me about. And in that 302 it says that Sonny Franzese has told an informant that he just came back from a meeting with the Queens people and that they're very upset with Gotti Jr. Further, Sonny Franzese is basically saying, on behalf of the Colombo Family, "We don't have a problem if you want to have him killed." Pretty specific, but Kim says, "I don't remember. I don't remember."

So I ask him, "How long have you been a prosecutor?" He says, "I was there six years." I ask him, "What units were you assigned to?" and he says, "I was four years in the Organized Crime Section."

"Okay, well, I'll show you this 302 now. Does that refresh your recollection?" and with a straight face, looking at it he says, "No."

"Well," I ask, "did you know an individual by the name of Sonny Franzese?" and he shakes his head, "No."

Now, I've got four people on the jury who are shaking *their* heads because they *know* who Sonny Franzese is. This Assistant U.S. Attorney with six years experience—four in Organized Crime—says he doesn't recognize the name?

At this point I'm crazed because the jury doesn't know what the 302 says. They just know I showed it to him and I'm asking him questions. And I'm trying to put out as much information from the 302 as possible, but I can't read it out loud, because it's not in evidence.

So I go to the Judge. I ask for a sidebar, "Judge, I'm sorry, we're ready to end the case, but obviously I'm getting sand-bagged here. I need to call the agents who made the 302."

The judge says to the prosecutor, "All right, well, when can you have the agents available?" And they say, "I don't know, Judge. Let us check. Oh . . . they're not available. They can't be here for three or four days." So the judge says, "All right. Why don't you just stipulate to the 302 and let him put the 302 in?"

So now the prosecutor goes and talks to Ted Otto and comes back saying that the government refuses to stipulate to their own 302. Can you imagine this, this is their document.

Well at that point the Judge, who's been killing us throughout the trial and couldn't give a spit for us is now upset. Now he's upset with their attitude, "I'll go so far, but now you guys are being ridiculous."

Then, in a stage whisper, loud enough for the jury to hear, he says to them, "You get those agents in this courtroom tomorrow. I want them here tomorrow."

With that they go back, talk amongst themselves and they come back, "All right, Judge, we'll agree to the 302." [Charlie said during the interview, they didn't want to put the agents on the stand.]

So now I stand up in front of the jury and read this document which lays out the whole thing that had just been shown to this witness who was saying it didn't refresh his recollection about the death threat, and that's it. I look at the jury and I can feel it. At which point I say to the Judge, "We're finished, Your Honor. We rest."

We could not have had a more powerful close to the defense of this case then letting the jury appreciate the lengths the government was going to in order to hide the truth.

Joe O'Kane

One of our most important defense witnesses we had to have produced from USP Canaan, a federal prison in Pennsylvania—Joe O'Kane. He gave his testimony through a wired up jaw that had been broken in prison or in transit to my trial.

He was forty-two and no stranger to the prison system.

He had previously served five years for assault in the first degree and attempted murder charges of which he was innocent, as was confirmed years later by cooperating witnesses, charges that were dropped *after* he served those five years.

O'Kane was indicted again in June, 1999, on racketeering and murder charges. He was found guilty, and received a sentence of life plus fifteen years.

O'Kane testified that he was no stranger to John Alite. He knew him since grammar school and, in the eighties up until about 1990–1991, he was Alite's partner in the drug business, and a close friend. After Grosso had been murdered by Alite, they took over Grosso's drug trade which operated out of the appropriately named White Horse Tavern.

O'Kane went on to testify that Grosso had been murdered by Alite because it was personal. Gebert and Grosso had shot at Alite in front of his mother's house.

On the stand, O'Kane was asked by my attorney, "Did Alite ever tell you that John Gotti had any role in the Grosso murder?"

"Absolutely not."

With respect to my alleged involvement with the drug business, O'Kane was asked, "Did you ever speak to Mr. Gotti about drugs?"

"No sir."

"Did you ever pay Mr. Gotti any of the proceeds from your drug business?"

"Absolutely not."

"Did Mr. Gotti ever ask you to pay him any money from your drug business?"

O'Kane looked directly at my lawyer, and emphatically said, "Mr. Gotti at the time didn't even know we were dealing drugs."

"Did you ever have a conversation with Mr. Alite, concerning his relationship with Mr. Gotti and the topic of drugs?"

"Yes," O'kane said.

"Can you tell us what Mr. Alite said to you?"

"John Alite told me, if I was ever approached by John Jr. or his cousin John Ruggiero, and I was ever asked if he and I were selling drugs, just deny it 'til the end. Never admit it. And I never did," O'Kane said.

"Did Alite ever say to you whether John Gotti knew that you and Alite were in the drug business?"

"What time frame are we speaking about?" O'Kane asked.

"Late eighties."

"There was a time," O'Kane said, "it wasn't the late eighties. In the late eighties, John Jr. had no idea we were selling drugs. Into the early nineties Alite had approached me and said John was inquiring if him and I were selling drugs."

"And what happened after Mr. Gotti found out that you and Alite were indeed selling drugs?"

"I would say it was probably six months to a year after the first time. Alite beeped me and I met him. He said that he had a serious argument with John, stating that John had told him to stop selling drugs. 'I don't want you around me anymore,' [quoting me]. So John told him get away."

Carnesi then asked O'Kane about a change in Alite's financial status after I had chased him. He said, "After John Jr. chased John Alite from Queens, pretty much New York, his finances dried up because he was no longer selling drugs or doing any activities he was doing."

From testimony it was made clear that Alite had used my name all over the place, in the streets, even at night club doors to avoid having to stand in line to get in.

O'Kane explained on the stand that "John Alite lived on John Jr.'s reputation. And would throw the name all over the place any chance he got. Whether it be a problem or a night club."

It was also made clear that Alite had no loyalty to anyone except himself. O'Kane related how, after he refused to help Alite set up people for robberies that O'Kane knew, Alite had *him* robbed, tied up, and pistol whipped.

Alite, ironically had told O'Kane that he was the only reason he would come back to the neighborhood, the only guy he wanted to see, that he was the only man that Alite could trust.

O'Kane knew me from the neighborhood; we had played football together on occasion as kids. The FBI wanted to get to know Joe also. He testified that, at USP Canaan, he was told he had a visitor, and when he appeared at the visiting room, he ran into Agent Ted Otto sitting waiting for him. (Similar to my scenario in March, 2005, at the MCC, although of course, that wasn't Otto sitting there in my case.)

"The agent said, 'My name is Agent Otto,'" O'Kane said. "He called me Joe. 'My name is Agent Otto, Joe. I understand you are doing a life sentence and we want to give you a number.' I didn't know Agent Otto, but from reading the newspaper and John's previous trials, I know Agent Otto was the case agent on John's trials."

So it was obvious he was being approached by Otto to cooperate against me, in exchange for a significant reduction of sentence time. But O'Kane, unlike his ex-friend and partner in the drug business, Alite, had ethics, and would not violate his own principles and beliefs in what was right. He would not testify against me.

With respect to Otto's offer, O'Kane testified, "I told him to go fuck himself, and if you need to speak with me, just get in touch with my attorney, and I walked away."

"Has anyone from the defense ever indicated to you that they have the power or the authority to have your sentence reduced?" Carnesi asked.

"No sir," said O'Kane.

"When you finish testifying here today, where do you expect to go?"

"Hopefully, I will go back to the penitentiary I just came from in Pennsylvania."

"To complete that life sentence?" Carnesi asked.

"Yes sir."

★

Under a withering cross-examination from experienced Assistant US Attorney Trezevant, on loan to New York from his home base Tampa, O'Kane withstood the rapid fire questioning without changing his testimony one iota. Truth is a strong fortress no matter how much an outsider tries to break it down.

One question on cross, I will always remember, Trezevant asked, "If you provide any information here in this courtroom against Mr. Gotti, there are consequences that can happen to you correct?"

O'Kane fired back, "If I was going to provide information towards John Gotti, I'd be home with my family and my son right now."

★

Joe O'Kane finished testifying and was excused from the stand. I remember watching him as he was escorted out of the courtroom by the marshals, to be brought back to the MCC.

I felt mixed emotions.

First, gratitude that a man such as O'Kane even existed. He stood by what he believed. Tony D'Aiuto, one of my attorneys, had taken an immediate liking to O'Kane. "He's doing the rest of his life in prison, lost his marriage, and will be away from his son, and doesn't complain," observed Tony.

Tony had asked O'Kane about the realities of doing life, and what a day to day struggle it must be. Joe's response was, "The five years I had done were harder. I was doing time for something I didn't do. My father, who was a cop, had always taught me to take responsibility for what you do in your life. That's what I'm doing. No easy way out, being a man and taking responsibility."

"How does your son feel not having his father?" Tony asked him.

"My son knows I love him more than anything in this world, and when he's older, I know he will understand."

My second feeling as O'Kane left was sadness. His only future home, until his death, would be within prison walls.

What I didn't know at the time was how soon that death would come. As per Joe's wishes, he was returned to USP Canaan to serve out the rest of his life sentence.

On Sunday April 25, 2010, Joe O'Kane was found lying dead in his own blood in his cell, stabbed more than a dozen times. A guard found him there at 9:45 PM.

Railroad Job

Summations had not yet been made; the trial was over, the deliberations yet to begin. I had sat and borne witness to the federal games which had been played throughout this trial. They had withheld documents from us until the eleventh hour, they attempted to restrict valid use of our evidence, they had brought on perjured testimony through the mouths of murderers.

But whatever had taken place, the submission of evidence by both sides was done, and only attorney arguments remained before jury deliberations.

However, dramatic events were still to come.

An anonymous letter had reached Judge Castel's bench, claiming that two jurors could not get along, and the heat of the dispute between them would nullify there being an impartial jury that could deliberate to a verdict.

Supposedly, a heated argument had occurred when one juror, who had been accused of creating a hostile environment amongst the panel, referred to the other as a hater. A person designated as "Juror #7 was accused of having a foul mouth, and being decidedly pro defense. So said Juror # 11.

The letter had been sent by US mail. This, in itself, would make its origin and validity suspect, because pursuant to the explicit instructions of the court, if there are any juror problems or questions, they are handed up to the bench through the jury foremen, or the marshal, not by postal service.

By using the mail, there would be no way to put a face to the complaint—unless a juror would admit to having mailed it.

Upon receiving this letter, and in consideration of the circumstances of its delivery, Castel conducted in camera *voir dire* questioning of the individual jurors, to find out what the problem was and who sent the letter.

Each and every juror denied sending it.

My attorney was perplexed. A posted letter claiming that two specific jurors were going at it head to head; something which would likely only be known to a juror, and yet none would claim authorship to the letter.

Could this be other than what it was on face value?

The juror #7 complained of was an Afro-American woman, and my attorney, Charlie Carnesi thought the letter to be race motivated. Juror #7 had given indications by her body language during the trial, of her favoring Carnesi, and made it a point to say hello to him every morning. Juror #11 during trial, had, after finally being disgusted by the Alite testimony, turned her chair away from the witness stand.

These actions did not go unnoticed by Agent Ted Otto, who made notes of juror reactions throughout the trial, and made notes during the actions of Jurors #7 and #11. I did not have access to the content of the notes, but I was witness to the timing of the making of them. (I sat right behind Ted Otto during the trial.)

The judge, in his decision on the issue, which was put on the record with a long prologue about justice and the jury, and whatever else you might want to have on a record on appeal if you are a judge, booted *both* jurors.

When Judge Castel put his decision to remove these two jurors from the panel, my mother, who had been sitting every day in the courtroom, could no longer control her outrage.

She jumped to her feet and yelled, "This is a railroad job! Enough is enough! They're railroading you; they're doing to you what they did to your father! Why don't you just take him out back and shoot him? You lying bastards! You should all be ashamed of yourselves, you fucking lying bastards!"

I tried to calm her, "Please, Ma, I got this, I got this. I can handle it."

The marshals moved towards my mother, and I warned them, "Lay a hand on my mother and I'm coming over!"

My sister Angel, who was with my mother, realized the potential disaster in the situation, grabbed my mother and hurried her out of the courtroom.

This of course, did not happen in the presence of the jury, but the media witnessed it, and of course they published stories about it in bold type.

Castel warned that another outburst like that would cause my mother to be barred from the courtroom, as well as my other family members.

I instructed my mother not to return to court, to avoid any further problems.

★

It had become obvious to me now, the tremendous toll that had been taken on my mother from all that had happened to her, my brother Frankie's death, my father's repeated incarceration and wasting death, and what had been done, and was being done to me.

I watched her being led from the courtroom, sobbing; a very rare occurrence for this lioness of a woman.

But every person has a point where enough is enough, where rage becomes outrage, and where the injustices in a courtroom require outcry—despite it not being due and proper form. She had reached hers and reacted.

I loved her for it, I respected her for it, and I was angry at myself for what my earlier life choices had brought upon her. I was also angry at the government for not acknowledging what they had long known—that I had left the Life, at this time, more than a decade past, and not only were they now unjustly making me suffer, but torturing my mother in the process.

★

We broke early that day.

The scenario I had just witnessed in court accompanied me as I walked through the tunnels back to the MCC. When I was returned to my cell block, I placed a call to my attorney W. Adam Mandelbaum and instructed him to come visit me the coming Saturday.

I will let him tell you what occurred:

"When I saw John in the third floor visiting room at MCC, he did not look like his usual self. Some of the self-assurance was gone, and some more than usual anger was present in his words.

"I told him about the change I saw, and changing the subject, he instructed me to reach out to the government with respect to a possible eleventh hour plea deal. I was shocked, especially when he told me that he would accept up to twenty years.

"I looked at my friend and bore witness to his exhaustion.

"I told him, 'You make this kind of a deal, and you will get out in your sixties, your kids will have grown up without you.'

"John told me that he believed it was time to end all of this tribulation, and have his family move on without the constant burden of him being on trial.

"I was torn as I left the visit and headed out on the Lower Manhattan streets.

"On the one hand as a friend, I didn't want anything to do with it, for although being ever the pessimist, I believed he would at least get a hung jury on this. On the other hand, as one of his lawyers, I had to respect the instructions of my client, no matter how strongly I disagreed with him.

"It was his life in the vise, not mine.

"Upon my return from the prison, pursuant to John's instructions, I informed his family members of his considering taking a plea, if both sides could work it out. He didn't want his family to be taken by surprise, in the event this took place."

Letter from Home

On Sunday morning at MCC, I received an unexpected visit from my attorney Tony D'Aiuto. He brought with him a letter from my mother that was to be read in front of him, and he would take it back after reading it.

She reminded me in the letter that a twenty year plea was tantamount to a life sentence. My children would be permanently damaged by it, my wife would basically be alone for most of her future, and there was no guarantee I would get out anyway after serving my time—the government had taught me that lesson already.

Further, she reminded me that my father had always stood straight and tall and spit in the face of the enemy. He never took a plea, and he never forgot that he had a son that he loved very much, every day he was in prison.

She asked me in the letter, what was the purpose of what I was contemplating. Joe O'Kane, Matthew Morris, Brian Lindemann had all stood up for me in court at risk to themselves—certainly at no benefit to themselves. My attorneys, my friends, my family had all stood by me in this fight—and now, at the last second I was going to throw in the towel?

After reading the letter, I knew the answer. No plea, no deal, I see this fight through to the end, regardless of what that end might turn out to be.

Let's go back to my attorney Mandelbaum, and hear his words.

Sunday night, I couldn't sleep. I wanted to disappear inside a hole and never come out. I might wake up the next morning, go to court, and following my friend and client's instructions, engage in lawyering that would ruin his life and the lives of his family. I might take a plea that I didn't believe in taking on his behalf, and earn the undying hatred of his family—all of whom I had over the years become close to.

But they didn't write the code of professional responsibility to please me. I had specific instructions from my client, and I couldn't without his consent, deviate from them.

So Monday I arrive in the courtroom at 500 Pearl Street. John's attorneys did a double take in seeing me, as I had already testified at trial, and had no purpose being there.

They quickly recognized my purpose, and Charlie Carnesi said to me, "What are you doing here?"

I'm here for moral support, I told him.

"Fuck you," he said, "you're here to take a plea."

I told him I was here representing a client's interests and instructions, and I needed to speak to John.

I came through the well to a bullpen behind the courtroom, where John sat alone, his hands cuffed together. He greeted me with his usual, "What's up pal."

He could see the misery in my face, and told me, "Don't worry about it, I'm not taking a plea."

I felt instant relief. But not for long.

"If I get convicted, I'm telling you now," he said, "draw up divorce papers and have my wife served."

Once again I was shocked, but I understood what he meant. He wanted her to be free, to have a house not subject to forfeiture, and go on with her life. The government had already indicated to Carnesi that in the event of a conviction, they would push hard for John to be sentenced to ADX Florence, in Colorado, the highest security prison in the country.

He didn't want his wife to go through what his mother had gone through.

★

The other attorneys were informed by Mandelbaum of my decision, and closing arguments would be taking place, as there would be no deal pursued.

In Summation

AUSA Honig and Trezevant in their summations wanted the jury to accept the testimony of John Alite as truth, and to weigh it heavily on the prosecution's side of the scale of justice that would determine whether or not they had proven their case against me beyond a reasonable doubt.

They mocked and belittled the value of the testimony of our defense witness, Joe O'Kane, referring to him as a drug dealer. They derided our withdrawal defense, reminding the jury that one doesn't just leave the mob, you can't quit the Life. They had asked for a jury determination of "guilty" that would send me away for the rest of my life.

Then satisfied with the arguments that they made, they thanked the jury for their attention, and resumed their positions at the prosecution table.

My attorney, Charles Carnesi, sprang to his feet, no notes, no outline in his hands, just a passion for justice and a strong desire to make sure the jury knew that the prosecution witnesses were of little account, that the defense witnesses had nothing to gain in coming forward, and perhaps much to lose, and that I, John A. Gotti, had left the Life some ten years before the trial started.

"I will take one Joe O'Kane over ten Joon Kims," Charlie said. "The one, gains nothing from testifying in this trial, he could have gone to the government, made a deal, and like he said on the stand, be home with his wife and kids. But instead, he refused to abandon his sense of right and wrong, and at substantial risk to himself, took the stand and told the truth.

"Joon Kim? An embarrassment. His testimony disgraceful."

Charlie had worked himself up to fever pitch, when he told the jury:

> What is this trial really about? It's about courage. It's about the courage of defense witnesses with nothing to gain, much to lose, who took the stand to tell you the truth. Not like Alite, who made his bargain with the government to get out of prison, regardless of what he had to say.
>
> It's about the courage of my client, a man who was once in the Life, who paid for his crimes with many years in prison, who had the courage to leave the Life, had the courage to tell that to his father, to whom the Life was everything, had the courage to accept the consequences which might include his being killed for leaving the Life.
>
> My client willingly accepted responsibility for what he had been, what he had done, and a decade ago made the decision to change his ways, despite great sacrifice. You can understand and appreciate that courage, you can accept the testimony of

those who gained nothing by coming forward, and send my client back home to his wife and children.

That's what I'm asking for here today. A verdict of not guilty. Send John home.

Deliberation

Themis. The goddess of justice. A familiar image to all. She is blindfolded, and with one hand holds a scale, and with the other, a sword.

Arguments finished, it was time for the jury to retire to the deliberation room to determine my fate. The sword was now once again hanging over my head.

With the consequences being freedom and a return to my family on one hand, and spending the rest of my life in a super max prison in Colorado, locked up for twenty three hours a day, I was understandably anxious. To say the least.

Normally, on Veteran's Day, the Federal Courthouse is closed. Not in my case. Judge Castel had ordered the court be open so that deliberations could begin on November 11, 2009. Was this a tactic to achieve a rapid verdict, having jurors come in on what normally would be a day off for them?

I believe once the reader learns of the other judicial practices during deliberations, the determination of the reader will be that the Judge was guilty of putting undue pressure on the jury to achieve a verdict quickly—before Thanksgiving.

So there I was in the bullpen on Veteran's day—alone. Completely alone, as mine was the only trial going on, the only proceeding going on in the entire courthouse. None of the usual sounds of chains, keys, marshals—nothing. A perfect opportunity to second guess myself, my trial tactics. A perfect opportunity to wonder how, when, and where we had fucked up in my defense.

I didn't know it at the time, but jury deliberations would be spread out over twenty-one days, perhaps the longest period of any case in recent history. Each day I wondered, will it be today—*what* will it be today?

Will the sword fall on my head today?

Despite the optimism of my trial counsel, I steeled myself to be ready for the worst. I did not want to add a crushing disappointment at the last minute to a life sentence. On the other hand, by preparing for the worst, if a not guilty verdict did come in, I could add joyful surprise to my return home.

Each time I was taken from the downstairs bullpen to go back to the courtroom, the adrenaline in my body would go into high gear. Would it be a final verdict? Each time the jurors sent a note to the judge, I had to go back to the courtroom, and I had to endure the feeling of those fight or flight hormones raging in me while belly chained and handcuffed.

Eight days into deliberations, the jury sent a note back to the judge. Up to the courtroom I go, expecting the worst.

They were deadlocked. It was Thursday afternoon.

But Judge Castel pushes on and reads to them, what is, in effect, an Allen Charge, (which we discussed earlier). To remind the reader, this is the charge to the jury where the judge tries his best to have them render a verdict, it puts significant pressure on a jury to do so, and it is in normal judicial procedure, to be given only once.

After hearing Judge Castel's instructions, my attorney jumped to his feet, (once the jurors had been excused), and inquired as to whether or not this was in fact an Allen Charge.

The judge said it wasn't. Now, having been there, and being a certified paralegal, and having some experience with criminal trials, I know that what the judge read was a *de facto* and *de jure* Allen Charge. My attorneys agreed.

But having heard what the judge said, I knew that I might hear this again, I knew he would be relentless in pushing the jury for a verdict. Judge Castel wanted a verdict before Thanksgiving, because, he *said,* he was concerned that around a holiday table, jurors would be talking about this trial—the most publicized trial in America at the time

The judge, gave the jurors Friday off, and had them resume deliberations Monday, the 23rd of November.

Maybe he figured with a three day weekend, they would come back ready to render a verdict. If so, he figured wrong.

Tuesday, November 24, 2009. Once again, the jury sends in a note they cannot render a verdict. Deadlocked. The second time within six days. It's is very close to Thanksgiving, and it doesn't look like they are going to give the prosecution anything to be thankful for.

I was right about the Allen Charge. On November 25, 2009, with the jury still deadlocked, Judge Castel read to them what he then acknowledged to be an Allen Charge, and then after having given the second Allen Charge in reality, he excused them for the Thanksgiving Holiday, and ordered them to return on December 1, 2009.

So what was my Thanksgiving holiday like, at MCC waiting for a verdict? Each face of the jurors came to mind as I tried to analyze what their decision would be. I felt some of the jurors were favorable, I felt some were hostile. In some judgments I turned out right, in some wrong.

Holiday season always makes one think of family, of home, of food shared amongst loved ones. It had been two years since I had celebrated the holidays with my family, (when I was still on parole), and as I sat in my cell I realized that there was a good chance that I would never have a Thanksgiving or Christmas with my family again.

Christmas—my favorite time of year. And part of me thought that there was some possibility that yes, I would be with my wife and children for Christmas 2009. But I had to suppress that thought, both in my mind and in the minds of my wife and friends.

I was allowed three hundred minutes of phone time a month, so I budgeted each call to be no more than ten minutes each. I called my family at my sister's house, where they traditionally celebrate Thanksgiving. My wife said, "It's a downer you not being here, but you'll be home soon."

I had to correct her. "First, why is it a downer? I'm healthy, the kids are healthy, you're there with the rest of the family. Second, don't say I'll be home soon, especially in front of the kids. What will be will *be*."

In a holiday call to my friend Steve Dobies, whose daughter, Victoria, is my goddaughter, he too expressed the opinion that soon I would be home. I corrected him also.

I didn't get much sleep that extended weekend. Then, like it does everyday, the sun came up, and the morning of December 1, 2009, began.

My prison morning began like every other one. As usual, at five in the morning my door was opened and I had to get ready for court. Brought to the shower around 5:15 AM; then to await transport to the courthouse.

When I was dressing, my shoes were missing, the guards couldn't find them. An omen? I wouldn't wear someone else's shoes, and I insisted that mine be found. Finally they were, and I remembered that they were the shoes I wore for the last verdict which resulted in a hung jury.

I went to court.

I spent the morning in the bullpen. Then, around noon, I was notified there was another note to the judge from the jury, and that I would be brought up after the lunch break.

I was brought in through the side door, and sat at the defense table. The entire courtroom was packed with press and the public. Standing room only. The overflow of people heard the proceedings in another courtroom where a live feed had been set up.

As I looked around, I saw the tension on the faces of my family, I saw some strangers in the benches fingering rosary beads. I noticed law enforcement on one side of the courtroom, many of them smiling, assured that they were going to hear those words that had long been denied them.

On the other side of the court sat the public. There was an air of expectancy—almost tangible.

"All rise."

I rose.

"Be seated."

I sat.

The jurors filed in stoically, and sat down.

Judge Castel turned to the jurors and said, "I have received your note," and he opened it again, and read it out loud. "We are hopelessly deadlocked."

The judge looked up from the note, and looked at the prosecution table and the defense table. (The defense table was directly behind the prosecution.)

"I have no choice," said Judge Castel, "I must now declare a mistrial."

At least two jurors, and even the judge's clerk Florence McCarthy, began to cry. My sisters were hysterical crying, I had tears down my face as well. The law enforcement side of the courtroom was no longer showing smiles; on the defense side, it was as if everybody sighed in relief in unison.

Or so it seemed to me. Once again, I was tried, and a jury could not make a determination. My fourth full trial. My fourth hung jury. Of course, I was feeling joyful, but I also knew that a mistrial is not a verdict, and technically, I could be tried again.

Would I be tried again?

I was brought out of the courtroom and into a separate room to be processed for bail. The press crowded around us, pen and papers at the ready.

As the prosecutor must sign off on the bail papers, AUSA Honig, in front of all of the journalists and cameramen, walked into the room where I waited, signed what he had to sign, then did what he didn't have to do. He had the class to shake my hand, look me into the eyes and say, "John, I want to wish you good luck and good luck with your family."

I thanked him, and he walked out of the room alone, but was accompanied by my respect. I had always felt, throughout the trial, that the Southern District did not want to try this case, it was imposed upon them. I believe that AUSA Honig, personally, did not want to try this case.

I was given bail, and walked out a free man on the evening of December 1, 2009, to the waiting throng of reporters and public. Several jurors were also waiting to see me. They came over and wished me luck, and one, who was a school teacher, gave me a tearful hug, and said, "We tried so hard to get you home for Thanksgiving."

"I appreciate everything you have done with all my heart," I told her.

I climbed into a waiting car with Charles Carnesi, and once again I was heading home.

Epilogue

So now you have heard my story.

Perhaps it might be thought of by some as an epic journey of a man from one life to another very different one, told on a cool autumn night. If one wishes to be poetic, perhaps it is a saga of the rising of one soul from the Inferno through Purgatory, and out again into the daylight.

Whatever you may wish to call it, know that you can call it truthful. Heartfelt.

The cigar that I have been smoking has gone out, and it has been forcibly crushed into an ashtray, a fitting image for my days as a criminal which are now some sixteen years in the past. The days of extortion, loan sharking, and other racket staples of what we called The Life, are to me now, nothing but dead cold ashes.

They will forever remain so.

Now, after reading my book, you have an accurate picture of who my father was, who I once was, and what I have now become. I idolized my father, who idolized a certain type of life—that of the 24/7 in your face gangster.

He died firm in his belief that the street was his only road to be taken. I lived long enough to know another road was opened to me, one where there were no victims and no vicious victors, just regular people trying to make a life for themselves and their families within the legal boundaries of our society.

It is a better path.

There have been, and there will continue to be, inaccurate tales told of who the Gottis were and are, penned by those who get their information third hand and from sources with an agenda. Those authors that are not concerned with the truth of matters; who will publish inaccuracies for a quick profit to an eagerly awaiting audience.

Our society has indeed been fascinated by the charming outlaw that my father was, and the press has obviously been attentive to the events in my life, whether it was a dramatically staged arrest, a series of unproven accusations made by those who would say or do anything to stay out of prison, or long deliberating juries that resulted in four mistrials, which set me free.

It is unfortunate that my former life is at times glorified to our young people in the media. I fell victim to such glorification when my greatest goal as a young man was to follow in the footsteps of my father, whose character, charisma, and power held me in awe.

It is my hope that, along with setting my story straight in this book, I might positively influence readers, and make them realize that the street life is no life to live, because of the destruction to victims, perpetrators, and the families of both.

★

This book is not intended to be an indictment of law enforcement per se, but the implication of those few in it who play by their own set of rules, bending the system to achieve their desired outcomes; granting absolution to career criminals that are often times more culpable than those against whom they are used as witnesses.

These abuses of power help create the potential for far more dangerous criminals, who have reason to believe that they can do whatever they want as long as they can trade up by cooperating against others. This can cause them to be far more wanton in their illegal actions.

How is this "ends justify the means" approach any different than what the mob does to achieve its goals? Law enforcement should be about impersonalized justice. To view a defendant as a personal trophy, as a stepping stone to career advancement regardless of whether or not he is actually guilty of the crimes charged, is inexcusable.

There are of course, many fine individuals engaged in law enforcement, and that they arrest people in the Life is within the proper exercise of their duty. I understand that, and accept it.

However, when the government no longer plays by its own rules, and violates both law and morality, that is something that needs to be exposed to the public. I trust I have done that.

★

I often run into people on the street that come up to me and express their feelings about what was done to my family, and their heartfelt wishes of good luck to me and mine. There are others, I'm sure, who felt that we got what we deserved, and I can understand that, as long as there is no hypocrisy in condemning us, but praising those in that same criminal world that cooperated with the government.

I'm sure that there are others who see me and still think I am in the Life; that my withdrawal from mob life is only a ruse.

I cannot be responsible for the thoughts of another individual.

My responsibility here was to tell my story to you, the reader, as clearly and truthfully as I could. I refuse to accept the government and its cooperators writing our history. Hopefully, I have entertained you. Ideally, I have provided somewhat of an education about what happens behind the scenes in the Life.

My greatest wish is that I may keep some young people attracted to the imagined glitz and glamour of the Life from entering those portals where all hope is to be truly abandoned.

In writing this, I also feel it is my duty as his son, to protect my father's reputation—not to whitewash it, but to make sure that others don't tarnish it further with untruth. This work is also an explanation to my children of who their grandfather and father were, and who I am now. They bear my last name, and are subject to potential prejudice because of its history, and peer pressure from those in the old neighborhood who might expect them to take up the mantle anew.

In a letter to Eric Holder, June 24, 2009, wherein I sought a fair trial; when I was convinced I would spend the rest of my life in jail, I wrote:

> I was a kid who became a punk making mistakes who then developed into a man making the same mistakes on an even larger scale. Maybe in some strange way I deserve some suffering as punishment for those very mistakes. If by truth not lies I will acknowledge that suffering and endure it. What about our children, they should not suffer. As a father and uncle I have spent my life trying to keep all of the children in my family on the right path so as not to make the same mistakes I have made. Unfortunately my being there for them may be ephemeral. I now feel the need to write you in the hopes of some justice, if not for myself but for the future of our children.

Those dark thoughts during dark times have long echoed in my head. But now the sun is coming up. The path this morning looks bright.

★

I declared myself, and did become a civilian in 1998, contrary to the belief of those both in the Life and in the government.

From 1998–2008 the government had used over fifteen prosecutors and more than one hundred cooperators (many of whom were violent felony offenders who in the aggregate had committed nearly a hundred murders and hundreds of assaults and robberies) to bring cases against me.

Those cooperators soon found their freedom regained after testifying, and many of them were returned to their communities with the help and support of their government handlers.

Made in the USA
Lexington, KY
01 February 2016